A Worldview of Everything

A Worldview of Everything

—— *A Contemporary First Philosophy* ——

Brian Cronin

EDITED BY
Mark T. Miller

PICKWICK *Publications* · Eugene, Oregon

A WORLDVIEW OF EVERYTHING
A Contemporary First Philosophy

Pickwick Publications
An Imprint of Wipf and Stock Publishers
199 W. 8th Ave., Suite 3
Eugene, OR 97401

www.wipfandstock.com

PAPERBACK ISBN: 978-1-5326-6099-3
HARDCOVER ISBN: 978-1-5326-6100-6
EBOOK ISBN: 978-1-5326-6101-3

Cataloguing-in-Publication data:

Names: Cronin, Brian, author. | Miller, Mark T., editor.

Title: A worldview of everything : a contemporary first philosophy / by Brian Cronin; edited by Mark T. Miller.

Description: Eugene, OR: Pickwick Publications, 2022 | Includes bibliographical references and index.

Identifiers: ISBN 978-1-5326-6099-3 (paperback) | ISBN 978-1-5326-6100-6 (hardcover) | ISBN 978-1-5326-6101-3 (ebook)

Subjects: LCSH: First philosophy. | Metaphysics. | Knowledge, Theory of.

Classification: BD331 C766 2022 (print) | BD331 (ebook)

11/28/22

Contents

Diagrams:

Preface

THE CENTRAL FOCUS OF modern philosophy is to give an adequate account of human knowing. Descartes made contributions with his clear and distinct ideas, his Cogito, intuition, and his confidence in the power of human reason. Hume was more skeptical and critical, more down to earth, and he saw no need for real causes, relations, substances, nor invisible entities like souls or God. Kant tried a complicated compromise distinguishing the appearance that we can know because of our sense intuition, and the thing-in-itself which we cannot know because we have no intellectual intuition. Husserl pinned his hopes on a transcendental reduction, a return to the things themselves, a rejection of the natural attitude, and turning philosophy into a rigorous science based on intuitions of essences. Each of these great figures have spawned schools of followers, not always noted for their fidelity to the particular tradition, who have splintered, qualified, added and subtracted to the babel of voices. These movements have culminated in the skepticism of postmodernism with its rejection of metanarratives and embrace of diversity. Many of the students that I taught in Duquesne assumed that philosophy was about having opinions, and were unappreciative of the difference between informed and uninformed opinions.

I was introduced to a version of Neo-Scholastic philosophy in the early 1960s. It was in Latin, dogmatic, abstract, related to nothing in the real world or to the science of the time, devoted to the definition and division of concepts such as being, substance, nature and soul. We searched the library looking for something more inspiring and some of us found this in Bernard Lonergan's *Insight: A Study of Human Understanding*,[1] which had accidentally been added to our library. At first it meant absolutely nothing to me.

1. I was reared on the original edition published by Longmans, Green and Co. in 1958. The critical edition is the Collected Works of Bernard Lonergan, Volume 3, published in 1992. All references in this work are to the critical edition.

After a year, I began to understand individual sentences and paragraphs. I bought my own copy in 1965 and continued to read passages on and off, convinced that there was something new and important here, but not quite able to grasp what it was. A lifetime of reading, reflecting, teaching, and writing followed and gradually all the pieces began to come together. It was a natural process of intellectual development: asking questions, being puzzled, finally understanding and being able to express and confirm the truth and value of ideas—pivoting from parts to the whole, from images to ideas, from logic to method, from vague hypotheses to formulated explanations, from theories to interiority, from lower viewpoints to higher viewpoints, from teaching to writing, from knowledge of philosophy to self-knowledge, from study of history to a personal conviction. Lonergan's work was an inspiration and a map of the terrain but all along I took very seriously his exhortation, "the point here, as elsewhere, is appropriation; the point is to discover, to identify, to become familiar with the activities of one's own intelligence; the point is to become able to discriminate with ease and from personal conviction between one's purely intellectual activities and the manifold of other, 'existential' concerns . . . ."[2]

In 1980 I was appointed to teach philosophy in a seminary in Tanzania. For the first few years I taught the history of philosophy, but then did a PhD at Boston College to prepare to teach a syllabus based on Lonergan's way of thinking. I then returned to initiate a first cycle philosophy program for African students in Arusha. It was relatively easy to transform the traditional Scholastic structure into a course focusing on personal intellectual development of students, on their appropriation of the structure of their own minds, on the practical relevance of philosophy to understanding the world in which we live. Each subject could be taught by a process of appealing to personal experience and describing the actual process of understanding in examples, projects, solving puzzles, discovering solutions. These could be compared with experiences of knowing described by psychologists, written about in biography and autobiography, and transformed into theories of knowledge by philosophers. Teaching was a positive experience as the content was relevant and important, the students were enthusiastic, appreciated the projects and became familiar with their own processes of knowing.

A major difficulty was lack of textbooks for this kind of course. *Insight* has been criticized as too detailed, too dense, too obscure and above all too long! But it is a classic and will remain so for centuries. Generations of philosophers will be grateful for the richness, precision, exactitude of definitions ant terms, and solutions to age-old disputes in philosophy and theology. It

---

2. Lonergan, *Insight*, 14.

is head and shoulders above any other text in the modern or contemporary field of philosophy. It is 785 pages long in the first edition, and I was disappointed to reach the end. However, there does exist a real problem of communicating Lonergan's thought to academia, to scientists, philosophers, students and the culture in general. Very valuable work has been done in preserving the heritage of all his writings, published and unpublished.[3] He has faithful followers but not a wide influence on academia as a whole or the culture. But he has so much to offer. The problem is that popularizing, simplifying and clarifying his thinking requires good judgment on what to leave out and what to emphasize. I have faced many of these judgments in teaching and writing and can only hope that I got it right.

I wrote *Foundations of Philosophy: Lonergan's Cognitional Theory and Epistemology* (1999) to make it easier to teach these topics and to make this pedagogy available to a wider audience. I jumped to *Value Ethics: A Lonergan Perspective* (2006) as it seemed the more urgent in the light of confusions on the foundations of moral philosophy. This applied the method of self-appropriation to judgments of value, decisions and moral actions, thus integrating a fourth level of consciousness with the three levels discussed in my previous book. It focused on the question of value, deliberative insight and judgment of value as an integral part of a complete cognitional structure. I moved to Duquesne University in 2011, and after some years teaching, wrote *Phenomenology of Human Understanding* (2017). It put the content of my first book on foundations of philosophy in a clearer, more coherent, critical and contemporary context. It simply reiterates the position of a critical realism where the real is that which is experienced, understood, judged and evaluated to be correct.

This present text has emerged from that context and has been taking shape over the last twenty-five years. I spent three years full-time on Post-Doctoral Fellowships in Boston College (2003, 2009–11) working on this text, but it just would not come. My research time in Duquesne has been devoted almost entirely to organizing this material. It was easy to sketch out topics and visualize what is needed to be said, but difficult to get that down on paper in a coherent form. I was not intending to produce a simple paraphrase of Lonergan's text in *Insight*. This text is not just another theory to be added to all previous efforts but an entry into a new mode of thinking—a metaphysics based on self-appropriation of one's own structure of knowing, a metaphysics moving from self-consciousness to self-knowledge. I aim to present it as a coherent text with its own beginning, middle, and end. A

3. See the Collected Works of Bernard Lonergan published by Toronto University Press and the website "Bernard Lonergan Archive."

stand-alone in that sense, but not in the sense that it does not build on the viewpoint and the conclusions of previous books.

I acknowledge an enormous debt to Spiritan Missionary Seminary in Arusha, where the first steps towards this worldview were taken. I was given regular leave to do four post-doctoral fellowships in Boston College, and my teaching load was taken up by others. I owe a debt to Boston College for the fellowships and for the resultant discussions, workshops, courses, and advice from the specialists in Lonergan studies who teach there. I owe a debt to Duquesne University for accepting me into their community of philosophers, allowing me a light teaching load, and giving me time to finish this book. I owe a huge debt to Mark Miller who edited the text very closely and made numerous suggestions about a better ordering of the ideas, about corrections, and improvements.

Brian Cronin, 2021.

Introduction

WHY ANOTHER BOOK ON philosophy? Why a book on philosophy during a pandemic? What is the use of philosophy anyway, at the best of times? Perhaps these reactions spring to mind when one reads the outrageous title, *Worldview of Everything: A Contemporary First Philosophy*. Of what conceivable use can that be?

For those who view philosophers as scholars living in an ivory tower, irrelevant, utopian, obscure, and out of touch with reality, it is natural to deride such a futile exercise. But there is an alternative view of the vocation of philosophers as people who think seriously and explicitly on the truths and values operative in a society, who realize the import of general principles, truths and priorities on particular decisions and actions. We are all philosophers in that we cannot avoid adopting general principles by which we judge and decide our actions from morning until night. We all seek to understand correctly the big issues of the day, priorities, elections, friendships, health, leadership, truth and falsehood, good and evil, praise and blame. Philosophy is a natural development of the human mind, continuing to ask questions, to solve problems, to discover the big picture, to keep everything in perspective, to search for the meaning of human life, to articulate a contemporary wisdom, and to make the world a better place for humans to live more humanely. Such is the notion and function of philosophy that pervades the present text.

I thought at one stage to use the title *A Theory of Everything* for this text. Scientists and authors have been fascinated by the notion of a theory of everything, it seems such an attractive ideal and a noble aspiration.[1] Most efforts toward this end seek to combine classical Newtonian physics

1. For example: Barrow, *Theories of Everything*; Weinberg, *Dreams of a Final Theory*; Hawking, *The Theory of Everything*.

1

with Einstein and quantum mechanics. Is there a theory that combines the macro and the micro, classical and quantum, gravity, space, time, and the speed of light? Is there a theory of everything? Such is a worthwhile aim but unfortunately, there are limits to theories. The notion of theory is too restrictive for my purposes. A theory is abstract; it prescinds from the concrete. But "everything" must include the concrete as well as the abstract, knowing as well as the known, the subject as well as the object, the humanities as well as the sciences, the potential as well as the actual, the immanent as well as the transcendent!

Further, a unified theory of everything is often thought of in terms of physics. That would be a tremendous achievement for physics, but sadly would not include the knowledge of common sense, chemistry, biology, anthropology, the human sciences, philosophy, and theology. Physics encompasses all realities only in so far as they are material and subject to the laws of physics, but there are many other realities and laws that, for some reason, are excluded or else reduced back into physics. "Everything" must include everything. If you aspire to unify everything, you are looking for a philosophy or worldview that encompasses all the hard sciences, all the human sciences, all disciplines and skills, all commonsense knowledge, all knowing and known, and any other knowing that I might have left out.

Metaphysics is traditionally the term for the study of all of reality. Thus, I thought at one time of entitling this book, *Metaphysics for a Post-Metaphysical World*. But the term "metaphysics" is not exactly in favor these days. It is very often used in a derogatory sense as impractical, useless, up-in-the-air. Whole schools of philosophy deny the possibility of a discipline that studies the whole of reality; there are those who revel in the diversity, particularity and uniqueness of human cultures and languages, and abhor any attempt to formulate metanarratives or overall explanations of such variety. Post-metaphysical thinking denies the possibility of a single unified view of everything—but that is precisely what I am presenting. I use the term "worldview" as a more acceptable substitute for "metaphysics."

I use the term "worldview," from the German *Weltanschauung*, as equivalent to first philosophy but in a slightly looser sense. Philosophy as a technical, explanatory, professional discipline can be somewhat specialized and off-putting; it seems to be reserved for academic professors or full-time scholars, whereas I like to emphasize that philosophy is for everybody. Everyone has a worldview, namely, a set of presuppositions, principles and notions that unifies everything in their experience. Worldviews can be quite mistaken, incomplete, vague, incoherent and so on, but we all operate out of that worldview which is uniquely our own. In this text we are trying to establish a correct, comprehensive, critical, contemporary worldview as the set of most general principles from which we should operate and deal with the concrete situations of everyday life.

I ended up using the term "first philosophy" as a subtitle, harking back to Aristotle who saw no need for a word such as "metaphysics" for what he was doing.[2] It is not a reference to Descartes, or to Levinas or anybody else. First philosophy for Aristotle was the search for the first principles and causes of everything, a study of being in its many senses, an analysis of substance, and the notion of Unmoved Mover. Using these various approaches and terminologies, Aristotle achieved for his time and place an overall view of how everything fits together. Many new ideas, methods and technologies have emerged since, and so we need to seek again a unified view of everything at the level of our times—a worldview that incorporates and integrates this new knowledge, expertise and understanding.

There is only one discipline appropriate to the task of understanding everything and from the time of Plato and Aristotle it has been called philosophy. Each of the particular sciences cuts off a part of being and studies that part from the limited point of view of biology or astronomy or medicine or sociology or whatever. But wisdom cannot limit itself to any one part of reality and must encompass and aim at an understanding of everything, which Aristotle referred to as "being." How does one go about studying everything? It cannot be a question of becoming a walking encyclopedia, a know-all, a universal scholar of all disciplines. The days when that was possible are long past. What we are aiming at is an overall view of how and why everything fits together, an understanding of the unity that lies behind the multiplicity of everything, the pivot being the knowing and the known. We are looking for the first principles and causes of why everything happens and exists. What kinds of things are there? Where did they come from? What is the purpose of the universe? What is the purpose of our short human lives?

The Real Difficulty

The real difficulty in grasping this approach to philosophy is that it is not just a new theory of everything but is a development of the human mind that goes beyond theories to interiority. Theories are reasonably easy to understand. A theory is an explanation that seeks to relate things to one

---

2. An editor of Aristotle's works, Andronicus of Rhodes, found a collection of writings of Aristotle on the general theme of first principles and causes, substance, being, first philosophy, and God. He put them together in one book which he called the *Metaphysics*, simply because they came after the *Physics—meta* meaning "after" in Greek.

another rather than to oneself. Theory is a jump into measurement and definition, seeking precision and excluding relativity to the observer. Geometry and other forms of mathematics are almost pure theory. We can cope with theories. Most of our scientific knowledge is theoretical or derived from theories. Theories demand a certain asceticism and concentration but, in the end, we understand. Theories represent an enormous leap above the relativism and vagueness of common sense and personal description. But they also embody deficits of their own which call for a further development in understanding.

Most systems of philosophy have been presented in the mode of theory. Certain principles and general axioms are accepted as true and basic and unquestioned. These basic principles are then expanded, applied, and elaborated in various relevant areas. Concepts are defined, divided and subdivided; logic is developed and utilized; coherence in the resultant system is valued and achieved. Theoretical problems, thus, are solved in this context of systems of axioms, principles and concepts.

But further questions arise, such as: how does theory relate to common sense; what are the advantages and disadvantages of theory; what are the criteria for the best theory, simplicity, or beauty, or generality, or verifiability or falsifiability; how and why does one theory replace another? The weakness of theories is that their foundational definitions and axioms can be changed quite arbitrarily. New data can undermine the most sophisticated or elaborate theories. We need an understanding of how theories function in the development of understanding in a discipline, what role do they play, and how and why they change. Hence our focus returns to the question of human understanding and the possibility of a frame of reference that goes beyond theories to interiority.

Scientists will spontaneously appeal to their own data to justify their conclusions and that is right and proper. But if you are a philosopher and you want to present a theory of knowledge, to what data do you turn to justify your conclusions? I would hold that you can only justify a theory of knowledge by presenting data which shows how knowledge actually occurs, what are its stages, its dynamic, its parts, its activities. Epistemologists can only justify their theories by appealing to their own data, which in this case is the actual conscious process of knowing, as it occurs in your mind and my mind. Harvesting the data on "the activities of knowing" is difficult. We can only know the minds of other people mediately, indirectly, through their descriptions and interpretations. We can only become familiar with the workings of our own minds by a process of self-appropriation involving describing, differentiating, naming, identifying and pinning down our own actual experience of understanding.

Introspection has always been suspect as a method in psychology as also in philosophy; but the reality is that it is only by some form of introspection or retrospection that we can describe human cognitional activities, differentiate them, line them up in an order of dependence and thus understand what we are doing when we are knowing. Theories need logic to ensure the coherence of conclusions with premises; interiority needs method to ensure that all affirmations about experiencing, understanding and judging are based on the reality of how the human mind spontaneously works in this way to produce true judgments. The process of knowing is difficult to pin down because it is dynamic, it is constituted by a series of different, distinct, subsidiary activities rather than being one single activity, and above all because it demands reflection and self-knowledge.

Interiority involves an intimate familiarity with the actual processes of conscious, human knowing. That is the springboard to a precise, accurate, comprehensive account of understanding in both the sciences of the parts and a worldview of the whole. That is the mentality pervading this text. That is what makes it difficult for theoretical philosophy or theoretical metaphysics to grasp. Unfortunately, there is no way of getting around this difficulty; it has to be taken head on. First philosophy is a call to self-knowledge which provides the framework for understanding our universe in all its diversity in unity, its detail and simplicity. A detailed, systematic elaboration of the characteristics of interiority will be presented in chapter 1.

In the *Phenomenology of Human Understanding,* I used a method of self-appropriation to give an accurate, verifiable, detailed account of human understanding. Humans achieve knowledge by questioning what they experience, by understanding and formulating hypotheses, by reflecting on the sufficiency or insufficiency of the evidence for verifying the truth of the hypothesis, and by evaluating the discovery in terms of its implications, possibilities, uses for the good of humanity. This process represents a critical realist position that can be contrasted with inadequate accounts of human knowing found in the empiricist, materialist, analytic, and continental traditions. Our account was found to give objective knowledge and was not open to basic revision. The method explicitly focuses on actual experience of how people come to understand and to know. It appeals to biographies, psychologists and sociologists, various accounts of aspects of human knowing. But the critical source of data is one's own experience of questioning, thinking, understanding, criticizing, judging, and evaluating. The chief benefit of all this self-appropriation is the discovery of the criterion: "the real is the verified; it is what is to be known by the knowing constituted by experience and inquiry, insight and hypothesis, reflection and verification."[3]

I would like to have published that text as Volume One and the present text as Volume Two, but I was not so prescient at the time. That would express more clearly the relationship between the two works. The second flows from the first and has to take for granted many of the achievements of that first text. Briefly, that first text answered the question, "What are we doing when we are knowing?" This second text answers the follow-up question, "What do we know when we are doing that?" The first is about knowing and the second is about the known. The first book establishes clearly the process of human knowing; this second text focuses on the broad outlines of what is to be known when we do that. The suggestion is that if the activities of human knowing form a basic and consistent structure, surely that which is known will in some fashion mirror that basic and consistent structure. In other words, the reality that we know will mirror the process by which we come to know.

What we are attempting here is not just a scholarly rehabilitation of metaphysics, not just an academic exercise, but a vision of the function of metaphysics in our daily lives, in our culture and politics, in the sciences, and in the university. Metaphysics matters. Although it seems to be far removed from the concrete details and decisions of life on the ground, our individual metaphysical principles influence and actually determine what those decisions will be. Positions taken up on issues of metaphysics have practical applications and implications that influence every detail of our emotional, social, cultural and ethical lives.

Aims and Intentions

Let us formulate clearly our aims and intentions so that we can understand clearly what we are doing. I suggest five prongs to this attack.

1. Our main aim, as the title of the book suggests, is to formulate a worldview that will be: *correct*, in the sense of true and accurate to the data available; *coherent*, in the sense of everything working together with no contradictions or friction between parts; *unifying*, in the sense of seeing the many interrelations and interdependencies between parts; *critical*, in the sense of worked out methodically according to clear criteria; *verifiable*, in appealing to sufficient evidence and understanding,

---

3. Lonergan, *Insight*, 277.

whether of the data of sense or data of consciousness;[4] *comprehensive*, in the sense of including everything; *therapeutic* in the sense of including values and goodness, promoting progress and reversing decline. At the same time as we promote such laudable aims, we work against and reject worldviews that do not rise to these high standards.

2. The worldview we aim at is a kind of wisdom that understands how everything is related to everything else, how all the parts and details relate to the whole, how the knowing relates to the known. Our knowledge varies from the very specific and particular, to the very general and universal. Between these two extremes there is a spectrum or continuum in terms of generality or particularity. Knowledge of the specific is usually the knowledge of common sense as well as the knowledge of the specialist, the scientist, knowledge of practical skills and applications to concrete situations. On the other hand, there is the kind of knowledge which consists of general principles, universal causes, understanding the whole, which is a characteristic of the philosopher. Although the general and the particular seem far apart, these kinds of knowledge are intimately related, influence one another, cannot be separated, like the whole and the part. The general worldview of the whole sets the context, interprets, criticizes, transforms and unifies the knowledge of the specialist. But where would the whole be without the parts! The scientist, the people of common sense, the specialists, provide the material details, the parts to be unified into a whole. If one's worldview is healthy and correct then it will promote a correct understanding, interpretation and unification of the parts. If one's worldview is twisted, narrow, naive, or incorrect then the knowledge of the sciences and common sense will likewise be twisted and incorrect. Philosophy is not some abstract discipline irrelevant and separated from all the other disciplines. Wisdom is the ability to grasp the big picture, to see the unity between the many parts, to integrate all human knowledge into a single healthy worldview.

3. We aim not just at understanding but also at "healing and creating"[5] the universe in all its aspects but especially its culture and science. Knowing is incomplete if it does not include knowledge of the good

---

4. Data of sense focuses on the contents of what we see, hear, remember, touch, understand and know. Data of consciousness is our awareness of the operations of seeing, questioning, thinking, concluding, and evaluating as mental activities. See chapter 1, section 3.1.

5. Lonergan wrote an article on "Healing and Creating in History" in vol. 16 of the *Collected Works*, 94–104

and produce fruits in good decisions and actions for individuals and society. A salutary worldview promotes such goodness and reverses the evil effects that an inadequate or false worldview will inevitably produce. Good actions, policies and programs will only emerge from good decisions aiming for objective progress and not from self-interest, deceit, pride, or ignorance. Good decisions emerge from a correct set of value judgments that establish an objective order of priorities and ends. Good judgments of value will only emerge from a basis of correct judgments of truth about science, about climate, about causes and diseases. Good judgments of truth will only emerge from the effort to understand correctly, to grasp the sufficiency of evidence, to link the evidence to the conclusion.

4. We aim to promoting the shift from theory to interiority. Lonergan has not just produced a new theory of knowing, he has ushered in a new mode of awareness of the process of knowing and how that gives us a new control over meaning. I have great sympathy with those who find Lonergan a hard read. It is a hard read because we start reading thinking that it is a new theory; but it is not a theory. It is an invitation to go beyond to the source of theories, the source of culture, the source of philosophy, in the unrelenting desire to know and the criteria and norms operating in our efforts to understand. It is an invitation to self-awareness, self-understanding, self-affirmation, self-evaluation, self-control and full human authenticity. Sadly, our educational systems are moving more and more in the direction of short-term gain, immediate practicality, get the students into the job market as quickly as possible, give them the style but not the substance, the procedures but not the underlying understanding. Professors are told to prepare them for the "real world." As if history, chemistry, literature, physics, mathematics, philosophy and theology had nothing to do with the real world!

5. We also aim at promoting a greater familiarity with the thought of Lonergan. Reading the secondary literature that popularizes and simplifies Lonergan's work—like this text—is not enough. This text may serve as an introduction, but so many matters of substance have been left out, so much detail and richness of illustration, so much depth, that I almost apologize for the poverty of this text. But I hope that its focus on Lonergan's metaphysics will make it worthwhile to those searching for helpful introductory material.

Most of the ideas presented here originated in the writings of Bernard Lonergan, SJ (1904–84), particularly his magnum opus, *Insight: A Study of Human Understanding*. In Aristotle and Aquinas metaphysics preceded epistemology, which was consequently elaborated in metaphysical terminology and concepts. Lonergan has reversed the order and it is only after a detailed study of human knowing that he attempts to extrapolate to a metaphysics. The focus of modern and contemporary philosophy is on the question of human knowing, its scope and limits. The turn to the subject is typical of Western philosophy after Descartes. Lonergan completes the turn to the subject by finally identifying the sequence of cognitional activities that constitute correct critical human knowing. Having done that, he is in a good position to move on to metaphysics. He recognises a parallel between the activities of knowing and the contents known; the structure of knowing is reflected in the structure of the known. Lonergan's presentation relates these two structures, presenting epistemology and metaphysics as complementary and advances in one stimulating advances in the other. His treatment of metaphysics in chapters 14–18 of *Insight* is brilliant, coherent, original and practical. However, it is also somewhat detailed and inaccessible to those who are not professional philosophers familiar with the background. Hence, this text seeks to present Lonergan's worldview in a manner accessible to scientists, students, professors and all who wonder about the structure of the universe.

This approach is philosophical rather than theological or religious, not because the latter methods are illegitimate or unimportant but because they introduce a dimension that is beyond our scope here. We will inquire about the transcendent but only from the point of view of universal human experience and understanding. Many people get their unified view of everything from belief in a religious perspective. Thus, you can have a worldview based on Christian teaching, or Hindu, Buddhist, Islamic, teachings, or African Traditional Religions, and so on. Personally, I am a Christian following the Roman Catholic tradition, a member of a missionary congregation, and this position informs my philosophical worldview. But any religious perspective supposes the existence of the world, that we can know reality, that there are moral norms underpinning our behavior. Christian theology is described as "faith seeking understanding"; it might help theologians if they have some idea of what it is to understand. There should be no conflict between theology, science, and philosophy. Each is seeking the truth and if truth is found in any part, it must be compatible with the whole. Unfortunately, philosophy has been conspicuous by its absence in the debates between scientists and theologians and thus regarded as irrelevant to culture and education. I think it has a vital role to play in these areas.

The central thesis then is that we can identify and affirm the four levels of our human knowing in experiencing, understanding, judging truth and judging values, because the evidence is in our own minds and is accessible to everyone. We can extrapolate from these structural components of one knowing by noting that we experience the sensible, we understand ideas and forms, we judge what is real and true, and we appreciate what is of real value. For millennia epistemologists have struggled to find a comprehensive correct account of human knowing and metaphysicians have struggled with terms like matter and form, potency and act, being and substance, the real and the good. What an extraordinary unifying insight it is to discover that the basic structure of human knowing gives us a way of defining and controlling metaphysical terms! Knowing composed of experiencing, understanding, judging truth and value, has a counterpart in the content that is known as potency, form, existent and good. Epistemology and metaphysics are parallel and complementary and mutually inform one another.

Summary of Text

Part 1 of the text—the first three chapters—deals with the methodological problems involved in this new, interiority-based approach to a worldview of everything. A correct understanding of Aristotle's notion of first philosophy is our starting point. But so much has changed in philosophy, culture, science, technology and social organization since then that we cannot be content with repeating Aristotle. Many of these changes represent progress and authentic development of clear differentiated thought underpinning a new worldview. Is there a method by which we can systematically and critically reach such a worldview? I propose a method of isomorphism by which we move from an appreciation of the invariant structure of the activity of knowing, to a parallel invariant structure of all that is to be known.

Part 2 of the text—chapters 4–8—outlines the structure of the elements of the universe from a "synchronic" or structural point of view. We start to implement that method by assigning a clear meaning to the term "being." In our universe it would seem that being is invariably constituted by the elements of the sensible, the intelligible, the actual and the good. From a structural or static point of view, we can differentiate every item of the known universe into these basic metaphysical elements, whether it be a tree, an atom, a galaxy, or a person; in the field of physics, biology, economics, or anthropology; we can differentiate anything known or to be known into these four invariant elements. However, we differentiate in order to integrate; we analyze in order to synthesize; we tear apart in order to put together again. That is how understanding works. In these chapters, we identify these four elements; we ask how they are defined, how they are related together; how they constitute a unity; and what kind of wisdom emerges from our analysis.

Part 3 of the text—comprising chapters 9–14—recognizes that our universe is also dynamic, has a history, and develops over time. We study the universe from a diachronic perspective. We summarize this dynamic worldview of everything under the term "generalized emergent probability." Order and complexity emerge in the story of our universe. There is diversity but there is also unity; there is differentiation but also integration. We note the emergence of substances, things, and unities over time. We note that things have properties and that properties inhere in things. We note that *physicists* identify subatomic elements, atoms, and the elements of the periodic table. *Chemists* examine the complex compounds that emerge from combinations of elements and there is an increasing level of complexity in organic chemistry. *Botanists* classify plants and trees in terms of classes, orders, families, genera and species, subspecies and varieties. The less complex ground the emergence of the more complex. Similarly, *biologists* identify the simplest of cells but note how they complexify, become multicellular living beings, from which emerge fishes, crustaceans, bacteria, reptiles, mammals and so on. The history of our universe is a story of emergence, from subatomic to atoms, to molecules, to living cells, to plants and animals, to human persons.

The human person is the culmination of all these processes of emergence. The human is dependent on and shares so many characteristics of our physical, and chemical universe, our botanical and biological ancestors, but emerges with a new characteristic: that of intelligent, reasonable, responsible and transcendent potencies. What emerges is the ability to be conscious, to feel, to sense and to act; to ask questions about what we experience; to understand the laws and regularities operating in our universe; to verify true accounts and reject mythological stories; to be able to evaluate discoveries and apply them in a technology; to learn to live well in a society, to love and to act with freedom and responsibility. All this makes human beings the peak of the known universe, the greatest achievement of the process of emergence. It does come with a downside, namely, the struggle between self-interest and detached intelligence, between in-groups and out-groups, between war and peace, between progress and decline.

In our final chapter, we ask the ultimate question about God. To be fully human is to be on the way to something more than human. From the beginning, humanity has manifested an aspiration to transcendence, has believed in a transcendent being, and offered sacrifice, worship, praise and thanksgiving. Every culture has given its own shape and form to these religious practices and beliefs. We can truly say that humans are "*homo religiosus.*" Philosophers approached the transcendent by way of asking about the ultimate origin and end of all things. Is the universe a random accident or is it completely intelligible? Philosophy shows our openness to the transcendent by way of our propensity to ask ultimate, unrestricted questions. Questions lead to answers and answers change our ways of living. So, the history of humanity shows both a universal openness to transcendence and a variety of religious experience, worship, ritual and beliefs.

Part One: The Notion of First Philosophy

1

Foundations

All men by nature desire understanding.[1]

Deep within us all, emergent when the noise of other appetites is stilled, there is a drive to know, to understand, to see why, to discover the reason, to find the cause, to explain.[2]

The question we have identified as first in rank—"Why are there beings at all instead of nothing?"—is thus the fundamental question of metaphysics. Metaphysics stands as the name for the center and core that determines all philosophy.[3]

Just as metaphysics can exist only in a mind and can be produced only by the mind in which it is to be, so also metaphysics can begin only in minds that exist and it can proceed only from their actual texture and complexion. Bluntly, the starting point of metaphysics is people as they are.[4]

Introduction

(I usually start each chapter with some relevant quotations highlighting the central issue of the chapter, presenting contrasting views on the question, and hopefully arousing interest. These issues will be clarified and explained in the course of the chapter, some quotes being accepted, and others being rejected. The quotes from Aristotle and Lonergan above situate the beginning of philosophy in the desire to know. This chapter identifies the

1. Aristotle, *Metaphysics*, A, 1, 980a.
2. Lonergan, *Insight*, 28.
3. Heidegger, *Introduction to Metaphysics*, 19.
4. Lonergan, *Insight*, 422.

desire to know and shows how it works towards a philosophy of everything. I would rephrase Heidegger's question and pose it as, there *is* something, but why?)

WE START IN THIS part 1 by elaborating how we intend to achieve this worldview of everything. There are critical foundational questions to be answered here. Many philosophers would consider such an ambition to be in vain. Most scientists do not see any role for philosophy in their understanding of the universe. In this first chapter we establish the basic structure of human knowing. I have done this previously in the *Phenomenology of Human Understanding*, but I feel it is necessary to establish briefly here how human knowing works and how we can be confident in affirming the truth of laws, principles and facts. After that we will be in a position to establish a method for achieving the aims of first philosophy (chapter 2). We will relate first philosophy to the sciences (chapter 3), and then start outlining a critical worldview (parts 2 and 3).

What Kind of Foundations?

Aristotle was a philosopher who worked in the mode of theory. He developed his concepts and principles throughout his life in his books on logic, his Physics, his Ethics, and especially in the *Metaphysics*. Lastly, he wrote *On the Soul*, where he poses the question, what is thinking? It is natural that his answer came in the theoretical terminology that he had developed. Thus, in his answer he distinguished active and passive intellect, material and immaterial reception of form, potentially and actually intelligible, images and ideas. Aquinas adopted the same approach and further defined, divided, and applied this terminology to the process of understanding in extraordinary detail. Aristotle, Aquinas and the Scholastic tradition dealt first with metaphysical concepts and later understood the process of knowing in terms of these theoretical concepts. They took the validity of the basic structure of knowing for granted and did not have to face the critical challenges of deconstruction,[5] "brain in a vat,"[6] everything is absurd,[7] and other radical, sceptical, approaches to human knowing.

Much has changed since the time of Aristotle. The empirical sciences have declared their independence of philosophy, have developed their own

5. A notion initiated by Nietzsche.

6. How do we know the external world is real? Perhaps the brain is in a vat with all the nerve endings of the senses connected to mechanical stimuli! A recent debate among Analytic philosophers.

7. See Midgley, *Are You an Illusion?*

methods, specialized, proliferated, invented instruments, measured precisely and applied their discoveries in technologies of transport, medicine, communications and construction that have transformed our human way of living. As of old, each science cuts off a part of reality be it physics, chemistry or biology; it sets up its department and devotes itself to developing and applying its laws and principles within its own field. The sciences develop largely by specialization, by more and more detailed exploration, observation and implementation in the most minute areas. More than ever because of this departmentalisation we need a metaphysics to develop a worldview of everything, to understand how all the parts of all the specialities fit together, to understand the causes and principles common to all scientific disciplines and to integrate the parts into a unified worldview of the human person in an evolving universe.

The moderns preferred the turn to the subject and find it difficult to even understand the terminology of Aristotle and Aquinas. They preferred the vernacular language and to develop their own theories about human knowing—now a central topic. The theory of knowledge took central stage, and it determined the possibility and limits of metaphysical knowledge. An empiricist epistemology leaves little or no room for metaphysics. Kant elaborated a detailed theory of knowledge which gave very little room for metaphysics. Although the concepts and terminology change, the mode of theory remains. And so we have rationalist theories, idealistic theories, Marxist, nihilist, structuralist, postmodern, empiricist theories, phenomenological theories, all competing with one another in schools and none of them quite solving the problem.

Theories are usually based on certain axioms and definitions from which you elaborate positions and conclusions as in Euclid's geometry. But can such principles be presupposed, can they not be questioned and changed, they may be shaky foundations. What is the starting point for a presuppositionless philosophy?

Is it possible to work out a correct and adequate first philosophy, which will retrieve the achievements of the past two millennia and speak to the challenges of the third millennium? Is it possible to be methodical, critical, precise, and relevant for our times? Can we discern the genuine achievements of modern and contemporary philosophy? Can we build on foundations that will be really impregnable? Can we learn from mistaken worldviews and find the fundamental cause of error and of evil? These and other questions, we hope to answer. In general terms our approach is to start from where you are and describe particular actual acts of human understanding and judging. Describe the individual cognitional activities in detail. Knowing is not a big undifferentiated blob; it is not a black box or a mystery. Discern the sequence of activities and characteristics involved in moving from a question to an answer. Knowing is a spiral of developments in questioning, imagination, awareness, intelligence, clarity, judgment and differentiation. Theories tend to lose touch with concrete reality. One fact can destroy the most grandiose of theories.

How do we find foundations for our approach to a contemporary first philosophy? Lonergan suggests that a contemporary philosophy should be structured around three basic questions. The *first* asks the question, "What do I do when I am knowing?" When we seek to know, we first ask questions about what we experience in order to understand correctly. There is a sequence of activities which we must perform to find the correct answer. If we identify this sequence, there emerges a cognitional theory, namely, a pattern of the mental activities involved in knowing.

The *second* question is, "Why is doing that knowing?" This deals with self-affirmation, the notion of being and objectivity. If we perform the above activities, we know beings and being. Objectivity requires that we ask every relevant question, do not go beyond the evidence, and do not let bias enter into our reasoning. Absolute objectivity is not constituted by sensation alone but more broadly by what our intelligence grasps as true from evidence sufficient to support a conclusion. Knowing is knowing being, including things that are not physical, such as love, friendship, or quantum realities.

The *third* question is, "What do I know when I do that?" In other words, what is the content of our knowing, of asking and answering questions? What is the broad structure of all that is to be known? It is the question for first philosophy to put in contemporary terms. This is the primary question of this book. We are not looking for the detailed answers to every particular question under the sun, but the general unity and structure underlying all particular detailed answers. We will proceed point by point to identify this new notion of first philosophy.

Describing Human Understanding

We start with a description of human understanding from a purely psychological point of view to get some grasp of the concrete details of the sequence of activities that produces items of human knowing. From these foundations we will extrapolate to a metaphysics and a worldview of everything. We are completing the turn to the subject, not leading to subjectivism or relativism or emotivism, but by way of authentic self-appropriation. At the end of the day our only access to the detailed stages of human knowing is through attention to how our own minds work.

One obstacle to the study of human understanding is that we think we know it already. We have been understanding and knowing all of our lives especially in a formal educational setting and so we take for granted that we know what "knowing" refers to. But such "knowing" is just an undifferentiated "blob" or black box. Discussions of theories of knowing are conspicuous by the absence of real, concrete, detailed examples of human understanding and knowing. But it is from that point that we start in order to differentiate the parts, to keep our feet on the ground, to appreciate the complications and subtlety of the process of understanding.

Consciousness

Let us start with the experience of being conscious.[8] "Conscious" is an adjective as in, a conscious act, a conscious motivation, I was conscious of X, I am conscious of my appearance, etc. This is an experience. Cognates would be, to be aware, alert, paying attention, awake, and the like. We are unconscious when in a deep sleep, under anaesthetic, after suffering a blow to the head, and perhaps when we are dead. We know the difference between being unconscious, being semi-conscious, and being fully conscious. It is crucial to identify for oneself this experience of being conscious and its opposite being unconscious, and to distinguish consciousness which is more a state from cognitional activities such as seeing or understanding or evaluating. Describe various states of being conscious, describe mental activities that we perform when we are conscious. Explore the difficulties of focusing your attention on some problem to the exclusion of all else. Identify activities of remembering, imagining, thinking, getting an idea, and coming to a conclusion. Take possession of your own mind. Mindfulness, meditation, analysis of problem solving, examining your conscience, becoming aware of implicit bias, and the like, can help. Above all distinguish being conscious from the cognitional activities you perform.

Data of sense is what is given in experiences of seeing, hearing, touching, smelling, tasting, and often remembering and imagining. As given, the data is undifferentiated, unquestioned, preconceptual, unnamed, but the experience establishes the possibility and perhaps stimulates the occurrence of questioning, understanding and knowing. The sciences are massively oriented in the direction of data of sense and do extraordinarily successful work on the macro and micro world. However, they are usually very poor on the knowledge of the subject, the experience of human knowing, human valuing and deciding. By *data of consciousness* we mean attending to the experience of thinking, imagining, deciding, feeling and other mental processes. We shift the focus of our attention from external data of sense to the activities by which we see, think about, analyze and

---

8. I devoted chapter 2 of *Phenomenology of Human Understanding* to describing and explaining consciousness.

know; we shift attention from the content of knowing to the activities of knowing. We focus on the ideas, the images, the thought processes, the fantasies and imaginings that go on in our minds. The data of consciousness is given in the sense that we perform these activities before we know what we are doing. We spontaneously imagine, think, ask questions, search for understanding. All these activities precede our reflective attention and efforts to identify these activities. The experience precedes identifying, naming and understanding this sequence of cognitional activities. But if you want to formulate a theory of human knowing, would it not be advisable to start by attending to what actually happens in the mind when we do science, or calculus, or solve a crossword puzzle. We would be astonished at the foolishness of a botanist writing a book about forests, without actually having visited a forest in his life. How can we expect to know about human knowing without having experienced, visited, attended to, identified, taken possession of the data of consciousness that is the starting point of our study? Self-appropriation shifts attention from the content of knowing to the activities involved in knowing. Therein lies the rub.

We can describe what it is like to be conscious, but can we define it? I suggest that consciousness is an awareness of self that is immanent in our awareness of objects or contents. If we are studying calculus, we are focusing on numbers, infinities, equations, and the like, but we are also concomitantly are aware that it is "I" who is trying to understand. We are focusing on the content, ideas, figures and equations but there is an immanent awareness that it is myself who is the subject of the activity. A conscious act of seeing necessitates a subject seeing, the activity of seeing and something that is seen. There is only one seeing which incorporates a subject and an object—a person and a content. Consciousness is simply the abstract substantive by which we refer to this experience. I give a precise meaning to consciousness as that awareness of self, which is concomitant with our awareness of objects, but is usually in the background. Many authors use the term consciousness to refer to anything that goes on in the head. That way lies utter confusion. A dog that is awake is conscious, but that does not mean that he is thinking deep thoughts.

Our natural focus, whether we are operating in the realm of common sense, science, or philosophy, is towards the object or content of our knowing, rather than our acts or operations of knowing. Just as you can shift your awareness from sights to sounds, you can also shift awareness from the content of cognitional acts to the activities by which they are made known. There is an enormous advantage in focusing on these activities as you can then discover the basic structure of human understanding and knowing. If you consider the activity of seeing you note that the possible objects of sight can be nearly infinite while the act of seeing is basically the same in all cases.

One act of sight can see any number of combinations of colors, shapes and sizes. I could spend a year describing everything I can see out my window. But there is only one activity of seeing. Similarly, if you consider the activity of understanding, you can again recognize that the content of any act of understanding is a quasi-infinity, while the basic act of understanding remains fundamentally the same. If you think of the books in your library, add the libraries of the world, add the sciences, languages, specializations and disciplines of a university, then you realize how much there is to be understood. But throughout all areas of potential understanding, the one act of understanding retains its basic structure; it is similar in all cases, which is why we use the same word for all these acts of understandings.

Similarly, we often criticize and reflect on whether what we have understood is true or false; we listen to the radio, read the newspapers, but we do not believe everything we hear or read. We look for evidence, plausibility, credibility, check the source of the communication and so on. We are constantly on the alert for fraud, lies, exaggerations, misinformation, fake news, and the like. But reflection and criticism are basically the same in all cases. Similarly, we evaluate the weather, the food we eat, the professor who is teaching, the clothes people are wearing; we evaluate our friends, our politicians, our leaders, our teachers, our phones and our computers; we make our own free moral decisions about our own actions. But the activity of evaluating, judging the value of, is fundamentally the same. Similarly, there are many global religious traditions with an enormous variety of practices, traditions, beliefs, ways of worshiping, celebrating, behaving and praying but there is a common core of something like "holiness" underlying all these practices. Shifting attention from the quasi-infinite contents of our experiencing, understanding, judging, evaluating and worshiping to identifying the basic cognitional activities achieves an enormous simplicity and unity of our activities of knowing.

We can differentiate levels of consciousness according to the relevant mental activity. If we are simply operating at the level of seeing and sensing, then we have experiential consciousness. If we are asking questions or trying to solve puzzles, we are operating at the level of intellectual consciousness. If we are criticizing and reflecting and trying to work out true or false, then we are operating at the level of rational consciousness. If we are trying to decide what is right or wrong, good or bad, better or best, we are operating at the level of personal or moral consciousness, also called conscience. If we are praying, worshiping, meditating, then we are operating at the level of religious consciousness.

We are aware that asking the reader to focus on their own operations or activities of knowing, is novel pedagogical strategy. It is difficult but the rewards are great indeed. For example, instead of focusing on Archimedes' discovery of the notion of density, we would focus on what kind of mental activities he performed before, during, and after his discovery. Could he do it without understanding, without experimenting, without getting ideas, without checking conclusions? Take any examples of real historical discoveries, study the biography and the details, and imagine what was going on in the head of the scientist. Then turn to your own experiences of correct understanding. In self-awareness you have access to the activity of imagination and intelligence, to images and ideas, to bright ideas that work and brilliant ideas that are useless. Describing mental activities is an empirical scientific activity, because they are part of our own experience, and we have direct access to how knowing works. We just don't pay much attention to these activities, usually. In attending to the experience of thinking and knowing, we are following the same steps as the empirical scientist, except that our attention is directed to the data of consciousness rather than the data of sense. To our surprise perhaps we can discover the difference between imagining and understanding, between thinking and knowing, between images and ideas. Perhaps also we might discover the almost infinite flexibility and creativity of human intelligence! Freud described his own dreams in meticulous detail. Surely then we can also describe examples of problem solving, ideas emerging from images, judgments emerging from evidence and arguments!

Self-appropriation then is the method. Our focus in this section on consciousness is to justify this possibility of describing our own process of knowing. It means attending not so much to the contents to be known but to the basic activities by which they become known. This is not private unverifiable unrepeatable introspection, but a collaborative process of sharing experiences, checking and helping one another, comparing observations and enriching our self-knowledge. If one can describe one's feelings, dreams, motivations, intentions, symptoms, fantasies, memories, hopes, then surely one can describe our processes of asking questions, understanding ideas, judging propositions and deciding, what is the best thing to do. Students can discuss different mental activities, can correct or improve descriptions, share what is common and notice what is different. It is not rocket science, but it does require maturity, effort, and concentration.

Human Understanding

To understand is synonymous with having an insight. To have an insight is to have a eureka moment, an Aha! moment: we get it, we grasp the point, we see the solution, a bulb lights up. These are colloquial terms for an experience which I hope you can recognize in your own life. We are puzzled by a position in chess; we think of various possibilities, we eliminate some, go back to others, we get our ducks in line, we understand, we make the right move. The clearest examples are to be fund in puzzles, chess, bridge, sudoku, card games, simple geometrical or mathematical or mechanical or practical situations. Studies in the human sciences such as economics, sociology, psychology, history and the like are often quite complicated, and it is not easy to isolate a single clear example of understanding and judging. Further, there seems to be a pattern in the emergence of an insight. We move from puzzlement to effort and tension; we reach a brick wall, we take a break; we come back to the problem, and it hits us immediately, we get it. We write it down, check it out and are mightily relieved. We can identify and describe five distinct characteristics or activities in the process of understanding.

First, we have the desire to know, we are puzzled, we are interested, we want to find the solution, it is annoying when you cannot fill in the last word in a crossword puzzle. If you are not interested, not motivated, do not care, are not paying attention, then forget it; you will never understand. The more interested or devoted or concentrated you are, the more likely you are to understand.

Secondly, we must do what we possibly can to reach understanding. This may involve research, going to the library, looking up dictionaries, consulting Google, or simply thinking, analyzing, looking for examples, images, memories, or similar problems, hoping to precipitate understanding. Thinking takes time.

Thirdly, there is a receptive element in understanding. It comes suddenly and unexpectedly. We recognize this when we use expressions like, it came to me, I got it, it dawned on me. One moment you do not understand; the next moment you have it; but you do not know where it came from. We are not in complete control of the emergence of an act of understanding. We do what we can, we provide the conditions for the emergence, but it cannot be forced, it is not automatic. Some students understand immediately, some have to struggle, some will never get there. In certain mathematical calculations you follow the rules, and you will get the right result; you have a procedure to follow. But more often we are in the dark and have to work out a method to reach the solution. This is the creative moment in understanding something new.

Fourthly, when we get an insight, an idea emerges from an image. Images are from the senses, visual, tactile, audio, olfactory, taste or sensory motor images of movement, place, speed and the like; we use our memories and imaginations. We manipulate images, data, memories diagrams, in order to produce understanding. This pivoting from images to ideas is the crucial element in the act of understanding.

Images are sensible whereas ideas are intelligible. You can have an infinite number of images of a triangle, but there is only one correct definition or idea of a triangle. Every human person is unique in the sense of being a different size, weight, color, age, sex, from a particular place and time; but all are human persons, all share the idea or definition of a human person.

Images are particular whereas ideas are universal. Archimedes experimented with one particular chalice, at one particular time, in one particular place. But the idea of specific weight refers to every material or liquid at any time or in any place.

We need the images to get the insight. If you want to communicate an insight to students you present particular examples, illustrations, diagrams, that might spark an idea, a law, a regularity, or a solution. As Aristotle put it: the active intellect throws light on phantasms so that the potentially intelligible becomes actually intelligible and is received into the passive intellect. He actually knew what he was talking about.

Fifthly, once we get an idea it becomes part of the habitual texture of the mind. It is easy to have the same insight again. It is easy to remember something that you have understood. There are moral habits like kindness or patience which become habitual, easy and pleasurable when we have attained them. There are intellectual habits of concentration, inquiry, criticism which become easier the more they are exercised. Ideas, laws, principles are understood and taken for granted and we move on to further matters. Our minds are formed and informed by ideas. A doctor thinks like a doctor; a philosopher thinks like a philosopher; that is what seven years of study will do to you.

Perhaps we could add a note on what an act of understanding is not. It is not an intuition, namely, it is not a vision, not a single act of intuiting, not a direct contact with reality, not taking a look. In my use of terminology an insight is a full act of human understanding as defined above; it is complex, mediated by images and language and context, unique in its own right, and fundamentally different from acts of sensation. Intuition is a very common way of misinterpreting understanding as simple, single, direct contact, touching reality. Seeing and hearing and touching do not give us a model for the act of understanding. Understanding involves a sequence of mental activities and we can get stuck at any of the steps on the way. Attend to your own personal examples of understanding. Do not take my word for it. The great advantage of self-appropriation is that you can see for yourself.

Human Knowing

Direct understanding as explained above gives you an idea, but as we know to our cost, a possible idea is not necessarily a correct idea. An idea is a possibility, a hypothesis, a possibly relevant explanation or solution. An idea brings us halfway to knowledge. Descartes made the mistake of thinking that all clear and distinct ideas were true. This is a major misunderstanding still infecting much contemporary philosophy. But it is not hard to pick out examples of very clear and distinct ideas which are palpably untrue, and somewhat confused, vague generalization which nonetheless are true. Insights are a dime a dozen. We have to persevere and ask further questions, namely, is it true, is it correct, how do I know that it is right, how do I know that it will work. This is the critical question.

A further act of reflective understanding is required. It is a further act of understanding and therefore will arise from questions, will involve activities of research and thinking, will have a receptive aspect by which the insight comes, an idea emerges from images and the idea passes into the habitual texture of the mind. The idea in the case of a reflective insight is a grasp of the relation between the sufficiency of the evidence and the evidence entailing the conclusion; it is a grasp of the relation between evidence and conclusion. It is intelligence at work in the search for true knowledge. Nowadays we use the expression "evidence-based knowledge," as if there were a true knowledge for which there is no evidence! The proximate criterion of truth is the sufficiency of the evidence for the conclusion in any particular example. The remote criterion of truth is the desire to know operative in asking all relevant questions, being free from bias, assessing the evidence and the arguments connecting the evidence to the conclusion. A reflective insight is needed in all examples of commonsense knowledge, scientific knowledge, knowledge in any discipline or skill, and even in philosophy and theology. It is the reflective insight that grasps the connection between evidence and conclusion and the necessity of positing the judgment. The judgment adds no content to the reflective insight except the affirmation of truth or falsity. If you start looking for further evidence then you have not yet affirmed the judgment, you are still assessing the evidence. Affirmation or denial however is crucial. It is the difference between possibility and reality, legend and history, alchemy and chemistry, pseudo and real, fiction and non-fiction, magic and science, fake and real. In our judgments we take a personal stand, we define what we believe in, we move from opinions to truths. It has taken two and a half millennia to realize that human knowing is a simple process of asking questions about what we experience in order to understand and formulate hypotheses; further, that possibilities are not conclusions, so we go further to ask if our hypothesis is correct, if there is enough evidence, and if the data entails the conclusion. Such is a judgement of truth or of fact.

Judgments of Value

The process of knowing truth may finish there but more often than not a further question will arise as to, what is the best thing to do with this discovery or truth or explanation. Questions arise as to implications, applications, and implementations. So, you question the value of your idea, explore possibilities, identity advantages and disadvantages, and eventually judge, what is the right thing to do. Another question is asked—the question of value. Another insight is required, in this case a deliberative insight. And then a further judgment emerges, a judgment of value. There is a further sequence of activities required parallel to those for the judgment of truth. A deliberative insight is sought, and we see the five characteristics of insight operative again. There are activities of researching, investigations, observations; ideas and concepts and principles are thought about. But there are also receptions by which the idea comes, it pops into your mind; you do not have full control of the process. A deliberative insight then is grasping the sufficiency of the evidence, which entails a conclusion regarding the value or worth of what is to be done. Once you have understood the worth of something, the idea passes into the habitual texture of the mind and becomes part of your habitual value priorities.

There is a feeling element that enters into the process of knowing truth and value from the very beginning and it is the desire to know. This is a feeling experienced as an Eros of the mind, the search for truth, intellectual curiosity, love of wisdom. The intellectual or philosopher is not a dispassionate creature forced by circumstances to study and write and teach; rather one who is passionately devoted to understanding, one in whom the desire to know dominates all other desires. Solving puzzles at the level of understanding is joyful and entertaining and relaxing; not much is at stake except winning or losing, getting it or not getting it. When it comes to judgments of truth we are more personally committed, more is at stake, it may be a question of a jury pronouncing a judgment of guilty or not guilty. We feel obliged to make a correct call and are satisfied that we have done all that is necessary to judge correctly. Feelings come more to the fore in judgments of value as more is at stake. The desire to know is not just seeking information but includes the desire to make the world a better place, to become a good person, to grow and realize potential, to be of benefit to others, to love and to beloved, to have moral principles and live by them. A correct feeling orientation greatly facilitates correct judgments of truth and value. A distorted feeling orientation will inevitably distort the proper unfolding of the process of knowing truth and value and their implementation in decisions and actions.

It is always tempting to oversimplify the process of knowing and reduce it to either experiencing alone (empiricism) or understanding alone (rationalism) or judgment alone (a kind of idealism). But knowing is a complicated discursive process uniting all these activities in one seamless process starting with a question and finishing with an answer. The great advantage of self-appropriation is that we can check it for ourselves. Take examples from your own discipline, or skill, or academic field and identify examples of insight and note the characteristics of the act of human understanding. It is indeed difficult to isolate individual acts of understanding from our habitual orientation to making sense of the world. But it is enormously rewarding. It provides you with solid foundations on which you can build a worldview of everything.

Diagram One: Cognitional Structure: Transcendental Imperatives, Levels of Consciousness, Questions, Activities, Receptions and Products.

Imperatives	Levels	Questions	Activities	Reception	Product
Be Responsible	4. Evaluating	Questions of Value	Evaluating Worth, Goodness, Merit, Use, Importance	Deliberative Understanding	Judgments of Value
Be Reasonable	3. Judging	Questions of Truth	Criticizing, Checking, Reviewing,	Reflective Understanding	Judgments of Truth
Be Intelligent	2. Understanding	Questions for Intelligence	Thinking, Research, Observation, Images, Ideas	Direct and Inverse Insights and Higher Viewpoints	Formulations, Definitions, Expressions
Be Attentive	1. Experiencing	Desiring, Instinct, Sensing, Feeling	Remembering, Seeing, Imagining	Hunting, Feeding, Reproducing	Gestures, Actions, Sounds

Identifying the Activities of Knowing (Diagram 1)

As explained above, a diagram is an image which might help to explain ideas or relations. Diagram 1 illustrates these many cognitional operations in more detail and in such a way that one can see the sequence and the parallels between the various activities. We divide the activities into four levels which are identified and named in the second column. The diagram is an attempt to represent clearly the sequence of cognitional activities involved in any act of knowing truth and value.

Level 1. Experiencing. This represents activities of sensing, feeling, seeing, hearing, tasting, smelling, touching, remembering, imagining, desiring, reflex actions and reactions. It includes a vast multiplicity of images, symbols, affects, reflexes, instincts, responses, sensations, even unconscious influences.

Level 2. Understanding. The process of human knowing starts with questions about what you have experienced. Your interest is aroused; you focus your attention; you are puzzled; you seek for a solution; you ask any of the multitude of questions of why? Where? When? How? What? How many? And so on. We search our memories for anything that might help to answer the question; we do a bit of thinking, try to make connections, speculate on possible causes, and try out different explanations. We remember relevant examples; we classify, define, contrast, connect; we proceed to search for an answer by manipulating the data, the images, the clues, in order to produce an idea through an act of understanding.

Understanding is both active and passive. We do the active part of thinking, imagining, putting one's ducks in a row, but then it comes, we get it, we have a eureka moment, it dawns on us, we get a possible explanation or hypothesis. That possibility may not be very clear, so you work on it make it clearer, formulate a definition or draw a diagram or identify a cause, and put it into words; thus, we produce clear formulations, definitions and expressions in language or diagrams or equations.

Level 3. Judging. That concept or definition may or may not be correct, so in level three one asks the critical question, is it correct, is it the right solution, will it work? You review your work, examine the connection between the data and the conclusion, reflect on the sufficiency of the evidence, check with examples, find further evidence, do the crucial experiment. You become convinced, you get the connection, you see the necessity of the conclusion, it comes to you, you have a further insight. Finally, you utter or produce a judgment, an affirmation or a denial, a yes or no, or a probability.

Level 4. Evaluating. In many cases the question of what to do with the discovery or explanation arises and so you move to level four. You ask about the worth of the discovery, what is the best thing to do, what action follows? A range of alternative courses of action suggest themselves. You review your experience, your understanding of possibilities, your judgments of fact with a view to evaluation and appreciating. What is the best thing to do? You have a further insight into the sufficiency of the evidence and the connection between the hypothesis and the conclusion. You utter a judgment of value, affirming or denying what is the best thing to do.

Deciding and putting into practice will follow and, needless to say, are of some importance. However, we are concentrating on the knowledge of truth and value that precede action. One can identify these individual specific steps in a complex survey investigating some new data and coming to a considered conclusion and recommendation. However, most of our knowledge becomes habitual and passes into the habitual texture of the mind. We do not have to repeat such a sequence of activities before deciding whether we will drink tea or coffee. An example of knowing such as, "the table is red," is a new and difficult insight for a child of about three years of age; but for an adult after thousands of similar insights it is routine, automatic, habitual, and does not reveal the complexity of understanding. However, we cannot exclude any of the named activities completely from authentic knowing, evaluating, and choosing.

The diagram is not to be taken too literally. In practice some activities are conflated or have become so much part of the habitual structure of our minds that we cannot recognize them as separate distinct activities. Nor do our minds always proceed sequentially from question to conclusion. Our actual thinking may seem to be a chaos of ideas, images, memories, fantasies, all jumping about in a jumble of activities. But retrospectively, we can see that our knowing is a structure of interrelated activities. Later activities always depend on the correct completion of the earlier. It is hard to see any steps being excluded or jumped over without the structure being weakened or destroyed and our resultant judgements and decisions becoming unreasonable and irresponsible. This sequence of activities represents an answer to the age-old question of how we know. The diagram can be applied to common sense arguments about when is the best time to plant, or who is the best player on the field, or who is the best person to vote for. It is valid as a simple presentation of scientific method which we can define as "theories verified in instances." This is not logic but method. It is the method of experiencing, understanding and judging truth and value. It is flexible enough to be applicable to all specializations, disciplines and methodologies.

Cognitional theory identifies the individual stages involved in this sequence of cognitional activities. We refer to them quite simply as experiencing, understanding, judging truth and value. Each activity can be explored, examined, defined, and qualified, to be clear about what is meant. Refer to books and other theories of knowledge, by all means, but also attend to your own mind to sort through the myriad confusions and discover a basic simple procedure of human knowing. This explanation of our cognitive procedure identifies and formulates each activity and relates them together in an ordered sequence. A theory relates things to one another; we are relating twenty-four boxes to show how they are related to one another. You would be right to ask further relevant questions such as: Have we left anything out? Is the order correct? How does it compare with other theories? I believe from years of study, teaching, and self-examination that it seems to cover everything.

In addition to being comprehensive this theory is foundational and not open to basic revision. It can be improved with a more nuanced appreciation of certain stages and the language to describe them. But if you want to revise the sequence of activities, you are forced to have recourse to those very same activities. You would be obliged to look at the data, the examples, the experiences; you would need to understand the deficiencies of the old theory and the advantages of the new; you would have to affirm that the old is deficient and the new is truer and better. To do a basic revision you would need to invoke the very sequence of mental activities that you are trying to overthrow. Further, the evidence for the truth of this theory is available directly to yourself; you can examine examples of your own understanding and judging in an intimate and detailed way.[9] Although we refer to this as a theory, if we recognize these activities in our own minds by self-appropriation, we have reached interiority.

The crucial element in all this is a personal appropriation of all the activities that lead up to judgment. Appreciation of the importance of the judgment is a moment of intellectual conversion. Knowing that understanding and judgment are the criterion of truth and not imagination or images of "in here" and "out there," is an intellectual liberation. We can know for ourselves what is true and false and do not need politicians or intellectuals, or social scientists, or journalists, or philosophers, to tell us. There is a foundation for truth, and if you have established those foundations, you can refute the vast array of sceptics, relativists, nihilists, and others who deny the possibility of truth.

Where do the imperatives in the first column of activities come from? They do not come from logic, or a priori, or theory, or clever thinking. They come from observing how your human mind works. The norms are immanent and operative in the activities of attending, understanding, knowing and evaluating. They can be called transcendental imperatives in this context simply meaning, applying universally across the board to every human knower of whatever time and place. There is a good way and a bad way of doing everything including the activity of knowing. It helps if you are attentive, intelligent, reasonable and responsible. You will not go far if you are

---

9. Lonergan gives a concise summary of these mental activities in, "Cognitional Structure," in vol. 4 of *Collected Works*, 205–21.

inattentive, unintelligent, unreasonable and irresponsible. These terms are not just vague slogans but have a precise meaning in relation to the cognitional activities performed at that level.

To be attentive means to be alert, to be awake, to notice anomalies, to attend to the data. Attention on the one hand can be sustained, concentrated, focused, heightened, to pay close attention to. Or it can be cursory, hesitant, to pay little attention, to be easily distracted. Attention focuses on data of sense that is for some reason potentially significant or important; this is the beginning of the process of knowing. Alexander Fleming[10] noticed a green mould on one of his petri dishes that was killing bacteria. He could have thrown it in the bin, but he paid attention to this anomaly and discovered penicillin. In the process of knowing, attention shifts from data to ideas, to causes, to evidence, to images, to conclusions, to applications; attention shifts from data of sense to data of consciousness. Without paying attention, nothing happens. How often does a teacher exhort her students, "Please, pay attention, this is important!" If a teacher does not have the attention of her students, not much real teaching can occur.

To be intelligent is to ask the pertinent questions, to make connections, to get new ideas, to understand easily and quickly, to pick out what is relevant, significant, meaningful. We are all familiar with intelligent people as well as the slow to understand. We experience for ourselves the struggle to be intelligent and to understand. There is understanding which is vague and general, and an understanding that is clear, formulated, and defined. This imperative does not arise out of logic; on the contrary logic is an attempt to formulate specific techniques of understanding by deduction or induction.

To be reasonable is to ask the critical question, is it true, is it correct, will it work, am I sure of this solution? The word "reasonable" can be used in many contexts with vague related meanings. Here it is used in a quite specific sense to identify the insight into sufficient evidence that leads to a true judgment. Bright ideas are wonderful, but often they are not true. The question of truth sets off a series of review questions, assessment of evidence, further relevant questions, has any data been left out, and so on. Neo-Scholasticism lost many of the genuine insights of Aristotle and Aquinas, but they held on to the distinction between simple apprehension and the judgment. Simple apprehension is a bright idea, a direct insight into a possibility. Judgment affirms the truth or falsehood of the proposition on the basis of evidence.

10. Alexander Fleming (1881–1955) discovered penicillin.

To be responsible is to recognize and follow the norms that are immanent and operative in our knowing of truth and values, our deciding, and living. A sense of moral obligation is part of being human and if it is absent, one is classified as a psychopath or sociopath. A sense of moral obligation is not produced by a syllogism. Although judgments of truth certainly inform judgments of value, you cannot reach an "ought" merely from an "is." To be human is to be obliged. Good and evil are categories that apply to children, to youth, to adults, to all. The distinction applies to values, decisions, actions, and consequences of action. An ethics of value makes this explicit as the foundation of moral norms.

To be in love is a further dimension that perfects responsibility. It can take the form of love of marital love, of parents for children and children for parents, for your country, for your God. Philosophy has been defined as love of wisdom. Love cannot be required by law, cannot be produced by force, but is natural to humans and its total absence would be a complete aberration. Aristotle wrote in his Nicomachean Ethics (Book 9) that it is the love of friendship that makes friends act justly to one another. In many cases love is the driving, affective force in a person's life. It provides the mass, momentum, drive of one's decisions and actions.[11]

The transcendental precepts can be reduced to the level of cliche, banal, vague and useless. But when we consider that it takes eight hundred pages[12] to describe and analyze the activities of human knowing and that the transcendental precepts are the norms immanent and operative in those activities, then we realize how important they are.

From Cognitional Theory to Epistemology

Our first question was, what do we do when we are knowing. We answered this first question by describing in detail various examples and experiences of the process of human knowing. Although what goes on in the mind is complex and confusing at first, a certain pattern emerges when we study the process over time. It always seems to start with an experience, whether sense experience or simply self-consciousness. Then it moves to a question, a stirring of interest, or a desire to understand. Instinctively we think about the problem, look up dictionaries or data bases, google it, experiment, gather examples, think backwards and forwards. We wonder what criteria must be satisfied for the answer to be correct and we try to satisfy these criteria. Finally, exultantly, we get the answer, we get an idea, we

11. See Lonergan on Feelings in *Method in Theology*, 30–34.

12. The first edition of *Insight* was 785 pages. The critical edition is 875 pages.

discover an explanation, the criteria set in the question have been satisfied. We usually stand back and consider the issue carefully before we affirm that the answer is correct. We are often then confronted with the question of implementation: what do I do about this, what is the best way to implement or exploit or use this new discovery? That too may take some time until we finally judge what is the best thing to do and then decide to do it. We describe the various activities, classify them into groups, notice the sequence in which they emerge, note the key questions that motivate the process, note the dependence of the later on the earlier, set up a diagram to illustrate the levels, the sequence, the key questions. Now we have an explanation of the process of knowing where the terms define the relations, and the relations define the terms. We have reached a cognitional theory verified in our own experience of knowing.

Now we need to answer the second question which is, why is doing that knowing? Grammatically, this is a rather awkward way of putting it, so let us try to rephrase the question. Why is it that when we perform these activities, a subject truly knows an object? What is this mysterious capacity we have to know things that are distinct from ourselves? Can we be sure that we are attaining a genuine objectivity and truth in performing these activities of knowing. In the light of our contemporary situation of deconstruction, subjectivism, relativism, skepticism, we must take a further step to justify confidence that personal subjects can have reliable knowledge of objects and content, that are really distinct from the subject. If we can guarantee that genuine objectivity has been attained then we have reached an epistemology, namely, a critical account of the subject knowing, a general account of what is known, and a clear real distinction between the knowing and the known. If we can do that then we have a guarantee that genuine objectivity has been reached.

Why is doing that knowing? We will posit three interrelated judgments that together establish, the reality of the self or subject, the reality of the content or object, and the real distinction between the two. Together the three judgments establish the objectivity of the process of human knowing. The three judgments will be: (1) I am a knower, (2) this is a computer, and (3) I am not this computer. We can make these judgments; we can know that they are true, because knowing is constituted by the sequence of activities we have already identified in our diagram. Let us examine them one by one and fit them into the wider context of self-affirmation, being, and objectivity.

(1) Self-Affirmation

Can I affirm the first judgment, that I am a knower? Can we affirm that as conscious subjects we perform the activities described in diagram 1?

Self. We will define what we mean by self, as subject or person in chapter 13. For the moment let us be content with an uncritical meaning given in common sense. For us to be conscious is for a subject to be aware of an activity or a content and at the same time to be aware of him or herself. There are many cognitional activities but always the one same subject as center and integrator common to all conscious acts. The activities of knowing are conscious and require a self. To deny this is to declare yourself unconscious. I am conscious of myself as a subject of all these various activities, and, at the very least, I know that I am performing the activities of experiencing, understanding, and judging.

Affirmation. To make a valid judgment you need a sufficiency of evidence and a link between the evidence and the conclusion. In this case—judging that I am a knower—the evidence is in your own experience of being conscious and performing the activities of experiencing, understanding and judging constantly. There is hardly a moment in the working day when we are not either experiencing, understanding, or judging, and hence knowing truth and value.

Alternatives. To judge that I am not a knower, or that I know nothing, or that I do not perform any activities of experiencing, understanding and judging, is deeply incoherent, absurd, and self-contradictory. To judge that I am not sure, that I need to think more about this, is reasonable, but in the end either you are a knower or incoherent.

(2) The Notion of Being

We will devote the whole of chapter 4 to the meaning of being. For the moment let us just assume that the term refers to something that is the objective of our knowing, like a computer, a house, a dog, a law of motion, or whatever. The judgment, "this is a good computer," is just one of a multitude of judgments that we are entitled to make, if there is sufficient evidence and a link between the evidence and the conclusion. We can distinguish between the activity of knowing and the object or content of knowing. Later we will establish the position that the content of all correct knowing is being.

(3) Objectivity

The judgment, I am not this computer, closes the circle of three judgments which now establishes the principal notion of objectivity. It is not hard to make the judgment, I am not this computer. Putting our three strategically chosen judgments together we have established a self as a conscious subject, a content which we will call being, and a real affirmed objective distinction between the knowing subject and the being that is known. This is a notion of objectivity based on reasonable judgments and not based on some incorrect interpretation of the correspondence theory of truth based on an imagined "in here" and "out there." The principal notion of objectivity affirms a real distinction between the subject and the object and between objects themselves. It asserts the existence of pluralism rather than monism. We establish the principal notion of objectivity in the relation between our three strategic judgments (I am a knower, this is a computer, I am not this computer). Together they establish an objectively real universe in which the subject knowing is really distinct from objects known, and the known objects are distinct from one another.

The absolute notion of objectivity refers to the notion of truth. If you sent an abusive email to your friend this morning, there is nothing in the whole world that will ever change the truth of the fact that this morning you sent an abusive email to your friend. You can apologize, retract, delete, affirm the opposite, say you didn't mean it, claim it has been misinterpreted, and the like, but even God cannot change the fact that you send that email, at that time, from that place and it was abusive. The absoluteness belongs to the truth of the statement, to the extent that it is true, not that the statement is a necessary or universal truth. What is is, and what is not is not. Of course, things can change and what is true here is not necessarily true there, it is raining here, but not there. A true statement, to the extent that it is true, in the context in which it is true, from the perspective of the statement, is absolutely true and nothing can ever change that.

In these three chapters of *Insight* (11–13) Lonergan makes a transition from a "knowing" identified simply as the performance of specific mental activities, to the critical position of real human knowing as a subject, understanding and knowing an object or content that is distinct from him or herself. Lonergan does this by his very strategic analysis of self-affirmation, being and objectivity He exploits the work he has done describing the sequence of activities involved in "knowing" and sees the necessity of accepting human knowing as it actually operates and not some theory of how it should or could operate. He accepts the actual potential and limits in the process of human knowing and the inherent normativity of the operations.

Epistemology is not just an exploration of a multitude of clever theories of knowledge but an affirmation of the actual activities and norms of human knowing. It is an impregnable position because it is based on ranges and ranges of facts accessible to everybody. Further, to claim that this is a mistaken account involves a contradiction between performance and content. The content claims that such an account of knowing is wrong; but to make such a claim is to experience conscious thought, to understand the defect, to formulate a better account, and to affirm that as true.

The position on knowing that is reached through this procedure is based on three interrelated judgments. If the judgments are true, the consequent position on critical knowing is true. Most other approaches to knowing are based on an implicit, imaginary notion of a subject in here coming into contact with an object out there. Such imaginary scenarios spawn false problems and false solutions. Knowing is through judgments, not through imagination. Counterposed to the correct position on self-affirmation, being and objectivity, you have an imaginative counterposition dominated by the paradigm of self in here knowing reality out there. Lonergan's approach is to start from authentic subjectivity in order to reach genuine objectivity. "For it is now apparent that in the world mediated by meaning and motivated by value, objectivity is simply the consequence of authentic subjectivity, of genuine attention, genuine intelligence, genuine reasonableness, genuine responsibility."[13] There are many spurious, distorted, notions of subjectivity in our contemporary culture. Genuine subjectivity invokes the human activities of knowing in all their complexities, is inspired by the desire to know, and can attain an authentic objectivity. There is no other way.

We have now answered the second of Lonergan's questions, namely, why is doing that knowing? There remains the third question, what do I know when I do that? That leads us into a worldview and a metaphysics. We have established the foundations on which to build and can now devote ourselves whole-heartedly to answering that question in the rest of this text.

From Description, to Theory, to Interiority

Describing is a normal and indispensable part of human knowing. Technically, describing means *relating things to yourself*, as you see or hear or perceive them. You describe the movements of the heavenly bodies from your own perspective, and in that context the sun rises in the East, moves across the sky, and sets in the West. The observer who is describing is the center of the world, and terms like left and right, big and small, up and down, take their

13. Lonergan, *Method in Theology*, 248.

meaning from the observer's point of view. Descriptive judgments as to size, warmth, number, capacity, can be vague, relative, ambivalent, and ambiguous. Science gets out of this limitation largely by transitioning to explanatory knowing, usually by way of measuring or defining. Thus, we enter the world of theory. A theory is an explanation that *relates things to one another*. In a theoretical context the earth rotates on its axis every twenty-four hours, and revolves around the sun once a year. A thermometer relates heat to the expansion of mercury. Size is determined in relation to a standard of length, and the same for weight, heat, sound, and so on. With theory, human knowing can become very precise and independent of the observer's position. Theory is a jump into measurement and definition, which tries to exclude relativity to the observer. Geometry and mathematics are almost pure theory. Natural sciences start with description but jump into theory very quickly, as they measure and define more and more accurately.

Aristotle was a theoretical philosopher because he set about defining his terms, relating them to one another, setting up systems of relationship between the virtues and vices in the pursuit of happiness. Aquinas represents a high point in the development of a systematic account of philosophy and theology with the emphasis on clear definitions of terms, the division and interrelations of terms, and setting up a system of terms and relations. Einstein articulated a special theory of relativity and later a general theory of relativity, asking how to understand space and time, what are the implications of an absolute speed of light, is gravity an attraction or a curve in space-time. To answer these questions, he had to work out the math. His findings were pure theory, but they also had practical implications and applications in both the macro and micro world. We can cope with theories, because most of our scientific knowledge is theoretical or derived from theories. They demand a certain asceticism and focus but in the end we will understand.

However, all theories have basic weaknesses: they are open to basic revision. If the axioms of the theory are changed, the theory must be revised. Theories are governed by the logic of coherence, correct definitions and divisions. If new data is found, this can instantly invalidate a theory. The defect of theory is that it cannot account for its own advantages and disadvantages, its strong and weak points; it cannot account for its own demise. It cannot understand the difference between description and explanation, verifiable and unverifiable images, between ideas and images, the criterion of what is real, developments in understanding, and higher viewpoints. Theories are open to revision for many reasons. They have their usefulness but need in the end to be superseded. Theories are static and are governed by logic. Interiority is dynamic and is governed by method. Theories are open to basic revision, while the conclusions of interiority are not open to basic revision.

What then is this interiority that is not open to basic revision? Interiority is a development of human intelligence that starts with an awareness of the actual processes of human knowing. It recognizes the defects of descriptive knowing and theoretical knowing. It is an advance in self-knowledge that includes the ability to understand theory but goes beyond it to appreciate the advantages and disadvantages, the function and provisional purpose of theories.

Firstly, interiority is characterized by awareness of the actual processes of human intellectual knowing and by appropriation of the series of mental activities, which together constitute human knowing. It calls for a self-knowledge not just of our feelings and dreams, our motivations and character, but of the very processes by which we see, hear, think, imagine, remember, understand, criticize, evaluate, conclude, and judge. Firmly grasping the activity of human understanding is the foundational characteristic of interiority; not as it happens in the abstract, but as it happens concretely in oneself. This is not just another theory about human knowing; rather, it is judging all theories about human knowing in the light of what we actually do in order to know.

Secondly, if we grasp the activity of human intelligence then we understand the source of all languages, cultures, common sense conclusions, philosophical systems, empirical science, historical knowledge, mathematics, and the multitude of products of human intelligence. Grasping the source of this quasi-infinite variety of products means that we can see that they have something in common, they conform to a common structure, and that even though they seem to be contradictory, they can also contribute to a single goal of comprehensive understanding of all things in the unity of a single perspective. Such comprehensive understanding is something human beings desire by nature. But while we cannot fully understand everything, we can intend, desire, name, point at, move towards ever greater understanding; we can grasp our unlimited desire to know and compare it with the limits of our achievement.

Thirdly, awareness of how understanding unfolds reveals that there are norms that are immanent and operative in that unfolding. The rules for correct understanding are immanent or natural in human intelligence. Following Lonergan, we encapsulate them in the imperatives: Be Attentive, Be Intelligent, Be Reasonable, and Be Responsible. We know when we have reached a correct conclusion; we do not necessarily need somebody to tell us. We do not need to depend ultimately on an authority, teacher, or tradition. We can attend to the data, think the matter through to the end, assess the relation between the conclusion and the evidence for the conclusion, ask all relevant questions, exclude all alternatives, and posit the conclusion as certain, highly probable or just probable.

Implementation of these immanent and operative norms is not necessarily easy. It requires some wisdom gained by experience and trial and error. But it is possible, and ultimately, we do not need to depend on an external authority. Each of us must eventually determine whom to believe, which tradition to follow, what can be appropriated and what needs to be transformed. We can and must take responsibility for our own conclusions. Hopefully, they will be reasonable, defensible, and demonstrable and not the result of an arbitrary choice, nor of blindly following a person or tradition. What gives us hope is the fact that each of us has internal criteria or guidelines for making authentic judgments, whether with our common sense, our theory, or our interiority. The transcendental precepts are a natural impulse to be faithful to the deepest and best inclinations of our hearts and minds.

Fourthly, we do make mistakes, but strangely we can reflect further and discover our own mistakes and learn from them. This testifies to our natural, internal guidelines, a kind of internal compass. Because of this compass, we can investigate systematically the typical sources of misunderstandings and false judgments. We can notice that we did not attend to all the data, and read all the reports, or that we jumped to conclusions on insufficient evidence. We can recognize that we did not think the thing through, realize the implications of a statement, clarify precisely what we meant, delimit clearly the extent of our competence. We can recognize when temperament interfered either rashly in pushing us into premature conclusions, or timidly in unreasonable hesitation in positing a conclusion. We can recognize many biases, prejudices, ulterior motives, much twisted affectivity, which interferes with the proper unfolding of the process of knowing. And going to the basic root of all misunderstanding in philosophy and science, we can recognize the dialectic operating in our knowing between elementary animal knowing with its criterion of the real in sense, and properly human knowing with its criterion of the real in correct understanding and judgment. There is a self-correcting process operative in our sincere search for knowledge.

Fifthly, the criterion of truth operates proximately in that in any particular concrete example the theory or explanation is verified in the sufficiency of the evidence. In a broader context the criterion of truth is that the desire to know is satisfied and all further relevant questions have been asked. The criteria operate in particular statements and in general statements, in scientific examples, and in philosophical positions. We are familiar with scientists verifying their theories with measurements and experiments. But philosophers must also appeal to experiencing to justify their position. They must ultimately appeal to the data of consciousness, to the authenticity of their knowing process.

Sixthly, in interiority, basic method (not logic) rules. The basic method and foundation of all methods is the discovery of the invariant pattern of knowing, namely, experiencing, asking questions about what we experience, and then seeking to understand and judge correctly. Implicit in all our inquiry and seeking are the natural, internal imperatives to pay attention, be intelligent, be reasonable, and be responsible to do the right thing. These principles apply universally. Particular areas will require more specific methodologies, techniques, best practice, rules of procedure, protocols, use of instruments, and all the details particular to a specific scientific or a professional field.

First Philosophy as Contemporary Wisdom

Wisdom is a special kind of knowledge that is long-term, reflective, comprehensive, integrated, heuristic, and contemporary. Sadly, wisdom is conspicuous by its absence from public discourse, politics and culture. Skills, trades, business, technology, and practical disciplines are valued more than the wisdom of a life well-lived. Let me try to imagine what a contemporary wisdom might look like.

(1) Long-term. Wisdom takes the long-term view, thinks in terms of centuries, does not pander to the vagaries of the media, does not seek to be a weekend celebrity. Wisdom does not prioritize short-term expediency, immediate profit, or the narrow view. Wisdom thinks things through to the end. You expect the wise person to take a view based on long-term, sound priorities and not short-term expediency or convenience.

(2) Reflective. The philosopher is reflective, does not jump to rash judgments, is concerned about the truth and not the historical details, seeks for a foundation other than the authority of renowned historical figures. The wise person could also be a scholar. But a scholar who knows all the details of an issue is not necessarily a wise person.

(3) Comprehensive. You expect the wise person to know and care about the whole and not have a narrow view. Wisdom is a higher viewpoint. There are sequences of higher viewpoints. There are acts of understanding which take previous acts of understanding as their data. The mind spirals up to

a grasp of the unity of everything. Young people may be clever, prodigies, knowledgeable; but they are rarely wise. Wisdom takes time and experience.

(4) Integrated. You expect the wise person to do what they think is right, to be mature, respectful, honest, tolerant, patient, magnanimous, willing to put up with temporary suffering for the sake of long-term peace and progress. People tend to recognize and respect a wise person. Wisdom is associated with age and experience of life. Though not every old person is wise, very few young people are known for their wisdom. The wise person is one to whom people go for advice: a psychiatrist, counsellor, elders, grandparents, retired politicians, the people who have been through it all. The philosopher is critical of authorities, of sources, of positions, of conventional wisdom, of public opinion, of political correctness; s/he speaks with the authority of his own convictions and his own foundations.

(5) Heuristic. The wise person recognizes the limits of their knowledge but also anticipates how it can be extended and what that will imply. Love of wisdom or search for wisdom reminds us that wisdom is acquired over a lifetime of experience, suffering, study, reflection, action, rights and wrongs, successes and failures, births and deaths. A wise person is aware of their own ignorance and constant search for further understanding. They are not afraid to admit their ignorance, and to admit, "I do not know." Socrates reckoned this to be the characteristic of the wise person: to know one's own ignorance.

(6) Practical and Theoretical. The philosopher is not only wise in matters of theory and interiority but is also a good person in terms of virtue, and value, and seeking the good. The philosopher embodies within himself what the good life means, what human happiness means, and finds fulfilment in a life of contemplation. The wise person does not just teach wisdom to others through words but is a living embodiment of practical wisdom, in family life, politics, in finance, in education.

(7) Tolerant. The history of philosophy is a history of disagreements, misunderstandings, controversies, between very intelligent people. Progress is made by uncovering false assumptions, making necessary distinctions, going into more detail, accepting the limitations of one point of view. A hermeneutic of suspicion must be combined with a hermeneutic of retrieval. Progress in philosophy will always involve a dialectic—progress through conflicting views. We are all part of that dialectic.

(8) Contemporary. Someone who is wise must be familiar with our contemporary situation. A good philosopher today will do for this age what Aristotle did for his. Wisdom for ancient Greek society responded to the situation of the time. Wisdom for today is in response to a technological, differentiated, pluralist, global society. The wise person can see through the cover story. S/he can operate in terms of developing correct positions and reversing false ideas. She can read the signs of the times. A wise philosopher can appreciate the empirical sciences, the challenge of climate change, the scourge of AIDS, inequalities, injustice, the need for collaboration, independent thinking, critical thinking, and not following fads. This is a wisdom of interiority more than a wisdom of theory.

Summary and Conclusion

Such are our foundations. They are indispensable if we are to proceed to build a correct and basic worldview. Focus on the process of knowing is a necessary preliminary but our main focus now is the content of the knowing and to identify the overall structure of the universe and how it works. Just as we have found an invariant structure of activities, which constitutes and unifies human knowing, can we discover a parallel, invariant, unifying structure in the content of the known? Can we move to discerning the kind of universe we are living in, the overall characteristics of everything, the principles and causes operating everywhere? My contention, of course, is that this is possible, for it is what we are doing. Chapter 2 will discuss the method and parts 2 and 3 will deliver some results.

2

Method: From Knowing to the Known

Now let us say that explicit metaphysics is the conception, affirmation, and implementation of the integral heuristic structure of proportionate being.[1]

Finally, the foregoing account of potency, form, and act will cover any possible scientific explanation. For a scientific explanation is a theory verified in instances; as verified, it refers to act; as theory, it refers to form; as in instances, it refers to potency.[2]

At this point, metaphysics may be defined as the study of the ultimate cause and of the first and most universal principles of reality.[3]

Simplifying to the extreme, I define postmodern as incredulity towards metanarratives.[4]

Introduction

YUVAL NOAH HARARI WROTE a book entitled, *Sapiens: A Brief History of Humankind*. It has proved to be very popular and tells the dramatic story of the development of humans from the Cognitive Revolution to the Scientific Revolution and beyond. The facts, the dates, the sequence of events seem to be quite correct. The details are perhaps accurate, but the big picture of what it means to be a human person is very limited. The worldview permeating this history text is one where humans are just another species of animals. It is implied that the purpose of human beings was to control

1. Lonergan, *Insight*, 416.
2. Lonergan, *Insight*, 458.
3. Alvira et al., *Metaphysics*, 4.
4. Lyotard, *The Postmodern Condition*, xxiv.

and dominate nature. Religion was a purely human invention to explain how things happen and how gods can be propitiated and manipulated. We have made ourselves gods by dominating and destroying other animals. For some reason, liberalism, communism, capitalism, nationalism, Nazism are now religions. He is not optimistic about the future as he is of the opinion that we do not know where we are going. He has little to say about the discovery of language, of writing, of engineering, of philosophy and poetry. He has nothing to say about the mind, understanding, libraries, thought, ethics, culture, law, order in society, politics, human rights, equality, and genuine religion. The factual details of the story may be correct but the worldview permeating the story distorts, twists, deforms, misinterprets, and impoverishes the human subject of the story. Despite the wars, failures and difficulties, the history of humankind is a story of the emergence of intelligent, rational, ethical, loving, religious, human persons from the dust of the earth; we as far as we know are the peak of evolution. In our first chapter we have been distinguishing the big picture and the details, the specialists and the generalists, the first philosophers and the scientists. I present Hariri as an example of a writer who is probably correct on the details, but seriously deficient on the big picture of the human subject.

We readily engage with the details of scientific discoveries; we readily appreciate aspects of our culture, which touch us every day. But we so often take for granted the more important background values and truths which we do not notice and do not question. However, if we get the big picture wrong the details will be distorted, importance will be attributed to the wrong events, trivialities will be regarded as significant, the correct meaning will be lost. The big picture we are talking about is first philosophy, a worldview of the whole. It is easy to check the dates, the places and the facts of history but more difficult to notice and critique the big picture. We are claiming that we can develop an explicit and correct big picture as a universal framework for everything else. And the big picture is first philosophy.

There are many false philosophies infecting our culture and science and doing enormous harm to everybody. We have emphasized the importance of a correct worldview to inform, to transform and unify our science, our culture and our knowledge. There are several dubious current worldviews such as: a materialist worldview, an idealist worldview, a reductionist worldview, an organicist or holistic worldview, Marxist or Hegelian worldview; atheist, agnostic, or theistic worldviews; relativist, subjectivist, or nihilistic worldviews. How do we know that they are deficient? Our task now is to find a method to arrive at a first philosophy that will be correct, explicit, balanced, comprehensive, sophisticated, and true. Can one find a basis for methodically working out the main features of the structure of our universe and our place within that structure? What we are looking for is a correct worldview and a critical understanding of the first principles and causes operating in our universe. We have a way of checking various concrete facts; can we find a way of checking the worldview on which the facts depend and attain significance?

Henceforth, we are embarking on a project of working out an explicit worldview, the principles and causes operating in that worldview, including the place of human beings in that universe. We hope to do so methodically, step by step. We will try to do it critically in the sense of taking nothing for granted and giving reasons and evidence for every step of the way. We hope that the resultant worldview will be verifiable in the sense that it is not arbitrary choice, it is not a speculative guess, but is the result of thinking and reasoning on the evidence before us, leading to a necessary conclusion.

This chapter then will focus on the method of reaching that conclusion based on the parallel structure of knowing and being, which I will call "isomorphism." It is perhaps a new idea deriving from a slightly novel approach to the ordering of philosophical subjects. It does not depend directly or in principle on the conclusions of the empirical sciences but is fully consonant with those conclusions. Further chapters in the second part of the text will take up individual issues concerning aspects of our universe one by one.

We are now asking the third of Lonergan's questions, namely, what do we know when we perform the activities constitutive of human knowing? We are interested in the content of all types of knowing, including common sense, science and philosophy. We will attempt to organize the totality of that known into an intelligible unity. What are the parts of reality, and how do they fit together? What principles and causes are operative in the whole of the known?

Questions That Evoke First Philosophy

Empirical science dominates our culture. Philosophy is regarded as a rather peripheral occupation, which has oft been pronounced dead,[5] but still seems to keep resurrecting. Let us defend the notion of philosophy as necessary, distinct and complementary to that of the empirical and human sciences, as the product of continuous questioning. We distinguish

5. For instance, Hawking and Mlodinow, *The Grand Design*, 5: "Traditionally these are questions for philosophy, but philosophy is dead. Philosophy has not kept up with modern developments in science, particularly physics."

between philosophy and the sciences, not by definitions and logic, but by the kind of questions that are asking in the two disciplines. Philosophers ask questions about the whole, about general principles and causes, about how everything fits together, about truths and values, about what does it all mean for a living a human life. Scientific question will relate to the details of their own discipline and are readily recognizable. Here we aim at a preliminary notion of first philosophy by identifying the kind of questions we are trying to answer. These questions are preliminaries to our definition of first philosophy which we will later in this chapter.

I take my cue from Aristotle who distinguished clearly between the special sciences and first philosophy. The special sciences cut off a part of being and study that part from a limited point of view, such as medicine studying health, and astronomy studying the heavenly bodies. But besides that, we also we need a discipline of first philosophy to study being in general, being as being, everything, from the most general point of view possible.[6]

(1) First Philosophy Must Encompass Everything

The distinctive characteristic of the discipline of philosophy is that it enquires about everything. We seek an answer to the question, what kind of a world are we living in? Each of the empirical sciences cut off a part of being and limit themselves to an understanding of the principles and causes related to that part. Philosophy includes in its subject matter all the materials of all the sciences, all real and possible worlds, the infinite and the finite, the present past and future, the known, the unknown, and the process of knowing. It includes the objective and the subjective, the data of sense and the data of consciousness. We ask broad questions about everything, and it is, by definition, the task of philosophy to try to answer them. Within philosophy, the branches of cognitive theory and epistemology study the process of human knowing, discerning a structure therein, and thus a parallel structure in the known. The philosophical branch of ethics and politics notes the presence of good and evil in human affairs as a fundamental aspect of being human. Because the human sciences are encompassed in the scope of philosophy, a philosopher must learn from sociology and psychology, history and economics, literature and art, prose and poetry, comedy and tragedy, language and communication. Philosophy must also note the urge to transcendence manifested in the religious aspirations of every culture in the world until the present day.

---

6. Aristotle, *Metaphysics*, IV.1.1003a, 17–30.

I like to use the term a "worldview" because it is somewhat more informal and looser than the term first philosophy. While there is a similarity between the terms, "worldview" and "first philosophy," they are not quite the same. Aristotle thought of first philosophy as an academic achievement of the highest importance; and so it was. My point in this text is that each and every one of us, educated or uneducated, scientists or philosophers, farmers or fishermen, have developed our own worldview, our own interpretation of what is important and what is not important, what generally is good and what is bad. We develop a worldview because the mind seeks a big picture; it tries to fit all our knowledge into a coordinated framework. Our worldviews aspire to be comprehensive, but they are likely narrow and limited, implicit rather than explicit, uncritical rather than critical, incoherent rather than coherent. We tolerate contradictions, gaps, confusion and ignorance. We do not usually devote time to defining our general principles and priorities. Yet it is in the light of these very principles that we make all of our daily, concrete, decisions and actions. These principles have implications, and we follow out the applications without fully realizing why. We are implicitly all first philosophers, because we have adopted general principles by which we judge some things as true or false, some as good or bad, some as important or unimportant. We do this as individuals belonging to a society and so a society develops a set of meaning and values that people share in common; we receive from this culture and make out own contribution to its development or decline. It is a rather incoherent, incomplete, uncritical set of beliefs and values, because the individuals do not devote time to working out a coherent set of first principles. Political correctness embodies assumptions about what is true or false, good or bad, but these assumptions are usually incoherent, contradictory, and keep changing.

(2) From the Broadest Point of View

As philosophers who inquire about everything, we must seek for the kind of understanding proper to that level of generality. The philosopher is not an encyclopaedist; she is not expected to know everything about everything. Nor is philosophy a random accumulation of unrelated facts. It aims at a basic understanding of the whole, the big picture, the broad lines of all there is to be understood. The philosopher is content to construct a framework into which all the details or parts find their proper place and hence can be understood in their context. He will seek to correctly and adequately establish the causes, principles and characteristics of the universe as applied to everything: the intelligibility appropriate to the whole. A biologist will study a frog from the viewpoint of understanding its biology; a physicist will study a black hole from the point of view of density, size, gravity, and so on, from a physicist's point of view. A doctor will study a patient from the point of view of their health, symptoms, treatments, and the like. The first philosopher will be interested in all of these instances insofar as they are included in a worldview of the whole cosmos. The philosopher is interested in everything in so far as each concrete instance adds richness and detail to a general philosophical worldview. "Metaphysics, then, is the whole in knowledge but not the whole of knowledge."[7]

(3) Specializing and Generalizing

Knowing can move in two directions—that of generalizing and that of specializing. Both of these are authentic forms of knowledge, but they play a different role in advancing understanding.

Specialization is the form of knowing with which we are most familiar. Here we are talking about field specialization, namely, the narrow range of data in which we happen to be interested. We are at home in concrete, practical, short-term, limited pursuits. We are at home working in the garden, fixing a broken bicycle, cooking a good meal, planning our budget. The workplace becomes more and more specialized as tasks are allocated and supply chains are extended, and professionals know more and more about less and less. Common sense specializes in the practical, the local, the short-term and hence it is a specific development of intelligence particular to each situation, village, area, family, and culture. Scientists are also familiar with specialization, as they focus on the details of a smaller and smaller area of data to make new discoveries, such that progress in science seems to be by way of more and more specialization. We have little difficulty accepting that and dealing with that kind of specialized knowledge or skill. In the context of sciences, it is easy to see when things have gone wrong, because there is a criterion of verification operating. The results are tangible, measurable, verifiable and usually fairly concrete. We are happy in that world.

Generalizing is a kind of knowing that goes in the opposite direction. It is defined as extrapolating from the particular to the general, from a limited number of cases to all cases. The limited number of swans that I have seen in my life are white; therefore, all swans are white. One politician is seen to be corrupt; therefore, all politicians are corrupt. One person with malaria has a headache; therefore, all people with malaria must have headaches. It is inductive knowing and is in principle a legitimate process of knowing but

7. Lonergan, *Insight*, 416.

can be abused in hasty, unjustified, generalizations. In generalizing the range of application of the proposition becomes wider and wider. The specialist knows more and more about less and less, (until—as the old saying goes—he knows everything about nothing!). The generalist knows less and less about more and more, (until he knows nothing about everything!).

Science heads in the direction of specialization; philosophy heads in the direction of generalization. Aristotle recognized the need for the special sciences, each of which brackets off a part of being and strives to attain an understanding of that part. By "science" he meant systematic knowledge through causes and the highest science was philosophy because it sought the first principles and causes of everything. Hence Aristotle recognized the need for a distinct science to cover the whole of being and reach a general understanding of the whole. This science he called "first philosophy." When doing first philosophy one would seek to construct a general view of the whole, to define principles and causes valid across all areas, to discern what all the sciences have in common, to coordinate their conclusions, and see how they fit together within a vision of the whole of being. Generalizing is a legitimate procedure of understanding but can easily go wrong, because such overall understandings are not readily verifiable, difficult to measure, are general and not particular. That vision of the interrelations of the parts in the whole I am calling a first philosophy.

The two kinds of knowledge, the general and the special, are complementary and coexist in the one mind and influence one another enormously. The general worldview is the integrating structure, the context into which all particular instances of knowledge will be fitted; it is the big picture. If one has a materialist worldview then somehow all particular scientific results and discoveries will be made to conform to that framework, even if it requires a little pushing or forcing. Everyone's worldview includes an ethical dimension, and so we make particular decisions in the light of general principles of what is of value, worthwhile, or important. A hedonist and a puritan will react differently to an invitation to a party. Interpretation is a major part in all our knowing, and we interpret on the basis of many general presuppositions. We impose our ideas on the text as well as taking ideas from the text. In other words, our worldview contains our principles of interpretation and will thus influence how we interpret. Our worldview will push us in certain directions of research: What are we interested in? What are we trying to achieve? What is important or not relevant? A worldview directs our interest, guides our decisions, evaluates courses of action, coordinates all the parts into a whole. Our worldview matters.

Even within each discipline there are hierarchies of specialized studies and further generalizations. In history you can start with the detailed biography of one individual, then fit that in the context of the person's time and place, a larger context of the country or continent, and eventu-ally world history. History can be specialized and detailed, or alternatively a general outline of a larger picture. All sciences specialize but they also generalize. Both processes are legitimate and verifiable All their results are either true or false or probable. Deduction is a process from general principles applied to specific instances. Induction goes in the opposite direction from particular facts to general principles; both processes are a normal part of human thinking and knowing. Particular statements are usually easier to verify because they are concrete and close to the data of sense. General statements are harder to justify because they encompass a larger amount of data, which constitutes the evidence for the truth of the generalization. But for the same reason general statements have impor-tance because they encompass so much ground.

The philosopher is the supreme generalizer as he devotes himself to understanding everything. He formulates principles and causes applicable to everything. The aim of this book is to clearly identify these general prin-ciples by which we all operate. For the most part they remain implicit: we have our priorities and principles, but it is hard to name or express or reflect upon them or make them explicit. But wouldn't it be much better if they were opened up to the light of day? Wouldn't it be better to work systemati-cally towards a worldview that is correct, differentiated, critical, relevant to our current situation, coherent, and normative? Can we work methodically towards such a position? Can we uncover some of the many false or incom-plete worldviews that are part of our contemporary culture? Reaching a cor-rect, explicit worldview is a real challenge particularly in the contemporary perspective which prioritizes the sensible and specific, the scientific and computer-generated reports. I hope to establish step by step a method of reaching such a worldview, to outline the structure of the universe and the unfolding of the history of our universe. I hope to show that just as scientists have their concrete and effective ways of verifying their hypotheses, so also the philosopher or the generalizer has a method of verification available for the most general of philosophical statements.

(4) Higher and Lower Viewpoints

Progress in knowledge is not just the addition of more and more facts to our encyclopaedia or data base. It also requires the integrations, connections and generalizations that one makes when learning more about a subject. There is a process of moving from lower viewpoints, concerned with limited data and experience, to higher viewpoints when the data and experience is significantly widened. This is true not only for philosophy, but also in the concrete, detailed investigations of the particular sciences. When a person performs various operations in different fields s/he uses a single mind, and the human mind will always try to introduce coherence into one's thinking. For example, a first-year student in the university may study four or five different subjects that may not directly relate to one another. The student will endeavour to understand, learn, remember these different topics at first without any sense of how they fit together or contribute to the ultimate goal of the discipline. In second year, the student will go on to study topics more related to their major interest. In both years, s/he may become confused by the different subjects which do not seem to merge with one another. But usually in the final years the student is required to work on a capstone or synthesis paper or project that would relate material from one course to the others, to see how the parts are related to the whole, to integrate what has been differentiated. This is a movement to a higher viewpoint. The aim is not to remember everything that has been taught from year one to year four but to learn to think like a doctor, or a physicist, or a philosopher. Each step in this development is an act of understanding which integrates more and more material into one mentality or viewpoint. At each stage we ask questions about the relevance or significance of various topics because we need to integrate them into the whole. Philosophy represents the highest viewpoint in integrating all knowledge, science and common sense. (We will do a detailed treatment of successive higher viewpoints in chapter 13.)

(5) Ultimate and Proximate Questions

Another useful way of identifying our spontaneous move to philosophy is to distinguish proximate and ultimate questions. Philosophers tend to ask ultimate questions and the empirical scientists ask proximate questions. You can ask why a particular car will not start, or you can ask why car companies make cars that sometimes do not start. There is the specific, proximate question of why my baby is sick versus the general, ultimate one of why we have a universe in which babies get sick. There can be a series of causes, some proximate, some remote, some primary and some secondary. One can explain that lightening is caused by static electricity, but further questions arise: why does electricity need to be earthed, what is the connection between electricity and magnetism, what is the electromagnetic spectrum, what role does that play in the evolution of the universe, when did the universe start, and what was there before the big bang? Proximate questions are easier to answer than ultimate questions. Ultimate questions ask, where did the universe come from, what is the purpose of human life, is there a creator God, and the like.

(6) Meaning of Life Questions

There are few who have not looked at the stars and asked themselves, where do I fit in this vast scheme of things? Is it all just a monumental accident, a meaningless random occurrence, or is there somewhere, somehow a value and special meaning to our individual existence? One can seek a religious answer or a philosophical position or both. We may not have the opportunity to devote time and energy to seeking for an answer or we may have been given an answer by our parents, culture, church or education. But even these, we test out against the lived experience of autonomy. This text will work towards a philosophical view that understands the whole and evaluates the role of the human person in the overall scheme of things. We recall the oft-quoted statement of Socrates, that the unexamined life is not worth living.

(7) Knowledge of Good and Evil

From time immemorial humanity has aspired to a knowledge of good and evil. The theme features prominently in the biblical narrative of the garden of Eden and the entry of evil into the world. Mythology often features an original state of pure goodness with sickness, death and evil intruding as an addition or a punishment for a fault. Humans encounter evil in everyday experiences and activities where the ramifications of evil acts and evil people are immediate and palpable. Understanding the stars, nature, the purpose of human life is one thing—understanding evil adds a dimension of difficulty being so intractable and unavoidable. Our approach to a worldview will incorporate the dimension of goodness and its absence as an integral, constitutive dimension of our view of reality.

These spontaneous aspirations are indeed vague, deeply felt and in some ways fleeting. Our task now is to follow them up, to make them explicit and explanatory, to devote time and effort to respond to these in a comprehensive critical philosophical worldview. These vague aspirations are our starting point. Our end point hopefully will be a philosophy rooted in concrete experience, responding to felt needs, but at the same time critical, explanatory, and a worldview fit for purpose.

A New Path to a First Philosophy—Isomorphism

It is almost impossible to overemphasize the importance of the discovery of the invariant structure of human knowing that we engaged in our first chapter on Foundations. In a sense it is the end of a history, the culmination of three millennia of reflection on human knowing. At last, we have found closure; a communal verifiable process of self-appropriation; we have a self-correcting process in place; we have scientific method pinned down; we can apply scientific method to data of consciousness as well as data of sense. All the incomplete accounts of human knowing in the history of philosophy can be seen as contributions to the clarification of this one single goal. Now that we have achieved clarity on the structure of human knowing, can we use this as a springboard to clarity on the structure of the known?

Diagram Two: Isomorphism of the Activities of Knowing with the Known

One Knowing	Intent Of Knowing $\longrightarrow$	Content Of Knowing	One Known
Evaluated	JUDGING VALUE $\longrightarrow$	Value, Good, Worth	a good
Verified	JUDGING TRUTH $\longrightarrow$	True, Real, Exists	is
Theory	UNDERSTANDING $\longrightarrow$	Intelligible, Idea, Essence	Computer
In Instances	EXPERIENCING $\longrightarrow$	Sensible, Visible, Data	This
	DESIRE TO KNOW $\longrightarrow$	BEING (Everything)	

Basic Invariant Structure of Human Knowing

The position outlined on human knowing is important in itself, but also pivotal for our project of working out a first philosophy. The invariant structure of human knowing is the foundation we are going to use to formulate a correct worldview, the big picture of the universe. Without a personal appreciation of the structure of human knowing, then the edifice we build on that foundation will be meaningless. We are now moving on to the next step in the argument and invite you to refer to our diagram 2 on "The isomorphism of the Activities of the Knowing with the Known." The left-hand side of the Diagram summarizes the position we have reached on knowing. Let us just enumerate those claims as a reminder of where we have reached.

1. We are claiming that all human knowing involves activities of questioning, experiencing, understanding, judging truth, and judging

value. Common sense knowing, scientific knowing, knowing in the human sciences, knowing in various disciplines, knowing even in philosophy and theology, invoke these activities. One can usually refer to four levels of activities, namely, experiencing, understanding, judging truth, and judging value.

2. There is a sequence of activities where each activity depends on the correct performance of the previous activity and prepares the way for the next. The sequence is ordered; it is an ordering of emergence and dependence. I identified thirteen different activities of knowing, put them in sequence and presented them in a four-level structure which we can summarize as experiencing, understanding, judging truth, and judging value.

3. Knowing is discursive, complex, takes time, and involves many activities. It has both active and receptive aspects. It is NOT one, single, simple, direct, contact, or intuition between the knower and the known. We can only appreciate real human knowing if we focus on concrete examples, describe in detail, differentiate activities and levels, and recognize these in your own experience.

4. The structure or sequence of activities is not open to basic revision. I am not claiming that it cannot be improved, nor that it cannot be made more differentiated, nor that it cannot be made clearer. But I am claiming that the basic structure cannot be fundamentally changed. Nothing substantial can be added nor anything substantial be subtracted. Because any attempt to do so would involve questioning, experiencing, understanding, and judging.

5. An explanatory theory relates things to one another and prescinds from the perspective of the observer. This is precisely what makes it explanatory and not descriptive. If you look at diagram 2 you will see how the activities are related to one another in a hierarchy of four levels. Terms are defined by relations, and relations are defined by terms. The left-hand side of this simple diagram presents a theory of knowledge. It is different from a Kantian or empiricist theory because it derives directly from observation of one's consciousness, from self-appropriation, from interiority. It is descriptive in the sense that it describes activities. It is explanatory in that it defines these activities and relates them in a structure. In this case description and explanation coincide rather than diverge—the more you describe cognitional activities the closer you come to the invariant structure—the better you understand the structure the easier it is to describe the activities.

6. An epistemology examines the basic notions involved in understanding the process of knowing. Knowing involves a subject and hence we affirm the existence of a self. It involves an object, which we identified with being. And it involves objectivity, namely, the real distinction between the subject and the object.

7. I am claiming that this structure of human knowing is common to all human beings, at all times and in all cultures and in all places. Humans enjoy a rich diversity of culture, language, environmental conditions, religions, modes of production, ways of celebrating. But the same cognitional structure is operating underneath all this diversity. Everyone I have met in my life operates using this basic method. I have never had a student whose mind worked in a substantially different way.

8. Lonergan defines method as, "a normative pattern of recurrent and related operations yielding cumulative and progressive results."[8] Here we are not thinking of rules, instructions, techniques, procedures, methodology, laws, logic or any other procedures which if followed by a dolt will automatically achieve the desired result. We are identifying the fundamental, transcendental desire to know which pushes us to attend, to understand, to judge correctly and evaluate responsibly. These are the norms which are operative in all our activities, in all the sciences, in all disciplines and skills and hence we call them transcendental in the sense of applying in all circumstances. We are implementing this transcendental method in extrapolating from the operations of knowing, to what is known in those operations. We hope to set up a worldview which will yield cumulative and progressive results.

Intentionality of Activities

You can move from that structure of the activities of knowing to the invariant structure of the objects known because of the principle of isomorphism by which the activities and objects are proportionate or parallel. The term isomorphism refers to something that has the same shape, form or structure as something else. The term is often used in biology and mathematics. Here we are using it to indicate a parallelism between the structure of the activities of knowing and the structure of the content of the known. This is our pathway into a metaphysics or worldview. The principle of isomorphism simply states, "if the knowing consists of a related set of acts and the known is a related

8. Lonergan, *Method in Theology*, 4.

set of contents of these acts, then the pattern of the relations between the acts is similar in form to the pattern of the relations between the contents of the acts."[9] If we find that the activities of knowing and the objects known are parallel or proportional, then this confirms our metaphysical hypothesis and also our theory of knowledge. But why is there such an isomorphism/ proportionality/parallelism? It is due to intentionality.

"Intentionality" was a category in classical Scholastic philosophy that has been adapted by modern phenomenologists. This turn to the subject is achieved by introspection or intentionality analysis. It is noted that all of the activities involved in human knowing are intentional in the sense that each intends or is directed toward an end proper to itself. Intentionality asserts that knowing is a transitive activity in the sense that a subject intends an object through some operation of knowing and that the object is distinct from the subject. The activities of knowing, experiencing, understanding and judging, are intentional; they intend an object specific to themselves; they pass beyond themselves. The pure desire to know intends being, intends to know everything, is open to know and question everything. The more specific components of knowing intend what is specific and proper to their activity. Let us consider each level of activity and their specific intentionality.

Experiencing intends the sensible or imaginable; by its very nature and definition it intends what can be experienced, what can be sensed, what is sensible, what can be detected by the senses or instruments used to extend the range of the senses. You cannot, strictly speaking, experience the intelligible. It is understanding that apprehends the intelligible. Hence, there is a proportion between the intention of the activity, the activity itself and the content intended in that activity. Acts of sensing intend the sensible. Acts of seeing intend what is visible, acts of hearing intend to detect noise, acts of imagination play with images. Though there is a proportion between the seeing and the seen, they are distinct. One is an activity and the other is the content of the activity. The activity is usually one and the same simple act of seeing, but the content can be any of an infinite number of objects; there is one basic structure of seeing but a quasi-infinity of colors, shapes and figures to be seen. We are going to call the content of acts of sensing "the sensible" or "potency" (since they can potentially be understood), but this will be further qualified, defined and clarified in chapter 5.

Understanding. Aristotle defined the act of understanding in terms of the active intellect throwing light on phantasms so that the form is abstracted

9. Lonergan, *Insight*, 424.

from matter and received in the passive intellect. Lonergan defines the act of understanding in terms of the question operating on the data so that the idea emerges and is expressed in a definition. Understanding is intentional; it intends an intelligible insight/idea/hypothesis. Specific intelligible contents are infinitely varied but we can generally refer to the content of the act of understanding as the "form" or the "intelligible." We will later devote chapter 6 to further specifying this definition.

Judgment of Fact. After one understands, the further question arises as to the truth of one's idea or theory or proposition. Reflective understanding organizes the evidence and judges the connection between the evidence and the conclusion. Then we utter the yes or no, affirmation or denial of a reasonable judgment. Reflective understanding is also intentional; it is an activity that intends a content. The content of the act of judging we are going to call "act" or "actual," "existence." This will be further defined in chapter 7.

Judgment of Value. Finally, we often ask a further question as to the value of what we have discovered, how it might be implemented, or what is the best thing to do in the light of a scientific or medical discovery. The value question arises, and the mind seeks to answer it by gathering evidence for or against various alternatives, by being moved by our conscience to do the right thing, by working out the probable consequences and implications, and finally issuing in a judgment of value. Questions of value intend the good in the question, understand the good in the various alternatives, grasp the good in the deliberative insight and affirm the good/value in the judgment of value.

We can talk of a "notion" of the sensible, a notion of the intelligible, a notion of truth and a notion of value. Before we experience any particular thing, we already know that it must satisfy one criterion, namely, it must be sensible. Before we understand any particular problem, we already have a question which sets the criteria that the answer must satisfy; it must be intelligible. Before we judge, we know that the truth must satisfy the condition of sufficiency of evidence for the truth. Before we evaluate, we realize that there are good and bad alternatives which must be sorted out. We intend before we know. An all levels there is a process, a procession, a series of activities, a heuristic operating to guide the process to a successful completion. That heuristic guides us to our notions of the sensible, intelligible, true, and good/valuable.

Diagram 2 lays out simply and clearly how the activities of knowing on the left-hand side correspond to or are "isomorphic" with the contents of the known on the right-hand side. It is an extraordinarily unifying insight to note that basic activities of knowing are paralleled in the content that is known in these activities. It would seem to follow that the relations of sublation and dependence in the activities of knowing are paralleled in the relations between the elements known. Similarly, the sequence in the emergence of the activities of knowing seem to be reflected in the sequential emergence of things in the real world. Aristotle did recognize that sensing and understanding in some way was reflected in matter and form but did not go further. But to recognize that the full range of activities of knowing are reflected in the full range of that which is known was not recognized until the twentieth century! At first it seemed to me to be an arbitrary, artificial construct, useful in its own way but without foundation. With further familiarity and musing I realized not only that it was so, but that it must necessarily be so. The key idea to grasp this necessity is the notion of intentionality.

The epistemology discussed above paves the way to consider a metaphysics of proportionate being. By proportionate being I mean the being which can be questioned, experienced, understood, affirmed and evaluated as good by a process of human knowing. We are excluding for the moment transcendent being which cannot be experienced directly by humans, even though we can extrapolate certain notions and attribute them to God as we will do in our last chapter. Now it is time to focus on the known, namely, what is experienced, what is understood, and what is affirmed as true and evaluated as good. Let us explain the columns of the diagram one by one.

It is to be noted that the diagram is an example of explanatory terms and relations where the terms define the relations, and the relations define the terms. It is analogous to the periodic table of the chemical elements where even if an element is missing, you can assign its properties and mass from its relations with the other elements in the table. In our diagram the activities of knowing are related to the proportionate content of the known. We are working on a parallel between the knowing and the known. The activities of knowing we have explored in cognitional theory and are found to be intimately related with one another in a structured way. The contents of the knowing are related in a parallel fashion. Hence we have found that the basic components of one knowing, experiencing, understanding, knowing truth and knowing value, are isomorphic with the basic elements of the known, potency, form, act and value. This is a brief presentation to the overall isomorphism of knowing and known. In part 2 each of the metaphysical elements will be identified in greater detail.

Diagram 2 suggests a simple example of judging/knowing: "This is good computer." Parallel to each activity of knowing is the content known in that specific act. (1) The computer is sensible: it can be seen, touched, opened, broken, used, thrown away, or whatever. It has weight, occupies space, can be disassembled into component parts. It can be *experienced* as *data*. (2) But the computer is also intelligible: it can be identified and classified as laptop or tablet. From the viewpoint of common sense, it seems to be a computer. From the point of view of metaphysics, it can be seen as an essence, a form, a universal, realized in a particular. It is something to be *understood* as an *intelligible essence/form*. (3) We are not always certain at first sight that it is a computer. So we look carefully, switch it on, identify the keyboard, hard drive, and screen. We *judge* the *truth/reality/existence* that it is a computer. (4) Further, it is good computer if it functions well as intended by the manufacturer and as used by the purchaser to store files and access the internet. It might be a bad computer, in which case it does not function as intended, is too slow, has very little memory, and often crashes. It makes a difference whether it is good or bad and that difference is verifiable in using it. We can *evaluate* a computer as *good* or *valuable*. Although there are four distinct elements, it is one computer that is sensible, intelligible, real, and good.

You can substitute any other judgment for this particular example. The weather is good today; cigarettes are bad for your health; he is a good person; this is a good bargain; water is H_2O; Newton's laws of motion; Einstein's theory of Relativity, and so on.

From Activities to Content

Just as there are four basic components of all human knowing, so we are asserting that there are corresponding elements of being, elements of the proportionate universe intended in each of these activities. Just as the activities are distinct and have distinct intentionalities, so we are asserting that there are four distinct elements of the universe of proportionate being, namely: *potency, form, act,* and *good*. These are heuristic definitions. We are determining the shape of our universe and asserting that in general it is complex and fourfold. Thus, we have distinguished the four basic elements of the universe of proportionate being. We assert that they are distinct, which does not mean separate and unrelated. We will consider the relations that exist between these elements as parallel or isometric to the relations between the activities of knowing in the following section.

We are proposing the above diagram as an overall skeletal framework for our elaboration of the universe of being. Just as there is one process of knowing there is also one object known. Just as there are four components of knowing, so there are four elements of proportionate being, namely, potency, form, act and the good. These are the terms we are assigning to the elements at the moment. Later we will have an opportunity to see why these terms are particularly appropriate and other terminology is not so suitable.

What we are doing now is metaphysics and not empirical science. We are assigning heuristic notions to cover all our knowing and all possible to be known. We are asserting only that in any complete term of human knowing of being there must an element of potency, an element of form, an element of act, and an element of value. As metaphysicians, we do not give specific answers to specific questions. We are asking about the universal properties that must be satisfied if knowledge is to be knowledge of the universe of proportionate being. Whether it is common sense, science, the human sciences, other knowledge disciplines, the fourfold structure of human knowing will be reflected in the fourfold structure of proportionate being.

Such is the hypothesis of isomorphism. It is extraordinarily unifying in relating all activities of knowing with all that is known or to be known. However, just because it is neat and plausible does not mean that it is true. Where are the facts to back it up?

The diagram of Isomorphism presents us with two ranges of facts that serve as a heuristic for the method and content of our knowing. First, we have a range of facts about human knowing, its activities, the characteristics of these acts, and the pattern that relates these acts. These are facts which we ourselves outlined in our study of cognitional theory and can be verified by applying empirical scientific methodology to the data of consciousness. We are performing these activities every day. We appeal to our students to pay attention; we give them examples so that they will understand; we present arguments and data to show that the explanation is true. You can continue to show the value of the correct explanation in applications and implementations that will benefit mankind. Sadly, many accounts of human knowing present a truncated, simplified, distorted account, but we are now in a position to appeal to the facts and give a comprehensive correct account.

The second range of facts is about the known, about the conclusions of empirical sciences, about the nature of the parts of the universe. Astronomy tells us about the stars, biology tells us about life, geology tells us about the earth and its history, anthropology and the human sciences tell us about human persons in all their details. History tells the story of all aspects of the development of the universe and human beings. This is indeed a vast and ever-expanding range of facts, which expand exponentially in all areas. How do we bring some sort of order into these ranges of facts? By noting that every scientific discovery is a result of theories verified in instances. Scientists deal with data which is sensible; it can be observed, researched, experimented upon, expanded, remembered, and imagined. To prove a scientific theory, you have to be able to point to some instance, at some time, in some place, that shows the theory to be true. It is a theory or a hypothesis or a possible explanation that needs to be proved by recourse to data. Hypotheses emerge from acts of understanding, we get an idea, it dawns on us, we assign a possible solution to our problem. Verification is a special act of human understanding that grasps the sufficiency of the sensible data to justify the conclusion; that the hypothesis is correct and can be affirmed. Every time a scientist makes a correct discovery in his field, he is affirming all that we have said in epistemology about human knowing, and all that we are saying as metaphysicians about the known.

Both of these ranges of facts about knowing and about the known are concrete, verifiable, true or false, synthetic a priori judgments. These two ranges of fact are now affirmed to be isomorphic, namely, parallel, proportionate, mirroring one another, of the same structure. The relations between structure of the knowing is isomorphic with the relations between the structure of the known. However, the two ranges of facts do not have the same value. Our primary starting principles are the facts about human knowing. We start with these facts because they are directly accessible to each of us in our own consciousness and can be verified by each individual by the simple process of self-appropriation. Further, the facts about human knowing form a relatively simple unity. There is an infinity of things we can ask about, but only one pure desire to know issuing in particular questions. There is an infinity of things to be understood, but only one single activity of human understanding. There is an infinity of things to be judged, but only one basic structure of judgment. Surely then the activities which are all intentional can be used as a template for the unity and structure of the contents of acts of sensing, acts of understanding, and acts of judging. Hence our metaphysics will depend primarily on the range of facts about human knowing and only indirectly on the range of facts from empirical sciences about the contents of the known. However, it is significant that the facts about the universe revealed in the empirical sciences are fully consonant with the anticipations of our worldview. They fit in perfectly.

We are going to use this structural similarity to define being, the metaphysical elements, substance and accidents, genera and species, finality, development and generalized emergent probability. Our clue will always be the invariant structure of our human knowing reflected in the structure of the contents known in that particular activity.

"The process, then, to explicit metaphysics is primarily a process to self-knowledge."[10] It is the structure of our knowing that we are using to move to the structure of the known. But as we have seen the process of

10. Lonergan, *Insight*, 422.

self-appropriation of the activities of our knowing is long and difficult. It presupposes a certain amount of maturity, a reflective temperament and an integrated personality. Like good wine it improves with age. It is a process from self-consciousness, to self-understanding, to self-affirmation, to self-evaluation. It develops from a latent stage, to a problematic phase, and finally to explicit metaphysics. Everyone is potentially a philosopher; we all have a desire to know and feel the obligation to understand correctly the true and the good. But not many have the advantage of leisure, education, good teachers, and financial backing to be able to devote themselves to the search for wisdom. The metaphysics is problematic when we notice the difficulty of answering the simple question, what is real? Is it real because we can see and imagine, or because we can correctly affirm its existence? To persevere in sorting out the problem of knowing and recognizing the intentionality of all operations of knowing will eventually lead to an explicit metaphysics. Hence metaphysics exists primarily in human minds and only derivatively in books.

It is not in any way easy to attain an explicit awareness of the invariant structure of our human knowing. It takes years of awareness, reflection, maturity to reach a point where we can really identify the process of human knowing and overcome our instinctive presuppositions about how knowing works. Hence Lonergan's statement that an explicit and adequate metaphysics will depend on an explicit and adequate self-knowledge.

One Knowing, One Known

The diagram might give the impression that the activities of knowing are atomistic, that they are separate and independent from one another. But they are laid out in ordered sequence. The columns on the far left and the far right show that knowing is one and the known is also in some sense one. The activity of physical, biological seeing is a cognitional activity in itself inasmuch as it is part of one process; the eye sees what is visible. But seeing by itself is not knowing. It is elevated to be part of human knowing when intelligence asks questions about what is seen in order to understand. The act of human understanding needs images, data, the sensible in order to get ideas. Once we understand, we ask a further question as to whether our understanding is correct or not. To ask this question about the truth moves us beyond direct understanding to a reflective act of understanding. When we seek or intend the truth, we cannot do that apart from data and images or apart from ideas and causes. Similarly, the question of worth arises, and this cannot be answered without reference to the sensible, the intelligible, and the true. The final stage, judgment of value, incorporates elements of the three prior stages of knowing and known to formulate the simple judgment, this is a good computer. There is one activity of knowing with four components that culminates in a judgment of value. Just as there is also only one computer which is sensible, intelligible, real and good, there is one process of knowing.

In parallel fashion, the known is also one. This is a good computer. One can distinguish the sensible, the intelligible, the real and the good about the computer but it is one computer. You can see the computer, understand what it is, verify that it is real computer by using it and affirm that it is good because it functions well. But it is one known, one thing, one substance, one unity of different elements. The unity of a computer is different from the unity of an army, or of a cat, or of a house.

The perennial danger of differentiating so explicitly between the sensible, the intelligible, the real, and the good is that we tend to think of them of separate and apart from one another. When we have discrete individual words, we tend to think that the word refers to a discrete, separate thing or part of a thing. As with the word "being" we tend to think there must be something separate and apart from individual things outside the mind to which the word refers. Many of the misunderstandings of Aristotle's hylomorphism spring from this tendency to separate matter as one thing, and form as another thing, and stick them together with glue. Our approach is to differentiate in order to integrate; we differentiate knowing into questioning, experiencing, understanding and judging only to clearly understand and strongly affirm the unity of one act of knowing. We differentiate potency, form, existence, and good, only to affirm their integration in one good computer, or one good human person.

Even the metaphor of levels can be taken too literally, as if we had to climb laboriously up and down from one level to another. In truth we are often working at different levels simultaneously: our attention can skip up and down in an instant, and we not only move from below upwards (experience to judging) but also from above downwards (judging to experience). Once we have reached a judgment this will have a feedback effect on further experience in research and thinking.

Relations between the Four Elements

The diagram presents the terms from the point of view of the knowing and the known. Now we have to consider the relations between the terms, using the principle that terms define the relations and the relations define the terms. Isomorphism also applies to the pattern the relationships operative in the knowing and a similar pattern operating in the known. The activities of experiencing, understanding and judging form a pattern of relationships. It is an ordered sequence; judging depends on understanding, which in turn depends on questioning experience. You can have experience alone, a simple biological seeing, for example. But as soon as intelligent questions arise you begin sorting out what you see in order to understand. You are still physically seeing but the seeing is informed by questioning. The higher activities depend on the earlier ones. In the judgment knowledge incorporates elements of experience and understanding. That is the pattern of relations of dependence operating in the activities of knowing. By isomorphism we will expect that the same pattern of relations will be found in the content of the known.

There is a kind of hierarchy of emergence and dependence in the unfolding of the individual activities of knowing. There is a similar hierarchy of emergence and dependence within the objective correlate of proportionate being. Let us examine this hierarchy in the knowing and then the corresponding hierarchy in the known.

Knowing usually starts when we ask questions about what we experience. But we can have many experiences about which we do not ask questions. Experience can occur without the further acts of questioning, understanding and judging. There are many things that we experience, and we take them for granted, pay no attention to them and hence do not proceed to understanding. Sometimes we do not ask the question; sometimes we ask and find it difficult to answer. Experience is then the bedrock, the necessary starting point for all human knowing. Without experiencing you cannot have understanding. But even with experiencing you need not necessarily proceed to understanding.

If we do ask questions about what we experience, an idea might emerge. We might proceed to understanding, to having an insight, a eureka moment. Ideas emerge from images; they are dependent on images for emergence and for development. We cannot think without images. The more appropriate the image the sooner the idea will emerge.

Experiencing and understanding can occur without the further act of judgment occurring. You can consider all the possibilities, but the judgment can remain elusive. The judgment emerges when there is a grasp of the sufficiency of the evidence for this particular judgment. The judgment emerges but is dependent on the sufficiency of the evidence. You can understand a theory but still suspend judgment as to its truth. When reading fiction, you are understanding and enjoying but the critical faculty has been switched off. When reading history, you are very much aware of the need to judge and read critically. Hence, you can have experiencing and understanding without a judgment of truth; but you cannot have judgments of truth without previous experience and understanding.

Experiencing, understanding and judging can occur without passing into the area of evaluation. Pure science or philosophy may aim at the truth and only the truth. Many sciences claim to be value-free. It is possible to have a judgment of truth, which is not a judgment of value. However, more often than not there are questions about application, questions of value, questions of, what is the best thing to do when these circumstances arise. And so, the question of value arises with the need for a judgment of value. When the question of value arises, evidence for and against the proposed value judgment is considered, and if the evidence is considered sufficient the judgment of value emerges. On the other hand, it is not possible to have a correct judgment of value without a previous experience, understanding, and judgment of truth. The judgment of value emerges from and is dependent on previous cognitional activities.

So, there is a kind of hierarchy of emergence and dependence operating in the activities of knowing. The same hierarchy is to be found in the proportionate metaphysical elements of what is known in these cognitional activities. We will be dealing with these metaphysical elements in great detail in part 2 of this text but allow me to sketch the relations between them here.

You can have potencies that are not realized. They remain potencies but are never or may never be actualized. A seed does not necessarily result in a tree. A child does not always survive to adulthood. Only some blocks of marble are turned into statues. Only some persons become good philosophers. Emergence depends on certain degrees of probability and hence emergence occurs contingently and not necessarily.

An old Scholastic adage says, "when the potency is ready the form emerges." Form emerges from and depends on potency. If the potency is not there, the form cannot emerge. If there is no real potency, there can be no real form. Form depends on previous potency. Potency is limited. An avocado seed can become an avocado tree but cannot become a mango tree. The child has the potency to learn any particular language but has not the potency to become an elephant.

Potency and form of themselves belong to the world of possibility. Act adds existence, the real, truth. Form, which is first in potentiality, now becomes an actuality. Existence is not a predicate floating around in the air looking for a form. Possible forms remain possible until they emerge and actually exist. Existence is added to form; it is contingent existence. It exists for a time and then ceases to exist. You can ask the question, does it exist or not exist, about all forms or essences. That is an intelligent and reasonable question. Our universe is a succession of informed matter emerging from unformed matter, existing for a given period of time, and then ceasing to exist.

Just as judgments of value emerge and depend on previous activities of knowing, so the emergence of new actual forms in our universe depends on previously existing forms and realities. The story of the universe is a history of the emergence of atoms, emergence of galaxies, emergence of our solar system, emergence of life, of vegetation, of animals, and finally we human persons arrived on the scene. Each step in the process depends on the previous developments and functioning on the lower levels.

Polymorphism of Human Consciousness

We have presumed in our discussion in this chapter that we are consistently operating in the intellectual pattern of experience. In other words, we are presuming that the motivating dynamism of our inquiry derives from the pure, detached, unrestricted desire to know. We are taking for granted that we have accepted a correct understanding of the process of knowing, that it arises from desire to know, refers to what we have experienced, grasps an explanation or cause from the data, verifies this hypothesis through accumulation of evidence and its connection with the conclusion. We accept judgment of ideas verified by data as the criterion of what is real. Since we are deriving our metaphysics from our cognitive theory, we must be clear about the process of knowing so that we can be clear about what is known in these operations.

Many however do not operate on the basis of a clear understanding of the process of knowing. Many are confused about the activities of knowing and consequently are confused about the structure of the known. Many are unable to distinguish the many activities of knowing from one another. In any such cases isomorphism will not work as a pedagogy or in principle. Lonergan uses the term "polymorphism" to refer to those who are confused or wrong about human knowing and cannot on that basis be clear about the known. Polymorphism occurs when our accounts of the process of knowing are confused or inaccurate and do not conform to what we actually do when we question, observe, understand and judge. Clarity about knowing can lead to clarity about the known. Confusion about knowing can only lead to confusion about the known. The term "polymorphism" is not referring to mistakes in logic, or mistakes in data collection, or small misunderstandings or jumping to conclusions. It refers to very deep-rooted, fundamental bias in our human understanding and hence to conclusions about what is known.

The biological pattern of experience is the most common cause that tends to intrude on the intellectual pattern and thus distort the process of knowing. This happens because in the biological pattern of experience we operate in terms of a different criterion of the real. Cats know real food by smell, taste, looks, and its location in the place where food normally appears. We can dub this knowing as a "sense knowing" of the "out there now real." It is a sensible criterion, which works for animals, who can distinguish by their senses between real food and plastic. Sadly, because we too are animals and the criterion of intelligence makes a tardy entry into our lives, we tend to operate on the animal criterion of the real. We think of knowing as sensing, tasting, as what satisfies imagination, memory and instinct. We have no problem with the reality of trees, because they are clearly out there now real. But we have problems with causes, identities, substances, relations and the like, because we often cannot physically see them. There are many ways in which our theories about knowing could be fundamentally skewed and therefore polymorphic rather than isomorphic with the real world.

Another way of describing this basic confusion about knowing is when there is no clear distinction between operations of intellect and activities of imagination, when there is confusion between ideas and images. Intellect searches for ideas, for acts or understanding, for explanations, for solutions to problems. Imagination seeks images—visual, tactile, or auditory. Ideas emerge from images, but images and ideas are fundamentally different entities. Ideas are intelligible, universal, abstract, and general. Images are always sensible, particular, concrete, and specific. The idea of a triangle is quite different from an image of a triangle. We often have difficulty in philosophy or physics teaching an idea and then we invent diagrams, construct pedagogical images, or appeal to particular examples. In the process of knowing, the desire to know is the dominant dynamic, not the desire to imagine.[11]

There are many other images that can be used to show how our basic unquestioned assumptions about human knowing can be mistaken and distorting. It is difficult to appreciate isomorphism if you have not grappled with the polymorphism of your own experience. Nothing will make sense in the rest of this text unless you are operating in the intellectual pattern of experience. I devoted a chapter in my previous book on "understanding misunderstanding."[12] That chapter suggests many images and examples that

11. Cronin, *Phenomenology of Human Understanding*, 213–22.
12. Chapter 9 in Cronin, *Phenomenology of Human Understanding*, 205–37.

might trigger the required insight into a very common misunderstanding of what constitutes human knowing.

To understand polymorphism in the above sense, you need an inverse insight: an insight into the absence of an expected intelligibility. You need to understand that it is a mistake to believe that the criterion of the real is known simply through imagination and sensation. To uncover such deeply embedded faulty assumptions is no easy task, but it is important if we are to abandon an incorrect, distorted metaphysics and develop a correct, explicit one. Confusion about knowing inevitably results in confusion about the known.

Explicit Metaphysics

Lonergan defines explicit metaphysics as, "the conception, affirmation, and implementation of the integral heuristic structure of proportionate being."[13] This sounds rather difficult but when we break it down it begins to make sense. His basic idea is that explicit metaphysics works not by dictating the content of any of the sciences, but by anticipating the overall worldview of what is to be understood in the individual sciences. Each of the sciences studies a part of reality of proportionate being but it is metaphysics that provides the integrating framework or context of how the parts fit into the whole. Now let us look at the elements of the definition.

"A heuristic notion, then, is the notion of an unknown content and it is determined by anticipating the type of act through which the unknown would become known."[14] Heuristic comes from the same root as the "Eureka!"—I have found it!—of Archimedes. A heuristic is something that will help you to find what you are looking for. You may not know the precise content of the answer, but you know what you have to do to find the answer. It is a kind of anticipatory knowledge, guidelines that help one find and anticipate what one seeks to discover. Every genuine question implies a combination of something that is known and something that for the moment is unknown. You assemble what is known, you look to what is unknown, combine characteristics of known and unknown, work backwards and forwards, analyze and synthesise, and eventually the answer will pop out. To be able to formulate a question properly and clearly already puts us in reach of a solution: that is a heuristic.

You can outline a general heuristic method. In algebra we are told to name the unknown as "x," to combine the known and unknown in as many

13. Lonergan, *Insight*, 416.
14. Lonergan, *Insight*, 417.

equations as we can, and then solve the equations to find the value of "x." But this can be generalized to all fields of human understanding. Knowing is always a proceeding from the known to the unknown, from experience, to understanding, to judgment. Chess players do not become great simply by memorizing and being familiar with all the great games played by all the grand-masters and champions of history. They proceed by recognizing patterns, and structures, and combinations, and sequences, and tactics, and strategy, which are relevant to an almost infinite variety of actual positions.

The heuristic notion of metaphysics involves moving from the activity of knowing, to anticipating the general lines of the content of that knowing. We are not trying to determine precisely the specific content; we are anticipating the general structural lines of the content. We are not able to determine which particular substances exist; but we can anticipate the properties of substances in general because we know the kind of insight by which substances are grasped. This whole strategy of anticipation proves to be immensely useful, as we will see in the discussion of the metaphysical elements.

We are not now generalizing from the results of the sciences because we do not want to be directly dependent on the results of empirical sciences for our metaphysics. We have seen that empirical science is open to basic revision; its basic terms and relations and definitions and axioms can change overnight. We are looking for a worldview that will be permanent and stable even if it is not very specific. In metaphysics we are not looking for an encyclopaedic comprehension of everything about everything. We are looking for the integrating structure uniting all the contents of all the encyclopaedias.

"A heuristic structure is an ordered set of heuristic notions."[15] The simplest way to understand this is by looking at the best example of such a heuristic structure. We have discovered that knowing is one structure composed of the components: experiencing, understanding, judging truth and judging value. This is one structure with four components, and because it is isometric with what is known, we can anticipate that what is known will be one structure with four elements. In this way we can anticipate the unity of proportionate being and its four elements: potency, form, act, and good. This is a heuristic structure comprised of ordered heuristic notions. Such notions can be utilized in more detailed examples and can be very fruitful.

"Finally, an integral heuristic structure is the ordered set of all heuristic notions."[16] Later in part 2 we will systematically set out such an ordered set of notions on the four elements of metaphysics, potency, form, act, and good.

---

15. Lonergan, *Insight*, 417.
16. Lonergan, *Insight*, 417.

In part 3 we set out a worldview of generalized emergent probability comprising, conjugate and central potency, form, act; then explanatory genera and species, then understanding living things, and the human person. These are all heuristic notions. Put together like this they are an ordered set of all heuristic notions and, hence, an "integral heuristic structure."

All this is fine, but we have also to explain how metaphysics is the "conception, affirmation, and implementation" of that integral heuristic structure.

"Conception" refers to coming up with the idea of such a metaphysics at the level of thought, or possibility. It is a product of direct understanding. "Affirmation" refers to accepting this approach as the correct approach. It is not only a possibility: there is sufficient evidence to judge it to be the correct approach: it is a judgment. "Implementation" refers to deciding and acting to put the process into practice. Metaphysics is not a series of dry propositions to be buried in archives and learned tomes. It is a programme for the transforming and unifying of the knowledge of your own mind and also a programme to be applied to knowledge presented by others in books, articles and lectures. This is how metaphysics is so closely related to all the other branches of human knowledge. Metaphysics provides the framework and criteria by which we can unify our own knowledge of the universe and also embrace, transform, and criticize the thought of others.

Characteristics of This Metaphysics

We are not looking for an abstract understanding of being qua being. We are not looking for a metaphysics of all possible worlds. We are not looking for empty speculation, fruitless disputation, doctrinaire concepts, or even a merely scholarly, professional, academic, or theoretical metaphysics.

We are searching for a concrete understanding of this actual universe, our universe, and the role of human beings within it. We are looking for a flexible and practical understanding of the basic first principles and causes operating in this universe of ours. We leave the details to the scientists. We are looking for a broad framework which will function as unifying, integrating, and transforming every facet of our human knowing and doing. Our metaphysics is a universal frame of reference to unify all the results of all scientific investigations, past, present and future.

This philosophy includes as an integral part the judgment of value, how truth leads on to value, and hence how we can make the world a better place. Politics and ethics focus on the details of this program of improvement, but it is also overseen by the total view of the good of the universe. To understand the universe fully is to understand it as good, as developing, as getting better, and people, societies, cultures, nations, and individuals joining in that movement of progress. This worldview recognizes and promotes progress and recognizes and reverses decline. Thus, this metaphysics is strategically concrete and practical.

This approach to metaphysics will be stable. It is not a generalization from the present state of scientific knowledge about our universe. The sciences provide the material parts, the details, the content which can then be unified in a single worldview. Science advances at an ever-increasing rate. New facts are discovered, new instruments devised, new measurements taken, new definitions and principles are asserted, new hypotheses formulated, and theories tested in experiments. We are seeking a worldview that will be stable and constant over changes in scientific revolutions and discoveries. Hence, we are not taking our starting point from the results of empirical scientific investigations but from the invariant structure of our own knowing, which is not open to substantial change.

Our method makes metaphysics verifiable, because the sciences and common sense that provide the materials for metaphysics are factual and verifiable. Similarly, the facts and hypotheses about the structure of our knowing are also concrete, specific and verifiable. All the terms and relations in the structure of knowing are verifiable by self-appropriation. Every statement about the structure of the universe will be isomorphic with some element of the structure of our knowing. Therefore, metaphysical statements will have an empirical referent and will be verifiable. This will become clearer as we proceed and apply the method in various areas of proportionate being.

It also makes metaphysics progressive and purposive. The one integrating structure can become more explicit, more critical, more sophisticated, the more our understanding of the universe develops. Every development in the sciences or the humanities, in skills, technology, or other disciplines can be included in the development of a correct and differentiated worldview. The more you understand about the parts the more you can understand the whole. The clearer and more differentiated the sciences become, the clearer and more explicitly can their unity and interdependence be affirmed. Metaphysics is interdisciplinary in the sense that it unifies, incorporates, and transforms the contributions of all other disciplines and actions.

Conclusion

You may have been surprised to have seen no mention of being qua being in our notion of first philosophy. Discussion of being qua being has tended to become abstract, detached from reality, dealing with concepts rather than the real world. That way lies the road to nowhere. Metaphysics can and should perform a positive real function in the intellectual progress of humanity. That function is precisely to unify, to transform, to correct, to guide and assist all the varied sciences and disciplines and skills. A good metaphysics underlies, penetrates, transforms and unifies. A mistaken metaphysics eviscerates, destroys, impoverishes and distorts. We are looking for a correct worldview, which will transform and unify our contemporary culture and our contemporary science. Thus we turn in our next chapter to that precise relationship between philosophy and the sciences.

3

Philosophy and the Sciences

Accordingly, just as the scientist has to raise ultimate questions and seek the answers from a metaphysics, so the metaphysician has to raise proximate questions and seek their answers from scientists.[1]

The contribution of science and of scientific method to philosophy lies in a unique ability to supply philosophy with instances of the heuristic structures which a metaphysics integrates into a single view of the concrete universe.[2]

There is no formula that can deliver all truth, all harmony, all simplicity. No Theory of Everything can ever provide total insight. For, to see through everything, would leave us seeing nothing at all.[3]

The reciprocal relationship of epistemology and science is of noteworthy kind. They are dependent upon each other. Epistemology without contact with science becomes an empty scheme. Science without epistemology is—insofar as it is thinkable at all—primitive and muddled.[4]

Introduction

IN OUR FIRST CHAPTER, I aimed to establish foundations for a new approach to first philosophy and focused on recognizing the basic invariant structure of human knowing. Our second chapter showed how the notion of isomorphism can establish that the structure of the known will be isomorphic to the structure of the knowing. The intentionality of knowing is the key to

1. Lonergan, *Insight*, 533.
2. Lonergan, *Insight*, 455.
3. Barrow, *Theories of Everything*, 210.
4. Schilpp, *Albert Einstein*, 683–84.

this transition. Basing ourselves on this isomorphism we should be able to build a metaphysics that is not open to basic revision, that is progressive, that unifies and transforms the knowledge of the sciences and all other disciplines. We can develop a worldview that is correct, comprehensive, helpful and critical. That previous chapter may have seemed a trifle general so in this chapter I want to show more concretely how such a worldview would operate in relation to the empirical sciences.

My thesis is that the big picture and each of the particular sciences influence one another in a myriad of ways. A correct worldview will function in relation to the sciences as a unifying and transforming influence promoting the right questions and discouraging distortions. An incorrect worldview will point in the wrong direction, misinterpret data, distort the presentation of results, and promote decline rather than progress. In general, I hope to show that science not only can, but also must, also move from the world of theory into the mentality of interiority.

This chapter shows how neither science nor philosophy can stand alone. To think that science does not need philosophy is a dangerous illusion. Nature abhors a vacuum, and all sorts of strange, unquestioned ideas will usurp the rightful place of philosophy. For philosophers to think they can produce a first philosophy while ignoring science and its discoveries is to claim to know the whole, while knowing nothing about the parts. We will try to show the mutual interdependence and complementarity of science and philosophy in their methods, and their conclusions. We aim to harmonize the best of philosophy and science.

How Philosophy Impacts the Empirical Sciences

Everyone develops a unique worldview of their own. It may be comprehensive, correct, well-meaning, a set of practical priorities, what we consider important, and the like. For some these may be quite vague and implicit. However, such basic principles effect what we do with our lives, they inform every decision that we make, and have immediate concrete implications on how we live our lives. The "big picture" impacts on all that we do and conversely our actions will have a feedback effect on our principles.

It is somewhat the same when it comes to the relation between an explicit philosophy and the work of the empirical sciences. Aristotle conceived the empirical sciences as under the control of philosophy, as being in a subordinate position. Others would consider philosophy and science as belonging to separate realms and they work best in isolation from one another. Some would think that there is no longer a need for philosophy now that we have discovered the real sciences. My view is that they work in tandem and effect one another in a myriad of ways. This chapter aims to identify and highlight these influences and promote a view of the complementarity of the two field of thought. First, we say something about how philosophy impacts on the world of empirical science.

Metaphysics Underlies, Penetrates, Transforms and Unifies the Sciences

Lonergan describes how metaphysics functions in relation to all other disciplines saying that: "metaphysics is the department of human knowledge that underlies, penetrates, transforms and unifies all other departments."[5] Here he is explaining the relationship between metaphysics and the other empirical sciences and all branches of human knowledge as he understands it. For Aristotle and Aquinas metaphysics is the first and highest science; other sciences depend on metaphysics for concepts, methods, and principles; metaphysics is in no way dependent on lower sciences. Lonergan takes a quite different position. For him there is a very close interpenetration of the empirical sciences and metaphysics. The above quotation illustrates the function of philosophy; interested in all human knowing; providing a framework for unifying all knowledge; and correcting what is not based on sound epistemological principles. Philosophy is interested in everything and so must be interested and involved wherever correct knowing is taking place, in this case, in the sciences. Note that this relationship occurs whether the philosophical framework is valid or invalid.

Metaphysics *underlies* all other departments of knowledge. Any other department of science is simply one example of the unceasing wonder of questioning, leading on to insight into data, and the formulation of theories, to be verified in instances. The desire to know is the origin and source of commonsense knowing, of the empirical sciences, of human languages and cultures, of technology, production, art and skills and of first philosophy. Every empirical science invokes a criterion of what is real and implies a notion of truth and objectivity. These are implicit in every area of human knowing. It is the task of metaphysics to make these basic principles explicit. Yet they are presumed by all the sciences, and hence it is that metaphysics is said to underlie all the other areas of human knowing.

Metaphysics *penetrates* every other department, not in the sense of interfering in specifics where it does not belong, but in the sense that each department of science has cut off one particular area of being to be

5. Lonergan, *Insight*, 415.

studied; each science is restricted to one kind of data or area of being. But metaphysics deals with the whole universe of being—it excludes nothing. The contributions of all the sciences are contributions to our understanding of the concrete universe of proportionate being. Any advance in the empirical sciences is simultaneously an advance in philosophy. Biology studies frogs as an example of a living thing. Philosophy is interested in frogs because they are beings; they are included in the "everything" which is the material content of first philosophy.

Metaphysics *transforms* all other departments. Because all the sciences invoke some criterion of the real, it happens very often that the results of scientific inquiry are formulated with a view of the real, which is basically unsound. Newton was correct in all that he said about relative space, time, and motion because all these affirmations could be verified. However, when he formulated notions of absolute space, time, and motion nothing was empirically verifiable; he was satisfying his and our imagination and was perhaps also influenced by theological convictions. In that case he is operating on the criterion of the real as the out there now real of sense and imagination. Even Einstein formulated his conclusions with a determinist philosophy in the background. Darwin made some brilliant discoveries, but some of his followers interpreted these as an explanation of everything and as proving that God does not exist. Philosophy has the task of distinguishing correct positions from their opposite. Scientists are not usually good philosophers; they are most often naïve realists. They are often not aware of their philosophical presuppositions. Metaphysics, "is a transforming principle that urges positions to fuller development and, by reversing counterpositions, liberates discoveries from the shackles in which at first they were formulated."[6]

Metaphysics *unifies* all other departments of knowledge. Other sciences deal with special areas of being. But metaphysics deals with every area. Metaphysics is "the original, total question and it moves to the total answer by transforming and putting together all other answers."[7] The sciences have to presuppose metaphysics in the sense that they have to invoke some criterion of what is real and objective; as specialists they have some framework into which new discoveries can be fitted. But it is explicit metaphysics that in the end unites all the parts into a whole view of the universe. The whole cannot do without its parts. As Lonergan has already said in his Preface,

6. Lonergan, *Insight*, 415.
7. Lonergan, *Insight*, 416.

"But a unification and organization of what is known in mathematics, in the sciences, and by common sense is a metaphysics."[8]

Specific Areas of Influence

It might help to specify the areas in which presuppositions and general philosophical positions influence the process of scientific research. These unquestioned philosophical assumptions will influence: (1) the direction of research, (2) the interpretation of results, (3) the presentation of results, and (4) the implementations and applications of discoveries.

(1) The general *direction of scientific research* is set by the questions that are asked and deemed to be important and promising. Scientific method works in terms of scissors like movement of a heuristic upper blade and an empirical lower blade. The upper blade is the question, the hypothesis, the anticipated understanding and how to find it. The lower blade is the investigation of data guided by the hypothesis. These specific questions are often posed or determined by the worldview of the researcher rather than the data at hand. In a reductionist perspective the parts are of overriding significance; the parts are the cause of the whole; therefore, you study the parts but not the whole. Copernicus was much influenced by a kind of Pythagorean thinking and this, rather than any particular observations, led him to his heliocentric hypothesis. Biologists, who are convinced that humans are only marginally different from brute animals, will go out of their way to focus on the "intelligence" of animals. The search for the ultimate smallest particle is often interpreted as the search for the meaning of the universe: Crick and Watson thought they had found the "secret of life" when they discovered the structure of the DNA molecule.

If you think that the world is material and only material, then investigating the material particle is of supreme importance; hence materialists will study the brain and its neurons but not the mind, patterns of thinking, the characteristics of the act of understanding, and the like. What are things made of, the material cause, are the only questions worth asking. If physics is the only real science, then that is where all the real questions are asked. If the world is only material, then physics and perhaps chemistry are the only valid sciences of matter. Living things are not allowed to have souls, wholes, powers, unities, identities. Biology, botany, zoology and anthropology are just more complicated physics and chemistry.

8. Lonergan, *Insight*, 5.

Of course, many other non-philosophical factors influence the direction of research, such as, grants, the media, desire for fame, the high-profile cases with a promise of publicity, and so on.

(2) Interpretation of results. At one point in history the same astronomical observations could be interpreted either on a heliocentric or geocentric model. Copernicus had no really new or convincing evidence for his heliocentric option; his theory was even more complicated than the Ptolemaic. Galileo discovered the telescope and did produce convincing evidence in favor of heliocentrism. But the Bishops and Aristotelians were still able to disavow the telescope and continue to favor the geocentric interpretation. The same biological discoveries are often appealed to by evolutionists as favoring their position, and by intelligent design advocates as favoring their position. Darwin's genuine biological discoveries can be interpreted as compatible or as incompatible with theism; a theory of evolution is often embedded in a mechanist and atheistic worldview.

The Copenhagen Interpretation of quantum physics was followed by many other interpretations. It was not a row about the data but a row about the correct interpretation. Kantian philosophy and Earnest Mach's positivism were directly invoked. The discovery of the chemistry of the human genome can be interpreted as finding the ultimate secret of life, or as just another step in finding out the chemical mechanism for replication and for inheriting traits.

Interpretations are acts of human understanding. They will be correct if one operates in the intellectual pattern of experience, asks all relevant questions, excludes bias and unquestioned assumptions, and produces an interpretation based on adequate evidence. Interpretations are not arbitrary assertions; one interpretation is not as good as another; some interpretations are reasonable and correct; other interpretations are uncritical, biased, serving preconceived ideas, and responses to the wrong questions.

In many scientific writings you will notice the presuppositions of reductionism popping up when needed. It will be assumed that the whole can be explained in terms of the parts; that the higher can be explained in terms of the lower; that explanation means explaining how the smallest units or parts work. In some cases, you will notice an epistemology of constructivism being appealed to; meaning that we give meaning to reality by the constructs of our theories. Stephen Hawking and Leonard Mlodinow inform us at the end of *The Grand Design*, "We form mental concepts of our home, trees, other people, the electricity that flows from wall sockets, atoms, molecules, and other universes. These mental concepts are the only reality we can know. There is no model-independent test of reality."[9] They call their epistemology model-dependent realism. It is also pure conceptualism; if concepts are the only reality we can know, then we can know concepts, but we cannot know reality.

(3) Presentation of results. Every discovery in science can be presented either as a position or as a counterposition, as representing progress or decline. Darwin's genuine discoveries in biology are often presented as an antireligious argument, one which he did not necessarily share. Nature programs often present their discoveries in terms of the science of evolution replacing the need for God. Nature programs emphasize the similarities of humans to animals: animals think, animals use language, animals have feelings, animals are social; therefore, animals are just like humans and saving the whales is just as important as saving the babies. Notoriously, statistics can be used and abused to prove what you want. Cosmology often presents the history of the universe as if it can explain everything by saying that it all happened by chance. Humans are presented as cosmic accidents occupying an insignificant corner of an immense universe and could not possibly be the center or purpose or apex of the universe. But the same facts can be turned on their heads to show the wisdom, the power and magnificence of a real, ultimate, first cause, which some call God.

The Neo-Scholastic has an aphorism, "whatever is received is received according to the mode of the receiver." The same set of statistics can produce a "yes" to one person and a "no" to another. To one person a set of climate data proves that the climate change is real; but the same set of facts is brushed aside as a hoax by another. I present an ideal of how we know the truth and value by following a sequence of mental activities; and a philosophy based on that being done consistently and disinterestedly. In real life the whole process can be usurped by mistaken philosophical ideas, by deeply held commonsense presuppositions, by conspiracy theories, by common biases and the like. In reading scientific works it is essential to be able to notice the influence of such unstated positions.

(4) Applications. Priorities and value judgments belong to a worldview. Scientific discoveries are usually applied in technology, medicine, and other procedures crucial to human persons and societies. Such discoveries involve big money, politics, fame, strategic advantage, and the like. One's view of the human person, of society, of human values, justice, equality, will enter into such decisions. Nuclear science can be used to produce

9. Hawking and Mlodinow, *The Grand Design*, 172.

electricity or to make nuclear bombs. The worldview of the scientists will clearly condition how such decisions are made.

Positive Contributions of a Correct Philosophy

(1) A Correct Cognitional Theory and Epistemology. A philosophy that promotes the progress of the sciences is one that unifies and transforms all knowledge but especially that of the empirical sciences. This philosophy will embody an understanding of the structure of everything, how it all fits together, what are the principles that apply to everything. Philosophy should be able to say how common sense is related to science, and how the sciences are structurally related to one another. However, it will look to the sciences to fill in the details, connect with concrete specific realities. The specialists who work in the fields of physics, chemistry, botany biology, zoology and the human sciences study the parts. But parts can be isolated and cut off from the whole. We are looking for a correct framework into which everything will fit and will demonstrate how all the parts are related to one another. Just as a single tree by itself is just a tree; if it is part of a forest its value is enhanced, it becomes part of a larger system, and contributes to the functioning of that system. Similarly, the single sciences are unified and transformed when there are related in a correct worldview. For the moment we present the following framework as a hypothesis. Later, the rest of this text we will see that it is more than a hypothesis.

We have elaborated a correct, differentiated, foundationally based understanding of the sequence of cognitional activities that constitute human knowing. The foundation for all method is the norms and procedures that spontaneously emerge in the workings of the human mind as it performs those activities. We have laid out what we think these procedures and norms are in chapter 1 on Foundations. Many have thought of scientific method in terms of induction and deduction, symbolic or mathematical logic, verifiability or falsifiability, and the like. But the simplest, most accurate, most correct and all-encompassing definition of scientific method is "theories verified in instances," which is based on a general epistemology of experiencing, understanding and judging.

Understanding description and explanation are crucial because this distinction solves a historical problem of appearances and reality, common sense and theory, primary and secondary qualities, the thing-for-us and the thing-in-itself. Aristotle and the Scholastics had the distinction between *in se* and *secundum quid*, meaning *in itself* and *from a certain perspective*. From Locke onwards we had primary and secondary qualities variously defined and applied. But this suffered from the notion of the real implied in the distinctions; it was a naïve reality based on imagination and sense. Lonergan was the first to formulate the difference between description and explanation based on judgment and universalized to apply in all areas of human study, as we have explained earlier.[10] If one is not clear about description and explanation, it is hard to grasp the difference between ideas and images, verifiable images and symbolic pedagogical images, common sense and theory. Lonergan states, "The perennial source of nonsense is that, after the scientist has verified his hypothesis, he is likely to go a little further and tell the layman what, approximately, scientific reality looks like!"[11] The equations may be verified; but the images the scientist uses to communicate this to the public are not verifiable but are invented for pedagogical reasons.

Our epistemology also distinguishes between classical and statistical method, how to understand the systematic and also the non-systematic through probabilities. We recognize inverse insights and the degrees of probability in our laws and conclusions. In most cases scientists aim for high probability rather than absolute probability. Rather than depending on a vague commonsense notion of how we reach knowing, our position presents a correct, differentiated, verifiable, sequence of cognitional activities.

It is no longer sufficient that a scientist relies on a commonsense view of method, of worldview, of interpretation, of the criterion of the real, and the other epistemological and metaphysical ideas that underpin the whole scientific enterprise. A commonsense criterion of the real will appeal to images of in here and out there, the criterion will be imagination and not intelligence; knowing will be equated with looking, and will be considered as a simple direct contact between knower and known. Adam Becker published an excellent account of Quantum Physics with the title, *What is Real?* In the Copenhagen interpretation he claims, "there is no problem with reality in quantum physics because there is no need to think about reality in the first place."[12] The author counters by saying, "Yet quantum physics is certainly telling us something about what is real, *out in the world* (my italics). Otherwise, why would it work at all."[13] The book is an excellent analysis of the issue. He is very familiar with the various interpretations and also with the Vienna Circle, positivism, Ernest Mach, Quine, and the like. But he fails to clarify for himself and the reader what is the criterion of the real and he seems to be relying on a paradigm of in here

10. See chapter 1, section 6 above.

11. Lonergan, *Insight*, 278.

12. Becker, *What Is Real?*, 4.

13. Becker, *What Is Real?*, 5.

and out there. A more sophisticated criterion is needed for the intricacies and paradoxes of the new quantum world.

Most scientists will be operating on a commonsense criterion of what is real. We have shown that the real is not something imagined or presumed to exist independently of the observer. Rather it is that which is verified to exist through the experience and understanding and judgment of the scientist. Genuine objectivity is the fruit of authentic subjectivity, as we explained in our first chapter on Foundations.

(2) A Correct Worldview. In parts 2 and 3 we will present what we consider a correct worldview. It is important for the scientist to have a correct worldview because that will underlie, penetrate, unify and transform all his work. We give a short summary of that worldview here in anticipation of greater detail later.

1. Study Everything. Nothing to be ignored. We have claimed that the discipline of first philosophy is obliged of its very definition to study everything, to understand how the parts are related to the whole. It is interested in everything, includes everything, every new discovery or advance in knowledge is added to the store of what philosophy studies. It studies being which we equate with everything.

2. Everything can be divided into transcendent and proportionate being. Transcendent being is the ultimate, perfect, completely intelligible, first cause, infinite being, and transcendent, which we usually call God. Proportionate being is everything within the scope of our human capacity to ask questions about what we experience, in order to understand ideas and principles and laws, and to verify hypotheses with sufficient evidence; to evaluate and attain true value.

3. Proportionate being must be understood in terms of its elements, the sensible, the intelligible, the real and the good. These are principles or causes, or components or aspects of proportionate being, to be discussed in detail in part 2 of the text.

4. Across the whole field of knowledge and all of the sciences, you find a basic structure of things and their properties, substance and accidents, objects that are identified by their characteristics. The first basic division of proportionate beings is into things and their properties.

5. Forms are not chaotic or random but form a hierarchy of genera and species. An individual mouse is a subspecies of rodent, which is a subspecies of animal which is a subspecies of living things, which is s subspecies of

material composite thing. Biologists divide their specimens into classes, orders, families, genera, species, subspecies, individuals.

6. The sciences are to be understood as related to one another systematically on the model of successive higher viewpoints. The sciences are dependent on one another and related intelligibly to one another.

7. What is life? This is a question that needs to be asked. How is life different from non-living? What are the characteristics of living things and how are living beings in turn to be classified, organized and understood.

8. What is a human person? Give a structural account of the unique characteristics, potentialities, abilities, value of this being, who is conscious, experiences, understands, affirms and denies truth and value; who is morally obliged, free and open to religious experience. The text develops an adequate appreciation as to the value, the rights, the meaning of the human person.

Such is the framework that I propose as an integrating structure for a first philosophy which is obliged to see everything as related together in some way in one universe. The details will be outlined in successive chapters. The empty structure will be filled out with examples and data from the sciences. For the moment it is hypothetical or heuristic. Knowledge develops in a scissors like process of an upper blade and a lower blade working together to cut through to verification. The upper blade is the hypothesis; if you have a good hypothesis you are well on your way; the hypothesis is a heuristic, it suggests the direction you should aim at; it will help you to find what you are looking for. The lower blade is the data the material, the facts, the specific requirement that must be satisfied. We can think of the relation between first philosophy as upper blade and the special sciences as lower blade working together to gain true understanding.

From Theory to Interiority in the Sciences

Philosophy in these times is required to move on from theories of knowing and of being to a mentality of interiority, marked by an awareness of the cognitional activities that produce theories and results. It is the same thing for the empirical sciences. They need to move on from formulating theories to an appreciation of the advantages and disadvantages of theories, to the realization that understanding is not the same as having a theory, to pushing the potential of intelligence to the limit. The mentality of interiority is not a monopoly of philosophers. It is as much needed in contemporary science as in philosophy. Thomas Kuhn wrote about paradigm shifts in the history of science and caused consternation in the scientific community.[14] Some concluded that science was basically irrational and depended on a choice of paradigm. Some concluded that science was an arbitrary construction put together to produce the desired results. Others that science is better served by a theoretical anarchism than a normal method. From the point of view of interiority, it is a natural development of human understanding that new ideas take the place of old ideas, that new theories supersede old theories and that new paradigms replace old paradigms. The drive behind the whole enterprise of science is the desire to understand and to know. A correct appreciation of the structure and process of actual human knowing would be of great benefit to science. The sciences are no longer subordinate to philosophy in an Aristotelean sense. But neither are they free in invent theories of knowledge or to operate in the context of muddled notions of intellectual development. A critical realist philosophy is not contained in books, it is contained in minds. Entering the world of interiority is not about learning definitions and divisions, it is about a development and transformation of the mind. It is to implement that control of meaning in all the other branches of knowledge that we are involved in.

At the same time the philosopher learns from the sciences, because that is where philosophy gets its content, and that is where we learn the details of our knowledge of the universe of proportionate being, that is where the philosopher is in contact with the real, concrete changing world. Good science is always done in the context of the principles of critical realism. Good scientists assume these principles perhaps spontaneously and implicitly. Just as it is difficult to expect the professional philosopher to be also a professional scientist, so the reverse is equally hard to expect. But both can enter the world of interiority by a constant stream of questions, higher viewpoints emerging from lower, attention to the act of understanding either of the whole or the parts. Cooperation between philosopher and scientist is not only a desideratum but a necessity for progress in both disciplines.

How the Sciences Contribute to Philosophy

The sciences have been extraordinarily successful in pushing back the borders of the unknown in the micro and macro fields. It has done so by using mathematics, constructing instruments, applying discoveries in technologies, and using methods that produce cumulative and progressive results.

14. Kuhn, *Structure of Scientific Revolutions*.

The worldwide community is involved as scientific methods and research operate above national boundaries and independently of cultural and linguistic differences. In most aspects, science has been used to improve the lot of human beings, to produce food, to improve medicine, to foster education, to construct the infrastructure of our present way of life. Developments in scientific thinking have made it easier to realize that the human intellect is really a capacity to make and create all things. It has provided the material to be organized and transformed by a philosophical worldview.

The sciences have made a significant contribution to the formation of our contemporary worldview. From the point of view of astronomy, we have moved from a limited, geocentric, view of the earth surrounded by close heavenly bodies, to a realization that we are one planet in a solar system at the edge of a galaxy called the Milky Way, which is but one of the billions of galaxies that constitute our universe. We have moved from a notion of a world about six thousand years old, to a realization that the universe is about fourteen billion years old and our solar system about five billion. Our notion of the atom once a single solid particle now has about fifty-six subatomic particles. We had a notion of a basically static system of genera and species and now we realize that new species and subspecies are emerging and becoming extinct all the time. In biology we recognize the existence of different kinds of cells, bacteria, viruses, neurons, and the like. In physics we thought of space and time in commonsense terms and now have to accept the speed of light as an absolute, that events do not happen simultaneously, that gravity is not an attractive force between masses but the curvature of space/time continuum. It is the empirical sciences which pioneered and provided the basis for this transformation. But still these insights need to be interpreted, presented, integrated and applied correctly in a holistic worldview.

Method can be symbolized in terms of a scissors like movement; the hypothesis comes from above and the data from below and they work together towards a judgment. One can apply that to philosophy and science. While first philosophy represents the upper blade of the method, the sciences represent the lower blade. Philosophy provides the integrating structure, and the sciences provide the material to be integrated. If there is no lower blade, no data, no sciences providing the detailed, specialized knowledge of the real world, then philosophy would be quite empty, abstract and useless. First philosophy is the framework, and the particular sciences provide the material to be understood, integrated and verified.

The scientific revolution has provided a myriad of examples of scientific method at work. In this way the sciences have provided us with a multitude of examples of theories verified in instances. Because science is so specialized these instances of understanding at work illustrate again and again how understanding occurs. Understanding is no longer a black box but can be analyzed into a linked series of mental activities; each step in the series can be described and identified. The sciences have demonstrated clearly in numerous examples how we ask questions, about what we have experienced, in order to understand correctly. If we are clear on empirical scientific method, then we can also apply the same method to the data of consciousness and formulate a cognitional theory.

The sciences provide a model of a method that verifies and produces cumulative and progressive results. We find that the method of the special sciences is a prime example of the method of understanding in common sense, in all disciplines, in the human sciences and in philosophy. It is a method for understanding correctly. The same method can be used in the human sciences provided you make allowance for the fact that you are dealing with intelligent, reasonable, responsible, free and social beings. You can also use the method in philosophy as we are doing. The heuristic structure of first philosophy only comes to light when ranges of ranges of results from the various sciences call forth these integrations. Particular discoveries are not only a cumulative and progressive advance in the specific science, but also is an advance in the understanding of the whole and an understanding of how all the pieces fit together into an integrated whole.

Philosophy and the sciences overlap but yet are distinct disciplines. If you want to know, what is the essence of water, you ask a chemist and not a metaphysician. The chemist is competent in the field of the periodic table, chemical compounds, reactions, measurements, and the like. If you want to know, what is an essence, ask the metaphysician. The metaphysician is familiar with potency, form and act, essence and existence, substance and accidents, terms and relations, description and explanation, critical and naïve realism, theory verified in instances. The metaphysician provides the questions, the expectations, the integrating framework, and the general definitions and principles, whereas the sciences provide the specifics, the understanding of particular things from a limited point of view. The discoveries of the sciences help to correct and reorient some of the concepts of metaphysics. Discoveries in quantum physics require a rethinking of the notions of space and time and perhaps causality.

The empirical sciences hit on a method of proceeding and verifying, applied the method to every area imaginable, produced astounding results, transformed medicine, agriculture, technology, information technology, and the like. At the same time, the philosophers for the most part were marginalized by the success of the sciences and confined to the fringes, isolated, ignored, peripheral figures. The great esteem in which Science is held compares with the quiet disregard for the efforts of the philosophers. Philosophy is seen as irrelevant, metaphysics as empty speculation, having nothing to do with science or real life. The decision of philosophers to ignore the emerging sciences has left them in a limbo of abstract concepts with little contact with the real changing world. There is a great need for a recognition of the role of philosophy in unifying and transforming our contemporary worldview.

Can Philosophy Function without the Sciences?

I have made the point that common sense, and the sciences and disciplines deal with the parts and that philosophy deals with the whole. It would be very strange then if a philosophy could operate without paying any attention to the parts. We cannot expect philosophers to study the sciences in the same way that professional scientists do, but we can expect a familiarity with the methods, procedures, advances and applications of science. I feel that to understand philosophy it is necessary to be familiar with at least one of the empirical sciences. Is it possible to do good philosophy and to ignore the sciences, both the hard sciences and the human sciences? What happens to a philosophical school that explicitly looks down on the sciences as inferior and sets itself up as a purveyor of wisdom for the modern world? Let us take a brief look at how some philosophical schools did this and have paid the price. What actually happened after the sciences declared their independence from philosophy and went their merry way? What attitudes do contemporary philosophies adapt towards the knowledge and progress of the empirical science?

The Aristotelians of the time of Galileo considered themselves as superior; they thought that they had nothing to learn from empirical science; they thought that science was inferior and gave only superficial knowledge of the appearance of things. This attitude continues to permeate schools associated with Neo-Scholasticism or Neo-Thomism. With the notable exception of Lonergan, they continue for the most part to ignore the discoveries of modern science and continue to speculate about being, the transcendental properties of being, the definition and division of being and substance. This is a tradition associated with the Catholic Church, its Colleges, Universities, and seminaries.

The empiricist tradition focused on the sensible as what can be known and nothing else. According to Hume, understanding is a habit of associating images that happen to follow one another or appear side by side. In an empiricist philosophy the insights, generalizations and universal laws claimed by scientists are not logically possible. This does not fit well with a scientific understanding of theories verified in instances. Verification appeals not just to sensible data but to the correct understanding of that data; thus, there are at least three activities involved in correct knowing, experiencing sense data, understanding hypotheses and theories, and verifying sufficiency of evidence for the conclusion. The empiricist tradition, logical positivism, and linguistic analysis became narrower and narrower in their scope, excluded recourse to the data of consciousness, and more and more focused on language and meaning. Because they reject introspection, retrospection and self-appropriation they have no handle on the activities that constitute correct human understanding. An empiricist philosophy has little to contribute to the progress of science, and equally has nothing to learn from such progress.

The Kantian tradition centered on the justification of a priori synthetic propositions such as the empirically based universal laws of science. Kant laid down the a priori conditions for the possibility of this kind of knowledge. He legitimized propositions such as those of Newton, but the reality referred to in these propositions is subjective rather than objective. Its reality comes from the a priori categories of the mind rather than independently existing reality. Philosophy and the sciences were distinct disciplines with no overlap between them.

The phenomenological tradition learned little from modern science and contributed little to their studies. Phenomenological method was claimed to be empirical and scientific, a rigorous science. Heidegger in particular despised the empirical sciences and the technology to which it gave rise; he regarded it as superficial, a manipulation of nature, an attempt to control and dominate.

The existentialist tradition concentrated on subjective moods and states, choices, ethical dilemmas, the drama of life and its tragedy, its absurdity and its meaninglessness. They have little interest in the investigations of scientists.

Postmodernism has almost no interest or respect for the work of empirical scientists. However, they do use the terminology and images taken from modern science. Whether this is in the interests of enlightenment or obfuscation is a matter of debate. Alan Sokal and Jean Bricmont claim that postmodernists repeatedly abuse scientific concepts and terminologies, using them out of proper context, and turning them into a jargon to impress their readers.[15]

---

15. Sokol and Bricmont, *Fashionable Nonsense*.

In conclusion, I think we can see that contemporary philosophies have made little contribution to the development and progress of the empirical sciences. There seem to be two universes of discourse, that of the scientist and that of the philosopher. They seem to be continuing in splendid isolation from one another. As I see it, this is doing harm to both science and philosophy. In the end both science and philosophy are trying to understand the real world; there must be some complementarity in their various approaches.

My position would be that philosophy must accept some input from the empirical sciences in order to fruitfully attain theoretical wisdom. Philosophy if it is anything must answer basic ultimate questions such as, what kind of a universe are we living in, what are its first principles and causes, what is a human person and what is the meaning of a human life in the context of such a universe. How can one answer the question of what kind of a universe are we living in without some input from cosmology, physics, astronomy, geology, and the like? How can philosophy claim to know about the human person, if it ignores empirical psychology, sociology, economics, politics, history, languages, and culture? There cannot be a knowledge of the whole without a knowledge of the parts. There must be some kind of positive relationship between the human sciences and philosophy.

Complementarity: Wholes and Parts

Perhaps the easiest and clearest example to understand the complementarity between metaphysics and the empirical sciences is the relation between wholes and parts, so let us conclude with that. A quote from Lonergan puts it succinctly: "Metaphysics, then, is the whole in knowledge but not the whole of knowledge. A whole is not without its parts, nor independent of them, nor identical with them."[16] Metaphysics studies the whole, that is, everything from the broadest point of view, seeking the intelligibility proper to the whole. But the whole is not independent or separate from its parts, and so indirectly metaphysics will be studying the parts in so far as they constitute the whole. Nor is the whole identical with the sum of the parts; that assertion would amount to the whole being nothing, that there are only parts, a reductionist position. The unity of the whole does add something that is not merely the sum of the parts. A forest is more than the sum of the individual trees; the universe is more than the sum of all the galaxies; a living cell is more than the chromosomes, plus the membrane, plus the nucleus, plus the Golgi apparatus, and so on. The insight into the whole is distinct from the

16. Lonergan, *Insight*, 416.

insight into the parts. (This will be discussed in more detail in our chapter on Things and Properties.) Some might ask, which do we know first, the whole or the parts? My answer would be that they grow together. Understanding develops by pivoting from a better understanding of the whole to a better understanding of the parts and vice versa. If you want to understand the contents of a book, first get an overview of the table of contents, introduction and conclusion. Then tackle the first chapter, return later to the table of contents, proceed to the next chapter. Understanding of the whole develops along with understanding of the parts. First philosophy and the empirical sciences are complementary just as wholes and parts. They are inextricably linked together and progress or decline together.

Therefore, metaphysics and the empirical sciences should be understood as complementary. They depend on one another and are of benefit to one another. They cannot thrive separate and apart from one another. The sciences deal with specific questions from a limited point of view. But then we ask what is the significance of this part? How does it contribute to the picture of the whole? What are the implications for other fields? How does it fit into general presuppositions about how the universe is constituted, and what are its principles and causes? The sciences need such an integrating framework in which to fit their particular specialized results and it is the function of metaphysics to provide such a comprehensive and correct framework. Metaphysics for its part has nothing to integrate, if it is not for the contributions of the sciences, common sense and other sources of knowledge. Lonergan sees this mutual dependence as "the dependence of a generating, transforming, and unifying principle upon the materials that it generates, transforms, and unifies."[17]

It would be hard to overemphasize the importance of this shift in the understanding of the purpose of metaphysics. It is not superior to the sciences; it is not isolated and apart from the sciences; it is not a special kind of knowledge available only to those who have a metaphysical intuition; it is not the third level of abstraction, it is not an ontology of being qua being, it is not a claim to know everything. It does bring metaphysics down to the level of every human person who tries to understand the kind of universe he or she is living in. In the end as we shall see it means that we are all metaphysicians of some sort and that there is no avoiding metaphysical commitments.

---

17. Lonergan, *Insight*, 418.

Summary and Conclusions

We have reached a number of conclusions in this chapter, and it may be helpful to put them all together.

1. Aristotle's hierarchical system of control by first philosophy over the empirical sciences did not work and will not work. We are in an age of specialization and empirical science is highly specialized and can only become more and more specialized. Aristotle recognized the need for an overall view, for first philosophy, for the generalist. It was unfortunate that he subordinated the natural sciences to philosophy in the way that he did. Today we accept the independence of science in choosing its methods, questions, its concepts, research, observations, measurements, and mathematical arguments. But still, we defend the need for philosophy to articulate the big picture which should serve as a worldview for scientific thought. The problem Aristotle failed to solve was the proper relation of the special sciences to metaphysics.

2. Empirical science needs the background of a philosophical worldview and will invent it if necessary. The scientists of the classical period assumed the philosophy of mechanist determinism and more contemporary scientists assume the presuppositions of indeterminism and other philosophies. Science cannot do without some philosophical worldview, and it is preferable that it be correct, explicit and helpful.

3. No contemporary philosophical schools seem inclined to be of benefit to empirical science as this background worldview. Most contemporary philosophical schools either ignore the empirical sciences or actively despise them.

4. There is a problem of distinguishing and relating metaphysics and empirical science. Subordination of the sciences to philosophy in one hierarchical system does not work. Total isolation and separation of one from the other does not work. Metaphysics has a legitimate role in human knowing—the generalist. Empirical science has a legitimate role in human knowing—the specialist. There are two different kinds of knowledge, and they are rarely distinguished and related. Only confusion can result if the methods, purposes and functions of philosophy and empirical sciences are not clearly distinguished and acknowledged.

5. Each of us has evolved a worldview of how the universe works. At the same time, we have detailed knowledge of the concrete realities of our particular specialization. However, our minds are not divided into

compartments. Our worldview and our specialization interact and relate in many and varied ways. This chapter had identified some of these interactions.

6. Bernard Lonergan has a clear explicit treatment of the complementarity of philosophy and science in a way that is beneficial to both. It is the task of this text to show that such complementarity and integration are possible and of benefit for both philosophy and empirical science.

Part Two: Invariant Structural Elements of Proportionate Being

4

The Notion of Being

Just as the notion of the intelligible is involved in the actual functioning of intelligence, just as the notion of the grounded is involved in the actual functioning of reasonableness, so the notion of being is involved in the unrestricted drive of inquiring intelligence and reflecting reasonableness.[1]

The being which is the subject matter of metaphysics, being as such, is neither the particularised being of the natural sciences, nor the being divested of reality of genuine logic nor yet the pseudo-being of false logic. It is the real being in all the purity and fullness of its distinctive intelligibility—or mystery. . . . It is not enough to employ the word being, to say "Being." We must have the intuition, the intellectual perception of the inexhaustible and incomprehensible reality thus manifested as the object of this perception. It is this intuition that makes the metaphysician.[2]

If the interpretation of the meaning of being is to become a task, Dasein is not only the primary being to be interrogated; in addition to that it is the being that always already in its being is related to what is sought in this question. But then the question of being is nothing else than the radicalization of an essential tendency of being that belongs to Dasein itself, namely, of the pre-ontological understanding of being.[3]

Thus, being appears or presents itself in the very first act of knowing as that which is known when knowing takes place.[4]

---

1. Lonergan, *Insight*, 380.
2. Maritain, *A Preface to Metaphysics*, 44.
3. Heidegger, *Being and Time*, 13.
4. Blanchette, *Philosophy of Being*, 27.

Introduction

IN THIS PART 2 we are setting out to do metaphysics, in other words, to outline an integral heuristic structure of proportionate being, meaning by that an overall framework for integrating all the results, of all knowing, of the past, the present and the future. We are looking for a framework that will relate all the parts together, illustrate their unity, and facilitate further progress in understanding. We are making explicit the presuppositions and assumptions which good empirical science must have if it is to be interpreted, presented, developed and applied in a fruitful way. We are looking for a permanent framework into which the changing results of the sciences can be integrated in a cumulative and progressive way.

Let us remember that in parts two and three we are dealing with proportionate being, namely, the being that is known through experiencing, understanding, and judging truth and values. We call it proportionate because the known is directly parallel to the four components of the knowing and always includes a reference to the sensible, to instances, to some material element. Besides this kind of knowing there is a possibility of a knowing of transcendent being which does not include that element of the sensible in the same way. That possibility we will explore in chapter 14.

In developing our worldview, we distinguish between the structural, invariant elements over against the historical, developmental elements. In this part two, we are concerned only with the synchronic or structural aspects of proportionate being. They are permanent, constitutive elements which are always there in every example of the known of common sense, science or philosophy. In part 3 we will deal with the dynamic or diachronic perspective. Everything has a history, develops and changes over time. Every science has its history, and what is known in every science has a history, and we will lay out the broad contours of this aspect in part 3.

This chapter starts with the broadest of notions and proceed in the next chapters to more detailed specifications. We start with the notion of being, and then we will move on to the elements of proportionate being, namely, potency, form, act, and value, each of which will be elaborated in detail.

Our text is entitled *A Worldview of Everything*. Being is a technical philosophical term for "everything." Introducing a technical language in philosophy has the advantage that you can define clearly what terms mean and develop clarity and explanation. However, there is also the danger that the technical terminology takes on a life and meaning of its own, over and against real descriptions and explanations of science or common sense. As with the invention of the word "metaphysics" so also the invention of the word "being" was a mixed blessing, communicating an important notion but also giving rise to many misunderstandings. For the moment we are simply using the term to refer to everything, to the whole of the universe, and all its parts, and causes, and properties, and elements, and laws. If this is to be an integral heuristic structure, it must include everything and must integrate all the parts into some single overall view.

Various Attempts to Define Being

The history of philosophy has attempted from the beginning to use a technical philosophical term to express the idea of everything. Thus, the term "being" emerged very early on in the history of philosophy as a technical term with a defined meaning depending on how that particular philosopher understood it. Let me briefly run through some of the various meanings that this technical term "being" has been given over the centuries. The word has a history of development and decline. It is important to note these various meanings so that by contrast we can develop a precise, correct notion that will be the fruitful basis for a fuller expansion and explication. We will try to identify the range of meanings so that we will be able to formulate a new approach to the meaning of being.

Parmenides (530–440) is the one who seems to have invented the Greek term *to on*. He saw two ways, the way of, "it is" and the way of, "it is not." There was nothing in-between, no becoming, no changing; either it is, or it is not. "One way alone is yet left to tell of, namely, "It is." On this way are marks in plenty that since it exists it is unborn and imperishable, whole, unique, immovable and without end. It was not in the past, nor shall it be, since it now is, all together, one and continuous."[5] He was forced then to reject knowledge of the sensible as an illusion because the sensible is always becoming and changing. However, he still seems to have thought of being as material, "like the mass of a well-rounded ball, equal in every way from the centre."[6] This was not a very auspicious beginning to a long history. It flies in the face of common sense and blocks rather than promotes development in understanding.

Plato was much influenced by this distinction between a way of truth and a way of belief. It would seem that he identified the way of truth with knowledge of the Forms, which are spiritual, permanent and perfect; and the way of seeming with knowledge of the senses and of particulars, which he did not consider to be true knowledge. Thus, he separated the knowledge of

5. Guthrie, *History of Greek Philosophy*, 26.
6. Guthrie, *History of Greek Philosophy*, 43.

Forms from the knowledge of the senses and separated the world of Forms from the world of sensation. Being for him was one of the Forms. Any particular being participated in the perfect Form of being. To be a being was to participate or to imitate the Form of being. As well as the Form of being there was a Form of the real, of the good, of the one, etc.

Aristotle by contrast realized that the word "being" is used in many senses; it is an analogous term; the many senses are usually related to one primary meaning. It can be used to refer to substances or to accidents, to primary substance or secondary substance, to being or to becoming, to act and also to potency, to the particular and to the universal. Being is not a form apart from a particular substance, rather it is immanent in the substance. The answer to the question, "what is being?" is associated with the answer to the question of, what is substance? For Aristotle there seem to have been three kinds of substance, composite changing substance, the intelligences of the heavenly bodies and the perfect substance, namely, the unmoved mover.

It was Aristotle's notion of being that passed into Scholastic philosophy and theology particularly that of Aquinas. Nearly all the terminology and ideas of Aristotle found their way into the Scholastic synthesis of philosophy and theology. Aquinas' original contribution to the history of metaphysics was his understanding of the importance of the distinction between essence and existence; that in God essence and existence are identical but in creatures are really distinct. The word "being" continued to be used in many senses as a rich, helpful, diverse, analogous term.

However, with Scotus philosophy and theology turned in the direction of conceptualism. Metaphysics focussed on the definition and division of the concepts of being, substance, essence, nature, and the like. Metaphysics was considered to be on the third level of abstraction. The sciences were on the first level because they only abstracted from particular beings. Mathematics was on the second level because it abstracted from everything except quantity. Metaphysics abstracted even from quantity and focused on being qua being. Abstraction was conceived as leaving behind various qualities or quantities; it became an impoverishing abstraction. We have knowledge of concepts rather than knowledge of real particulars in the real world. This kind of metaphysics separates itself from the emerging sciences and professes to have a superior knowledge of essences, natures, substances, and souls. Being is defined as the concept with the widest extension and the narrowest intension: it applies to the widest categories of things but means very little. The metaphysicians discoursed eloquently on quiddities and natures, not realizing that the quiddity was what was to be discovered in a correct scientific understanding of the thing. These tendencies were embodied in the manualist tradition of Christian Wolff and become the subject called "ontology." The suggestion of Jacques Maritain (cited at the beginning of this chapter) that we know being by way of an intuition, an intellectual perception of the inexhaustible and incomprehensible reality, is neither in line with St. Thomas, nor in line with our own experience of understanding the notion of being. If being is given to us in a simple intuition and we automatically become metaphysicians, why do we have to do such painstaking analysis in order to understand? Marion in *God without Being* seems to imply that if we include God within being then we have somehow limited God to our human categories. Hector, in *Theology without Metaphysics*, suggests that human language and concepts automatically corrupt the theological enterprise. Empiricists rejected the notion of being because it was too general with no apparent empirical referent to justify it. Heidegger made lavish use of the terms, being, Being, being qua Being, Dasein, an ontic being and an ontological being, but these terms seem to lack specific meaning. He may have been influenced by his study of Scotus in his dissertation. The postmodernists reject the notion of being because it involves too much of a metanarrative. It is too global and general to fit in their own particular metanarrative. These are just some of the misunderstandings of the notion of being to be encountered in contemporary thought.

Why is it so difficult to formulate one of the key terms in philosophy from ancient times to the present day? I suggest four points which make it difficult to have a correct understanding of the meaning of being, which I will designate as reification, assimilation, conceptualism and the theoretical mind.

Firstly, the disadvantage of inventing the word "being" for everything is that you now have a word and instinctively we presume that if you have a word then you also have something distinct and separate to which the word refers. The presumption is that this word is like every other word and that it can be defined like any other word—that it refers to some specific content, some reality, some particular thing. It is reified and is thought of as a thing. The tendency is to then think that the scientist knows the superficial, empirically verifiable characteristics of things, but the philosopher knows things at a deeper level, in its very being, the reality as opposed to the appearances. The tendency is to think of being as apart from particular beings; it is behind them, superior to them; it is known only by the metaphysician. The philosopher obviously has a deeper understanding of things than the mere scientist and so posits a being apart from mere particular beings.

Secondly, being is a word; each word can be checked in a dictionary for its meaning; therefore, the work "being" must have a specific meaning. We tend to treat it like any other word and define it in terms genus and species, in terms of what it includes and what it excludes; it must have a definite meaning. Unfortunately, this does not allow for the fact that the notion of being is unique, as we will see, and it cannot be assimilated into logic, linguistics and definitions in the same way as other words.

Thirdly, most of contemporary philosophy is done in terms of theories, ideas and concepts. But being is neither an idea nor a concept but a notion as we shall see. An idea is a product of direct understanding, grasping the essential and leaving behind the non-essential. But being must include the essential and the non-essential. Being includes everything and we humans cannot have a direct understanding of everything. Neither is being a concept. A concept is a clear formulated definition of something by species and difference; it has a specific content. If being were a concept, then philosophy would consist in the definition of being and its many subdivisions. This was what the worst of Neo-Scholastic philosophy did. If being were a concept then it would have cognitional content and it could be defined by what it is, contrasted with what it is not. Further, concepts are usually abstract; they are formulations of the essential definition of the thing. Confusion arises when you presume that the notion of being can be treated as a concept.

Fourthly, we have already noted the characteristics of the theoretical mentality in chapter 1. Theory relies on logic, definition, coherence, concepts, systems, syllogistic arguments, and is usually static. In that mentality metaphysics is usually primary and epistemology comes in a distant second. We have dared to reverse the order and entered into an intimate familiarity with the process of human knowing before venturing into a first philosophy. Now we are beginning to reap the fruits of this approach as we can base our metaphysics on the verified, invariant structure of human knowing. As being is a unique notion I hope it is clear that we need a unique method for finding an indirect way to specify what it includes, how it is used, and why we need that strategy to be clear about what we mean by being. Hence, we will appeal to the intentionality of the desire to know to give us a heuristic notion of being.

The Notion of Being

Our method of isomorphism suggests the possibility that maybe in the patterns and structure of knowing, we will find the key to the patterns and structure of the known. That is the method we are using here in our attempt to define the notion of being. Note that all knowing starts in questioning and only proceeds by way of asking streams of further questions. We are considering the hypothesis that being might be defined as the objective that is sought in that stream of questions—that the desire to know is a desire to know being. In self-appropriation we focus on personal experience of questioning, leading to understanding and knowing. We refocus now on the experience of questioning as intentional—as intending to know everything. Hence for the moment we will proceed step by step to clearly elaborate this hypothesis and compare it with other attempts to define being.

We Can Ask Questions about Everything

Let us revert then to our experience of questioning. One of the characteristics of our questioning is that it is unrestricted: we can ask questions about anything and everything: there is nothing about which we cannot ask questions. The more questions we ask and answer, the more questions arise from our new discoveries. Questioning when it reaches answers closes off one topic or term, but it opens up further questions, which can go in many directions. This is an experiential fact: it is a matter of personal experience and the very nature of how the mind develops. Every question is a combination of what we know and what we do not know. If we knew everything, we would not have to ask any further questions. If we knew nothing, there would be nothing about which we could ask questions. We are in-between asking questions in order to expand our understanding, knowledge and expertise. There is no end in principle to this expanding stream of questions.

Is there a limit to the things about which we can ask questions? But to know a limit is to immediately ask questions about what is there beyond the limit. We can imagine and speculate and fantasize about what might be beyond the limit. The Big Bang is supposed to have happened in an instant some fourteen billion years ago. It does not take long for people to ask, what was there before the Big Bang. A lifetime prisoner is confined by limits but thinks and imagines what is outside. In the fifteenth century Europeans wondered about the geography of the Earth and sent ships off to explore the limits. There are limits to our solar system, but we can see and understand what is beyond. We suppose there is a limit to our universe but wonder what could limit our universe and what would we find beyond it.

Some might object that some things are unknowable. But we do ask about the unknowable. When we do that, we are already naming it, trying to understand it, differentiating it from things that are known, and delineating the characteristics of the unknown. Thus, we must know something about it or else we could not ask questions about it. Aristotle claimed the prime matter is unknowable. But that is not strictly true. He knew what he was referring to when he used the term matter or prime matter. It is that which is the material cause of our understanding, that from which we abstract ideas. Our first minimal understanding of something is by nominal definition: what is the correct use of a word. Our first act in specifying an unknown is to give it a name. Algebra is a powerful tool because its method is to give the unknown a name, namely x. Specify its characteristics. Combine the knowns and unknowns. Find the value of x. Some might contend that God is unknowable to us. But we can ask questions about God; we know that the notion of God is different from the notion of cats and dogs—we have a nominal definition of God. We know that we can never fully answer our questions about God, but we can intend understanding, even if it is mostly negative and analogical. We can ask questions about everything. The effort to show that our questioning is limited is self-defeating. Questioning intends a content that will satisfy the criteria set by the question. Contrariwise, we can say that "everything" is that about which we can ask questions and intend to understand.

In principle, the objective of our questioning is unrestricted, but in practice it is limited. Because of limitations of time and facilities and abilities, we will always be limited in what we know. Even the scholar with twenty-two doctorates will have to admit that there are many things that he does not know. But in principle the desire to know is unlimited. There is nothing that is explicitly excluded from our desire to know. For Aristotle the intellect was, *potens omnia facere et fiere*; namely, a potency to make or to become all things. The objective of the intellect was unlimited, it included *all* things. There is nothing, which is by definition excluded from the objective of our knowing.

The Meaning of "Everything"

"Everything" is a term which can be used in the context of common sense. A child understands when you use the term "everything." It is not technical, not clearly defined, hence might be used with a variety of meanings. I am using the term "everything" as an entry into the more technical aspects of the use of the term "being." First, I want to be sure that "everything" means everything. Everything is totally comprehensive and inclusive, includes both universal and concrete. Let me list some of the things that might be included in the term. I will list only some of them. If I were to list everything, we would, quite literally, be here forever. This is only a sample to make a point.

Everything includes: the finite and infinite; the material and spiritual; the past, present and future; here, there and everywhere; the known, the known unknown and the unknown unknown; the real and possible; the impossible and contradictory; images and ideas; dreams and reality; hallucinations and inspirations; the sensible, intelligible, real and good; good and evil; values and disvalues; univocal, analogous, equivocal; animate and inanimate; animal, vegetable, mineral; myths, fables, legends; language, thought, sound; the true and false; the subjective and the objective; the personal and the impersonal; contingent and necessary; creator and creation; substances and accidents; things and their properties; space, time and motion; being and becoming; static and dynamic; notions of multiple universes, multiple dimensions; causes, relations, identities; equations, numbers, operations, results; suffering and death; consciousness and anxiety; the concrete and abstract, the particular and the universal; tables and chairs; dogs and cats; trees and houses; and so on, and so forth, for ever and ever.

All of these are different kinds of things, aspects, causes, perspectives on the totality of the real world. They do not all have the same status. But "everything" includes all on this list and much more. Imagine everything that is stored in a library, all the ideas, the facts, the expertise, the history, the geography; imagine all that the human mind has thought about, all the results of all the human sciences, all the literature, music, prayer, experience, success and failure. All common sense, all science, all explanation, all of interiority, all of meaning and even meaningless.

The only thing excluded from the notion of everything is nothing. Again, we have to be careful; "nothing" means nothing. We are tempted to treat nothing as if it were some particular kind of something. A false statement is not nothing; it is a false statement. A hallucination is not nothing; it is a distortion of reality. A phoenix is not nothing; it is a mythological creature.

A Heuristic Definition of Being

We started with the notion of everything, which is intelligible, easily understood, part of the knowledge of common sense, but is also open to nuances and confusions because of lack of specification. We are going to move from that vague notion of everything to a strict, clearly defined, notion of being. How would a philosopher define this crucial notion at the heart of every philosophy?

We must accept that the notion of being is a unique notion; there is only one being; it is of a kind; it cannot be categorized according to genera and species as things are usually defined. Our strategy in pinning down the meaning of being is to accept that it is not a concept, but we may well be able to formulate a heuristic notion of being. We have a notion of everything, but we do not know everything. Perhaps we can use the process of knowing as a template for knowing being. Whatever being is if it comes to be known it will be known by cognitional operations which are familiar to us because we have written a book about them. The activity that might help us here in particular is the desire to know and the established truth that we can ask questions about everything.

Perhaps we can define being as, "the objective of the pure desire to know."[7] Instead of defining being as to what it entails, what is included and excluded, perhaps we could focus on the act of questioning by which we anticipate a knowledge of being; that is our method of isomorphism. Here we are implementing this method of isomorphism for the first time. In diagram 2 we noted that the desire to know intends being, namely, everything. The desire to know is isomorphic with the content to be known, namely, being. In other words, knowing is knowing being. Or contrariwise, being is the objective of the desire to know. It is the only strategy we have available to define being. We cannot possibly grasp the totality of being in all its detailed complexity and as yet to be known factors. Yet we know that when we advance in our knowing it will be by asking questions about what we experience in order to understand correctly. We can formulate a notion of being because we know by personal experience the unlimited desire to know, which intends knowledge of everything. Let us look at some of the characteristics of the desire to know.

It belongs to our nature to ask questions. All philosophy begins in wonder. We spontaneously ask, why? where? how? when? what? etc. Children pester their parents with persistent questions. The questioning is fundamental to our nature as human persons. It is prior to all knowledge. It is the presupposition of all knowing. If there is no questioning, there will be no understanding. It is not the formulation of questions that is at issue here, but the basic spirit of inquiry that precedes the formulation of questions. Preceding all language, formulation, understanding, concepts and propositions is the pure desire to know.

The desire to know is referred to as the *pure* desire to know. There are many things that can deflect or interfere with the desire to know. Much of our emotional orientation can prevent us from an objective discussion of socialism or capitalism; many of the traditions and values of our culture we are unable to question or criticize; much of our interest in knowing can be practical or self-interested, just to get a degree or just to get a job; many of our formulated questions can be designed to show off, or to catch the teacher out or to put someone down. It is not easy to be motivated only by the search

---

7. Lonergan, *Insight*, 372.

for truth for its own sake. It is not easy to be guided only by the precepts of being intelligent and reasonable. It is easy to be led astray by imagination, by emotion, by pride, by the desire to win the argument at all costs.

The objective is not the achievement. Our questioning is purposive; we are looking for answers; we indulge in questioning not just for the experience but with the objective of finding answers. We describe the desire to know as pure because there are frivolous questions, pointless questions, twisted questions. We define it as detached as we are operating the intellectual pattern of experience and are motivated simply to find the truth. Being is the objective of the pure desire to know. What are we aiming at when we are questioning and trying to know? What are we trying to achieve? It is not the activity of knowing which is the final end. We are trying to grasp something and that is the content. We are not just knowing for the fun of it; we are knowing so that we will understand something and know something. The objective is the content of knowing, the known.

You can define being indirectly in terms of what is intended in questioning. It is an indirect, second order definition. Yet it is not totally indeterminate in that we have experience of our own questioning. Being is what is now known and what is to be known in the future. Being is anything about which we can ask intelligent questions. All our questioning is intentional, it points to the answer, it provokes the activities needed to provide the answer. It recognizes the answer as correct because the question sets the conditions to be satisfied by the correct answer. Because being is a unique notion, we need this unique approach to pinning it down indirectly. It is by examining further the characteristics of the pure desire to know that we specify what we mean by being or by everything. We define being in terms of knowing. Knowing is already familiar to us. Then we have a way to indirectly determine what is being.

You can reach a second definition of being as "what is to be known by the totality of true judgments."[8] This is equivalent to the first definition. It is the "what is to be known," namely, the objective of the desire to know. We do not know everything yet, but we do intend to know in an unrestricted orientation. There is no other way to know than by judgment. Any other kind of knowledge of the real is illusory. Being will only be fully known in the totality of correct judgments. We have only a limited number of correct judgments. We know something about being, not everything. But if there were a mind that had reached a totality of correct judgments, then, it would have an actual exhaustive knowledge of being and of itself. There could be nothing that that mind would not know; that you would have to call the

8. Lonergan, *Insight*, 374.

Idea of Being or God. Finally, the judgments must be true judgments. By false judgments we do not know being. It is by correct negative judgments that we know of privations, the irrational, and of nothing. This definition of being is also a second order definition.

What Is a Notion?

We have to realize that Lonergan has a special technical meaning for the work "notion." In ordinary English usage the word is used in the sense of idea or vague general idea as in, "Have you any notion how to fix this car?" In Lonergan's sense a notion is an anticipation, a heuristic, an orientation, a desire, an intention, a tending towards. "A heuristic notion, then, is the notion of an unknown content and it is determined by anticipating the type of act through which the unknown would become known."[9] Just as hunger is orientated to food, and a foetal eye is orientated to seeing, so the notion of being is immanent and operative in the desire to know and spontaneously intends being. The notion of being precedes a knowledge of being. This brings us back to the realization that you cannot teach someone what something is unless he already desires to know, experiences and can understand. You cannot teach someone what being is unless they already have a notion of being. The notion of being is prior to judgments, prior to understanding and even prior to experiencing. Notion is not the same as idea. An idea is the content of an act of understanding. But we cannot understand everything, we cannot understand being, we cannot have a positive grasp of the idea of everything.

Plato put the problem in the form of the dilemma, how does a person recognize a being unless he already knows what a being is. But where did he get this unlearned knowledge of being? Plato's answer was in the form of the theory of recollection: knowledge is remembering what we knew before in a previous existence. We would give a different answer. Spontaneously as a child grows up, he/she begins to ask questions about what they see and hear, to understand language, to distinguish dogs and cats, and to make judgments of true and false, good and bad. How does a five-year-old do this? Because the notion of being is immanent and operative in the desire to know. It is the desire to know that is spontaneous in us. It is innate, it is not learned from a teacher or a book. Aquinas claimed that the first thing that a person knows is being. By this he did not intend that the child has an explicit knowledge of the metaphysical notion of being. Rather that all that the child knows from the very beginning of pointing,

9. Lonergan, *Insight*, 417.

sensing, experiencing and naming is being. Being includes all that we ask about, all that we see or hear, all that we remember or imagine, all the forms that are grasped, the definitions that are formulated, the judgments and evaluations that are affirmed.

This is not to say that we have actual innate ideas. To say we have innate ideas is to imply that there is some cognitional content that is innate. But a heuristic notion is not an idea, it is not a content; it is simply an orientation. Our minds are still a *tabula rasa*, a blank slate; we recognize being, because it is the very nature of the desire to know to know being, just as it is the very nature of the eye to see color.

We situate the notion of being in the desire to know, because it is the desire to know that initiates the process of knowing. Some ask whether knowing starts in experiencing or in questioning. I would hold that it starts in questioning. It is true that experiencing can precede the desire to know; you can have experiencing without having the desire to know. But unless you have the desire to know you cannot move from experiencing, to understanding and judging; you cannot move to knowing. Experiencing by itself is not human knowing. It is intelligent questioning of experience that produces knowledge.

Advantages of This Approach

1. This approach to give an indirect heuristic definition of being is intelligible, it is clear, it makes sense. It does what the word is supposed to do. We have taken as our base the invariant structure of human knowing. We are familiar with this because we have written a book about it. We are familiar with this from personal experience. Everything that is said about human knowing can be verified or repudiated with reference to one's own self-appropriation of the activities of human knowing. On that base we can define being as what is intended in that questioning and knowing. Hence, we can define being as the objective of the pure desire to know.

2. It unifies everything. If there is one human knowing there is one human known. If nothing is beyond the objective of the unrestricted desire to know then there is one worldview that encompasses everything. Someone might claim that there are an infinite number of universes; but if we were to know that, then there would still be one universe even though it would be infinite. Each new astronomical discovery expands or contracts our worldview; it is an advance in knowing that our universe is larger or smaller than we thought. One

universe, including the possibility of multiple universes, even an infinity of possible universes, including a First Cause if there is one. Being is all-encompassing and includes every hypothetical possibility which some day might be realized.

3. Our notion of being is open; it does not predetermine scientific discoveries; it can absorb any conceivable scientific discovery provided that it is genuine, true and real. Our notion of being is open to the future and inclusive of everything that is to be known. Every new discovery further specifies our notion of being. Our overall view of everything is based on the particular discoveries of the sciences and common sense, the spontaneous structure of human knowing as questioning, experiencing, understanding, judging and evaluating, and on the cognitional content of those activities the sensible, intelligible, real and good. We have used our method of isomorphism for the first time and cleared up the central notion of all philosophy, namely, the notion of being.

4. There is only one correct notion of being and this is it. There is only one correct way for the human mind to proceed to correct understanding and knowing. There are many variations, methodologies, strategies and tactics, in the various disciplines but fundamentally you must find questioning, experiencing, understanding and judging truth and value. Hence there is only one correct way of knowing being and only one correct notion of being.

5. But this is only the beginning of our journey. The notion of being derived from the above reflections is open and indeterminate. We could be talking about an idealist, or a monist, or a materialist universe. We have not yet specified how being is determined in this universe. We have set up a basic structure of the knowing and the known, both of which are beings. Our previous discussion of objectivity identified knowing in terms of experiencing, understanding and judging, with a subject knowing an object. We have exploited our familiarity with the intentionality of the process of knowing to define being as the objective of that knowing. Knowing is knowing being. We will proceed to further specify this rather open notion of being in succeeding chapters.

Unique, Puzzling, All-Inclusive, and Nuanced

It is puzzling because it is unique. The normal rules of logic do not apply; the normal rules of definition and division do not apply. Normal ways of thinking about cats and dogs do not apply. Normal scientific methods do not apply. The notion of being is unique because it is the only notion that must include everything, the known and the unknown, the universal and the particular, and everything else. There can only be one notion of everything; therefore, it is unique. We constantly attempt to apply the normal rules of definition to the notion of being, but they do not work. Hence, we are puzzled. Normal strategies do not work. There is only one unique strategy that works and that is the strategy of starting from the invariant structure of knowing and extrapolating to the invariant structure of the known and to be known universe of proportionate being. Our consideration of the notion of being is the first step in our outlining the general structure of our universe. We now have one word to encompass everything in the universe, namely, being.

Is a unicorn a being? The temptation is to say, No, because unicorns do not exist in the real world. But a unicorn can be defined. A unicorn is different from a dragon or a witch. A unicorn is a concept and a definition and hence an essence and hence a possible being. A unicorn is an object of thought although it does not exist in the real world. A unicorn is a something, an animal of mythology and imagination and therefore a being in some sense. A unicorn is a possible being. The Scholastics spend much time discussing possible beings. Even though they don't exist in reality they do exist as possible relevant hypotheses at the level of understanding, constructions of intelligence. There are an infinite variety of possible beings that can be conceived. But normally our knowing is purposive; we want to know the real world. Spending a lot of time on possible being is not a good use of limited time and not much help in understanding the actual concrete universe of proportionate being.

Do we experience being? Again, we must be careful. We only know being in judgment. But prior to judgment there is experience and understanding. Without experiencing and understanding there can be no judgment. Strictly speaking the object of experiencing is potency. Potency is a being in the sense that it is one of the metaphysical elements which along with form and act constitute an existing substantial unity. Potency does not exist by itself, but it is an element of the real. This will be explained in chapter 5.

Is being analogous or univocal? This was a point of conflict between Aristotle and Aquinas against Scotus. You can say that being is univocal in the sense that all particular beings are included in the general notion of being.

You can say that the notion of being is analogous in that the term being refers in different ways to particular beings; there is a real difference between a stone, green, God, the law of gravity, a centaur, becoming, what is in the mind, what is outside the mind. You can also argue that analogous, equivocal and univocal refer to concepts and not particularly to the notion of being. You are invited to continue to explore this notion of being by asking yourself, is evil a being and in what sense? Is the square root of minus one a being? Are numbers beings? Is existence a being? Do animals know being?

The notion of being *underpins* all cognitional contents. The notion of being is the beginning, middle and end of all our knowing. It is immanent in the desire to know. It selects data for understanding, it checks whether the understanding is correct. The process from questioning to a final solution can be long and difficult, but all along the line it is the notion of being that underlies all the activities we engage in in order to reach the final solution. In all fields of knowing, we are trying to know one particular aspect of real being.

The notion of being *penetrates* all cognitional contents. Being includes the concrete universe of proportionate being. The physicist trying to establish the laws of motion is trying to know being; the zoologist studying the behavior of ducks is knowing being; the logician studying the laws of thought is studying being; the mathematician studying logarithms and calculus and differential equations is studying mathematical being; the man of common sense who is trying to learn how to make a table is studying the properties of concrete being, namely, wood, chisels, saws, etc. Being is not something over and above what is known in the sciences. It is not the metaphysician who knows particular beings but the scientist. The metaphysician provides the method and the criterion, but the scientist provides the detailed content, as we have seen. The notion of being is concrete; all that is known in all of the sciences and common sense and theology is knowledge of being.

The notion of being *constitutes* all contents as cognitional. Knowing is knowing being. In judgment being is known, and in judgment what is known is known as being. In this whole section we have been answering the question, why is doing that knowing? Knowing is not purely immanent; it has a content; it has an object; the objective is being; in knowing the subject goes beyond himself to something other than himself; that is the nature of knowledge; it is the nature of being to be knowable; there is no unknowable being; we intend to know everything even though we will only know partially and indirectly.

Conclusion

Our achievement in this chapter has been, first, to break with mistaken notions of being and then to formulate precisely and in detail what is meant by being, how it is a unique and puzzling notion. We have elaborated on how the notion of being is pervasive; how every full or partial act of human knowing implies and presupposes our notion of being. We have used out method of isomorphism for the first time to great effect. We have taken a giant step forward in establishing a correct, comprehensive, critical worldview. We have established what we mean by being, namely, the objective of the desire to know. We are now in a position to further specify the invariant structure of that being, namely, that it is either proportionate or transcendent; and that proportionate being involves an element of the sensible, and an element of the intelligible, and an element of the actual, and an element of the good.

5

Elements: (1) Matter/Potency

Materialism is a form of philosophical monism which holds mat-ter to be the fundamental substance in nature, and all things, including mental states and consciousness, are results of material interactions.[1]

On the one hand, physicalism is a thesis about the nature of the world that we have considerable and perhaps even overwhelming reason to believe. . . . Rather the status of physicalism is more like the status of the theory of evolution or of continental drift. . . . Those who deny physicalism are not making a conceptual mistake, but they are, nevertheless, flying in the face not merely of science but also of scientifically informed common sense.[2]

Accordingly, the material can be defined as whatever is constituted by the empirical residue or is conditioned intrinsically by that residue.[3]

The standard picture does not view physicalism as true merely for selected bits of the world—merely for human or sentient or living beings, for example. Rather it is intended to be a very general and abstract doctrine that is true of the world as a whole, it is . . . a world-view or Weltanschauung.[4]

1. Wikipedia, s.v. "Materialism," last modified March 17, 2022, https://en.wikipedia.org/wiki/Materialism.

2. Stoljar, *Physicalism*, 13.

3. Lonergan, *Insight*, 540.

4. Stoljar, *Physicalism*, 15.

Introduction

IN OUR PREVIOUS CHAPTER we have established a notion of being as the objective of the desire to know. However, this is so general that it is compatible with many and varied philosophical positions. The task now is to further specify this basic notion of being and to start filling in the broad lines of the integral heuristic structure of proportionate being. The method we will be using will be the principle of isomorphism, namely, exploiting the intentionality between the knowing and the known. It might help to keep in mind diagram 2 in chapter 2 where this parallelism was explained. In this part 2 we are outlining the four elements of potency, form, existence and value as the four constitutive elements of each and every instance of proportionate being.

In this chapter, we focus on the first of these elements, namely, matter or potency, which will be identified, defined, and related to other elements. In subsequent chapters, the other elements will be specified, illustrated and defined. Here we consider matter/potency as the element of the real world of proportionate being that corresponds generally to experiencing. This is the first and the most difficult to understand of the four constituent elements of the universe. What is asserted here will become clearer in the context of the following three chapters.

Materialism as a Misunderstanding of Matter

Our difficulty in arriving at a philosophically correct conception of "matter" is that we think we already know what matter is even before we really start to think about it. We have an unquestioned, imaginative assumption about what matter is. People of common sense, scientists and even philosophers rarely question this assumption and simply put into words what they mean by this basic assumption. Thus, matter will usually be imagined as what is solid, can be measured, is visible, has weight, has extension, can be touched, can be kicked. Matter is the "stuff" of the universe. It is that out of which everything else is made. We imagine matter as a particle, a little marble, round, solid, smooth, impenetrable. And we have no difficulty asserting that it is what really exists out there, and even mind and consciousness are basically configurations of matter. This is a common undifferentiated descriptive attempt to say what matter is. We have to be a bit more precise and make certain distinctions.

Materialism as a philosophical system rests on the principle that only matter exists. This position has a long history. Some early Greek cosmologists presumed that everything in the universe was made out of some "stuff" and once you had decided what kind of stuff, then you could explain everything. This stuff was variously identified as water, or air or the infinite, or fire, and everything in the universe was made of configurations or mixtures of this stuff. Democritus came later and posited the existence of atoms and void only. The primary focus of these philosophies was how to identify the original "stuff" out of which everything was made.

Descartes formulated a mechanist notion of matter as extension, as the *res extensa*, the sensible, what can be sensed. "Thought" could not be sensed, so that must belong to another world of reality, apart from that of matter in motion. Newtonian science was built on an image of materialist determinism—the clockwork universe. The Enlightenment was to embrace this notion of science as the study of the material, natural world, and dismiss any talk of essences, forms, causes, laws, universals, or God, as unverifiable speculation.

Nowadays, materialism, sometimes called physicalism, seems to be the common assumption underlying much of modern science. This assumes that matter is real, that only matter is real, and that all explanations will be found eventually by some appeal to matter and how it behaves. This is often tinged with reductionism, which holds that if we find the smallest material part, and the laws pertaining to that part, they will eventually explain everything about the whole. In that case, the scientist espouses a philosophical position of reductionism, and presumes that it is correct and in no need of examination.

Materialism is a metaphysical position, a stance on the nature of reality. It is not in itself a scientific position, since the view that all is material is an assumption and cannot be proved within the ambit of scientific method. Science cuts off parts of material reality and aims at the intelligibility appropriate to that part. To deal with the whole of reality you must move into philosophy, so as to justify your philosophical method, to establish your criterion of truth, the meaning of self, of knowing, of objectivity and of being. Everyone is entitled to make philosophical assertions, but it is best to have studied philosophy seriously, to have reflected on philosophical method, understood the difference between philosophy and science, and worked out a philosophical position.

The negative implications of a materialist position are vast and ruthless. Any reality beyond the range of sensible experience is deemed to be eliminated. God, religion, spirit, selves, the immaterial, are obviously ruled out. Essences, substances, natures, genera and species, would also seem to be eliminated. Scientists like Dawkins and Hawking use their positions as biologists and physicists to promote an atheistic, materialistic metaphysics.

Each and every one of us starts off our conscious intellectual life with a global, imaginative, compacted, undifferentiated, notion of matter. Lonergan recounts his own surprise growing up when he discovered that air was real. Augustine famously spent long years before breaking with the assumption that if God is real, he would have to be material. Most modern materialist scientists continue to operate on an uncritical assumption that what is real must be material and by that they mean a "stuff." I tried to start a philosophical discussion with a biologist, but he walked away muttering, "We only deal with what we can prove," implying that science can prove its conclusions and no other discipline can prove anything. In the context of common sense one can never arrive at precise differentiated notions of matter, potency, form and existence. We must move to a precise explanatory notion of what these might mean in explanatory science and what they should mean in explanatory metaphysics.

Knowledge of Composite Material Things

As we move to identifying an explanatory philosophical definition of matter let us remember our method of isomorphism, whereby the components of the activity of knowing will be reflected in the structural elements of the known. Now there are different activities involved in a single process of knowing and for each of these activities there is a corresponding element of the known. Our method laid out in chapter 2 suggests we work from the basic invariant features of the structure of knowing, to the content intended in those activities and known in correct judgments. If we wish to specify how we know material things, then we must first look to the cognitional activity in which it is known, which we have generally summed up as, experiencing, understanding, judging and evaluating. We have explained the subject knowing in diagram 1 using the example of, "this is a good computer." Now we are moving to diagram 2 illustrating the isomorphism between each component of the knowing with the particular element known. So, let us examine "experiencing" and explore its many shapes and sizes so that we can move to the corresponding meanings of matter and potency. "Matter" is used in many senses and we are obliged to clearly distinguish the different uses. Let us start with the normal case, meaning, how we get to know material things such ordinary things as, acids, cells, trees, planets, houses, dogs and the like.

Sense knowing knows the sensible. Seeing senses color, size and shape; hearing intends tone, sound, noise, music; and so on with taste, smell, and touch. Animals coordinate the input from these senses in imagination, memory and instinct and by association and imitation learn to survive and thrive. Sensing is isomorphic with the sensible. But by itself it is only experiencing the sensible. Animals do not ask questions, or understand causes, or identify relations. They do sense the sensible in single, simple, direct activities of sensation and that is all. They operate in terms of sensible similarities and differences, associations between input from different senses, and memory of what happened before.

Humans have inherited all the senses of the animals, but we rarely operate in terms of sensation alone. It is hard to sense the sensible without some element of identification, naming and understanding intervening. One of the characteristics of understanding is that it passes into the habitual texture of the mind. We learn that water flows downhill, fire burns, that sharp knives cut, that rain wets; we understand causes, effects, the properties of things, how to relate to people and the like. Our education builds up a mentality of habitual expectations and principles of what happens in our world. Because our understandings have become habitual, we take it for granted and do not notice its effect on our mental operations. As adults we rarely revert to operating in terms of sensation alone. Our knowing does start with sensation but continues with questioning, understanding and judging.

Experiencing is a broad term that encompasses what we receive from our five senses as well as our imagination and memory, and even some learning by imitation, association and instinct. Experiencing is only experiencing. It is not the whole of human knowing. It is the indispensable foundation that makes human knowing possible. It is the beginning of full human knowing. We have treated of the full gamut of cognitional activities and just call them to mind here. Our point in this section is to highlight the activity of experiencing so that we can extrapolate to what is experienced. Our knowing usually starts with experience, we encounter something odd, and our curiosity is aroused. We ask questions, do research, understand. To judge that your understanding is correct you revert back to an experience. We defined scientific method as, theories verified in instances. The instances refer to experience. Our knowledge is evidence based.

We have given an adequate and correct account of the process of knowing so there is no problem in accepting our ability to know particular material things. We used the example of, this is a good computer. The sciences are justified in their statements about atoms, cells, trees, diseases, laws of motion, and all the rest of it. We justify our knowledge of things and also our knowledge of the properties of things which are understood utilizing the same structure of knowing. But can we identify and define the individual elements of the known, in this case, matter/potency? Now we have to make distinctions. First, we will examine matter as potency to form. Then we will consider matter as the empirical residue.

Potency as a Metaphysical Element

We are asserting that the structure of human knowing that we have outlined is invariant, not open to basic revision, and consists of four components of experiencing, understanding, judging and evaluating. Each of these structural components are intentional and consequently intend the material, the intelligible, the real and the valuable, respectively. The known is the content of the knowing but is really distinct from the knowing as we have shown in our section on objectivity in our chapter on Foundations. Hence a metaphysical element is an element in the known that is isomorphic with the structural components of the knowing. There is only one structure of human knowing common to all human beings of each and every culture and time and place. Sometimes it is developed, sometimes it is undeveloped, sometimes it specializes in practical achievements, or artistic works, or mystical practices, or theoretical reflection, it is the same human intelligence by which we recognize all as equally human beings. Similarly, we hold that the structure of the four metaphysical elements of being will be permanent and universal and applicable to all things and all properties across the board at all times and in all places in the universe of proportionate being. We are starting with the most basic of the elements and attempting to elucidate the meaning of matter as a metaphysical element, common in varied ways to all composite material things and properties. We cannot have a direct insight into what is potency, in the same way as we can have an insight into an apple or a donkey. We cannot further subdivide the metaphysical elements of the known into another potency, form, act, and value. We have reached a basic element that cannot be subdivided.

(1) Why Do We Refer to Matter as Potency?

Aristotle formulated the distinction between potency and act to explain "becoming" which he found to be common to all material things. He had to counter Parmenides who held that being is one and therefore does not change. It is not hard to understand that a medical student is potentially a doctor, but not actually a doctor; that a seed is potentially a tree, but not actually a tree; that a new car has the potential to travel a hundred thousand miles but has not actually travelled so far. Hence potency is a basic category in the understanding of all areas of our universe. There is potency in the knowing and potency in the known.

(2) Potency in the Knowing

When we are faced with a problem, we start a discursive process of sorting out data which is relevant and leave aside what we consider irrelevant. Archimedes had a problem of whether a crown was pure gold or was it mixed with cheaper silver. He had a laboratory, he had samples of different metals, he was not totally new to the field. He had designed boats and was familiar with things that float and those that sink. After all he was an engineer. I imagine he did various measurements, comparing how metals behave, how they mix, how some are heavier than others. He was looking for the clue that would enable him to solve the problem. In the baths he got the insight that what was relevant was the relation of weight to volume; everything else was irrelevant. He had discovered the idea of density or specific weight. With that he was able to weight the crown in water establish its volume and weight and compare its density with that of pure gold. Now he could focus on the data that was relevant and leave aside what was irrelevant. The relevant data of volume and weight were relevant; all else was irrelevant. The relation of volume to weight is taken up into the insight and the judgment; the rest is irrelevant, insignificant, unimportant. You will find with any puzzle or problem that you sort through examples and memory and images. You run with those you find promising, you abandon those that seem to lead nowhere. Some data is intelligible, and some is irrelevant. Some data is incorporated in the insight; some is left out. Potency incorporates what is potentially intelligible. The irrelevant is relegated to the empirical residue.

In the process of knowing, potency refers to the elements of experience that can be incorporated or included in an intellectually patterned experience. Examples would include the aspects of sounds, colors, shapes, that can be sensed and can be patterned or related to each other through an act of understanding. Potency is the data in so far as it gives rise to the idea. Potency is the evidence or instances which support an idea and give rise to the judgment. We are assigning a strict meaning to the term "potency." Animals do not know potency. We do not know potency by simply experiencing. Potency is only known in an indirect manner within the context of fully explanatory human intellectual knowing. Our diagram 2 on Isomorphism gives a simple example of a judgment, "This is a good computer." The "this" specifies the particular time and place and the uniqueness indicated in a sensible experience. That experience is the potency for understanding and judging. All human knowledge, including scientific statements or laws, can be analyzed into the components of potency, form, act and good.

Our epistemological position rests on the principle that human knowing begins in the senses. We ask questions about what we experience. Our understanding expands only to the extent that we continue to ask further questions about what we experience. Experiencing as potency is the foundation for this possibility of human understanding and knowing. Experiencing is potency in the sense that it is potentially intelligible, it is the beginning of our human knowing, it is that out of which our ideas and explanations, and theories emerge. We are told that Einstein saw a man fall off a ladder, but it took him eight years to understand the equivalence of gravity and acceleration. Darwin observed many phenomena when he visited the Galapagos Islands. But it took him years to understand, to formulate and to present his ideas on evolution of species. Without some experience there is no understanding or human knowing.

(3) Potency in the Known

Matter is in potency to form. In other words, matter as potency is what becomes patterned/organized by forms to actualize particular things. It is the ground of the reality of the universe. Just as there is no natural human knowing without experiencing; there is no reality to the natural universe without matter as potency to form. Potency is the "instances" referred to in our definition of scientific method as "theory verified in instances."

The difficulty in knowing potency is that we do not know it until the form has been realized. Who would have thought five billion years ago that living things could emerge? Who could have thought twenty million years ago that intelligent humans could emerge? It is only in relation to form that you can understand potency. In potency itself there is a lack of expected intelligibility. That is why it can be talked about, pointed to, indicated, but not directly defined; it is not directly intelligible; it is indirectly intelligible in relation to form. Potency is that out of which form emerges. Let us consider some examples or types of potency.

In its most general occurrence, potency is to form, as form is to act, as act is to good. Our universe and everything in it are examples of potency realized in form. This highlights the significance of potency. Matter is not just inert matter. Just as experiencing is the unavoidable starting point of knowing, so matter as potency is the unavoidable starting point of any form emerging as existing.

Higher forms can emerge from lower forms. It would seem that atoms emerged from the potency of pre-existing subatomic particles. It seems that the one hundred basic chemical elements emerged from the pre-existing potential of the atoms. It seems that living cells emerged from the pre-existing potential of highly complex chemical compounds and processes. It seems that all species of animals and plants emerged from the pre-existing potency of simple living organisms. It seems that intelligent humans emerged from the potency of highly developed primates. Understanding the story of evolution requires the philosophical notions of potency and form and actuality.

Living things are yet another example of potencies being actualized. Living things possess their being not statically, all at once, but by way of developing over time. Despite changing over time, a living thing is the same thing during its lifetime, from birth to death, generation to corruption. Living things develop over a linked sequence of stages, where the living thing is becoming more differentiated and integrated at the same time. A day-old bird has the potential to fly but usually cannot actually fly. An elephant has the potency to reproduce but that potency is only realized after ten years of growth. A human baby is not actually thinking but has the potential to think; a plant is not potentially rational at any stage.

(4) Definition of Potency

Lonergan defines potency as "the component of proportionate being to be known in fully explanatory knowledge by an intellectually patterned experience of the empirical residue."[5] Obviously, this is a heuristic definition as it does not define a specific object directly but defines the object indirectly by the cognitional act by which it can be grasped.

Let us explain this definition. We wish to identify four components of proportionate being, and the first of these components is potency. Potency is the component to be known, not by experience alone, not by description alone, but by moving into a fully explanatory context usually by definition or measurement. The definition of potency does not strictly apply in descriptive knowledge because of the relative and ambiguous nature of description. It applies perfectly only in fully explanatory knowledge where we are relating things to one another. In some cases, explanatory knowledge has not yet been attained. But we already know the kind of act by which it will be known in science or philosophy. Potency is isomorphic with intellectually patterned experience, meaning that we are operating in the intellectual pattern of experience, asking questions about what we experience in order to understand

5. Lonergan, *Insight*, 457.

and judge. Potency is the component of that experience that is taken up into the insight and the judgment, other elements being considered irrelevant. We will explain empirical residue later in this section.

(5) Potency as Principle of Finality

Potency is the metaphysical principle of finality because things first exist in potentiality before they exist in actuality. Our universe is a massive, variegated example of potencies as the source of forms, some of which continue to exist, and some of which become extinct. We will see later how the principle of finality operates in our universe, and how our universe is dynamic, and the fundamental source of this dynamism is potency. The undifferentiated becomes differentiated, the undeveloped becomes developed, the simple become more complex, the non-systematic becomes systematic and in all cases, we have examples of potencies being realized in new forms and new forms emerging from potencies. (We will elaborate on the principle of finality in our chapter on Generalized Emergent Probability.)

(6) Potency as Principle of Limitation

Similarly, potency is the metaphysical principle of limitation. The universe has its limits. Act is limited by form, and form is limited by potency. Correct judgments are limited by understanding; understanding is limited by experience of data. We know that things in our universe are limited in what they can do, how long they can last, what can emerge and what cannot emerge; what is possible, what is probable and what is impossible. Dinosaurs ruled the planet for a time but then the environment changed, and they became extinct. Water freezes at 100 degrees centigrade normally. There can be exceptions, but water does not have a potency to become a stone or a lump of iron. The potency of proportionate being is not an unlimited potential. The emergence of new things is strictly limited in time and space. Many conditions have to be fulfilled for the possibility of the emergence of new things. New things emerge intelligibly and in a limited manner. Everything has its limits.

The Empirical Residue

The question remains about the irrelevant, the insignificant, the data that is considered in a particular context to be useless. But the question of our knowledge of such data arises and we must make some attempt to answer it in some way. Perhaps we can know, not by direct insight but by the means of an inverse insight. So, let us examine the phenomenon of inverse insight and then use that to illuminate the difficult notion of the empirical residue.

Sadly, not everything in our universe can be defined clearly, grasped accurately, and articulated with confident conviction. Aristotle warns at the beginning of the *Ethics* that we should not expect of a science more precision than the nature of the discipline can provide.[6] Human affairs, ethics and politics, and perhaps even philosophy are the disciplines he has in mind. Sometimes we are in a confused state about some area because we have not even tried to sort it out. Other times no matter how we reflect, focus, analyze and research, we are still left in a state of perplexity and confusion. Reluctantly, we accept that there are degrees of intelligibility in our universe. Sometimes there is too much intelligibility as when we think about God and we are blinded. Alternatively, there is too little intelligibility as when we consider data that can be sensed but seemingly not understood and we fail to pin it down. An inverse insight may be necessary to grasp this lack of an expected intelligibility.

There are three characteristics of an inverse insight: it incorporates positive data, there is a lack of an expected intelligibility, and the insight occurs in the context of concomitant positive developments of human understanding. Let us illustrate with some simple examples.

The ancient masters of mathematics, particularly of geometry, were surprised to find that there was no clear formula for determining the precise length of the diagonal of a square in relation to its side. A square is the simplest of geometrical figures; four equal straight lines and four right angles. What could be simpler! But if you try to calculate the size of the diagonal, they found that it was what they called an irrational number. If the side is one, the diagonal is the square root of two. If you work out the square root of two in decimals, you find it goes on for ever and ever, the numbers always changing and never repeating. Here you have positive data on geometry of squares. Also, you have an unexpected irregularity or irrational number, where one would expect a square to be regular and rational. This was only discovered because of developments in geometry and would not be noticed by those struggling to count.

You take a book out of the library, let us say, *An Introduction to Plato's Sophist*. You are familiar with the text of Plato but hope to understand it better with the help of a competent guide. You read the book through, find it very difficult, and wonder why you are not understanding. You read again

---

6. Aristotle, *Nicomachean Ethics*, 1, iii, 1094b12–30.

slowly and identify certain contradictions and confusions in what the author is saying. You begin to suspect, so you read again and confirm that the author espouses a postmodernist position and is trying to impute the same to Plato. You identify the background suppositions, you note the consequent contradictions, confusions, and misunderstandings, and you regret the time that you have wasted. You have experienced an inverse insight. There is positive data, three hundred pages of it. You expect a commentator to be intelligent and competent, but you find the opposite. The author is not competent, not clear, not helpful, in fact a morass of misunderstandings and confusion. Yet it is a liberating experience because now you are learning how to distinguish good philosophy from bad, informed interpretations from arbitrary assertions, and progress from decline.

Normally, we understand by way of a direct insight into a regularity, a cause, a solution to a problem, and proceed to judge the truth or falsity of the insight: we attain true clear knowledge. In inverse insight we grasp the lack of an expected intelligibility, namely, something irregular, unsystematic, lacking intelligibility of itself. Importantly, if the inverse insight is correct, we have attained knowledge. To understand that an author is incompetent or has misunderstood is an important step in our understanding of philosophy or academia in general. To understand that there are degrees of intelligibility in the various aspects of our universe is a breakthrough. To understand the history of philosophy one is constantly pivoting from direct insights to inverse insights, grasping what the philosopher got right and realizing that he got many things wrong. Some aspects of the universe are regular, systematic, mathematical, predictable, deductible, uniform and are understood by direct insights. Some aspects of our universe are irregular, unsystematic, chaotic, irrational, unpredictable, unique, and can only be understood by an inverse insight. Inverse insights pose a challenge to us, but they occur in the context of important positive developments of philosophy, mathematics, and science.

Lonergan coined the term "empirical residue" as a modern equivalent of what was called prime matter in the Scholastic tradition. Put simply the empirical residue is the data left over after understanding. Understanding grasps a regularity or pattern in the data; but there is always a residue which does not fit into the regularity or pattern. When the detective visits the crime scene, he picks out what is important: the position of the body, the spattering of blood, a broken window, a blood-stained hammer, and a fingerprint. But so much in the room is unimportant, irrelevant to the case, insignificant in itself, and is just left behind as of no consequence. When we understand anything, we understand the form and leave behind the matter that is not relevant to the insight; we understand what is important and abstract from what is irrelevant and unimportant. Data that is unimportant, irrelevant, insignificant, peripheral, to the question at hand are examples of the empirical residue. It is empirical, positive data, but it lacks significance in terms of the question or investigation.

The empirical residue is grasped by an inverse insight because as much as we would like to have a direct insight into matter and provide a systematic definition, such an expectation is not to be satisfied. The only way we can understand the empirical residue is that it is "that from which understanding abstracts a form or an idea or a cause." It is the sensible as sensible which cannot be understood directly. Sensing experiences the sensible; intellect understands the intelligible. The sensible and the intelligible are distinct but not separate. If we were to understand the sensible directly then it would not be sensible but intelligible. We grasp the empirical residue as the sensible that is left over after understanding has been reached.

If you take the statement "this is an avocado tree"; presuming that it is true, it is a single item of knowledge of the real. To affirm it as true you must first ask a question about what you see, understand the definition of an avocado tree and affirm that there is sufficient evidence to confirm that this is truly an avocado tree. But concomitantly there is the avocado tree as sensible, unique and individual. There is the avocado tree as satisfying the definition of an avocado tree and you have enough evidence to affirm that this particular sensible presentation satisfied the definition of an avocado tree. The evidence is in the shape and color of the leaves, the appearance of fruit of a certain shape and size, ultimately you can check in an encyclopedia, or get a botanist's judgment. It is hard to think of the definition of an avocado tree without including some element of sensible potency, some data that is included in the definition, some image informed with an idea.

But the form of this tree is also particular and individual. As individual and as unique, the tree is sensible but not intelligible. Potency is the data that is relevant to the definition and incorporated in the definition. The empirical residue is what is left over after science, common sense and understanding have exhausted the issue. It is what can be experienced but may not be directly understood. The individuality and uniqueness is known by the roundabout way of an inverse insight. Inverse insights are either true or false; they are acts of understanding which are either correct or incorrect; such insights can add considerably to our knowledge of the universe.

Much the same occurs over a wide range of our knowing. We understand what is significant but leave behind what is insignificant; we pick out what is meaningful and leave behind what is meaningless; we pick out the relevant and bypass the irrelevant, and so on. We use the term "residue" to indicate the incidental, the insignificant, the meaningless, the irrelevant, the negligible that is abstracted from in an act of understanding; in that sense it is a residue, what is left behind by intelligence, what lacks immanent intelligibility.

Let us examine five classic critical examples of the empirical residue. In each case let us note the three characteristics of the empirical residue, namely, positive data, lack of immanent intelligibility, and a connection with compensating higher intelligibility.

(1) Individuality. Medieval philosophers and theologians were aware of the problem of knowing the individual as such and sought for a principle of individuality, namely, a philosophical reason why this piece of chalk is different from that piece of chalk, even though the pieces are materially identical in all respects. Aquinas appealed to *materia signata quantitate*, "matter as specified by quantity," as the principle or cause of individuality. Scotus appealed to a principle of *haecceitas*, "thisness," as the cause of individuality. But do you solve the problem of individuality by appealing to a principle or cause? If so, you are presuming a direct insight or cause as to why two identical atoms are still numerically distinct. Two identical atoms are numerically different; they may not be different materially in any respect; but one is "A" and the other is "B"; they are individuals of a species; each possesses its own individuality, its own uniqueness; but there is no cause or principle that can explain why they are different. They are individually different only as a brute matter of fact. You cannot explain numerical difference by way of a principle or cause; to do so would presume a direct insight into an intelligible cause. We appeal to an inverse insight; it seems strange at first but that is the nature of grasping the absence of an expected intelligibility, in this case an absence of immanent intelligibility. We think there should be a reason but there is none. Individuality as such is left behind as part of the empirical residue when we understand, "this is an avocado tree." There is no shortage of positive data in this case as most of the things and events that we encounter are individual.

This aspect of the empirical residue is related to a compensating higher intelligibility. Experiencing experiences what can be sensed, felt, imagined and remembered, what is given. But by itself that is not human knowing. Human knowing begins when we ask questions about what we have experienced in order to understand. Understanding grasps the explanation, the idea, the cause, or the answer to the problem. The empirical residue is the basis for the possibility of understanding, of generalizing, of abstracting, which leaves behind the individuality. All our intellectual operations and knowing begin and depend on this aspect of the empirical residue.

The empirical residue opens the possibility of abstracting universals from particulars, forms from matter. It means that scientific discoveries and laws are independent of where and when they were made. Scientists all over the planet can collaborate and share their particular research, inventions, measurements, and discoveries. Science research can then be progressive and cumulative. Furthermore, discoveries about the properties of potassium do not have to be repeated for every sample of potassium. Empirical science does not formulate laws for this potassium but for all potassium, not for this water but for all water, not for this living cell but for all living cells. That is how science works; that is how the universe of proportionate being is constituted

(2) Space/Time Continuum. Zeno, an early Greek dialectician belonging to the Eleatic school, held that Being is One and unchanging. One of his many arguments went as follows. If you want to go from point A to Point B, you must first pass through a point that is halfway between A and B. When you reach that point you still must pass through the new halfway point between yourself and B. And so on and on *ad infinitum.* The distances become smaller and smaller but never reach zero, so you can never reach point B. Thus, he concluded, motion is impossible, and all is One. He succeeded in puzzling his contemporaries.

If you are teaching geometry and ask the students to define a line, someone will surely suggest that a line is an infinite series of points. You explain that a point is "position without magnitude," and an infinite series of points without magnitude does not produce magnitude. But a line does have one magnitude of length and so the definition fails.

Space and time are continuous. They are not made up of actual parts; they are not discrete. A wall, a ruler, a table, are constituted by actual parts and are discrete. That is easy to understand and that is what we expect. But a continuum is different; it lacks immanent intelligibility. It is not made up of actual parts. You can suppose that it is made up of an infinite series of parts or points, but that remains always a supposition. It is hypothetical rather than real, potential rather than actual. If you remain puzzled that is because it is puzzling. Why does Zeno's argument not apply in the real world? Because it doesn't apply to a continuum. A continuum lacks expected immanent intelligibility. It belongs to the empirical residue.

This peculiarity becomes extremely important because it is the basis for the infinitesimal calculus. In calculus you suppose a division into an infinite number of parts; you perform whatever operations you need to do on paper; then you eliminate the infinities and what remains is the actual correct answer. This is a puzzle, but it works! And is of enormous importance.

(3) Particular Times and Places. We live our lives moving from particular places at particular times. So, there is an immensity of positive data about what happens where and when, and historians try to give us a snapshot of what they think is important and where and when it happened. Particular times and places may be important for the historian, but not so much for the scientist or the philosopher. There is no immanent intelligibility in the difference between particular times and places. Understanding usually abstracts from particular times and places. We cannot know the sensible as sensible by direct intellectual knowledge. Intellect knows form; sense intends the sensible as sensible. Inverse insight understands the lack of intelligibility of particular places and times.

Again, realizing that particular times and places lack immanent intelligibility is of enormous importance, for it makes possible invariant laws and definitions of science and philosophy. The discoveries of Archimedes in Syracuse at one time, in one place, with one material, in one laboratory, are abstracted from the time and the place. He discovered the idea of specific weight, the relation of weight to size and its importance for what floats and what sinks. But the idea is valid everywhere, for all time, and can be applied to a great variety of substances and liquids. Explanatory discoveries in the sciences are invariant; it does not matter where or when they were discovered or where and when they are applied. The time and place of discovery is irrelevant. Particular times and places are irrelevant to the invariant laws of science and philosophy; they belong to the empirical residue.

(4) Law of Inertia. What is it that causes an arrow to continue in motion even though it has long lost contact with the bow that fired it? Zeno posed this in one of his paradoxes and it remained a problem until the scientific revolution. The medieval philosophers postulated a force as a property or accident of the arrow; others thought of wind coming from the front to the back to push the arrow. Our experience of pushing and pulling, throwing and catching, inclines us to think of rest as the natural state of bodies and if they are moving someone must be pushing them to keep them moving. We think there must be a cause operating on something that is moving.

What is the cause of the continuous movement of the arrow? Sadly, they were asking the wrong question, which Galileo understood, and Newton formulated in his first law of motion, namely, bodies continue in a state of rest or motion in a straight line unless something interferes. The relevant question is not what is pushing the arrow, but what is stopping the arrow from moving forever in a straight line. However, there is no reason or immanent intelligibility as to why a moving body would continue to move forever in a straight line. When the question is asked in that way there is no intelligible response.

The idea of inertia is an inverse insight and turns the question upside down. You can give an intelligible answer to the question what is stopping the projectile from moving forever in a straight line. You specify friction, resistance and gravity as measurable, intelligible, verifiable answers to the question. Such a way of understanding is the key to mechanics, astronomy, momentum, projectiles and motion. Hence, constant velocity in itself lacks immanent intelligibility and belongs to the empirical residue. But when you turn the question on its head it becomes the basis for all modern mechanics of motion and changes of motion.

(5) Probabilities. Another important example of the empirical residue are chance occurrences. We define chance as the non-systematic divergence of the actual frequency from the statistical ideal. In other words, if the average rainfall for each year is fifty inches, the rainfall for this year may be more or less, but the pattern of actual figures turns out to be non-systematic and not open to precise prediction. The probability of a coin toss may be fifty-fifty but that does not preclude streams of heads or tails. Average life expectancy may be seventy years of age, but that does not mean that you cannot live to be a hundred. Meteorologists tell us that there is a ninety per cent chance that it will rain tomorrow. If it does not rain, we tend to think that the forecast was wrong. But that is not the case. Probabilities do not refer to single events but to sequences of individual events. After understanding probabilities, we can define chance as the deviation of the actual occurrence from the correct predicted probability of occurrence. It is the gap between the ideal and the actual that is unpredictable, unintelligible, and always lacks immanent intelligibility.

Understanding probabilities is of enormous importance because most of our knowledge of the concrete happenings in life depend on probabilities. Classical laws of physics and chemistry can predict with great accuracy in the abstract, but when it is put into practice all sorts of factors enter in and can influence the result. (We will give more analysis of probability in chapter 9 on Generalized Emergent Probability).

Definition of Matter

Now that we understand inverse insight and the empirical residue let me give you Lonergan's definition of the material. He defines the material as, "whatever is constituted by the empirical residue or conditioned intrinsically by that residue."[7] As we have seen the empirical residue is empirical in that it is sensible, data, individual, and can be experienced but not in itself directly understood; it is a residue in that it is irrelevant or un-important, or insignificant from the point of view of a particular insight, or law, or a definition. The five examples we discussed above are either constituted by or intrinsically conditioned by that residue. As well as the direct insights that grasp the systematic, recurrent and regular features of our universe, there are inverse insights that grasp the absence of an expect-ed understanding and so we realize that there are degrees of intelligibility in the various realms of proportionate being. We can talk intelligently and critically about what is grasped in inverse insights. Inverse insights give us real true verifiable knowledge of how our universe works. We will deal further with the absence of intelligibility in our final chapter on ultimate causes and the intelligibility of the universe as a whole.

Conclusion

Potency as a metaphysical element is not a thing, is not a stuff, is not a spe-cific material like water or iron or clay. We are trying to conceive of potency as a metaphysical element, as a constituent cause or principle of all propor-tionate being. The scientist seeks proximate answers to satisfy the needs of the moment. The philosopher seeks ultimate answers in terms of the whole universe of proportionate being, past present and future. The philosopher specifies the general form that correct answers must take.

What we are asserting is that we live in a complex universe that can be known by a variety of ways and disciplines. It is not simply the matter of the materialists; it is not just the idea as the idealists assert. It is not just in the head, *a priori*, as the Kantians might assert. It is a complex universe where the four elements of potency, form, existence and good, emerge, change, interrelate, develop, and sometimes decline. Not one of the elements can be denied or neglected. In every human act of knowing there is also a known and the known must include some element of potency, form, act, and good, respectively. Whether it is common sense descriptive knowing, or the knowing of astronomy, astrophysics, hydraulics, paleontology, and so on, then each specific answer must include some element that is sensible, some element that is intelligible, some element of verification of the real and some evaluation of its contribution to development or decline.

We have been continuously oscillating between the terms matter and potency. In general terms, we can view them as two sides of the one coin.

7. Lonergan, *Insight*, 540.

On the one hand, data of sense, the sensible, can be understood, is potentially intelligible, is the source and basis for all acts of human understanding, it is that from which our variegated, complex, enormous universe of proportionate being has emerged. In that context the data of sense is *potency*. On the other hand, there are aspect of the data of sense, that lack immanent intelligibility, that are left behind by direct acts of understanding. They belong to the empirical residue, they can only be grasped indirectly by inverse insights, and we refer to them as *matter*.

This will become clearer as we deal with the other metaphysical elements. Matter/potency is the most difficult to pin down precisely because of the lack of intelligibility it is harder to understand. Hopefully, when we have the full picture, we will then be in a better position to appreciate the richness, the diversity, the change, made possible by matter in potency to form.

6

Elements: (2) Form/Intelligible

When someone said that <u>Intelligence</u> *exists in nature, as in animals, and that He is the cause of the arrangement and of every kind of order in nature, he appeared like a sober man in contrast to his predecessors who talked erratically. We know that Anaxogoras openly made these statements.*[1]

Spontaneous order is being explored by physicists, chemists, biologists, and mathematicians and has been found to occur among elementary particles, among molecules, in complex systems, in living things, in the brain, in mathematics, even in traffic.[2]

Once one has understood, one has crossed a divide. What a moment ago was an insoluble problem, now becomes incredibly simple and obvious. Moreover, it tends to remain simple and obvious. However laborious the first occurrence of an insight may be, subsequent repetitions occur almost at will. This too, is a universal characteristic of insight and, indeed, it constitutes the possibility of learning.[3]

The faculty of thinking, then thinks the forms in the images.[4]

Introduction

IN OUR PREVIOUS CHAPTER, we established the notion of potency as a basic metaphysical element constitutive of the universe in which we live. There is an element of the sensible, of matter, of space and time, and it is within that context that we live and move and have our being. But is it the only

1. Aristotle, *Metaphysics*, A, 3, 984b15–20.
2. Watson, *Convergence*, xxviii.
3. Lonergan, *Insight*, 30.
4. Aristotle, *De Anima*, III, 7, 431b4.

metaphysical element? Is it the only reality of our universe? Are we already committed to become materialists? Is our universe a chaos of sensible events succeeding one another at random? Is there order in the universe and where does it come from?

The early Greeks asked about the material cause of the universe. Some said that it was made out of water, others air, others fire. Then they seemed to settle on the four elements: earth, air, fire, and water. The focus was on the matter out of which things were made. Aristotle then highlights the grand entrance of Anaxagoras,[5] like a sober man among drunkards, proclaiming that there must also be a principle of order, some answer to the question of formal cause, some explanation for the intelligibility of things. Anaxagoras realized that the world is not chaotic; it is not just a bundle of random matter; it is not unformed matter. It is ordered, it is patterned, it is according to law and reason, it is regular, it is intelligible; and these laws and intelligibilities are just as real and important as the matter out of which the universe is made. Aristotle realized that as well as answering the question about the material cause, what are things made out of, you also have to answer the question of the formal cause, namely, what is it? Seeking the formal cause is the more important and fundamental question.

In our day we need another Anaxagoras. It would seem that materialism or physicalism is the default position of most philosophers in contemporary philosophy, particularly for the empiricists and linguistic analysts. Most scientists, too, would seem to assume materialism as their default philosophical position. Materialists, subjectivists, reductionist, constructivists, argue the toss in the philosophy of science but all differ on the issue of how we know and hence what can be known. Endless arguments ensue but do not seem to achieve much. The issue is fundamentally an epistemological issue and can only be solved by reverting to an appropriation of the fullness of human knowing in experiencing, understanding and judging. Scientists seem to have been appointed as the repositories of contemporary "wisdom," when in reality as philosophers they are at the level of the early Greek philosophers, fixated on the raw materiality of our universe. We need someone to hoist the banner of intelligence, form, order, regularity, system, cause and identity. Maybe Lonergan is that person. I can see few others.

We reached our notion of matter by way of proportionality: the sensible is to the intelligible, as matter is to form, as experiencing is to understanding. Utilizing our method of isomorphism, we examined potency as the objective counterpart of intellectually patterned experiencing. We now

5. Anaxagoras (500–430). A Greek from Asia Minor, who founded a school of philosophy in Ionia. He introduced a principle of *Nous* or Mind to explain motion and order in the universe but did not develop the idea as Aristotle would do in terms of form.

ask, what is the counterpart of understanding? What is the content of acts of understanding? Cognitional acts have goals. They are intentional. What is the intentional content of acts of understanding? In a general sense we name them ideas or forms or intelligibilities. In every act of understanding there is a corresponding content, some form or idea or a law or order that is understood. The traditional terminology is form or idea. I like to use the term the intelligible, to highlight that the content of any act of understanding is by definition intelligible; but we also use such terminology as form, idea, law, order, pattern, relationship, etc.

Finally, let us be clear that at this stage we are considering order, intelligibility, form and idea as possible entities. We are prescinding for the moment from whether these are real or true, whether they exist or not, whether they can be verified or not, which requires a distinct act of reflective understanding. In the next chapter we will consider whether they are true, whether they can be verified, and how and where and in what way they are real.

General Description of Intelligibility

If matter were the only metaphysical element, we could start writing the conclusion to this book. If the materialist hypothesis is correct, then we have said all that can be said about our universe. But most readers, including materialists, would be very dissatisfied with such a premature conclusion. The material universe is that which is experienced; but there is a further dimension of the universe revealed by our ability to understand. We can understand many things and develop a science of all the areas we consider. What are these sciences aimed at other than to order the data of their discipline, to define and divide the elements, principles and causes, to recognize and promote further understanding? Our position is that whenever we perform an act of human understanding, we grasp some form, or order, or idea, or intelligibility, which is distinct but not separate from its material conditions. Our purpose now is to illustrate this truth and focus on the intelligibility of our world. We start with common sense, move on to science and then return to metaphysics.

Whenever we ask and answer a question, we grasp a form. Whenever we explain something to somebody else, we communicate an intelligibility. When we hear and understand the news of the day, we are grasping a variety of ideas about events, causes, explanations, possibilities. When we see or hear and do not understand, then, we have failed to grasp the idea or form, and will usually inquire further in order to understand. Understanding permeates all our activities, at home, at work, at play, in our conversations, and interactions with others. From waking to returning to bed again, we deal with things that tend to behave regularly, systematically, in an ordered and intelligible manner. We have little difficulty negotiating this multitude of forms because we can understand, we have learned how the world works and can negotiate this complex world, for the most part. What is it that we are understanding? We are understanding that our universe is not simply and solely brute, raw matter, that materialism is a defective, truncated position, that there is a metaphysical element of form or idea or intelligibility or order permeating every detail and corner of our universe. We do not know our universe by sensing alone but by sensing and understanding. By understanding we grasp the order, the laws, the diversity and richness of our multifaceted universe. We are having our Anaxagoras moment.

Let me tell a story which might help to illustrate the difference between the materialist/empiricist and ourselves. Three football referees were discussing the facts of life within the game. The first referee says, "I calls 'em as I see 'em." That is his philosophy of refereeing, and we can call it the empiricist approach. The second referee says, "I calls 'em as they are." We can take this as an expression of critical realism, which happens to be our position. Finally, the third referee says, "They ain't, until I calls 'em." We can take this as a constructivist position, which we will deal with towards the end of this chapter.

The first referee is an empiricist because he thinks that knowing resides in the seeing: that seeing is enough to make the call. If he knew some philosophy, he might embrace the philosophy of David Hume. The second referee is an Aristotelian. Aristotle defined truth "as a statement of that which is that it is, or of that which is not that it is not."[6] The third referee could be called a constructivist: we make it to be by our declaration.

Let us consider an example from soccer and focus on the first two referees. In soccer, if a defender deliberately touches the ball in the penalty box, the referee should call a penalty/foul. However, an accidental handball is not a foul at all, and play continues uninterrupted. How does a referee distinguish between a deliberate and an accidental handball? The referee cannot see into the mind of the player. But there are clues: did he move his hand towards the ball; did he move his hand away from the ball; were his hands in a natural position; was he too close to the ball to do anything about the ball hitting his hand. Simple seeing on its own does not solve the problem. Evidence, understanding, inference, beyond a reasonable doubt, all play a part in the referee's judgment. We do not judge by seeing alone but by gathering the relevant data,

6. Aristotle, *Metaphysics*, 4, 7, 1011b25.

knowing the rules, understanding relations between factors, knowing the distinction between deliberate and accidental, and judging the preponderance of evidence in favor of one judgment or the other. A referee who blew his whistle every time the ball touched a player's hand would soon be sidelined, as he would seem not to understand the difference between accidental and deliberate. Rules are an example of forms, as they impose order on games. Referees need to understand the rules as well as to have good eyesight. The rules for offside might take about twenty pages to explain, to define, to deal with exceptions and qualifications. You do not see a person off-side; you understand and judge that he has infringed on some aspect of the twenty-page definition of the off-side rule. Technology and video evidence reduces the margin for error, but a definitive judgment still depends on an interpretation of rules and hence on human understanding.

If knowing were simply seeing, then the materialists, the empiricists, the atomists, and the first referee would all be correct. We would be living in a universe of formless matter and there would be no room for causes, relations, connections, order, regularity, science, and the like. We would be living in a chaos of material things. But quite evidently, we are living in a relatively ordered universe. Water does not normally flow uphill. Milk will normally go sour if left out at room temperature. A ball that is kicked will normally move in the direction of the force exerted. If the weather clouds over, we expect it to rain. The sun seems to rise in the east and sets in the west regularly according to the seasons. The stars appear to revolve around the Earth in twenty-four hours and return to approximately the same position. If you combust hydrogen in the presence of oxygen you will get water. If you jump out of a plane (without a parachute) you expect to fall. Two cars crashing directly into one another at speed will do serious damage.

Of course, we could go on indefinitely enumerating the intelligible regularities, patterns and laws that constitute the order of our world and which we take for granted. These expectations or order are built up by understanding correctly and not simply by seeing or hearing. Humans spend about fifteen years of full-time formal education in order to be able to operate effectively as adults in the world. Why do they need fifteen years of full-time education? To understand how the world works, its physics, chemistry, biology and human sciences; its humanities, languages, communications, technology and culture; about laws, relationships, good and bad behavior, to develop useful skills. All of these areas require understanding because we are being taught about regularities, causes, patterns, expectations, techniques, relations, and laws. These insights pass into the habitual texture of the mind and build up a mentality that can very quickly sum up a situation, understand the cause, grasp differences, assign blame, and know what to do. Principles and causes are operating in the real world and our education helps us to recognize that. Unfortunately, we often do not advert to the reality of causes and principles and think of the real world out there simply as what we can see and touch, what is sensible.

At the level of common sense, the principles and causes and forms are experienced and understood but are not yet explicitly formulated or precisely defined. It is the sciences which have, each in their own area, established the basic laws of genetics, of chemistry, or motion, of particle physics, of astronomy, of medicine, and so on. These are usually explanatory, precise and correct.

Scientific Definition of Form

The sciences start by describing the data of their subject matter, but then they will go on to explain the data. The description may be the same as non-scientists would describe the data using common sense, but a scientific explanation moves to the precise relationships of variables in technical, theoretical language. A chemist will describe sulfur as a yellow powder with a sharp smell and it burns to produce noxious gases. But then s/he will go on to get the atomic weight of sulfur, fit it into its place in the periodic table, establish its valency, find out its main compounds, discover how it reacts with other elements or compounds and establish its essential characteristics. This is an explanatory definition or form. It is clear, verified, measured; it gives the essentials and leaves out the non-essentials; it grasps the particular essence of sulfur. That is the special kind of understanding, which is an explanatory science, meaning relating things to one another.

Each science discovers the elements and laws appropriate for that area of science. Chemistry studies the chemical elements and compounds and how they relate to one another; what compounds can be formed, how they combine, how they can be classified, how they react, the properties of each of the elements and compounds. All of these are specific forms, intelligibilities, order out of chaos, discovering what is there to be verified, the potentially intelligible becoming actually intelligible. Physics will do the same for energy, mass, movement, heat, light, subatomic particles, etc. In each case you have the scientist specifying particular laws, equations, causes and definitions. In each case you have examples of theories verified in instances, or forms informing matter.

As well as identifying the substances and units that make up the data of the science, the scientist will formulate laws that refer to the interrelations of these units. In physics you will have the laws of motion, laws of thermodynamics, laws of mechanics, laws of electricity, laws of radiation, etc. These too will be precise and explanatory and verified. They are intelligibilities to be grasped by investigation, formulating explanations and verifying hypotheses. You cannot verify relations without verifying the terms of the relations. So, we have a basic strategy of terms defined by their relations to one another; and relations defined by the terms of the relation. Terms define the relations, and the relations define the terms.

The sciences answer specific questions about areas of their subject matter. If you want to know specific forms go to the empirical scientist competent in that area. They are the ones to gather the data, do the research, conduct the experiments, formulate hypotheses, devise further tests or experiments, and verify in terms of sufficient evidence for the conclusion. We gradually understand, discover, and formulate correctly the laws and principles applying to each area of science. The philosopher by contrast studies essence in general, the components of the knowing process as well as all the elements of the known.

Form as a Metaphysical Element

Common sense finds a multitude of overlapping, merging, specific intelligibilities in a world that is described. The sciences find a multitude of explanatory forms whether as terms or as relations proper to their area of interest. The philosopher is interested in all intelligibilities. The philosopher considers forms in general; identifies the notion of form as that which is understood and basic distinctions between kinds of forms differentiated in various ways. We are trying to understand and define explanatorily the metaphysical element of intelligibility, examining its extent, and its relation to the other metaphysical elements. Common sense and the sciences and other disciplines give us a multitude of specific examples of intelligibilities. Is there a definition of form which will encompass every example of an intelligibility? Does every item of human knowing incorporate an element of intelligibility?

As the scientist seeks explanatory definitions of things within a specific field, so the philosopher seeks an explanatory definition of form in general, one that would pertain to everything that exists. Form or idea are the traditional terms used to refer to something that is understood, namely, an intelligibility. Form does not refer merely to shape or Rorschach, or pattern; it is not an image but an idea. Our diagram 2 on the isomorphism of activities of knowing with the content known, presents the terms, which are related to one another; it is an example of a form. The terms of knowing are experiencing, understanding, judging truth and value. The terms of the known are potency, form, act and value. The terms of the knowing are isomorphic with the terms of the known. The principles of sublation and dependence relate to the activities as well as the contents. Any example of human knowing can be analyzed in the framework of this diagram. The diagram gets meaning and concreteness when it is applied to particular examples. The structure is explanatory in that the terms define the relations, and the relations define the terms.

Lonergan defines form as "the component of proportionate being to be known, not by understanding the names of things, not by understanding their relations to us, but by understanding them fully in their relations to one another."[7] Form is anything that is understood in an explanatory context. Form is isomorphic with the act of understanding; form is the idea abstracted from the image; form is the content of an act of understanding; form is the intelligible in the sensible. Lonergan makes it clear that we are not talking about nominal definition, the correct use of words; nor are we talking about descriptive definitions, where the metaphysical elements apply only loosely. We are talking about fully explanatory human knowledge where things are defined in their relations to one another.

These forms, when verified, are just as real as matter and just as much part of the universe as the potency out of which they emerge. The forms do change but usually according to intelligible patterns and not chaotically. Forms are not eternal, not permanent, not subsistent; not apart by themselves, not unchangeable essences. Some subatomic particles can only exist for a fraction of a second, yet scientists have no difficulty naming them, identifying them, saying what they are, where they come from and where they go to. Aristotle had no difficulty with forms being generated and corrupted.

The forms exist, not apart from matter, not separate from matter but immanent in the reality of proportionate being. Parmenides had a notion of being as One, Unchanging, Eternal, Infinite and thought that all change was an illusion. Plato compromised and claimed there was one world containing many perfect, unchanging, subsisting Ideas and also a world of the sensible, with the two worlds being separate and apart from one another. Knowledge of the Forms was true knowledge because the Forms do not change. Knowledge of the sensible is unreliable opinion because the sensible is always changing. Aristotle's epistemology insisted on the close connection between intelligence and the senses. He insisted on the connection between form and matter and the reality of both. If you ask, where are the forms, the answer is that they are

---

7. Lonergan, *Insight*, 457.

where matter is informed. Where are Newton's three laws of motion? Wherever material bodies move in relation to one another.

Just as you cannot have understanding without human experiencing, so also you cannot have form without matter; they are not two things but one substance with a formal and material cause or principle. Essence, nature, and substance are terms often related or even equated to form. *Essence* means what is essential and excludes all that is not essential. *Nature* means the essence as the principle of operation; you know the nature of something by studying its activity, its movement, its change. *Substance* means the essence of a composite thing: what makes it to be what it is as a unity, identity, whole. We will distinguish substantial forms from accidental forms in chapter 10. *Form* is the formal cause that makes it to be what it is; the answer to the question, what is it?

We have difficulty understanding the reality of form because we have difficulty imagining the reality of form. But we acknowledge their existence in different ways. Take for example, laws of nature. We generally acknowledge that they exist, although from a materialist position, one might ask, where are Newton's laws of motion? If they are real, where are they? Show me and I will believe. But this is to fall into the trap of imagination. Our criterion of truth is not whether it can conveniently be imaged or sensed, but can it be correctly understood and affirmed. If this is a real cat, then you have matter and form and act; "this" refers to the sensible, "cat" refers to the intelligible form; "is" refers to exist, to act, to be real, to be affirmed. We do not have to imagine form as a ghost, or invisible entity, or "soul." What we experience is the potency, what we understand is the form, what we judge is the existent. In our terminology of isomorphism, experience is to understanding as potency is to form. Just as potency is defined in relation to experiencing, so form is defined in relation to understanding. Just as you cannot understand without first experiencing, so you cannot have form without emergence from potency.

Each of us faces the difficulty of moving from the dominance of sense and imagination to the position that the real is what is affirmed in a correct judgment. The law of gravity is real; it is a form; it is real and operative, immanent is all material things; it is not an imposition, not a construct imposed arbitrarily, not an a priori form, not a subsistent Form in Heaven. It is the immanent intelligibility of the universe of proportionate being. The forms are not separate and apart from potency but emerge from potency, continue to depend on potency but they are distinct elements from potency. To be distinct does not mean to be separate and apart. Potency is real. Form is real. Form is not potency and so there is a real distinction between form and potency. But in real things like cats and dogs potency and form represent what you experience and what you understand—they are two aspects of the one thing. Such is the position of critical realism where truth is the product of reflective understanding backed by experience and not unquestioned imaginative assumptions.

Variety of Forms/Intelligibilities

Our purpose in this text is to develop a worldview of everything. We are working towards an understanding of the structural features of the universe (part 2), and the dynamic, developmental stages (part 3). All the laws, invariants, relations, sublations, identities, definitions, and everything else that will be understood are forms, they are intelligible, and in our next chapter we will show that some are true and hence real. Let us here just call to mind some examples of these intelligibilities and what needs to be said about their scope.

(1) First Principles and Causes

It is found that certain principles apply in all the sciences and in all areas of proportionate being. Because they are so general and apply everywhere, it is part of the heuristic structure of first philosophy to study them. They are immanent and operative in all sciences, skills and disciplines. They are part of the habitual texture of the mind of the adult educated person. They are the prism through which we view our world and all that happens in it. Let us just identify some of them and move on.

Causality. There are different kinds of causality, which operate in many different ways and are fundamental to understanding how anything happens in any area. Cause is not to be confined to efficient cause; there are also formal, material, final, exemplary, instrumental, creative, etc. Causes are not the same as correlations. All sciences necessitate a sophisticated understanding of causes because they operate everywhere. Causes are either proximate or remote. Causes are known not by seeing alone but by understanding and judging. Causes produce effects. Often, they are invisible but that does not mean they are not real. We will give a more detailed treatment of causality in our last chapter on ultimate causes.

Finality. We find a directionality, a historical development, a directedness in all areas; this is presupposed in all the sciences. We recognize progress and decline. There is a principle of finality, and it operates universally across the whole of proportionate being (explained in chapter 9). Every science recognizes a general progression from the big bang, to galaxies, from hydrogen to helium to more complex elements, to solar systems, to life, to plants, to animals, to humans.

Relations. You could say that everything is related to everything else. But we need to be precise about what kind of relation, the basis of the relation, the implications of the relation. Descriptive knowing relates things to us; explanatory knowing relates things to one another. Terms are defined by relations, and relations are defined by their terms. This is a key to understanding each and every science. Also, there are mathematical relations, relations of causality, descriptive and explanatory relations, kinship relations, relations of sublation, relations of size and distance, and more.

Change. Everything seems to change yet something remains the same at least for a time. It happens across the board. But there are different kinds of change. We will have a chapter on substance and accidents (chapter 10) which will explore different kinds of change.

Space and time. Everything occurs in a particular place at a particular time. All proportionate being is limited and understood in terms of when and where. Scientists define space and time in various ways, as the notion developed from Aristotle, to Newton, to Einstein, and then quantum mechanics.

Unity. Unity is an analogous term and is used in many senses. In mathematics the unit one is the basis of all arithmetic, calculus, algebra, and the rest of mathematical specialties. Each science has the units that it studies whether it be atoms, molecules, cells, plants, animals or humans. There are unities of aggregates, artefacts, cities, armies, clouds, and so on. Any act of understanding unifies a range of data in various ways.

Truth. In our next chapter we will discover that the true is very close to what is real. In epistemology we reach truth in correct judgments. The sciences reach the real when they verify theories in instances. The notion of truth is relevant across the board in all disciplines.

Value. Again, we all have our value priorities, and they affect everything that we do. We note the goodness of the universe; the goodness of particular beings; the goodness of nature; the goodness of persons; the goodness of families; the goodness of order in society; the goodness of procreation; the goodness of work; the goodness of life, of peace, and so on.

(2) Are Forms Immanent or Transcendent?

How do we resolve the debate between the Platonists and the Aristotelians, between those who place the reality of the Forms in a world apart and those who assert that the forms are immanent in matter? We have indicated the difference between Plato and Aristotle above in section four. But from our point of view, what are the crucial arguments? We start with the epistemology and move on to the metaphysics.

How do we arbitrate between different epistemologies? We can do so through direct, personal recourse to the facts of human knowing. We can advert to how our own acts of understanding occur and how they relate to operations of imagining, remembering, and sensing. We perform acts of understanding all the time and with a little self-appropriation we can grasp the conditions, the characteristics, the stages, the levels the modalities of human understanding. In my experience and that of many others, such self-appropriation would verify that the Aristotelian position is consonant with personal experience and so we elaborated an epistemology of experiencing, understanding and judging, as one process of knowing unfolding on four interdependent levels of operation.

If our principle of isomorphism is correct, then the pattern of relations of potencies, forms and acts will be proportionate to the pattern of relations of experience, understanding, judging and evaluating. But understanding depends on experience, emerges from sensing, is something new and different, but never separate and apart from experiencing. The data of sense establishes the possibility for insights to occur. Insights are ideas emerging from images under the influence of intelligent questioning. In parallel fashion we notice that in the universe forms emerge from potency; they do represent something new but continue to depend on the sensible conditions. A tree emerges from a seed, but the later stages are always dependent on the earlier stages. Water emerges from a mixture of hydrogen and oxygen given a spark to start the reaction. Without hydrogen and oxygen, you cannot have water. Life can apparently emerge from non-living given sufficient time, the necessary conditions, the material preparation, the requisite chemicals and electrical energy. Life cannot continue unless the conditions continue to be favorable. To put this more generally, forms depend on material to become real or actual. Forms are immanent in actually existing things.

Scientific method is based on the method of theory verified in instances, or one might say, forms verified in matter. It is an empirical method where the truth must be verified in an experiment, or experience, or observation, at a particular time and place. Scientific laws are verified not just in the head but in reference to instances, examples, observable sensible consequences.

The laws are forms and the instances, examples, and consequences are the matter. Scientific method would seem to imply that the forms exist potentially in the data. Scientific laws are discovered and verified by reference back to sensible experiences. They are not constructed and imposed arbitrarily on reality; they are not invented or chosen by social classes, or elites, or ideologies, or power mongers. They are immanent in the matter.

Positing forms that are transcendent would seem to be quite arbitrary and useless. There is no evidence whatsoever for such a world, which by definition is beyond the world of science. Aristotle's arguments against such a world are extremely cogent. As Ockham put it, entities are not to be multiplied without necessity.

(3) Are Forms Universal or Particular?

As soon as you claim to make a real correct distinction between a dog and a cat, you are committed to some theory of universals. On the one hand, this dog is particular; Fido is unique, a certain size, color, sex, age, state of health, weight and temperament. You can see the particular dog, touch it, call, feed, hold, scold, chase, play with, and the like. Every other dog you meet in your life will be different; each will not be physically identical but have a different size, color, temperament sex, age and state of health. Each is unique, particular, an individual, a never to be repeated instance of a dog. Dogs come in many breeds of varying sizes, colors, shapes and configurations. Yet we have no difficulty recognizing them all as dogs. We recognize them all as dogs, not because of sensible similarity, not because they all look alike, but because you understand that they all fit the definition of a dog, belong to the species of dog, and are specifically different from cats. We automatically distinguish between particular dogs of varying sizes and breeds, and the idea or definition of dog which is a universal definition.

We have an idea of what a dog is, and a cat isn't. The idea is learned over years, over a lifetime. It is learned by understanding this is a dog, this is also a dog, and this is another dog. Although they are all different, we call them all dogs for a reason. We develop our definition of the species of dog, which expands and contracts the more we know about the difference between dogs and cats. A professional dog breeder, or zoologist, will have an explanatory understanding of the evolution of dogs, the development of different breeds of dog, the domestication of the dog. They can write books about the species of dogs, its variety and essential characteristics. Nowadays, this may be done in terms of DNA. What is at work is human understanding. It is identifying the sensible, particular in terms of belonging to a species, a class, a category, a universal. You are classifying this particular dog in a category as an idea or essence or nature that is specific to all dogs but different from all cats. Where is that idea? Each dog is an instance of the idea, and is also particular, individual and unique. The idea of a dog is instantiated in each particular dog. The idea as universal definition is in the mind, imperfectly in the minds of us who know little of dogs, but clearly, precisely, explicitly in the mind of dog breeders and evolutionary zoologist.

Similarly, each cat is an instance of the species of cat, unique, particular, concrete and different from all other. Each satisfies the definition of cat, as a species, as a category, as a universal. The essence of cat exists in this particular cat as particularized; after all, it is a cat. The essence of cat exists in the mind as an idea, a species, a definition. To distinguish between cats and dogs, we invoke the difference between the species and recognize that cats are not dogs, and dogs are not cats. This is how understanding works. This is how we distinguish between chalk and cheese, hydrogen and oxygen, trees and forests, wood and plastic, a bacterium and a virus, a bicycle and scooter, and we can go on for ever and ever distinguishing all the different species, individuals, classes, artefacts, living things and all their varying characteristics. It is how the world works; it is how the human mind works.

Forms exist as universals in the mind. Archimedes formulated the basic law of flotation: a body will float if it is lighter than the volume of liquid that it displaces. This is an insight, or a set of related insights, which exists in the mind of someone who has understood the terms and relations of the law. The law does not specify what liquid, or what solid, where or when, how or why. It exists in the mind as an idea, a relation, a definition, a universal law. It exists first as a possibility and then after many applications and experiments as a verified law, as a judgment. In the real world wherever masses relate to one another in terms of displacement or flotation the law of flotation applies. Our universe is such that material bodies relate to one another in terms of this law and others. There is an intelligibility about who and what will float, and it is expressed in the law of flotation. The law is verified in instances, in examples, in data, in experiences, at particular times and places. The law does not have to exist in a noetic heaven waiting to apply itself to floating bodies whenever the question arises. It is a characteristic of our human knowing that we grasp the universal in the particular. It is a characteristic of our universe that things happen according to law; as well as the sensible there is also the intelligible, as well as the potential there is also the actual. The sensible is real; the intelligible is real. That is the kind of universe in which we live. It is not a static universe of pure forms. It is not a chaotic universe of raw, random, unintelligible matter or chaos. The vocation of the scientist and the philosopher is to discover the immanent intelligibility in the data of sense. We accept the classical moderate realist position which states that forms exist as universals in the mind but exist only instantiated in reality. This is not just an arbitrary choice of theoretical positions but a presupposition of modern scientific thinking.

(4) Different Methods Anticipate Specific Kinds of Form

We distinguish four ways of asking questions characteristic of four methods of understanding reality.

Classical Method. The forms characteristic of classical method will express direct intelligibilities, definitions and properties, which are very satisfying and yield laws of great generality. Classical method seeks regularities, universal laws, the systematic. Most scientific work up to the time of Einstein was done in expectation of reaching this kind of direct intelligibility. Archimedes, Euclid, Ptolemy, Copernicus, Galileo, Newton, Einstein formulated an extraordinary array of laws of motion, gravity, light, mass, acceleration, time and space, movement of heavenly bodies, culminating in Einstein's simple law of the relation of mass to energy.

Statistical Method. The forms characteristic of statistical method are not universal and systematic relationships but probabilities, averages, frequencies, or rates. It is not so satisfying because the laws change from place to place, and from time to time; you recognize a lack of an expected intelligibility. Yet to our surprise we discover that we cannot do without this kind of form and that most of our knowledge is cast in statistical format. Probabilities, averages, frequencies, rates, are still abstract laws and hence are forms, even though they are the result of inverse insights and lack the intelligibility expected of classical laws.

Genetic Method. You have forms characteristic of genetic method, namely, understanding how things develop. This involves putting together many insights into successive stages of development as well as from different points of view such as, anatomy, physiology, biology and psychology. Living things are generated, live, grow, move, age and die. All laws applying to all stages are relevant to the understanding of life.

Dialectical Method. You need a special method and set of ideas to reach an understanding of human conflict, of linked but opposed principles unfolding in individuals, groups, nations and their history. When we study the history of philosophy, we often find a series of conflicts, disagreements, controversies, arguments, even wars, over opposed positions. Can such opposed positions be considered as contradictory contributions to the clarification of a single goal? Can we explain disagreements? Can we see the reasons for misunderstanding? If we can give intelligent answers to these questions, then we are grasping reasons and hence forms. If it is something that is understood, then it is a form.

Conclusion

A full act of human knowing involves the four activities of experiencing, understanding, judging and evaluating. We are working on a principle of isomorphism which states that parallel to such acts of knowing there are also the contents known in these acts. These contents will by definition be potency, form, act, and value. Although we distinguish four activities and four contents of these activities, it is one knowing and one known. Form is first grasped as hypothetical in direct acts of understanding. Some of these are verified in the data and so are affirmed to be real: hypotheses become judgments. The theory of phlogiston is just as intelligible as the theory of combustion, but only the latter is judged to be true. Horses can be defined, but so can mythical beasts, like centaurs and unicorns. Our next task is how to distinguish the merely notional from that which can be affirmed, verified and stated as true and real. Let us now turn to the third metaphysical element that of "act," "the real," or "the true."

7

Elements: (3) Act/Existence

Our own position, as contained in the canon of parsimony, was that the real is the verified; it is what is to be known by the knowing constituted by experience and inquiry, insight and hypothesis, reflection and verification.[1]

In my talk, I argue for a new concept of existence: According to the view defended "existence" is appearance in the field of sense. The main argument for the view presented as an elaboration of the Kantian-Fregean insight that existence cannot be a proper property. . . . My own view is that there are transfinitely many fields of sense . . . which distribute modalities over a certain domain of objects associated with them. In this context I will argue that there is no all-encompassing field of sense . . . and that this necessary non-existence entails that all sense is contingent.[2]

Yet quantum physics is certainly telling us something about what is real, out in the world. Otherwise, why would it work at all?[3]

Indeed, the strangeness of quantum phenomena has led some prominent physicists to state flatly that there is no alternative, that quantum physics proves that small objects simply do not exist in the same objectively real way as the objects in our everyday lives do.[4]

1. Lonergan, *Insight*, 277.

2. Markus Gabriel, handout for talk on "The Meaning of Existence and the Contingency of Sense" (Duquesne University, March 9, 2012).

3. Becker, *What Is Real?*, 5.

4. Becker, *What Is Real?*, 5.

Introduction

FIRST, LET US CLARIFY the traditional and the more contemporary terminology used in this chapter. The basic terms used are "act," "existence," "actual" and "the real."

Act is the traditional metaphysical term referring to first act, the act of existence. We are discussing the triad of potency, form and act. We have elaborated on the metaphysical elements of potency in chapter 6 and form in chapter 7, and now we consider what has "act" to do with all that. First act is the act of existence, second act is existence as a specific thing or event. That use of the term first act is familiar to Aristotelians but may not be familiar in the contemporary world of philosophy.

The terms "existence" and "essence" came into prominence in the Middle Ages, when their relationship was a topic of great concern and controversy. The questions focused on whether existence was an attribute or a property, whether it was really distinct from essence, how can you define existence, and whether essence and existence were really distinct in God. The term existence largely overlaps with that of first act.

I use the term "actual" as equivalent to "act" as in an actual thing, an actual attribute, an actual event, something which is actual rather than notional, or virtual, or merely a possibility. In the full sense of first act, the term actual refers to existence. The most important thing one can say about something is that it exists, that it is actual; after that you can expound on its characteristics.

Finally, in contemporary culture we are more at home using the terminology of real, fact, or true as opposed to unreal, fantasy, or untrue. I have defined the real as what can be affirmed in a correct judgment. Hence, it is closely related to what is true. I do not use the term real as the out-there-now-real, as opposed to the in-here-now-real. In other words, the real is not simply physical objects, but it includes subjects and our consciousness. What is real is what is true, and what is true is what is real: whatever is fact belongs to the real world. The negation of these terms would be "does not exist," "is not actual," "is not real," "is false," "is fictional." What is fictional belongs to the imaginary world of fiction. We are appealing to the real/true as the criterion of correct judgments versus mistakes, lies, flights of imagination. Add together all the true statements that can be made about the universe, and you have the real world. Again, this largely corresponds with first act, or existence. Hence, we will use these terms interchangeably, as the context favors.

Science has revealed to us the history of the cosmos, of our solar system, of planet Earth, of the emergence of life, and eventually of human life.

We witness a stream of things coming into existence and going out of existence, emerging from potency, surviving for a time, struggling, dying, and becoming extinct. It happens to individual things, to species of things, to whole genera of things. Our hold on existence is precarious and dependent on many conditions. There is a considerable difference between something that exists and something that does not exist. Hamlet asks the question, "To be or not to be?" as he considers the possibility of killing himself. To exist or not to exist is of some importance.

Hence, we are led to a consideration of existence as a metaphysical element. Is it part of the universal invariant structure or nature of our universe and all that is in it? How is it to be defined? What is the cause of existence? What is the cause of coming into existence and going out of existence? Our contention is that existence is not something that can be ignored or taken for granted. It is the third of our metaphysical elements as we follow through our program of isomorphism of knowing and the known. This is to be understood in conjunction with our earlier reflections on potency and form. Forms may or may not exist. Acts of direct and inverse insights give us possibilities, hypotheses, forms or ideas. The performance of reflective insights assesses the evidence and arguments to judge whether the hypothesis is true, belongs to the real world, to actually exist. Again, since we are speaking as first philosophers, and not as empirical scientists, we are concerned with the totality of our universe and want to understand the first causes and principles operating in every area of the universe. We find that existence is a constituent metaphysical element of our worldview and hence of some importance.

Misunderstandings

Although distinguishing existence from essence is not a particularly difficult topic, it is constantly misunderstood. Permit me to try to identify some major sources of misunderstanding.

(1) Existence as a Concept with Specific Content. A distinguished visiting lecturer came to Duquesne from the University of Bonn to address us on the topic of "The Meaning of Existence and the Contingency of Sense." He seemed to take the position that existence can be defined as "appearance in the field of sense." All that remained was to explain the notions of appearance, and of field of sense, which he seemed to do very eruditely, quoting Carnap, Frege, Putnam, Schelling, and others. Now, can you define existence in a form of words? Can you give a content to the notion

of existence? Is existence a concept that can be defined, stating what it is and what it is not? Is existence amenable to the standard form of definition of what it is and what it is not? If we try to understand existence, we instinctively turn it into an essence to be defined by what it is and what it is not. But on principle, you cannot define existence in the normal manner because in doing so you turn it into an essence—the one thing it is not. How do we get around this difficulty?

In this text we have taken the position that the only adequate method to articulate the basic structural elements in the world of proportionate being is by way of isomorphism with the invariant structure of human knowing of truth and value. Being can only be correctly defined as the objective of the pure desire to know. Potency can only be defined as an experiential element in an act of human understanding. Form can only be defined as the content of acts of understanding. Neither being, nor potency, nor form can be defined as concepts, which express what are their essential properties or specific characteristics. Similarly, with existence. The only adequate way to understand existence and nonexistence is to parallel existence with the human acts of reflecting and judging. The notions of being, potency, form, act and good are so basic and universal and permanent and structural that they can only be defined as the intentional content of human questioning, experiencing, understanding, judging truth and judging value.

(2) Knowing as Merely Understanding. It is very common to have a great idea and to assume that it is true without further critical questioning. An insight can be so exciting, so inspiring, so breathtaking, that we assume that it is true and correct. It is common enough to analyze the human act of understanding, but rarely do we find a complementary analysis of the act of judging and hence fully human knowing. Descartes asserted that all clear and distinct ideas are true. He did not distinguish between simple apprehension and judgment which was a staple pillar of the Neo-Scholastics of the time. Not only did he not grasp that a direct insight is an insight into possibility, but he also did not realize that a further reflective insight and judgment is needed to affirm that a hypothesis is true or exists.

Knowing is not just experiencing and direct understanding. Further critical questions arise which are precisely: Is this theory true? Is this explanation correct? Does this essence exist in reality? Is this idea also real, verified, shown to be true with a sufficiency of evidence? There is a direct act of human understanding, which grasps the essence of something; there is a further reflective act of human understanding, which affirms that it is a correct answer to the question. The critical question, the question for judgment, is a distinct further question beyond that of simple understanding.

The answer to the question for judgment pivots on the sufficiency of the evidence and the connection between the evidence and the conclusion. If the evidence is sufficient to indicate a conclusion, then the person issues a judgment of affirmation or denial. Human knowing reaches a term; it is then a complete item of knowing.

Aquinas was much clearer than Aristotle in his epistemology on the difference between a simple apprehension (direct understanding) and a judgment. A simple apprehension was the activity of abstraction from phantasm grasping definitions, essences and forms. But it was only in the judgment that the truth, reality, or existence of these forms was affirmed as true or false. Truth resides only in the judgment. He was also clear that the judgment was the result of a special act of reflection on the grounds of reasoning to justify the truth or falsity of the judgment.

Corresponding or isometric to this distinction in his cognitive theory, Aquinas was able in his metaphysics to grasp the distinction between essence and existence, as well as the crucial importance of this distinction. Thus, he affirmed that in anything outside of God there is a real distinction between essence and existence. Nothing in the universe of proportionate being exists necessarily of itself. Every created being gets its existence from outside; it is not the cause of its own existence; it is a contingent and not a necessary being. He has a notion of one Creator, and everything else is a creature that is given existence by the Creator. Of course, in affirming such a real distinction, he was not imagining existences as floating around waiting to be joined to a possible essence. He was simply understanding a crucial truth about the kind of universe we live in, that it is contingent and not necessary, that it does not exist in its own right, that it could have been different, and that essences are coming into and going out of existence all the time. The only necessary being in the full and strict sense is God, the creator and cause of the existence of every created, contingent thing, whether material and spiritual. Aquinas affirmed clearly that in God essence and existence are identical, whereas for all else that exists, they are distinct. Many Scholastics for some reason had great difficulty with this distinction and it became a kind of cause célèbre in the history of Scholastic philosophy.

(3) Imagination as the Criterion of Knowing Existence. When we assert that there is a real distinction between essence and existence, this tends to be misunderstood (that is, imagined) as two separate things floating around until they get together to form a real existing thing. When Aquinas affirmed the real distinction in contingent things between essence and existence, but no such real distinction in God, this sounded too abstruse and difficult for the imagination to bear. So, later scholars subjected it to refinements,

misunderstanding, reservations and rejection. For us, "really distinct" is not to be understood as physically separable, or as readily imaginable. Existence is not a concept or a thing or a property but a metaphysical element to be understood indirectly by analogy with the act of human judgment.

Contemporary philosophy abounds in confusion between the imaginable and the intelligible. Since Hume defined ideas as "faint images" there seems to have been a complete failure to distinguish images from ideas, and imagination from intelligence. A correct understanding of human knowing assigns a proper place to imagination as providing data and images from which ideas emerge through questioning and intelligence. This distinction requires discipline and clear thinking. The criterion of the real is sufficiency of evidence and a link between the evidence and the conclusion, grasped in an act of reflective understanding. The common misunderstanding of the "correspondence theory" of truth holds that if, "what is in here" corresponds to, "what is out there" then one has understood the truth. But this is not understanding but imagining a correlation, which is actually impossible to make.

Plato affirmed the reality of Forms but felt it necessary to somehow imagine them as existing in a world apart, perfect, unchanging, eternal. But is this a necessity of intelligence or imagination? In the early Middle Ages it seems the "ultra-realists" tended to the Platonic position, affirming that universals were real not only in the mind but also outside the mind somehow on their own. Aquinas was a moderate realist following the path of Aristotle that universals are universal in the mind but individualized in things. The Nominalists denied the reality of universals outside the mind; there are only individuals, words are a *flatus vocis*, a convenience with no metaphysical value. It is not hard to see how the intrusion of imagination can distort correct understanding.

Suarez maintained that the distinction between essence and existence in creatures is merely notional: in the mind only and not real. Our contention is that it is a real distinction. It is real because essence is real, existence is real, and essence and existence are really different. They are not the same; they are really distinct and different. To be really distinct does not require things to be separate and apart. We are not claiming that you can have essences and existences floating around by themselves in some vague nether world. But where essences do exist, they exist because a real act of existence has made them to exist. Existence is added to essence from the outside in all contingent beings. Possible essences are different from real essences, just as hypotheses are different from correct judgments.

(4) Existence as a Property. A further misunderstanding is to reduce existence to the status of any accidental predicate or property. For example, "Fido is white; Fido exists" are two statements that are similar in structure. Their similarity makes it seem that both "white" and "existence" are accidents or properties. Whether Fido is white or not refers to a minor property or predicate. It is minor because he could be black, brown, etc., yet still exist. But if he does not exist there is not much point in asking, what color is he, and expecting a true answer. To exist and to be white cannot be treated as if white and exists were both accidental properties. Logicians can tie themselves in knots if they treat existence as a predicate at the same level as the nine categories of Aristotle attributed to substance.

Act/Existence as a Metaphysical Element

Using the isomorphism of knowing and the known, Lonergan can define act as "the component of proportionate being to be known by uttering the virtually unconditioned 'Yes' of reasonable judgment."[5] The metaphysical element of act or existence is isomorphic with the activity of judging; it is what is intended in questions for reflection, grasped in reflective insight and expressed in a correct judgment. We need to distinguish between judgments that are formally unconditioned and judgments that are virtually unconditioned.

A judgment that is formally unconditioned is a judgment that has no conditions whatsoever. The judgment is true in itself, of itself, not because of the premises, not because a cause has operated to make it true, not because it happens to be true, but because of its very nature and definition it is true. There is only one example of formally unconditioned and that is the existence of God. "God exists" is a judgment. But there are no conditions that determine the existence or non-existence of God. There are no causes outside himself or before himself that make God to exist. The judgment does not have any formal premises that cause the conclusion. There is no real distinction in God between essence and existence. This is an objective principle, but from the subject's point of view there are many factors conditioning their personal affirmation of the existence of God.

---

5. Lonergan, *Insight*, 457. A "virtually unconditioned" thing is a possible being that actually exists. It is a contingent or conditional being with all of its conditions for existing being fulfilled. A virtually unconditioned judgment grasps that all of these conditions are fulfilled. In our times "virtually" can mean online rather than face to face. In Lonergan it means, "all conditions are actually fulfilled."

A judgment is virtually unconditioned if there are conditions for a correct judgment to be made but all the conditions happen to be fulfilled. "It is not raining here now," is a judgment. It is true because the sun is shining, there are no clouds, there is no precipitation happening and the ground is dry. The conclusion ("It is not raining here now") is a virtually unconditioned because all the conditions for its truth happen to be fulfilled. There is only one judgment that is formally unconditioned, namely, the existence of God. For everything else outside God, there are conditions that must be fulfilled for the judgment to be true.

Clearly, the things in this world of proportionate being are not necessary, they come into existence and go out of existence all the time. We are familiar with the story of evolution and its series of extinctions and its series of emergences of new things that did not exist before. We are all familiar with our precarious hold on existence where our average life span varies from fifty years to eighty years. We are familiar with certain subatomic particles whose life span is measured in terms of nanoseconds. Our earth, our solar system, our galaxy, our universe all seem to have a beginning, a middle and surely an end, at some indeterminate time in the future. Change is all around us, and that means coming into existence and going out of existence.

The only way to correctly understand act or existence is to see existence as isomorphic with the cognitional activity of judging. Where the distinction between understanding and judgment is lost—as in Descartes—the corresponding distinction between essence and existence becomes meaningless. Where the distinction between experiencing and understanding is lost—as in empiricism—then it is doubly meaningless. Where epistemology becomes a total muddle as in some forms of existentialism, then too the relation between essence and existence becomes a muddle.

Some examples may help: The theory of combustion and the theory of phlogiston are equally theories, equally grasped by acts of direct understanding, equally intelligible as explanations. The theory of combustion is true, while that of phlogiston is not. This is discovered by the outcome further experiments and data. A horse or a centaur can be defined. But horses exist and centaurs do not. A biography is intelligible as a historical account, but fiction is simply a work of imagination, a grasp of a possible essence. Whereas the historical account attempts to present what actually happened, presenting evidence for every assertion along the way, fiction is allowed to go in any direction it pleases.

To move from direct understanding to reflective understanding is to move from grasping possible essences to grasping really existing entities. One of the defining characteristics of judgment is that it adds no further content to the definition or theory; it simply affirms as true or denies as false.[6] If further content is added, then the theory is being refined and adapted and must await a further final judgment of true or false. In parallel fashion, we note that existence adds nothing to the essence except existence, reality, actuality. It does not add new content, it does not add new attributes, it does not add new properties, it does not change the definition, it is not an added accident, it simply and only adds existence/reality/truth.

But surely that is of some importance! There is a difference between fiction and fact, between astrology and astronomy, between magic and science, between legend and history, between a novel and a historical account, between alternative medicines and evidence-based medicines, between the witch doctor and the medical doctor, between living in a world of fantasy and living in the real world, between the world of the child and the world of the adult. Existence is something distinct from essence. It is something added to essence. It is known only by way of a correct judgment. Just as there are many different kinds of judgment, so there are many different aspects of the real universe in which we live. Such judgments form the basis for the formation of our worldview.

All the statements and laws enunciated by physicists, chemists, biologists, zoologist, anthropologist, if they are true are real and belong to the real world in which we live, move and have our being. Knowing is isomorphic with the known. But our knowing is limited by time and aptitude and nature. The content of the totality of correct judgments is what constitutes our universe. Put the content of all true statements together and you have a full account of all that exists and does not exist in our universe of proportionate being. The principles and causes that we elaborated in chapter 6 on the Intelligible, if they are true, they are real, they exist, they are part of the actual universe.

Act or existence is then the third metaphysical element of proportionate being constituting a unity with potency and form to affirm one reality in the world of proportionate being. Isometric with this one structure of being is the single invariant structure of knowing. In other words, parallel to experiencing, understanding and judging is one reality constituted by potency, form and act.

What Is Real?

In our previous chapter on the Intelligible, we spoke of causes, relations, the content of direct insights, forms of every kind, but we were considering

6. See chapter 1 and chapter 3, section 3 above.

them as mere possibilities. We were unable to affirm their reality because direct understanding of intelligibilities grasps only possible solutions or forms. However, now that we have treated of the role of judgment as the criterion of the real, and now that we have defined existence as the metaphysical element corresponding to true judgment, we can emphasize the reality of potency and form in any judgment. In a true judgment knowledge comes to a term, no further content is added to the hypothesis, and experiencing and direct understanding are incorporated into the judgment. In parallel fashion referring to the known content of the true judgment, we can now affirm that potency is real, that form is real, and they really exist. There is one process of knowing from experiencing, to understanding, and to judgment. There is a parallel process in the known when potency is the basis for form, and form is the basis for the existence of all things and properties and events in the real world. Potency, form, and act are real, distinct metaphysical elements. They are the constituent elements of every area and corner and niche of the real world. We cannot understand anything about our universe unless we include some element of the material or potency, some element of intelligibility, ideas or forms and some element of existence, of actuality, of belonging to the real world. Scientific method includes these three elements in the simple formula as theories verified in instances, namely, forms, really existing, in a particular place and time.

We have no difficulty imagining that matter is real. We sense matter in space and time, out there now, through seeing and hearing and tasting and grasping. We have no difficulty imagining matter as existing as a stuff, as a particle, as a wave, as a lump of coal. Our definition of matter as a real metaphysical element is, however, not based on such easy imagining but on the difficult process of direct and inverse insight and explanatory definition. All true knowledge has to be grounded in evidence, in instances, in the sensible. Conspiracy theories are conspicuous by their lack of concrete data or evidence for their conjectures. To have recourse to non-evidence-based medicine is to play dice with your health. Criminal trials are structured around concrete witness testimony, forensic evidence, circumstantial evidence, both for and against the defendant.

We do have great difficulty imagining that form is real; we ask where it is and what does it looks like. If natures and laws and universals are real, then where are they and how do they work? We can imagine stuff existing, but we cannot imagine laws as existing in the same way, in the same state. Consequently, we were pushed to distinguish clearly between imagination and intelligence, between sensing and understanding and between the two criteria of the real, one operating in the world of sense and the other operating in the human knowing of experience, understanding and judging.

I gave two short quotations at the beginning of this chapter taken from Adam Becker's book entitled, *What Is Real?* It focused on controversies emerging from quantum physics. When he does explicitly examine the notion of the real, he mostly appeals to logical positivism and the Vienna Circle, a group of philosophers who tried to limit philosophy to the sensible, excluding understanding and judgments. Although he does cite about twenty other philosophers, sadly, there is no resolution, just endless confusion about the criterion of the real and how it is to be applied in the difficult field of quantum physics. Our position is straight forward and worth repeating as a mantra, "the real is the verified; it is what is to be known by the knowing constituted by experience and inquiry, insight and hypothesis, reflection and verification."[7]

For those who do not distinguish between imagination and understanding, endless confusion arises. It has taken a long time historically to be able to distinguish between two criteria of the real. Imagination tends to dominate and moves our thinking in false directions. It is not the imagination that determines what is real but intelligence and reason, understanding and judgment. These are more intangible faculties and more difficult to pin down. The materialist position is really that imagination is the criterion of the real; we can imagine matter and so it is real; we cannot imagine form and so it is not real. The idealist tends to think of the ideas as real but belonging to a world apart, a world of forms or Ideas.

Our worldview incorporates the three metaphysical elements so far examined in a unity of a single world with a rich diversity of potencies, forms and actual things and events. The three metaphysical elements we have so far examined are not three separate things but the three elements that constitute any existing and real composite thing. Imagination pushes us in the direction of three things stuck together somehow. But intelligence grasps the notion of distinct but not physically separable. What we know we know by experiencing, understanding, and judging; what is known is some intelligibility instantiated in particular data and really existing for whatever time and space allotted to it.

Conclusion

Our world is complex, rich, dynamic, diverse, sensible, intelligible, and real. It is known, not in the simple manner of looking, but in the complex manner of being aware of, understanding, and affirming existence. The materialists affirm the reality of matter but there is no intelligibility, there is nothing to

7. Lonergan, *Insight*, 277.

understand. The indeterminists affirm that it all happens by chance. But our world is shot through and through with order, organization, causes, laws, regularities, systems, intelligibilities, which assign a reason for what happens, when it happens and how it happens. There is an element of chance, but it is circumscribed by regularities and causes and order. The worldview that is emerging in our examination provides a positive, helpful, overview of the whole world of proportionate being, into which all of correct modern scientific understanding can fit.

Once one knows the truth about what is real, what exists, one spontaneously wonders about its value. One wonders if particular things and the world in general are good or bad. What are they good for? What is their worth? How do we distinguish good from bad? That is the question for our next chapter.

8

Elements: (4) The Good/Value

Every art and every investigation, and similarly every action and
pursuit, is considered to aim at some good. Hence the Good has
been rightly defined as "that at which all things aim."[1]

For central and conjugate potency, form, and act have been defined
heuristically in terms of cognitional acts; if there were more or
fewer basic types of cognitional acts, there would be more or fewer
metaphysical elements.[2]

And so it was. God saw all that he had made, and indeed it was
very good.[3]

Terminal values are the values that are chosen; true instances of
the particular good, a true good of order, a true scale of preferences
regarding values and satisfactions. Correlative to terminal values
are the originating values that do the choosing: they are authentic
persons achieving self-transcendence by their good choices.[4]

Introduction

WE HAVE EMPHASIZED THE point that metaphysics is the integrating structure
into which all our knowledge of sciences, common sense, history, theology
and scholarship should find their appropriate context. Being includes everything, and so we come to ask about the good and its place in relation to other
elements in the universe of proportionate being. We are now seeking for a
meaning to the term "good," its definition, its extension and intension, how

1. Aristotle, *Nicomachean Ethics*, 1, 1, 1094a1.
2. Lonergan, *Insight*, 523.
3. Genesis 1:30b–31a.
4. Lonergan, *Method in Theology*, 50.

it is to be related to our notions of substance, existence, the intelligible, the sensible, and human persons. Metaphysics seeks a unified view of everything, and so it must be able to assign a meaning and definition and place to the notion of the good. How it does that is the purpose of this chapter.

"Good" is of course a very traditional term in both common sense and philosophy and theology. Discussions and efforts to define the good have been made since the time of Plato, Aristotle, Epicurus, and the like. In the nineteenth century the new term "value" appeared on the scene. It had a major role to play in Marx's labor theory of value and in Nietzsche's transvaluation of values. Phenomenologists made some effort to examine where values come from, how they are evaluated, and how they are related to feelings.[5] The word is widely used nowadays in daily conversation and in professional philosophy and theology. It even has its own branch of philosophy, called axiology.

An important difference between the terms good and value is that the former cannot be used as a verb, but the latter can. As well as talking about values such as honesty, loyalty, bravery, and so on, we can also value something, evaluate a problem, and perform evaluations. Thus, the word can be used for the cognitional process of evaluating and also for the product of such a process. This makes it easier for us to continue to use a method of self-appropriation to examine the process of evaluating, to identify the intention of such a process and to define the product of such a process as a value. We can continue to use our method of isomorphism between the structure of the process of evaluating and the values that are being understood, defined and known in that process. Hence, the transition from "good" to "value" facilitates the transition from theory to interiority.

We need to distinguish between the study of the good in ethics and politics and how it is dealt with in metaphysics. In chapter 14, we will focus on the human good as studied in an ethics and politics. Just as we respect the autonomy of physics, biology, historical scholarship, so we recognize ethics as the proper place for dealing with the concrete details of good and bad human behavior. It is in ethics that we study how to make judgments of value and how understanding, feeling, will, and spirit enter correctly into evaluating particular human actions. We recognize different kinds of value such as, vital, social, cultural, moral, and religious, as well as terminal and originating. It is within the discipline of ethics that we elaborate on the topic of moral conversion, what it means to be a developing moral subject, and what it is to have a healthy moral society in which to live. Ethics and politics are highly specialized areas of competence requiring many different

---

5. See Cronin, *Value Ethics*, 55–58, for short history of "value."

treatments to diverse questions of detail. We are not questioning the competence of experts in these various specializations.

The role of metaphysics in treating the good is a more general than that of ethics or politics. Metaphysics functions as a heuristic regarding the good, and thus considers the good as part of its broad, integral heuristic structure of proportionate being. If the structure is to be an integral structure, then it must include everything, so surely it must include the notion of the good and value. Hence, our question is the metaphysical question: Where does good/value fit in our worldview of the total universe in which we live? What part does it play, what does it mean, how does it relate to our overall integrating framework of knowledge? The notion of good or value is a rather fundamental consideration of our universe that is dealt with in first philosophy and must be recognized as of foundational importance. It is important because it is the basis for all human decisions and actions. It cannot be left as an afterthought, a post-script, or an additional entity. We will be claiming that the good/value is a constituent, intrinsic element in everything, and so we must deal with it as a structural metaphysical element. How are we to do that?

My approach is that we consider the good/value to be a metaphysical element along with potency, form and act. Let us consider this as a hypothesis, formulate it clearly, assign advantages and disadvantages, deal with difficulties as they arise and then reassess our position. This is a disputed question among Lonergan scholars. We will devote some attention to that issue later in the chapter. Can the notion of the good/value be integrated into our basic schema of cognitional structure, intentionality, and the isomorphism of knowing and known? To see how the good or value should fit in with the metaphysical elements requires some background work in epistemology, and so we start with a review of how judgments of value fit in with an integral cognitional structure (§2). We then proceed to examine how the element of good/value fits in with our diagram of isomorphism (§3). We are then in a position to give a definition of the good similar to that by which we defined potency, form and act (§§4–5). For purposes of clarification by contrast we will consider the notion of evil (§6). Then we will deal with some real as well as imaginary difficulties (§7).

Integral Cognitional Structure

In *Insight*, Lonergan worked out a three-level structure of cognitional activity in terms of experiencing, understanding and judging truth. It was a magnificent achievement culminating over two thousand years of communal effort to objectivize the knowing process of the human mind. Within this context he worked out his metaphysics of potency, form and act. When he moved to *Method in Theology*, he expanded these three levels to four and usually called the fourth level that of "deciding." From the point of view of clarity and pedagogy and even logic, I find introducing "deciding" here slightly unfortunate. There is no doubt that deciding is a crucial aspect of a human person and has a central role in human development, conversion, and human activity. But does it fit in a diagram of human *cognitional* activities? Deciding is a volitional activity: deciding is willing, assenting, consenting, agreeing with a certain action. One cannot choose (at least not well) without first knowing, just like one cannot judge without first understanding. Deciding takes on many forms and roles, times when it is present or absent, and when it is habitual or erratic, intense or superficial, emotional or rational. It is an omnipresent factor in human activity; an action is not a fully human action unless it is free. Deciding cannot be absorbed into a diagram of cognitional activities without causing confusion; it does not belong there and needs a treatment and even a diagram of its own.[6]

Lonergan defined metaphysics as the integral heuristic structure of proportionate being. In that context he dealt with the three metaphysical elements of potency, form and act which are isomorphic with experiencing, understanding and judging truth. But can metaphysics be *integral* if it leaves out knowledge of the good, making judgments of value and knowing good and evil? Surely an integral cognitional structure should assign a proper place to the question of value, deliberation, evaluation, and the judgment of value. Knowing values is a cognitional activity. What you decide to do after such judgments of value is a volitional activity, an act of will, of deciding and moves into another dimension of human consciousness. Hence, I think there is much to be gained by presenting a four-level cognitional structure incorporating in its proper place knowledge of the good and of value. I get some encouragement from Lonergan's own words when he was discussing, "The Meaning of the Metaphysical Elements."

> For central and conjugate potency, form and act have been defined heuristically in terms of cognitional acts; if there were more or fewer basic types of cognitional acts, there would be more or fewer metaphysical elements.[7]

He was probably not anticipating that the three elements he had identified would be increased or decreased. However, he clearly links the metaphysical

---

6. See chapter 7, "Deciding Free and Responsible," in Cronin, *Value Ethics*.

7. Lonergan, *Insight*, 523.

elements to the cognitional notions and activities that intend and produce them. Moreover, he himself later identified a notion of value and realized that this was distinct from the notion of truth, and hence required a distinct judgment of value over and above the judgment of truth. He later spoke about the question of value, deliberation and evaluation, as the cognitional activities to justify concluding with a true judgment of value.

> Value is a transcendental notion. It is what is intended in questions for deliberation, just as the intelligible is what is intended in questions for intelligence, and just as truth and being are what are intended in questions for reflection.[8]

An integral cognitional structure must explicitly include the question of value, the evaluation process, and the emergence of a judgment of value. Thus, I have included values in diagrams one, two and four. The statement "this is a computer," and "this is a good computer," are two quite different statements. The structure of the two judgments of truth and value are the same but the intention, the content, the affirmed, are different.

As I indicted elsewhere,[9] I do not think that Lonergan had fully integrated the judgment of value into fully integral human knowing and was not clear on whether it arose from apprehensions of value, feelings of value, deliberation or evaluation or how these terms were to be correctly understood and applied.[10] A three-level structure was a monumental achievement; a four-level structure incorporating knowledge of value would add considerably to that achievement and would produce a truly integral worldview. In his later writings Lonergan seems to have acquiesced in the idea of a fifth level of consciousness where all specifically religious activities take their proper place. There is certainly much to be said in differentiating faith, hope and charity, grace, salvation, prayer, worship, and the like, from moral philosophy, metaphysics, ethics and politics.

There are many advantages in presenting an integral cognitional structure incorporating the question of value, the insight that grasps the sufficiency of evidence for worth or worthless, the connection between that evidence and the proposed affirmation, and the necessity of asserting the judgment as a true or false judgment of value. Sadly, the term "judgment of value" is often used colloquially in a pejorative sense, as if a judgment of value were arbitrary, divorced from facts, a feeling preference, or a merely personal opinion. It needs to be shown that a judgment of value is structurally similar

---

8. Lonergan, *Method in Theology*, 35.
9. Cronin, *Value Ethics*, chapters 5–6.
10. Cronin, *Value Ethics*, chapters 4–5.

to a judgment of truth and emerges from the intelligent activities of asking and answering questions responsibly. Judgments of value are judgments, therefore affirmations, and therefore either true, or false, or probable. Let me illustrate some of the advantages of incorporating the judgment of value into the diagram of integral cognitional structure. (It might help to refer back to our basic diagram 1 of Cognitional Structure.)

(1) *The judgment of value fits in perfectly well as the apex of our desire to know the universe of proportionate being.* In a complete account of cognitional structure there must be four levels, and the fourth level must include the question of value, deliberative insight, and the judgment of value. This fits in perfectly with the other levels of cognitional structure and is parallel to judgment of truth but has a different intentionality. It is parallel in the sense of being a product of the desire to know and the act of understanding producing a word or expression or a judgment. The structure of the judgment of value is similar to that of the judgment of truth. The difference is in the notion of value that is operative rather than the notion of the intelligible or the notion of truth. Just as the judgment of truth refers us back to data and understanding relevant to the judgment, so the judgment of value refers us back to data, to understanding relevant to the value judgment, also refers us to relevant truths known from prior judgment of facts. A prospective value judgment sets us off in search of relevant memories, images, examples, ideas, concepts and laws, scientific truths, relevant happenings, possible consequences, implications, repercussions. We sort out those that are relevant with a view to providing justification for or against the prospective judgment.

Judgments of value are verifiable in the same way as judgments of truth. The judgment of value is justified by the sufficiency of evidence for its truth, the link between the evidence and the conclusion, the conviction of closure when you have asked all relevant questions. The judgment of value is at the apex of cognitional activities; it presupposes and depends on the integrity of previous activities. It focuses on asking and answering questions of value, such as: What is this worth? What is the best thing to do? What are the possible consequences? What is the right thing to do? What is the profitable thing to do? Judgments of truth usually have practical implications and possible applications, and these usually involve choices and hence values. Answering the value question should normally precede decisions and actions.

(2) *Value judgments are ubiquitous.* They are a crucial part of our knowing. There is no avoiding values. Any account of knowing that excludes

judgments of value is fundamentally incomplete. While we readily accept that politics, religion, aesthetics, and other areas of life are pervaded by value judgments, we sometimes believe science to be value-free. But all scientific activity is shot through with values and value judgments, from the choice of topics to the use of methods, the allocation of resources, job choices, salaries, remunerations, institutions, government policies, rewards, and the like. It is not as if the question of value can be excluded or left as an added extra. Some have aspired to a value-free science and a value-free sociology and claim to exclude values from certain areas of academia or government. Such aspirations, if examined, are seen to be an illusion for the very claim that an area is value-free, is already a value judgment on what is the best way to proceed in this particular area. Any judgment about good, better, best; bad, worse, worst are value judgments by definition.

The question of value naturally, spontaneously and inevitably arises. It is a crucial question having a feed-back effect on all areas of human knowing, living and doing. Einstein though he was doing pure science, but his discoveries led to the possibility either of making atomic bombs or of producing electricity. All discoveries of pure science can be used for good or evil. Pure science and its discoveries nearly always lead to applications that involve value judgments. Judgments of truth are nearly always followed by judgments of value.

(3) Cognitional structure is what we discover when we appropriate the spontaneous cognitional activities and processes of the human mind. This fundamental structure of knowing is not open to basic revision. If you attempt to revise it, you must invoke those very activities in order to attempt the revision. This is a valid point not only for the judgment of truth but also for the judgment of value. If you want to revise the fourfold levels of cognitional structure, presumably you judge that such would be a good thing to do! There is a spontaneous, correct procedure to be followed to reach a knowledge of the good and value. It is not an arbitrary process, not a preferential choice, not an emotivist embrace on the basis of feeling alone. To attempt to revise the procedure for making a judgment of value, you are obliged to make a judgment of value! All that Lonergan says about the judgment of truth in *Insight* can be applied to the appropriation of the judgment of value.

(4) The affectivity proper to judgements of value may be deeper and more personal than those associated with judgments of truth. But judgments of truth do have an affectivity, an intentionality. After all, the driving force is the *desire* to know. When we want to know, we judge truth as a good, even if implicitly. There is a feeling component to the work of a scholar, a researcher, and

experimenter; he or she just wants the right answer; it may have no further implications. It may end up in a journal, which few will read. But we want it to be correct, we would be ashamed to make a mistake.

The intentionality of a judgment of value can be much more personal, intimate and affective. Our values are more important than our knowledge. Our values are that on which our decisions and actions are based. Questions of conscience and moral worth may enter in. The affectively mature person feels happiness in acting on real values. The hardened criminal is quite happy stealing, as long as he can get away with it.

The deepest and best inclination of the human mind is the desire to know. To desire is to be in an affective state. There are desires that are superficial, sensitive, temporary, biologically or culturally based, strong, with little reference to intelligence or reason. But there are also affective states belonging properly to the intelligent and reasonable and responsible element in the human person, namely, the desire to know, the Eros of the human mind, the love of wisdom, the passion for truth, commitment to goodness, and the like. The affectivity proper to judgments of value may be deeper and more personal but is in continuity with the affectivity proper to judgments of truth. Judgments of truth and judgments of value belong in the same diagram.[11]

(5) *The judgment of value sublates the judgment of truth.* (i) It adds something genuinely new. A value is different from a truth. A good book is different from a book. (ii) It enhances the value of previous cognitional acts. A judgment of value depends on the truth of the facts on which it is based. Action in response to climate change presupposes that the consensus of the scientists on climate change is true and accurate. (iii) It leaves previous levels intact. It does not interfere with the investigations of scientists or the value of sensing or the need to think and ask all relevant questions. (iv) It continues to depend on all these previous levels and activities. For example, if new evidence will indicate that the current consensus on climate change is wrong, various value judgments, decisions, and actions will also need to change.

In the end, a diagram is only a diagram. In it we are trying to present a clear picture of emergence, relations, dependence of cognitional operations on one another, the parts constituting a whole. "Levels" is a metaphor and must not be taken too literally; levels are an invented pedagogical image to represent distinctions and relations of activities and contents. From this section we see that value judgments emerge from a series of cognitional activities, are an integral part of cognitional structure, and

11. I analyze the cognitional, affective, volitional, and integrative aspects of judgments of value in great detail in *Value Ethics*.

bring the series of cognitional activities to a term. Let us now ask whether it is helpful or not to consider the good as a metaphysical element in the sense we have already defined.

The Good as a Metaphysical Element: Definition

At the beginning of the chapter, we quoted Aristotle's famous definition of the good as "that at which all things aim." Aristotle identified the supreme and final end of human life as happiness, which is desired for its own sake and not for the sake of anything else. In this way he comes to define the good as an object of desire, not as the means to an end, but for what is most desirable for its own sake. This position needs clarification and qualifications. There are many desires, and they are not always for the good. There are many goods, which are rarely desired such as chemotherapy, amputation, economic austerity, or confrontation. To desire the good would presume we know what we are desiring, and in that sense, knowledge comes before desire. Rather than defining the good in terms of appetite or desire or aim, it would seem to be a better course to try to understand the good through appropriating judgments of value and as philosophers to assert that in some sense everything is good and desirable in different ways.

We have already seen how the three metaphysical elements of potency, form, and act can be defined in an indirect but real manner by using the principle of isomorphism. Thus, we were able to define being as the objective of the unrestricted desire to know. We were able to line up potency, form and act as the contents of experiencing, understanding, and judging. As we are familiar with the activities of our own knowing, so we have indirect knowledge of the content of our knowing, that is, the known. There is a proportion between the activity of knowing and the known, but there is also a real distinction between the activities of knowing and the contents of that are known. The relations of sublation and dependence between the activities of knowing are parallel to those between the respective contents of the known. Through this isomorphism, we have been able to define the metaphysical elements with a precision and control over disputation impossible for Aristotle or Aquinas. We are well on the way to working out an integrating framework for all of human knowing including knowledge of the element of value.

With the notions of being, potency, form and act we were unable to give a direct definition of these notions by species and difference. Similarly, we are unable to give such a direct definition of the good. But we are familiar with the process of asking value questions, deliberating, and positing judgments of value. Hence it seems not only possible but also necessary to use the principle of isomorphism to define the good or value. To know the truth of a statement you must understand the statement, ask the critical question (Is it true?), assemble all the evidence relevant to answering correctly, understand the sufficiency of the evidence for an affirmation or denial, and affirm the appropriate conclusion. Similarly, for the judgment of value, there is a hypothesis regarding a possible value, a notion or feeling or question of value, a deliberative insight into the evidence for the judgment, the judgment of value affirmed and uttered and the process coming to a term. It is by personal, direct, explicit, familiarity with the process of making value judgments that we derive an indirect definition of the content of the value judgment, namely, the good.

We reached our definition of act or the actual as a metaphysical element by saying that the real is what is experienced, understood and correctly affirmed. We now propose to define value as what is experienced, understood, affirmed as true, and affirmed as a true value. Doing that we can now define the good in general as, what you reach when you (1) ask questions about value, considering all relevant information, facts, perspectives, (2) grasp the sufficiency of the evidence to entail the conclusion in a deliberative insight, and (3) affirm the value judgment in a fully explanatory context. In the example, this is a good computer, we can line up the components of experiencing, understanding, judging truth and judging value with the metaphysical elements of potency, form, act and value. Any and all judgments of value can be similarly lined up. In a fully explanatory manner, we can define the good as what is known in a virtually unconditioned judgment of value. We pass many judgments of value on the goodness or badness of people, things, events, activities. Mostly we do it well. We are evaluating all the time. We are knowing what is valuable, what is worthwhile, what is important, what is good, better, best, as well as bad, worse, worst.

Although Lonergan does not use the method of isomorphism in relation to defining the good, he does express the same idea in the isomorphism between originating value and terminal value. The subject (originating value) constitutes himself or herself by choosing objects (terminal value). Such choices are based on asking genuine questions of value, sifting through one's feelings that apprehend possible values, deliberating openly and honestly about the factors involved, formulating a hypothesis, asking all relevant critical questions, posits the judgment of value with relevant qualifications and exceptions, where necessary, decides in favor of the best course of action, loves and wants the good, implements and moves on. We constitute ourselves as good persons by respecting the cognitional aspects, the affective component, the willingness to follow through in the context of a dialectical struggle to promote progress and reverse decline.

Parallel to the subject as originating value is the good as the objective to be achieved, the terminal value. The terminal value might be a building, a successful teaching assignment, an improvement in the good of order, a good policy accepted and implemented, a personal relationship established, a book published, a religious value promoted and accepted. Good people are the basis of a good society. Good people produce good terminal values. There is a parallel or proportion between originating and terminal values. That is isomorphism applied to the area of values and goodness.

Aristotle had much the same idea: Virtue is what a virtuous person does; the good is what is judged to be good by a good person. We are in fact back to Aristotle's definition of the good person as the standard and measure of goodness.

> Acts, to be sure, are called just and temperate when they are such as a just or temperate man would do; but what makes the agent just or temperate is not merely the fact that he does such things, but the fact that he does them in the way that just and temperate men do.[12]

On the side of the subject, we can become intimately familiar with how to make correct, unbiased judgments of value and how to be faithful to them in choices, decisions and implementation. On the side of the object or act, we can become familiar with the complexities, the details, the nuance of justice and temperance in the concrete goodness of a universe of emergent probability. Justice is what a just man will do in any particular set of circumstances.

Another perspective from Lonergan might also help; "Genuine objectivity is the fruit of authentic subjectivity."[13] This is not just a throw-away catchphrase but the whole thrust of his approach in philosophy and theology. Start with self-appropriation, with getting a grasp of how the mind works and how we reach truth and value in the real world. Establish how the individual cognitional activities culminating in judgment are the criterion of what is true and real and objective. Proceed to ask about worth, goodness, possible courses of action and evaluate with a view to changing the world for the better. With those structural elements of cognition in mind, shift attention to the contents known in all judgments and you can identify the objective world, in most general terms, the world of potency, form, act and value.

---

12. Aristotle, *Nicomachean Ethics*, II, 4, 1105b 5–8.
13. Lonergan, *Method in Theology*, 273.

These can be specified in more detail by the innumerable affirmations of doctors, economists, teachers, scientists and philosophers who are faithful to a method of theories verified in instances. We reach the objective world, not by excluding subjectivity but by way of authentic subjectivity. The objective world is, in all cases, constituted by the four metaphysical elements which are isomorphic with the structure of authentic human knowing.

The good is the fruit of authentic judgments of value. Familiarity with the process of knowing improves the chance that we will be better knowers—of both facts and values. Self-appropriation increases the likelihood of authentic subjectivity. Thus, it is well worth our time to gain self-knowledge, to know ourselves as judges of value. If we do, then we will be able to define the good or value as what we know when we authentically desire value, question it, come to understand it, and judge it as true. This is our definition of the good, namely, what an authentic person seeks in asking value questions; sorts out alternatives, possibilities, relevant perspectives and facts; affirms the preponderance of evidence inferring one position; and affirms that position in a judgment of value.

The Good as Metaphysical Element: Implications

In saying that the good is to be viewed as a metaphysical element in the same way as potency, form, and act, what are we committing ourselves to? What are the implications of taking this position? What does it mean to say that the good is a metaphysical element in this sense?

(1) It means that everything has a value. Being is the objective of the desire to know. Being is known integrally by experience, understanding, and judging truth and value. Every being in this universe of proportionate being is intrinsically constituted by the metaphysical elements of potency, form, act and value. This is a philosophical position. There are no exceptions in our universe. This is the big picture, the most general statement that one can make, that everything is good. The notion of the good is part of the integral heuristic structure of proportionate being.

Some might ask, how do we reach this position that being is convertible with the good, that is, intrinsically good. I would turn the question around and ask, do we or do we not value our universe and all that is in it? It would be strange not to value your own life and the immediate social, economic, and physical conditions that makes human flourishing possible. It would be hard not to appreciate our planet, our global village, with our multiple dependencies on other countries, and peoples, and nations. It would be hard not to value our solar system, our galaxy, our universe, and fourteen billion years of history. It would be hard not to value the kind of universe we are living in, defined as a generalized emergent probability, with four constitutive metaphysical elements at its core. We are of the universe, subject to its rules, emergent from its potencies, and forever tied to its fate. We translate the theoretical position that being is ontologically good into concrete judgments of the value of the universe, and of its crowning achievement, ourselves.

(2) The goodness of individual concrete things is to be identified and specified by individual people of all walks of life, whether scientists, philosophers, or ordinary folk. Everything has some value, from some point of view, in some way, depending on one's perspective. Each individual reality can be examined in its details to determine to what degree and from what point of view it is good. Just as there are degrees of intelligibility, so also there are degrees of goodness and degrees of worth.

(3) If we assert that everything is good, how is it that there is so much evil? We deal with that later in the chapter. In brief, our conclusion will be that there is nothing that is intrinsically evil in the universe. What we sometimes think of as evil we find to be a privation, a lack of intelligibility, an absence of what should be there. We noted that our universe is developing and hence heading towards completion and perfection—but has not arrived yet. From this negative argument that nothing is intrinsically evil, we can again affirm that all being is good.

(4) The metaphysics we are proposing does not have a specific content of its own. It is the special sciences, which parcel out all the areas and data and fields to be their content; it is the specialists who make specific statements about the truth and value in each individual area of research. The integral heuristic structure fits all these pieces together into a general worldview of the truth and value for the whole of the universe. Metaphysics has a function and a method to unify and transform all these individual contributions of people of common sense, of specialists, doctors, social scientists, politicians, and the like. Metaphysics unifies these contributions because it allows us to understand the parts by how they fit together in the whole. It transforms them because mistakes are often made and have to be corrected or excluded.

(5) Any other philosophical approach would seem to treat the good as an add-on, a postscript, an alien element, an extrinsic component. The beauty of the idea of the good as a metaphysical element is that it fits seamlessly into our definition of metaphysics based on our method of using isomorphism

to identify the four levels of the activities of knowing and the four elements known in these activities. I will deal with disputed questions later.

(6) Our worldview would include an ecological appreciation of the vast diversity of the natural world in all its wonder. We have insisted that an integral cognitional structure must include a knowledge of values attained in a judgment of value. An integral worldview of the universe must appreciate its value as a whole and the value of every detail, variation, and specialization that constitutes the whole. Being is essentially good; there is no being that is intrinsically evil.

(7) The advantage of defining the metaphysical elements in relation to the activities of cognitional structure is that all of us are personally familiar with the activities of knowing and evaluating. We perform these activities every day, and the more we pay attention to these activities, the more we can identify with the sequence, the process, the ups and downs of how we know truth and value. We can become very familiar with the varieties and details and all the processes of feeling, willing, understanding and transcending that go into them. In that way, we have an indirect control and understanding of the truths and values that are intended and reached in the activity of evaluating. We have an indirect but real way of defining particular goods and good in general.

(8) Applying Lonergan's method of isomorphism to the metaphysical categories of potency, form, and act brings an end to empty metaphysical disputation. So perhaps extending this isomorphism to knowing the good allows us to define the good in a verifiable way that avoids empty disputation on the good/value. You avoid empty disputation in metaphysics because every proposition in metaphysics has an empirical referent to the process of knowing which produced it. The process of knowing is a conscious process and so is accessible to anyone by way of self-appropriation. Similarly, any affirmations that a philosopher makes about value must be backed up by judgment of value and the process leading to such judgments. Values are either true or false. Affirming or denying values depends on the attentiveness, intelligence, reason, and responsibility of the subject. Values are not arbitrary or emotional preferences or choices. The good is the objective of a desire to know. People naturally have a notion of value, we wonder about value, we have deliberative insights into value, and through judgments of value we come to know the real existence of a true value. It is only authentic human persons who can attain authentic true values. Individuals acting in the context of a distorted consciousness will not attain a true pure notion of value.

The Good as Metaphysical Element: Applied

We distinguished the philosopher from the scientist by distinguishing generalizing from specifying. This distinction is also applicable for our understanding of the good. The metaphysician is a generalist; he/she generalizes from the multiplicity of judgments of value made in all fields of human understanding. He/she provides a framework of principles and causes into which the particular judgments of value of specific specialists find their proper context and home. As we emphasized from the beginning, philosophy studies the whole and the sciences and common sense study the parts.

This applies to the good as well. The metaphysician answers general questions about the good, especially in the field of methodology. The specialists in all sciences and disciplines answer specific questions about specific value issues. Specialists, such as economists, doctors, politicians, administrators, teachers, farmers and fishermen, are faced with making value judgments every minute of every day. Their work is permeated with choices based on evaluations. They have to make decisions which might have ramifications for many others. Usually, they will have adopted an implicit scale of values by which they judge specific situations. They have adopted a worldview regarding values. Metaphysicians have the luxury of working out an explicit correct worldview and might have something to contribute to guide and direct specialists. Let us identify the many ways in which the correct metaphysical position on the good will help individuals involved in the multitude of specific judgments of value, whether it be of common sense, science, practical disciplines, or religion.

(1) Avoidance of Common Misunderstandings. We have as a first task justified the process of value judgments by way of self-appropriation. Values are not arbitrary preferences, nor emotive choices, random behaviors, irrational statements, or mere opinions. Value judgments are answers to questions about the good, followed by deliberation and evaluation, followed by an affirmation based on all relevant experience, understanding and truths, followed by appropriate actions. Our position on the good already counters the many misunderstandings, distortions, and wrong ideas about good and value. These unbalanced and distorted worldviews are numerous and very common. Emotivism promotes the notion that values are arbitrary preferences based on emotion and desires. Subjectivism suggests that all value judgments are subjective and therefore relative, and therefore there is no room for objective values binding on everyone. Hedonism suggests that pleasure is the only worthwhile object of desire. Nihilism professes to have no values and despairs at arriving at any value,

in any case, for whatever reason. Materialists can only recognize vital and social values and would devalue cultural and religious values. Our position stands in sharp contrast with these positions.

(2) Cooperation with Specialists in Their Own Area of Work. Evaluations do not have to be explanatory or professional or erudite. Parents, politicians, teachers, farmers, biologists, doctors, businesspeople, economists, lawyers, policemen, fishermen, administrators, and the like, are constantly making concrete, particular, contextualized judgments about what is the best thing to do in the here and now. Some of these judgments will be correct and will promote progress and value in that particular area of human life. Some of them will be mistaken, distorted, biased and selfish and will promote decline. One can only hope that the self-correcting process of asking and answering questions will kick in and gradually promote progress and reverse decline. It is the metaphysician who can affirm that there is such a self-correcting process at work, that it is rooted in the desire to know and unfolds according to the exigencies of the four levels of cognition outlined in our diagram 1.

There is a goodness proper to the parts to be identified by specialists in every area. Everything can be individually affirmed as good by competent people from their particular perspective. There is nothing in a dictionary that cannot be qualified by the adjective good or bad. But there is also a goodness of the whole to be understood by the philosopher whose job it is to articulate a worldview of a rich and good universe. As philosophers we affirm that just as every concrete part of the proportionate universe will incorporate an essential element of the sensible, the intelligible, and the real, so also it will incorporate an element of goodness.

(3) Affirmation That All Is Good. From the position of the generalist, the metaphysician, we can affirm that everything that is sensible, intelligible, and actual is also good. All the particular concrete affirmations of value can be summed up in the position that the universe is all good. The position we are taking is that everything in the universe is good. This is a position based on our principle of isomorphism, "being is what is to be known by the totality of true judgments."[14] It seems to follow that the good is what is to be known by the totality of correct judgments of value. The metaphysician presents an integral heuristic structure of proportionate being which includes its worth. The good is concrete in the sense that in this universe it can only exist instantiated in individual concrete beings or persons or actions. The good is also universal in the sense that it can be generalized: all

14. Lonergan, *Insight,* 374.

things are good. It is not subsistent in the sense of Plato's notion of a World of Forms. We are developing the position that the intelligibility of the world and its reality are coterminous with the good of the world. We will deal with the problem of evil at the end of this section.

(4) Analyzing Goods as Potential, Formal, and Actual. One can also distinguish between potential good, formal good and actual good. A potential good might be a manifold, a chaos, a lack of order; it is good as it is, but it could be better. Possible solutions are proposed, plans are made, ideals are approved of and so you have a formal good; a theoretical solution but it is still up in the air. Finally, you have the implementation of the solution, the actual solution is realized, the situation has been improved. Children are potentially good or virtuous; they become good by doing acts of goodness; in the end they are actually virtuous, when the habit of virtue is instilled in them.

(5) Classifying Kinds of Goods. Good is an analogous term and can be applied to many things, principles, policies, and behaviors with nuances of meaning in each case. One can classify different kinds of goods. One can establish a hierarchy of importance between these kinds of goods. In most concrete situations many different values are at stake; some are conflicting, and some are complementary. One way of classifying values is to follow the five levels of human consciousness which we will specify in our diagram 4 on the Human Person. In that we distinguish vital values, social values, cultural values, moral values, and religious values in a hierarchy of values. Let us just sketch what we mean by this distinction.

By vital values we refer to the goodness of everything that sustains life; the atoms, molecules, the cells, the organisms, the environment, the development and proliferation of living things, the promotion of the conditions for living things and humans to flourish. Food, air, water, exercise, propagation, safety, security, material conditions, agriculture, work, buildings, and all that promotes conditions for human flourishing are vital values. An old adage claimed, *mens sana in corpore sano,* a healthy mind in a healthy body.

Social values would include social organization, the common good, the good of order, efficiency of a well-ordered society, the functioning of an economy and production, institutions for health, education, social welfare, communications, transport, infrastructure. We are social animals and depend on such social conditions and also promote or damage them by our way of life. We look after ourselves and our families but usually in the context of a wider community, state, nation, and world.

By cultural values we refer to the beliefs and values of the society. These are embodied in the educational institutions, the political processes, the media, entertainers, the policies enacted and enforced. Fascism, communism, socialism, capitalism, democracy, embody central truths about human living and the priorities for what they consider progress and decline.

By moral values we mean the values of the human person acting as a free and responsible person. A person can be aiming at self-satisfaction or at true values. To move from self-satisfaction to true values is a process of moral development and conversion that starts with obedience to external moral laws, moves to increasing autonomy, and eventually reaches the subject taking responsibility for his/her own becoming, as well as how her/his actions affect others and the environment.

By religious values we mean valuing religious experience, activities of worship, prayer, reverence, loving God and neighbor. This has to be included in a comprehensive view of human persons. We will deal with *homo religiosus* in chapter 14.

Good then is an analogous term. It applies at different levels and there are degrees of goodness. Nor are we denying the existence of evil in a modified sense. Being is good, this person is good, this apple is good, this policy is good, and so on. What does Genesis mean when it says, "God saw all that he had made, and indeed it was very good"?

(6) Degrees of Goodness. There are degrees of goodness just as there are degrees of intelligibility. It may be surprising to some that we affirm the goodness of the universe and yet there are so many floods, diseases, corruption, imperfections in the real world. Good does not necessarily mean perfect, or complete, or developed, or predictable, or static. In fact, our universe is emergent and embodies an element of chance, but is aimed in the direction of the developed, the more perfect, the higher, the better. We will describe this universe of generalized emergent probability in greater detail in our next chapter. Much of what we refer to as evils in the universe, such as earthquakes, extreme weather conditions, disease, accidents, are part and parcel of a universe that is emergent according to schemes of probabilities.

If you or I were creating a universe, it would probably be fairly small, flat, static, dominated by straight lines, circles and squares, and it would be perfect, or at least perfect as we would imagine perfection. It would be finished, complete, ordered to the nth degree; it would be mechanical, material, clockwork and boring. There would be no untidy chance, no freedom or imperfection, no living things that are born, eat and then die. In our world humans would always be happy! There would be no evil people or things. We have a rather limited notion of how to make a universe!

The universe we live in is thankfully much richer and larger than this anthropomorphic utopia. It is good in many dynamic ways: alive, striving, growing and developing. It is vast and diverse in the expanse of the galaxies and mysterious down to the smallest neutrino. It has regularity, system, permanence, stability built into it. But there is also room for chance, room for development, room for innovation and change. It is not a flat earth universe but multileveled, including subatomic particles, elements, compounds, cells, plants, animals of innumerable diverse genera and species. It allows for coincidences, for stability in some areas and variety in others, chaos, a matrix of mixtures from which sometimes something really new and important emerges. That is the kind of universe we live in.

No matter what Leibniz speculated on the best of all possible worlds, this is in fact the kind of universe we are living in, and it is wonderful to behold. We are not really in a position to say what a better universe might look like. We must face the reality of the kind of universe we actually live in and make the best of it.

There is a finality operating in our universe which we will identify in detail later. It is toward an ultimate end or goal that our world is dynamic, developing, purposeful, moving from incomplete to complete, from undifferentiated to differentiated, from unintegrated to integrated, from undeveloped to developed, from lower to higher, from chaos to order, from simple to complex. As metaphysicians we see the whole picture as moving from potency, to form, to act, to goodness and beauty.

Our universe is rich, diverse, multi-layered, beautiful, deeply complex, interrelated, supremely intelligible, unpredictable, in a word, awesome. The human beings that have emerged are similarly developing, multi-layered, intelligent, reasonable, responsible, and open to the divine. They are free beings, responsible for their own judgments and choices, capable of great goodness and holiness, but also prone to depravity and corruption.

(7) An Ecological Ontology. The attitude of ancient civilizations was to live in tune with nature, to respect its laws, to hunt, to gather and to plant in a sustainable manner. They took what they needed and left nature in good shape for generations to come. The modern period has seen a process where nature has been exploited, despoiled, and instrumentalized. The seas have been overfished, the land and air have been polluted with artificial fertilizer, insecticide, noxious gasses and not allowed to recover. Common sense just thinks of the short-term gain and not of the future generations who inherit poisoned land and depend on genetically modified seeds. Resources are exhausted, species become extinct, and human induced climate change threatens our very survival. We need to think of ourselves as guardians of the goodness of the earth and nature. We need to think of everything in terms of sustainability, in terms of future generations, in terms of preserving the

richness of nature. The planet belongs not to us but to future generations. We need an ecological conversion in terms of a change of our attitude to nature. Pope Francis' *Laudato si* issues a call to precisely this kind of fundamental shift in values towards respecting nature and its laws and richness, and living in a sustainable, simple way that does not destroy the environment. This fits well with our own affirmation of the goodness of nature, of variety, of richness, of the elements of our planet and universe that are good, not simply from the point of view of being useful, but in themselves.

(8) The Good of Human Persons. The peak of our universe is ourselves as human persons and our extraordinary capacity to experience, to feel, to understand, to judge what is true and good and beautiful, to make free and responsible decisions, to have a religious experience and to relate to God as Creator. As far as we know, we are the highest peak of development that the universe has reached. The finality of the universe from undifferentiated to integrated, and from chaos to order and the like, find their highest achievement in human persons. Our human intelligence is an infinite capacity to do and to make; artificial intelligence is but a pale reflection of the intelligence of the engineers and technicians, mathematicians and manufacturers who have managed to combine their expertise in computers, smart phones, data analysis and the like. We are different from bonobos and chimpanzees, not as a matter of degree but as a matter of a new higher species emerging as a new substance from the developed sensitivity of higher animals. We embody a responsibility for our own progress, for that of our neighbor, and for the good of the planet.

Humans encompass all that is good in animal sensitivity—feeling, senses, brain, ability to survive, to reproduce, and to thrive—with the added addition of intelligence, reason, knowledge of true and good, free decisions, moral responsibility, and a capacity to worship God. We experience love, forgiveness, compassion, empathy, respect, sincerity, and the like. In us the universe becomes conscious of itself through us. We have emerged from this particular universe. We depend for our survival on the proper use and care of this environment. We are one with the universe which has produced us. We take responsibility for the future of our earth. (The good of the human person will be dealt with more systematically in chapter 14.)

The Problem of Evil

All of the above may have sounded very optimistic. What of the evils of floods, diseases, earthquakes, droughts, breakdowns, pandemics, extinctions, dead ends, regressions, disasters, failures, in the history of the planet! What of the evil of human persons who kill, torture, extort, abuse, and manipulate other people and society as a whole! What of the hatred, the dishonesty, the viciousness, and the selfishness of people! And where does a good God come in, for surely a good God would not permit the suffering of the innocent or the triumph of evil. Our general procedure will be to show that no being is intrinsically evil in itself as an entity; evil is to be understood as a privation, an absence of an expected intelligibility. Evil can only be understood by means of an inverse insight, by which we understand the absence of something that we expected to be there. Let us distinguish three kinds of evil:

(1) Physical Evil. We have already asserted briefly that our universe is one of generalized emergent probability which will be elaborated in our next chapter. This means that the universe is dynamic and emergent: it is moving from potency, to form, to act and goodness: from incomplete to complete, from undifferentiated to differentiated and integrated, from developing to developed. The earth's tectonic plates are cooling and hence contracting and that inevitably causes earthquakes and volcanic eruptions. There is some kind of principle of survival of the fittest operative in nature by which the adaptable survive and the inflexible are left behind. There is a mixture of stable elements providing structure and continuity, and unstable elements being the womb of novelty and innovation. Extinctions leave the way open for new developments and adaptations. There is an element of probability, of unpredictability, of the possibility of failure, in all this, and it applies to the emergence of human beings as well as everything else. We have already compared our diverse, rich, emergent, complex, integrated, differentiated, immense universe with our imaginary human utopia of a perfect, static, repetitious, stagnant, aimless, determined, universe. We cannot condemn such physical evils as earthquakes, or diseases, as intrinsically evil. They are part and parcel of the kind of universe we live in, which is intrinsically good. Privations not only make way for new things but also for better things, more complex, interdependent, powerful, intelligent, free things. There is also a beauty and intelligence in the diversity and complexity favoring some things and not others.

(2) Human Evil. We divide human evil into basic moral evil and the consequences of such evil in society. Basic evil arises from insufficient love of the good; it arises when we are not committed sufficiently to judge what is the best course of action, and so we often choose the most pleasurable or selfish alternative. If we were committed to what is best for us as well as

for our family and the whole community, we would have made a different choice. This is the root of human evil or basic sin. It is an evil, but it arises from an absence, a privation, something that should be there but is not, namely, concern for the whole. Our basic orientation as human persons is to desire and to know what is true and good, to decide for and implement goodness and values. However, human persons also experience and desire the apparent good and are fundamentally free to choose whatever they will or not. Good choices build up the habit of virtue; bad choices build up the habit of vice. There is the possibility of continuous development towards a good character; and also the possibility of continuous decline towards selfishness and bad will. That is the root of human evil, and it is basically a privation, a lack of what should be there. Evil is not an entity, it is not a substance, it is the lack of responsible, committed, determination to fulfil one's potential as a human person. Evil is often defined as a negation of what should be there, for instance, inattentive, unreasonable, irrational, irresponsible, impatient, unnatural, disorder, irregular, unkind, unjust, impious, and so on. It just illustrates how evil is a privation, a negation, an absence of something that should be there.

(3) Consequences of Human Evil. No man is an island, and so the repercussions of that absence of commitment to human values and ensuing behavior reverberate from the individual to the family, to the community, to the city, to the nation, to the world. The social evils of disorder, division, civil strife, discrimination, injustice, corruption, can all be traced to this lack of conviction for vital, social, cultural, moral and religious values. Social disorder is a lack of order; corruption springs from a lack of integrity; discrimination arises from individual, group or general bias. What should be in an ordered, just, efficient, healthy, honest, society, is not there, and corruption of various forms take their place.

The condition for the possibility for human evil and corrupt societies is that humans are fundamentally free. It is the misuse of human freedom that is the source of personal and social evils. It is misguided to blame God for evils brought about by human choice to misuse the gift of freedom. If there were a universe without human evils, that would be a universe of humans who are not free. If humans were not genuinely free, would they be truly human or would they be at same level as bonobos or cows?

While human corruption and conflict are in themselves tragic, they present the possibility of greater goods to arise. They are a challenge to good people, an opportunity to overcome evil by doing good. Much of one's efforts in philosophy is to overcome misunderstanding and ignorance. Much of our work in politics is to overcome entrenched selfish or group-interests and dubious practices. Much of the work of moving towards an ethical society is to overcome the bias, the blindness, the violence that is so common. In overcoming these evils, we build better selves and societies.

Difficulties: Imaginary and Real

(1) *Imaginative Difficulties.* The difficulties we have with affirming that the good is a metaphysical element are similar to the difficulties we have with affirming existence as a metaphysical element. Existence adds nothing to this horse but existence; value adds nothing to this horse but value. However, to say that something exists is somewhat important and meaningful. To say that something is of value is even more important and more meaningful. We try to imagine existence as something separate and apart, waiting to be joined with essence and are not satisfied with the real as the content of true judgments. Similarly, we try to imagine the good as separate and apart and encounter the same imaginative difficulties as to whether it is real or not. Either we imagine it to belong to the real world of the Platonic world of ideas, or we cannot imagine it at all and so dismiss it as a chimera. But goodness is part of the real world. There are real, verifiable, and operative distinctions between good, better, best. There are degrees of goodness; there are levels of the good. There are vital, social, cultural, moral and religious values which are either true or false. The critical realist position is that the truth is what is affirmed in a correct judgment of truth. In parallel, we can say that the good is what is affirmed in a correct judgment of value. Knowing the good takes more than just imagination: it takes experience, understanding, judging truth and authentic appreciations.

(2) *From Theory to Interiority.* Traditional Scholastic metaphysics treated the good as one of the transcendental properties of being, along with truth, unity and beauty. An ontological notion of goodness affirmed the good to be convertible with being. Mostly they followed Aristotle in defining the good as the object of appetite. A theoretical approach starts with metaphysics, derives definitions and concepts from a vague process of generalization, but is not based on self-knowledge, and has no criterion for eliminating endless disputation.

An approach to metaphysics based on interiority starts with an epistemology based on self-appropriation and discovers therein a basic invariant structure of intentional activities. After distinguishing and relating those activities, this approach shifts the focus of attention from the activities to the content of these activities and discovers in that content the world of being, the distinction between proportionate and transcendent being, the four structural elements of the universe of proportionate being, and the criterion to distinguish real understanding of metaphysics from empty speculation. The criterion is that every metaphysical assertion must have some corresponding epistemological justification. If there is a cognitional content it is very relevant that it is known and can only be known by a process of asking questions, observing data, organizing and understanding the data, formulating the ideas or definitions to answer those questions, asking the critical question, reflecting on the sufficiency of the evidence and positing the consequent judgment of truth followed usually by the question of value, a deliberative insight and a judgment of value.

(3) Is Value a Fourth Metaphysical Element? Lonergan was asked on three separate occasions whether "good" could be considered as a metaphysical element in the same sense as potency, form and act. He did not embrace the idea; he seems to have excluded it; but he did not explicitly reject it.[15]

Michael Vertin, a respected Lonergan scholar, had previously accepted the idea of four metaphysical elements[16] but then retracted the idea. In a further article in 2003 he again asserts the position that the distinction between act as real and act as good is only notional. He states, "I contend that the distinction between potency, form (or first act), and act (or second act) are real distinctions whereas the distinction between act as real and act as good is merely notional."[17] For Lonergan a notional distinction occurs when: P is not Q; P is merely an object of thought; and Q is merely an object of thought. He gives the example of "a centaur is not a unicorn."[18] This does not seem to fit with the distinction between act and good. Although the meaning of a notional distinction may vary according to different authors, I would think that the distinction between real and good is more than a notional distinction.

Lonergan takes the position that the good is identical with being. He deals with the human good in terms of objects of desire, the good of order, and judgments of value. He generalizes from this to treat of potential, formal and actual good, "where the potential good is identical with potential intelligibility and so includes but also extends beyond objects of desire, where the formal good is identical with formal intelligibility and so includes but also extends beyond human intelligible orders, where the actual good

---

15. These texts are gathered together by Michael Vertin in "Lonergan's Metaphysics of Value and Love," 195–205.

16. Vertin, "Lonergan's Three Basic Questions," 227–28n11.

17. Vertin, "Acceptance and Actualization," 74.

18. Lonergan, *Insight*, 513.

is identical with actual intelligibilities and so includes but also may extend beyond human values."[19] He concludes that subsection by stating: "So the good is identified with the intelligibility intrinsic to being."[20] All this was written around 1953 and published in 1957. However, in 1965 Lonergan realized that there is a distinct notion of value, over and above the notions of the intelligible and of the actual. He spoke more of the question of value, deliberation and evaluation, and the judgment of value.

What then are we to make of the distinction between, the sensible, the intelligible, the actual and the good? Transposing the whole context into a framework of interiority analysis and a consequent metaphysics I would suggest the following:

There is a real distinction between the activities of experiencing, understanding, judging truth, and judging value. Each cognitional activity when it occurs is really distinct from the other activities. The relations between the activities have been defined in terms of emergence, sublation, and dependence. In a judgment of value, the four activities are subsumed into one knowing of a particular, real value, but the four activities are distinct from one another; they are not identical and do not become identical.

The contents of these activities are also really distinct from one another, namely, the sensible, the intelligible, the existent and the good. A good computer incorporates an element of the sensible, of the intelligible, of the existent, and of value. The contents are really distinct from the activities. The subject knowing, and the contents known are really distinct. We established the principal notion of objectivity by affirming that I am a knower, this is a computer, and I am not this computer.

Much ink was spilled on the question of the real distinction between essence and existence in the Middle Ages and up to the present day. The Thomist position is that there is a real distinction between essence and existence. The reason for the existence of this computer does not come from within the computer but from outside: the computer does not explain its own existence, it is not self-explanatory, it is contingent and not necessary. Existence is added from the outside, though we should resist imagining existence as a property or a spooky entity or as a thing in itself. Hence, we would affirm that there is a real distinction between form and act, between possible and real. Lonergan affirms quite explicitly: "Minor real distinctions are between the element or constituents of proportionate being, that is, between central and conjugate potency, form and act."[21]

19. Lonergan, *Insight*, 628.
20. Lonergan, *Insight*, 629.
21. Lonergan, *Insight*, 514; also 525.

I would propose that the same line of argument applies to the distinction between the actual and the good. They are really distinct even if it is a minor real distinction. Goodness is not a property to be imagined, not a spooky entity, not a thing in itself. The real is good in virtue of the fact that all that exists can also be affirmed to be good. Distinct does not mean separate or separable or apart from one another.

Is the good identical with the intelligibility intrinsic to being? We have two words, the intelligible and the good. They do not have the same meaning. The intelligible refers to form, to what is understood, to the idea or explanation. The good refers to the aspect of the intelligible, which is valuable, worthwhile, a value, as a good. A computer is an intelligible notion; a good computer adds the element of value or good of the computer. If we have two words intelligible and good and use them in different contexts with different meanings, surely there must be some distinction between the intelligible and the good. I suggest that it is a minor real distinction in Lonergan's sense.

Traditional metaphysics did not have a method for removing endless disputation. A methodical metaphysics based on the principle of isomorphism does give you a method of ending useless disputation. Statement of metaphysical distinctions must be rooted and justified by their cognitional correlates. That is what I have tried to do. The judgment of truth is different from the judgment of value not in its structure but in its intentionality. I conclude that the distinction between true and good is a minor real distinction.

Conclusion

In this chapter we have focused on the good as a metaphysical element. We have used the method of isomorphism noting the proportion between the good as originating in the subject and genuine terminal values. We have identified the judgment of value as on a level distinct from the judgment of truth and emerging from a process of questioning, deliberating, understanding and concluding. We distinguished the affective context of the judgment of truth from that of evaluating. We have concluded that the good is a metaphysical element of proportionate being, meaning that every proportionate being is ontologically and intrinsically good, that evil is a privation of goodness, that there are degrees and levels of goodness, that good is an analogical term. We have also seen that the good that is our universe is developing, emergent, works according to both classical and statistical laws and therefore there is an element of chance operating. We have discussed that it is good people who are the best judges of the goodness in policies, in morals, in decision making, in the good of order, in the goodness of human relationships. And we have considered when people fail to choose the good and instead commit evil with dire consequences.

We live in a complex universe of proportionate being. The temptation in painting the big picture is to simplify everything into one element or aspect or thing. The most common simplification to be found in modern culture is that the universe is raw matter, that matter is physical, that matter is the only reality of the universe, and that everything else is subjective, construction, imposition, or invention. Our method of self-appropriation and isomorphism of knowing and reality allows us to affirm with certainty that there are four levels of a basic, invariant, structure of knowing and that each level intends the objective proper to that level. That each of these objectives, the sensible, the intelligible, the real and the valuable can be affirmed to be a metaphysical element of the universe of proportionate being, namely, an invariant, structural, constitutive, universal element.

To have a correct, complete and critical overall picture of the kind of universe we live in is extremely important; it promotes good science, ensures the implementation of scientific method, and fits particular solutions into a big picture. To have a distorted notion of the big picture inevitably leads to wrong questions, wasted effort, distorted conclusions and lots of misunderstandings. The scientist needs the metaphysician just as the metaphysician needs the scientist.

Part Three: **An Emergent, Diverse, Ordered, Universe**

9

Generalized Emergent Probability

Just as cognitional activity is the becoming known of being, so objective process is the becoming of proportionate being. Indeed, since cognitional activity is itself but a part of this universe, so its heading to being is but the particular instance in which universal striving towards being becomes conscious and intelligent and reasonable.[1]

All that has been learned empirically about evolution in general and mental process in particular suggests that the brain is a machine assembled not to understand itself, but to survive.[2]

The true physics is that which will one day, achieve the inclusion of man in his wholeness in a coherent picture of the world.[3]

Like successful Chicago gangsters, our genes have survived, in some cases for millions of years, in a highly competitive world. . . . I shall argue that a predominant quality to be expected in a successful gene is ruthless selfishness. . . . Much as we might wish to believe otherwise, universal love and the welfare of the species as a whole are concepts that simply do not make evolutionary sense.[4]

Dynamic or Static Universe?

IN PART 2, THE argument focused on an analysis of the invariant basic metaphysical structure of each and every instance of proportionate being. Each known truth about the universe is somehow constituted by an element of

1. Lonergan, *Insight*, 470.
2. Wilson, *Consilience*, 105.
3. Teilhard de Chardin, *The Phenomenon of Man*, 40.
4. Dawkins, *The Selfish Gene*, 2.

potency, an element of form, an element of existence, and an element of goodness. Put very simply, our metaphysical elements can be defined simply as: potency is that which is experienced, form is that which is understood, act is that which is affirmed correctly to exist, and goodness can be affirmed in correct judgments of value. Each element is equally real and important, and the four together constitute the intrinsic structure of our universe. This analysis might be called horizontal, across the board, applying to everything in the realm of proportionate being, past, present and future. That analysis was based on an examination that could be called synchronic or static. It was a cross section of the universe at any particular time.

But the universe is always changing and developing, and so we have to consider it from a dynamic or diachronic point of view. The universe has a history, and there is nothing in the universe that can be adequately understood without understanding its history. In part 3, we now set out to do that, not as geologists or historians or cosmologists, but as meta-physicians. We will continue to use our method of isomorphism. There is a pattern to the development of the human mind that is reflected in the pattern of the development of the universe. Each chapter will recognize the particular parallel and proportionate similarities between the process of knowing and the dynamics operating in the known.

A static universe would be one in which everything continues basically the same for ever and ever. It was the common view of the universe up to modern times. It is vividly illustrated in the story of Noah in the Bible. A male and a female of each species had to be brought into the ark and saved from the flood; otherwise, there would be a permanent loss. The presumption was that God had created each of these genera and species and that is how they should continue for ever and ever. Not one of them could be lost because there was no way of recovery. Aristotle described a universe that had no beginning and no end. Although it changed, there was no overall direction to the change. Aristotle identified a hierarchy of genera and species, but he saw them as permanently established and had no idea of how they emerged or diversified, or how new species could come into being.

In a static universe it would be impossible for a higher form to emerge from lower forms. It would be impossible for life to emerge from the non-living, and it would be impossible for intelligent form to emerge from non-intelligent, and thus spiritual could not emerge from material. Sometimes it is presumed that being is static because the notion of being is regarded as abstract and abstract concepts as such do not change. But whether the universe is static or dynamic is a question of empirical fact. It cannot be presumed that the universe is static and that therefore higher forms cannot emerge from lower forms. Nor can it be presumed that the universe is dynamic; this is also a matter of empirical investigation. To resolve the issue, we have to attend to our own knowing and the proportionate known and discern whether being is static or dynamic.

In modern times, we have learned to think historically. We accept that the universe is also dynamic and changing. Any explanation must include a historical perspective. We can only understand things if we understand how they emerged, where they came from, and how they developed. Philosophers such as Hegel, Marx, Comte, Alfred L. Whitehead introduced us to various visions of a developing universe. German historical scholarship introduced this thinking into interpretation of texts, changing contexts of thought, and our own dependence on history. Above all, it was the biologist Charles Darwin who introduced the notion of evolution according to the survival of the fittest of all living things. Teilhard de Chardin integrated a notion of evolution into Christian thinking. Nowadays we tend to think in historical terms, presuming a changing universe, a developing situation, and a dynamic framework.

Lonergan rarely uses the term "evolution." I presume he did not want to be identified with Darwin and Neo-Darwinism. Instead, he uses the term "generalized emergent probability" to describe world process as a whole and the principles operating in this process. It is a fundamental answer to the question, what kind of a universe are we living in?

By using the term "generalized," Lonergan is emphasizing that these principles apply across the board, that the universe of proportionate being operates according to these general principles. It is not that everything is emerging or developing in the same way at the same pace. Rather, the process of emergence admits of failures, dead ends, static immobility, degeneration, decomposition, decline, in specific areas. But that does not detract from the overall process of a generalized emergence of new and higher forms. This chapter will refine our understanding of the principle of finality, as it applies to the knowing and the known (§§2–3), through an analysis of the notion of emergence (§§4–6), and finally the role of probability (§7). In the following chapters we will go into the details of how these principles operate on, things and properties, on genera and species, on living things, and finally on the emergence of human persons. It is hoped that we will then have a general notion of what kind of a universe we are living in, an overall heuristic for understanding any particular time, topic, area, or phenomenon, in the unfolding of our universe from the beginning to the unknown end.

Finality of Human Intelligence

One of the basic principles for understanding the dynamic aspect of the universe is the principle of finality. It is very important to formulate this principle of finality correctly and precisely to avoid confusion. Finality is an aspect of the basic framework for understanding in all of the explanatory sciences. It is often glibly taken for granted, misconceived, exaggerated or denied. It is not the same as Darwinian evolution. Some assume that things evolve and see no need to focus on the intelligibility of evolution or natural selection or a more general principle of finality.

We are not talking about purpose or final cause. We are not asking why God created the universe. We are not asking about the purpose of different organs or genera or species. We are looking for the immanent intelligibility of the being of this universe. We are not talking of a pull from the future on the present, nor a push from the past on the present. We are not talking of final cause, the purpose for which something is made. The final cause is extrinsic to the thing, but we are talking of intrinsic intelligibility expressed in the principle of finality. Nor are we talking of the beginning of the universe or the end of the universe, but simply the universe as we know it now. We are talking of the intelligibility of the whole as dynamic or static. Is it dynamic or static? In what way is that dynamism to be understood?

Our starting point as usual is the activity of knowing and so our first question is whether our knowing is static or dynamic. Now that is not a hard question to answer after all our self-appropriation of the experience of knowing. Central to knowing is understanding. Understanding occurs only in the context of a question, the tension of inquiry, the desire to know. The correct answer to one question closes off that question but immediately opens up dozens more. The answers to those questions do not lead to a blank wall but to further questions and further insights. The more you know, the more questions you can ask, and you want to know the answers. The development of understanding in depth and width never ends; it is relentlessly pushing forward. And thus, we recognise the pure, detached, unrestricted desire to know as the principle of the finality in the activity of understanding.

Development in understanding is a directed development; questions seek understanding, they focus on data to produce understanding. In other words, they have a finality. Understanding, when formulated, leads to the further question: "Is it true?" This further question seeks and leads to the reflective understanding and the judgment where knowledge reaches a term, and we start again on a new or related topic. Questioning experience, attaining understanding, and moving on to knowing, then to evaluating, is the intrinsic dynamic of knowing. In principle, there is no end to this process of asking and answering further questions. The whole process emerges spontaneously and unfolds relentlessly. Our knowing is incomplete and tends to completeness; it is imperfect and tends to perfection; it is undifferentiated and tends to differentiation and integration. It is a directed dynamism aiming from experiencing data, to understanding, to knowing, judging and valuing. The directed dynamism of intelligence can be seen also in the move from description, to theory, to interiority. Our knowing becomes broader, clearer, deeper, more complete, more integrated and comprehensive; we approach the ideal of wisdom. This directed, intrinsic dynamism toward wisdom is the finality of knowing. This is what we mean by finality.

Of course, this does not mean that we are always progressing. Sometimes we spend months in a blind alley, working on a false or misguided hypothesis, doing research that turns out to prove nothing. Sometimes the desire to know is smothered by other desires that are more easily satisfied. Sometimes ulterior motives intrude and the whole direction of our knowing is hijacked for power or for corruption or for personal self-interest. But the overall picture of the finality of inquiring intelligence is incontrovertible. Particularly in our early years we made great strides in broadening horizons as we move from kindergarten to primary school, from primary school to secondary school, from secondary to university, from undergraduate to graduate, from dissertation to teaching, from instructor to full professor. Nor are we asserting that this process is automatic or determinate or inevitable. Common experience reveals how difficult this path of intellectual development is. There can be breakdowns, cul-de-sacs, regressions, mistakes, exhaustion, deformity, or retreats. Individuals might succumb, but the overall pattern of development is clear and usually wins out in the end. We identify the dynamism of this entire process of coming to know as being governed by a principle of finality.

Finality of the Universe

The evidence for the intrinsic finality of the human mind is very familiar to us—just attend to your own mind and how it works. It is incontrovertible and overwhelming. If we pay attention to our own mind, we will find a yearning and a movement toward understanding, knowledge of truth, and knowledge of value. If our minds are dynamic, we can immediately conclude that at least one aspect of the universe of proportionate being is intrinsically dynamic. As we will show in the schema of genera and species, human beings have emerged from the universe, within the universe, according to the patterns, principles and causes of the universe of proportionate being. Humans emerged when all previous levels of genera and species had been established, and it seems we emerged only on this planet earth. Human beings emerged as conscious, intelligent, rational, responsible, free, and with a possibility of relating to God. Human beings emerged not as a peripheral, incidental, unimportant species, but as the peak of development of the universe. We are of the universe, and we display an intrinsic finality in our way of thinking, knowing, valuing, and doing. Thus, we can affirm that one important part of the universe is intrinsically dynamic. Consequently, it is clearly false to say that this universe is totally static; as some parts of the universe are simply, evidently, not static but dynamic.

Further, the principle of isomorphism leads us to expect a parallel finality in the universe of proportionate being. This principle states that the pattern of relations between the activities of knowing will have a parallel in the pattern of relations in the content of what is known. We have already applied this principle to the metaphysical elements of potency, form, act, and value from the point of view of the invariant structure of the universe. The principle of isomorphism would lead us to expect that parallel to the dynamism of intellect there is an objective counterpart in the dynamism of the universe. So it is no great surprise to find that potency gives rise to form, form is the possibility for actually existing, and what comes into existence must be appreciated. The principle of finality operating in the universe of proportionate being is the objective counterpart to the dynamism of the process of knowing. It will be our task to identify clearly what this statement entails.

It seems that the presupposition of all the sciences nowadays is some kind of evolutionary framework. Cosmologists tell us a story about the history of the development of the universe from the Big Bang to the present time. They tell of a development, from subatomic particles, to atoms of hydrogen and helium, to the emergence of the higher elements in the heat of exploding stars, to the emergence of galaxies. Then we are told of the emergence of planets, the emergence of planet earth, the emergence of life, the emergence of plants and animals, to the emergence of human beings. All the sciences seem to accept this picture and accept an evolutionary framework for each and every science. The sciences seem to confirm the presence of a principle of finality operating universally in the universe from the beginning to the present time. The operation of the principle of finality is sometimes interpreted as completely determinate and sometimes as total indeterminate. Both of these are extremes. Hence, our aims are to formulate the principle of finality in a differentiated, explicit, correct philosophical manner. We base ourselves on the principle of isomorphism: from the finality of human intellect, we expect a parallel finality in the

universe. It is gratifying to note that such finality is recognized independently in the sciences and is confirmed more and more as the sciences seek
further understanding.

"Basically, then, finality is the dynamic aspect of the real."[5] To affirm
finality is to affirm fluidity, movement, tension, approximations, incom-
pleteness, becoming. To affirm finality is to deny that the universe is static,
complete, inert, unchanging, finished. We have no difficulty affirming that
our knowing is dynamic rather than static.

We are asserting that this is an upwardly directed dynamism. Just
as questioning experience leads to understanding, and questioning understanding leads to judgment, and judgment of fact leads to judgment
of value, so also potency is the possibility of form, forms emerge from
potency, some survive and so actually exist. In that way we have a generic
dynamism of potency to form, and form to act. It is directed in the sense
that later developments depend on earlier developments. Forms cannot
emerge unless the matter is properly disposed. Higher forms presume the
pre-existence of lower forms. There is an upwardly directed dynamism
towards higher forms, towards differentiation, completion, and fulfilment.
This does not exclude blind alleys, breakdowns, extinctions, stability, de-
struction and death. But the overall picture is a universe that is moving in
a certain direction. It is not totally indeterminate; it is not only chance; it
is not pure chaos; it is not just going around in circles.

The dynamism of the universe is not a deductive process in the sense
that if you know one situation you can reliably predict what must emerge.
It is not a simple, single line of necessary development. Certain aspects
of world process, such as the movements of the planets, can be predicted,
but we still cannot predict if it will rain here tomorrow. There is no simple,
single law of finality operating with iron necessity along one line of development. It is not determinism in the mechanistic sense. Mechanistic
determinism visualizes the universe as a kind of huge mechanical clock
which ticks relentlessly on, according to fixed laws, along a predetermined
path. It is not that the goal has already been fixed and everything converges
on the goal. It is not the operation of classical laws alone but also includes
the operation of statistical laws and probabilities.

On the other hand, it is not totally indeterminate either. There is a
certain direction in which it is moving. Some are happy to assert that it all
happened by pure chance. If that were so, then the universe would be a chaos of unordered, unrelated entities and would be a total nonsense. Chance,
in itself, strictly defined is an absence of an expected intelligibility; we have

5. Lonergan, *Insight*, 472.

defined chance as the divergence of the actual from the ideal expectation of a statistical law. Chance is indirectly intelligible as you can give it a real verifiable meaning. An inverse insight grasps a lack of expected intelligibility, which is circumscribed by laws of the classical type. There is both order and disorder in the universe, the regular and the irregular, the systematic and the non-systematic, the ordered and the random, certainties and varying degrees of probability.

If finality is not completely indeterminate nor totally deductive or determinate, then how is the dynamism of finality to be understood? It is the "effectively probable realisation of possibilities."[6] Let me explain.

Potency is the possibility of form. If there is no potency, there can be no form. Potency is the foundation for the principle of finality. The forms, which can emerge, are those appropriate to the relevant potencies, or possibilities in the situation. If you have a multitude of subatomic particles, you have the possibility of atoms forming. For atoms to emerge, the temperature must be right, as well as the pressure, the material conditions, spatial distribution, and the like. If you have no subatomic particles, it is hard to think of atoms emerging from nothing. The existence of subatomic particles does not mean that necessarily, deductively, determinately, predictably, atoms of a certain kind must emerge. But the possibility is there for various kinds of atoms to emerge.

This emergence takes place according to schedules of probability. We have seen in cognitional theory that to understand any one event or happening, say an auto accident, you must understand the classical laws operating in the situation, speed, momentum, friction, centre of gravity, and the like. But you are also obliged to understand the statistical laws, the coincidence of a bald tyre, a goat on the road, sudden application of the brakes, a driver not as attentive as he should be, and so on. Classical laws deal with abstract regularities, while statistical laws deal with concrete probabilities. To know why something happens will always involve both classical and statistical laws and hence some degree of probability. The probabilities can be high or low.

By "effectively probable" we mean that if something is probable, if you allow a sufficient number of occasions, then in the end it must happen. This is explained in more detail below in a special section on Chance and Effective Probability.

This directed dynamism is realistic. It is not a utopia drawn up by a romantic idealist. It is not what we would like to happen or what should happen, if people were perfect. It is our objective understanding of the

6. Lonergan, *Insight*, 473.

real universe and the immanent intelligible principles according to which it works. It seems to be verified in the sciences and in common human experience of the events of life. It is not fanciful or vague or millenarian. Teilhard de Chardin is famous for his *Phenomenon of Man*, where he expounds a picture of a world in evolution towards higher consciousness, towards an Omega point. He tends to be mystical, vague, and utopian. It is not a clearly defined analysis of the immanent verifiable finality of the real world, which we are attempting to articulate.

Finality is universal or generalized. The principle applies to the totality of the universe, the intelligibility of the whole universe and all its parts. This does not mean that new forms are emerging everywhere. It allows for stability, for sterility, for breakdowns, for blind alleys, for extinctions, for mistakes. If everything were changing, the universe would be just chaos. Change demands that some things remain the same, while some things change. The universe we live in is a combination of permanence and change, stable and unstable, systematic and non-systematic. This seems to apply in the world of subatomic particles, in the periodic table of the elements, in the different kinds of living cells, in the vegetative realm, and in the animal kingdom. Even among human beings, you have the conservatives who generally resist change, and the progressives who favour innovation. The history of our planet attests to such vagaries in all areas of living and non-living.

Finality is nuanced. It is as concrete, as differentiated, as various, as are the multitudinous concrete beings and situations, and times and places of this world. It operates in different ways, at different times, in different places, on different things, and within schemes of recurrence. It is not one size fits all.

Finality is flexible. There is major flexibility that allows higher integrations of otherwise coincidental manifolds to emerge and therefore the emergence of new genera and species. But there is a minor flexibility where the same goal can be arrived at in a variety of different ways. One sees very many twists and turns in the evolution of species and environments.

So, that is how we see the principle of finality as the immanent intelligibility of world process. That is the dynamism of world process. It is the objective parallel to the pure desire to know; it operates in terms of potency, to form, to act, to value, in the same way as experience is related to understanding and to judgment.

We distinguish also horizontal finality from vertical finality. Horizontal finality is the tendency to develop along a fixed line. It is the tendency to repeat, to survive, to multiply the same things, to maintain the status quo. Living things reproduce and generally reproduce the same kind of living thing; this is horizontal finality. But there is also a tendency for new species to emerge given mutations, certain conditions and probabilities; this is vertical finality. Vertical finality involves a jump from a lower level to a higher level. It does involve a jump, an emergence of something new, a higher integration of already existing conjugate forms.

Potency is not only the principle for development, for horizontal and vertical finality, but also the principle of limitation. Judgments of value are limited by our judgments of truth; judgments of truth are limited by our acts of understanding and formulating hypotheses, understanding is limited by the range of data available through experiencing.

Human beings are limited because of the demands of sensitivity. Vegetative and sensitive life is limited by the requirement of all living things for environment, food, reproduction etc. Living things are constrained by the laws of chemistry and physics which continue to apply to them. So, it is the vast pool of subatomic particles which set the limit for what is possible in our universe. We do not know in advance what these limits are.

To conclude, our concern has been a philosophical exposition of the overall structure of the universe we are living in. Our method is largely that of isomorphism. In this section we have seen that knowing is intrinsically dynamic, although this forward momentum works in fits and starts, with breakthroughs and breakdowns, with surges of progress and bouts of decline. Similarly, we find that the universe is intrinsically dynamic, that it is a directed dynamism from the lower to the higher. This finality is intrinsic, directed, nuanced, flexible, not totally determinate, not totally indeterminate. The sciences usually assume a framework of evolution, which, unfortunately, is often misconstrued. Materialist presuppositions regarding evolution are too narrow and do not allow for the dynamic of intelligence and the dynamic of an evolving universe of forms. Natural selection is often conceived in a narrow and limited way. Evolution is also misconstrued as a kind of determinism, which is an exaggeration in that some events are clearly not determined. Indeterminism is an exaggeration in that there are clearly regularities and classical laws. The reality of the dynamism of our universe is sophisticated and requires great care to elaborate it accurately. The unfolding of the human intellect is both the prime example of finality in our universe and our clue to understand the complexities of the dynamism of the universe. We have attempted to offer a notion of finality that is verifiable, differentiated, nuanced and helpful. It will be helpful in that it promotes correct questions and directs scientific exploration of evolution and other topics in the right direction.

We have been putting together our worldview, or overall framework for understanding the universe—the integral heuristic structure of proportionate being. We have outlined the universal elements of potency, form,

act, and value. In subsequent chapters we will see how things and properties, genera and species, living things, and the human person fit into this
framework. We call our view of the world "generalized emergent probability." We have identified a generalized finality. Let us move on to the notion
of emergence, and how that fits into the picture.

Emergence in the Knowing

We have met the notion of emergence in passing already in this text, but
because it is so central, we now focus on it explicitly. The notion has roots in
classical Scholastic philosophy where it was understood that form emerges
from potency. There was a burst of interest in it during the first half of the
twentieth century in Britain in a movement called "Emergentism," and
it seems to be experiencing a revival at the moment. The term evolution
implies a universe that is always gradually moving in small steps by way
of adaptation and survival of the fittest and sometimes refers only to living
things. Evolution evokes the name of Charles Darwin and neo-Darwinians.
Unfortunately, it is also associated with anti-religious sentiments. Emergence
on the other hand more broadly implies new things coming from old, an
upwardly-directed dynamism that is universal and central to our understanding of everything in the universe. Emergence does not evoke the same
emotional reaction as evolution and is philosophically neutral. As usual we
will appeal to our notion of isomorphism to better understand emergence in
the process of knowing and parallel emergence in the process of the universe.
Note that emergence is very similar to the process of sublation. I use the two
terms in different contexts. Usually, emergence refers to new things coming
into being from predisposed matter, while sublation normally refers to the
relation of what has emerged to that from which it emerged.

The prime example of the process of emergence is the emergence of
ideas from images in the act of understanding. The pure desire to know
operates on the data of sense and from the images emerge ideas. This is
a discursive process; it takes time; it takes effort; it is not automatic and
immediate but does occur suddenly and unexpectedly. There is an element
of initiative and activity as we must fulfil the conditions for the possibility
of insight to occur, namely, researching, observing, thinking, remembering
and the like. The process involves manipulating the image, looking at data,
appealing to examples, remembering relevant experiences, looking for help,
and so on. But there is also an element of receptivity, of waiting for the
insight to come, receiving the idea, the solution, the definition. We have
described this process before, so there is no need to dwell too much on it

here.[7] The important point is that we are appealing to your own experience of understanding, not to an authority, a proof, or a dogma. Is this or is it not your experience of how ideas come to you? This is the primordial experience of emergence and provides the template for all other occurrence of emergence. From this basic experience we can formulate some of the basic characteristics of the process of emergence, namely, (1) that something new emerges, (2) it leaves the previous levels intact and (3) even enhances the value of the previous levels. As we have already identified the steps in the process of knowing we can be very brief here.

(1) What emerges is something new and different from the old. It is autonomous, can exist on its own. An idea is not an image. An idea is universal, abstract, intelligible, and can only be produced by intelligence. An image is particular, concrete, and sensible and is produced by the senses in conjunction with the sensible imagination and memory, usually under the influence of the question at hand. They are as different as chalk from cheese.

It is new, and the new is unexpected, unpredictable, not deductive; it is genuinely novel. For some mathematical problems, it is possible to apply the rules and find the solution automatically as perhaps a calculator will do. In these cases, the solution can be found deductively, automatically, and simply by following clear rules of procedure. But where did the rules come from? Who thought of the rules in the first place? How did you learn to understand and follow the rules? Insight is the answer to these questions. The rules emerged from the minds of people who wanted to simplify and systematize mathematical operations.

Ideas emerge in the mind suddenly and unexpectedly. Parallel in the universe emergence can be unexpected and surprising. There is no way of predicting the emergence of homo sapiens from primate ancestors. There is an element of surprise in our emergence; something new is being produced. Again, we appeal to our own appropriation of the act of understanding as a model of how things emerge. A truly new thing has emerged, come into existence, and is a reality of its own. Ideas emerge from images under the influence of intelligence.

(2) When one has an insight, the images and the imagination continue to function according to their own laws and capabilities. They are still needed. We cannot continue the process of thinking without images and imagination. We are constantly pivoting from the abstract to the concrete, from general laws to particular examples. Emergence produces new and higher realities, but it does not destroy or negate or transcend or do without the

7. Cronin, *Phenomenology of Human Understanding*, chapters 3–4.

earlier efforts, namely, that from which it emerged. It continues to depend on the earlier and previous; ideas need to be expressed in images and developed by way of examples and taught in a system of pedagogically effective ways. Sensation, the senses, the brain, the imagination, and memory continue to operate and to be of value. The proper functioning of all these is necessary for the further development of ideas and propositions and concepts and systems. Human intelligence continues to depend on the proper functioning of imagination and memory, sensation and brain functions. Even in explanatory realms of philosophy and theology we spontaneously create diagrams, use examples, and construct images in order to understand clearly.

(3) The results of the process of emergence, far from devaluing that from which it emerged, enhance considerably the value of its preconditions. Sensitivity reaches its highest point of development in man not in beasts. There is a feedback effect of intelligence back on sensitivity. The power of the human imagination is more flexible and creative that than of animals because of the influence of intelligence. It is intelligence that manipulates images, draws diagrams, imagines possibilities, and formulates hypotheses. This is the prototype of all emergence.

Emergence continues to play a part in further developments of the human mind. *Judgments of Truth* emerge from possibilities, from explanations, from ideas and memories in a complicated discursive process. *Judgments of Value* also emerge when we ask questions about its worth, possible applications, alternative uses, and the like. *Higher viewpoints* emerge from lower viewpoints. We teach children how to read by starting with letters, moving on to words, then sentences, then paragraphs, chapters and books. It is a process of emergence; something new does emerge at each step. Our four methods of procedure, classical, statistical, genetic and dialectic produce four modes of emergence. If emergence is a basic property of insight, then it will also be a basic property of the different kinds of insights characteristic of these four methods.

Our method of isomorphism suggests the possibility that because there is a process of emergence in the knowing, so there might be such a parallel process in the known. Emergence in all examples of knowing gives us the template for our consideration of emergence in the known. Let us turn our attention to emergence in the known world.

Emergence in the Known

We are in a better position to appreciate emergence in the known because we have the model of the structure of human knowing and because we have worked out notions of potency, form, act and value. Later, we will apply the notion of isomorphism to central and conjugate forms, to a hierarchy of genera and species, and to an understanding of living things. Emergence is a fundamental category for understanding proportionate being and comes in many forms.

To understand the emergence of the known, we should also distinguish between horizontal and vertical emergence. This is similar to our previous distinction of horizontal and vertical finality in knowing. In *horizontal emergence*, new instances of the same thing emerge. Chemical elements combine with one another to form molecules, but they too are chemicals. Hydrogen plus oxygen gives water, but the conditions have to be favorable: the temperature, pressure, mixture, and proportion must be right, and then a light or spark has to be applied for the change to take place. Rusting, combustion, composition and decomposition are examples of potencies being realized, of form emerging from potency, either to survive or not to survive, to contribute to development or to decline. Most of the processes examined in chemistry are examples of horizontal emergence.

Similarly in the life sciences. From acorns, only oak trees will emerge. Monkeys give birth to monkeys, mackerel to mackerel, humans to humans. There are multiple examples of emergence as it is the necessary condition for the continuation of the species. In genetic method we study the emergence of a series of sets of properties emerging in succession according to the principles of operator and integrator. To understand a frog, you have to grasp the sequence of stages of a frog, from spawn to tadpole, to moving to land, to growing, to mating, to reproducing, to aging, and to dying. There is a sequence to the emergence of the various stages. The later stages depend on the correct emergence of the earlier.

In *vertical emergence* some kind of higher entities emerge. When subatomic particles combine together to form atoms of hydrogen, helium, and the like, something new and different and higher has emerged. When living emerges from non-living you have vertical emergence. When intelligent and rational life emerges from sentient then too you have vertical emergence.

Atoms emerge from subatomic particles; molecules emerge from simpler basic elements; living cells emerge from complicated molecules; multicellular plants and animals emerge from single cells; intelligent life emerges from sensitive life. Higher forms can emerge from lower forms. These are examples of vertical emergence. How exactly they emerge can be studied by the sciences. Whether new species will survive depends on its adaptability, on the environment, and on the conditions of its emergence continuing to favour it. There are schedules of probability for things to emerge and to survive, and these are best studied by statistical method.

Living things emerged from non-living. How, where, and when, we do not know. But it is evident that all the preconditions were already in place, and then perhaps a spark or a bolt of lightning or an unusual sub-atomic event occurred, and there emerged a cell that reproduced itself. It might not have happened. It happened by way of a coincidence of favorable conditions. It was a contingent not a necessary emergence. Without it we would not be here.

This is our overall view of schema of emergent probabilities encompassing the systematic, the non-systematic, the living and the dialectical. That is world process as we see it. That is our worldview. It is an all-encompassing worldview of the kind of universe we are living in, what it is made out of, and how it works in general terms.

Chance and Effective Probability

We have rejected a determinist worldview and also its opposite a totally indeterminist worldview. We are steering a middle path between the two and crucial to that position is the notion of chance and effective probability. This section will try to formulate these notions clearly and simply. We have already identified the importance of probabilities when identifying the empirical residue and explaining the need for an inverse insight (chapter 5). Now we see that probability is an essential element in our worldview of the whole of the universe, applicable in all areas across the board. Classical laws define clearly what should happen, if there is not interference from other factors, if conditions are perfect, if samples are perfectly pure, if measurements are perfectly exact. Sadly, such conditions cannot be fulfilled in any concrete incident, condition, or situation. Once it is concrete there is a gap between the abstract law and the concrete event. In dealing with all concrete happenings, emergences, things and their properties we are obliged to have recourse to statistical probabilities. Probabilities try to fill that gap in our knowledge between the ideal law in our minds and the concrete complexities, and details of actual events.

We define a probability as the non-systematic divergence of the actual from an ideal statistical law. It is the non-systematic divergence of the concrete from abstract statistical probabilities. It is a non-systematic divergence, because if it were systematic, it would be a classical law. It is understood thorough an inverse insight, a grasp of the lack of an expected intelligibility. For example, if you have a statistical law that average annual rainfall in a certain place is sixty inches, you do not expect sixty inches to fall each year, but you do expect the actual rainfall will fluctuate around the average of sixty. But you expect this divergence from the average to be non-systematic, unpredictable, and uncontrollable. If the actual rainfall is regularly and consistently below the average, you suspect that the average has changed. Rates, frequencies, averages, probabilities, do not give you the same intellectual satisfaction as Newton's three laws of motion or Einstein's incredible formula $E=Mc^2$, which are examples of classical laws.

Chance is constrained by being surrounded by classical laws which continue to operate. Rainfall is determined by winds, oceans, temperatures, humidity, barometric pressure, and other factors. A slight change in any of these factors can change the amount of rainfall in a particular area. But the classical laws relating to wind, humidity, pressure, altitude and temperature remain the same. There are limits to statistical fluctuations because a plethora of classical laws continue to operate. For Aristotle, science had to be certain knowledge through causes, capable of demonstration and of necessary truths which could not be otherwise. Coincidence was not counted as knowledge, and neither his metaphysics, nor his logic, nor his mathematics had room for probabilities. This position in general prevailed until the nineteenth century when the first statistical enquiries were made, and probabilities were studied in mathematics. Darwin was one of the first to use probabilities as an explanatory tool in his theory of selection of the fittest. However, mainstream science was dominated by classicists until the discovery of quantum mechanics. Then it was realized that statistical methods were essential tools in every science and that space, time, and motion could not be understood without the notion of probabilities. Since then, probabilities have been used in all areas of science and statistics constitute an essential part of mathematics.

Chance is precisely the non-systematic divergence of the actual from the ideal. Probability theory says that tossing a coin repeatedly will give equal numbers of heads and tails. But any actual sequence of tosses will probably diverge from this ideal. But it will not diverge in a consistent, systematic way. This non-systematic divergence from the ideal is our definition of chance. It cannot be a systematic divergence because then there would have to be a reason, but there is no reason for this divergence.

Classical laws and statistical laws are complementary. To understand any event such as a particular plane crash, you appeal to both classical and statistical laws. Classical laws deal with laws of motion, power of engines, weight of plane, angle of ascent, etc. Statistical method deals with how often the conditions governing these laws are fulfilled. Was the wind gusting, was the automatic pilot working, did the pilot react correctly, was the pilot sober and of sound mind, were there birds in the area, etc.? This applies to every occurrence in the concrete. You cannot understand anything that happens to you or your family without taking this into account. Classical laws are direct insights into regularities and predictions, but statistical laws tell you when various conditions are actually fulfilled. Nearly everything that we know in the field of science and common sense is only known with varying degrees of probability. Most of the things that determine our life including conception, implantation, genetic code, development, birth, crop harvests, traffic patterns, education, money, falling in love, and all the rest of it, are governed by schedules of probabilities.

Schedules of probability keep changing. Probabilities of a snowstorm change and get higher as the occurrence comes closer. Probability of emergence of life becomes higher the more the conditions for that possibility are fulfilled. Emergence of life is impossible in some situations but are possible in others. Making an airplane was impossible for the Greeks but is possible nowadays. Probabilities are either true or false, accurate or inaccurate. Probabilities are verified not in reference to single events but to ranges of data over the long term. Probabilities can be high or low and can change when circumstances change.

"Effective probability" is a special term coined by Lonergan to express the idea that if probabilities are given enough absolute occasions in time and space, what will probably emerge, now effectively must emerge: probabilities become effective. If you toss a coin, the probability of one side coming up is one in two. One knows that if you toss the coin a few times and one side keeps coming up, it is only a matter of time before the other side turns up. If you toss the coin a sufficient number of times the other side must effectively turn up. You do not know when this will happen, but you know that eventually it *must* happen. If the probabilities are low, then huge numbers of occasions must to be provided to ensure that the probability is realized. If the probability is one in a million, then, on a million occasions the one thing should normally happen, but there is still a good chance it will not. If you provide millions more occasions, then you know that the one thing must effectively happen, but you do not know where or when. This is another way that Lonergan steers between determinism and indeterminism in his understanding of how the universe operates. It is not pure chance, for chance is the non-systematic divergence of the actual from the ideal, it is understood by an inverse insight, and it is not intelligibility but the absence of an intelligibility. The finality of the universe does not operate as a classical, determinate law operating on fixed rails, inexorably producing predetermined results.

Finality is this rich, subtle notion that a probability, given a sufficient number of occasions, will eventually effectively be realized. Putting it simply, we assert that if it can happen it will happen, provided you allow for necessary conditions and a sufficient number of occasions.

Some have difficulty accepting that our universe is governed by probabilities. They find it too close to randomness and relativism. But this is assuaged somewhat by the notion of effective probability. If it is possible for something to happen or to emerge, then, given enough occasions in the end it must happen. This is analogous to Murphy's law, which states that if something can go wrong, it will go wrong. However, the notion of effective probability is valid and of considerable importance. If it is possible for life to emerge from non-living, then given a sufficient number of occasions, when the conditions are favorable, then in the end it is bound to happen. This is similar for the emergence of higher elements, a planetary system, the emergence of intelligence from sensitive, and all the other cases of emergence that we have identified. This demonstrates the significance of a large universe with a long history: it increases the number of occasions for things potentially to emerge, thus ensuring that effective probability can produce a rich, varied, and dynamic universe.

Everything Is Interrelated and Interdependent

It is easy to think of and articulate a universe that is determinate and always determinate, predictable and intelligible. It is easy to think of and articulate a universe that is completely indeterminate, that is unpredictable, that is not fully intelligible in terms of classical laws. Unfortunately, neither of these models are satisfactory when applied to the complex reality of the real universe revealed by the sciences in all their details. Both models are extremes, while the truth is somewhere in the middle. We have tried to articulate a view of the universe that is verifiable in common experience, in the sciences, and in the application of mathematics to the realities we encounter. Our presentation established the broad, philosophical parameters of a correct worldview. It is the task of the scientists and specialists to fill in the diversity, the richness, the detail of the specific things and schemes found in our universe.

In our schema of generalized emergent probability everything is interrelated in a complex network of causes, components, elements, events happening in one space/time continuum in one universe of proportionate being. We have shown how the four components of one knowing emerge and are dependent on one another. The four metaphysical elements are similarly related to one another in terms of emergence and dependence.

The sciences are related to one another on the model of successive higher viewpoints in the knower and a process of differentiation and higher integrations in the known. The same laws of physics, chemistry, biology, botany, zoology, anthropology, and the like, apply from one end of the universe to the other, from the beginning to the end. These laws are complex, involving certainty and probability, universality and particularity. All human sciences are complementary to one another in studying the one human person from many different perspectives. The universe has a past, present and future. Everything must be studied in terms of its origins in history, its present state, and future possibilities. There is a single network of causes operating everywhere, formal and material, effective and final, exemplary and instrumental, and others identified in each of the sciences. Everything is intelligible in its various degrees, its absence or presence, positive or negative, central or conjugate, certain or probable, according to the methods of classical, statistical, genetic, or dialectic. The worldview of generalized empirical probability embraces everything, which is the purpose of metaphysics or first philosophy. The final unifying insight is into the First Cause, the First Mover, the Source of everything, the Creator, comes in our last chapter.

This is but a framework of central ideas, which apply across the board, but allow for the quasi-infinite diversity of details, qualifications, specifications, implementations, and realizations to fill out the full picture of the unique concrete reality of everything and every event. This chapter has given a kind of overview of the dynamic aspects of our universe. Now we are ready to identify some of the more specific characteristics of what is going on in the universe.

10

Things and Their Properties

Now the notion of a thing is grounded in an insight that grasps, not relations between data, but a unity, identity, whole in data; and this unity is grasped, not by considering data from any abstractive viewpoint, but by taking them in their concrete individuality and in the totality of their aspects.[1]

But the impressions of reflection resolve themselves into our passions and emotions, none of which can possibly represent a substance. We have therefore no idea of substance, distinct from that of a collection of particular qualities, nor have we any other meaning when we either talk or reason concerning it.[2]

A thing is the existing bearer of many existing yet changeable properties.[3]

Thus, we are seeking the cause (and this is the form) through which the matter is a thing; and this cause is the <u>substance</u> of the thing.[4]

Introduction

HAVING PRESENTED AN OVERALL picture of the finality of the universe, we now delve into the details, starting in this chapter with a distinction, which seems to apply across the board, between things and their properties, or between substances and accidents. Then the question will be raised as to how the vast variety of things or substances are distinguished and related to one another in terms of genera and species (chapter 11). A special class

1. Lonergan, *Insight*, 271.
2. Hume, *Treatise of Human Nature*, 60.
3. Heidegger, *What Is a Thing?*, 46.
4. Aristotle, *Metaphysics*, 7, 17, 1041b9.

of beings deserving separate attention are living things which seem to have emerged from complex, organic, chemical environments (chapter 12). Then, we will consider human persons who seem to be the peak of all of this development (chapter 13). A final chapter will expand the viewpoint of proportionate being to include transcendent being (chapter 14). We will continue to use the method of isomorphism to utilize the parallels between the patterns of relations within the activities of knowing and the pattern of relations among the known contents. In this chapter we proceed to talk about different kinds of forms, never forgetting that we are talking of potency, form, act and value, in other words, good forms existing in matter. We focus on form because of the centrality of the intelligible.

There is a shifting terminology covering this area. The traditional Aristotelian tradition uses the terms substance and accident or attribute. The Middle Ages tended to use substantial form and accidental form. The notions of substance and accident were mangled by the Neo-Scholastics, the empiricists, the Kantians and even Heidegger. For this reason, Lonergan disengaged himself from this verbal tangle and used the technical terms, central form and conjugate form. Things and properties are the more common terminology used to distinguish these two realities nowadays. Hence, on the one hand, you have substance, substantial form, central form, or thing, being more or less equivalent. On the other hand, you have accident, attribute, conjugate form, properties or predicates. I tend to use the terminology of thing and property as Lonergan does in the first part of *Insight* because it is most accessible but at a certain point, we will introduce the more precise terminology of central and conjugate form. We will identify a certain kind of act of understanding which grasps substance and another act of understanding which grasps accidental form. This applies across the board in all the sciences, all academic disciplines, all wisdom, and all truth statements. It applies explicitly in explanatory, theoretical positions but also works in a general way in description and common sense.

Here we begin the process of further specifying the kinds of forms that exist—the overall intelligibility of our universe. The question arises as to how many forms are there? Are they of different kinds? Is there an order of forms or is it a chaos? Can forms be classified into groups? Can forms change and in what way and how? The synchronic analysis of the elements of all proportionate being identified the elements common to all intelligibilities in any particular field, namely, potency, form, act and good. That was a useful exercise, but we can and must specify how particular forms emerge, come and go, how they are organized, how they differ, how they relate to one another. Thus, we will further specify the dynamics of our worldview of everything.

This is important because we are seeking the intelligibility of the world as to how it develops and changes. We spent chapter 6 on the principles and causes operative from a structural point of view. Now we do it from a developmental point of view. One of the basic distinctions between forms is that between things and properties, central and conjugate forms. This applies in all sciences, in all disciplines, in common sense and is crucial for our understanding of emergence and change. This distinction is the basis for the order of the universe, for distinguishing genera and species, inanimate, vegetative, sensate, and human, which constitute the hierarchy of levels of things in the world. It is fundamental to understanding the unity of the human person and the rejection of reductionism.

We continue to use the method of isomorphism. We are going to identify two kinds of insight which I will call "inclusive" and "abstractive." Isomorphic with these insights are two kinds of forms which we will call "central forms" and "conjugate forms." This distinction illustrates a basic structural aspect of the human mind moving from the known to the unknown pivoting from the notion of the whole to the characteristics of the parts, from central forms to conjugate forms and vice versa.

Historical Sketch

(1) Aristotle. Aristotle realizes the importance of identifying the properties or characteristics of substance, and it is a theme of his writing from the beginning to the end. In the *Categories*, he identifies ten categories of "things," the first of which is substance, and the other nine are accidents. By "accidents" he did not mean something unimportant or trivial as in modern English. Nor did he mean unintentional or coincidental as in a motor accident. By accident, he refers to the nine categories, which are not substances but properties, predicates, or attributes of substance. He considers certain ways of defining substance, namely: (1) as an individual concrete thing, (2) as a core of essential properties or essence, (3) as that which is capable of independent existence, (4) as a centre of change, (5) as substratum and (6) as a logical subject. He returns to the topic of defining substance in the *Metaphysics* and struggles mightily with whether the substance is a universal, matter, or even potency. In the end he seems to affirm that the substance is the essence, what is grasped in understanding, namely, the unity and identity of the thing.[5] He was followed by the medieval philosophers, who formulated the concepts of prime matter and substantial form. This treatment was theoretical and metaphysical but was largely correct.

5. Aristotle, *Metaphysics*, 7, 17, 1041a6–1041b30.

(2) Descartes. Descartes gives a formal definition of substance as: "Everything in which there resides immediately as in a subject or by means of which there exists anything that we perceive, i.e., any property, quality or attribute of which we have a real idea is called a substance; neither do we have any other idea of substance itself, precisely taken, than that it is a thing in which this something that we perceive or which is present objectively in some of our ideas, exists formally or eminently. For by means of our natural light we know that a real attribute cannot be an attribute of nothing."[6] We cannot see individual substances, but we have to presume some notion of substance to be able to think. Descartes goes on to explain that substances have essential attributes, and the essential attribute of mind is thought, and the essential attribute of matter is extension. There are only two substances or two kinds of things, thought and matter (*res cogitans* and *res extensa*). It would seem to follow that the substance of a material thing is itself extended. In another context Descartes gives a second definition of substance, "Really the notion of substance is just this, that which can exist by itself, without the aid of any other substance."[7] Here we can see that the word is beginning to be "reified" or "conceptualized." It is taking on a reality of its own: substance has extension and can exist by itself apart from attributes. Substance as a thing understood by intelligent definition in Aristotle, is being transformed by Descartes into substance as a "body" imagined to exist apart by itself.

(3) Locke and Hume. Locke attacked the idea of a substance as a substratum, an idea that had become common in the later Scholastics. He argues that we come to the idea of substance when we experience groups of qualities which occur together in time and place and therefore, we presume they belong to one thing. We get accustomed to use one word such as, gold, table, horse, and the like, to refer to this collection of properties. We suppose that there is some substratum wherein they do subsist and from which they do result and which we call substance. He defines substance as, "the supposed but unknown support of those qualities we find existing, which we imagine cannot subsist *sine re substante*, without something to support them."[8] For him the notion of substance is obscure and relative, even though he does not reject it altogether. Hume does go the whole hog and rejects totally the notion of substance because it cannot be sensed and therefore cannot be verified. What Hume is rejecting is the notion of substance as an imaginary "body." Although Hume correctly rejected this

6. Descartes, *Philosophical Works*, 53.
7. Descartes, *Philosophical Works*, 101.
8. Locke, *Human Understanding*, 218.

imaginary notion of substance, he was in no position to rediscover the true notion because of his scepticism and radical empiricism.

(4) Heidegger. Martin Heidegger is of interest to us because he wrote a book entitled *What Is a Thing?*[9] However, it turns out that he has very little original thought on the subject and, in fact, lines up with the decadent Scholastics, namely, what is left over after all attributes have been removed. After much preliminary musings, Heidegger finally concludes that the *thing* will never be found in the properties of things as they encounter us: "a thing is always something that has such and such properties, always something that is constituted in such and such a way. This something is the bearer of properties; the something, as it were, underlies the qualities. . . . It is a nucleus around which many changing qualities are grasped, or a bearer upon which the qualities rest; something that possesses something else in itself."[10] He concludes with a sort of definition of the thing as, "A thing is the existing bearer of many existing yet changeable properties."[11] He admits himself that he has arrived at a basically traditional notion of substance, as the foundation or what underlies, as the bearer of properties, the substance as opposed to accidents, the subject as opposed to the predicate. He is looking for something "behind" the properties that will be the substance or thing in itself. With the advantage of a correct epistemology, we will find that notion as a very defective way of accounting for things and their properties.

Despite the efforts of modern philosophers, basic confusion remains over how we know substance, how we know properties, and how substance and properties are related. Related notions of essence, nature, genus, universal, are likewise totally confused with real implications for our worldview. I think Aristotle and Aquinas were right on this issue, but our present generation has lost the philosophical concept of central and conjugate forms. Still, everyone, including scientists of all specializations, make an operational distinction between things and properties. Practitioners operating on the level of common sense or theory may not be too concerned about a technical definition of substance, but a philosopher who wants to understand the order of the universe and the unity of the human person cannot ignore this basic issue.

9. Heidegger, *What Is a Thing?*
10. Heidegger, *What Is a Thing?*, 45.
11. Heidegger, *What Is a Thing?*, 46.

Imagining Things

A child knows what a thing is and what is not a thing and in this, children are mostly correct. It seems such an elementary notion that we seem to arrive at it without thinking. But that is the problem. Our notion of thing is often an unquestioned assumption of what a thing must be. It must satisfy the imagination and not the intellect. We often assume a pre-intellectual, pre-conceptual, imaginative notion of what a thing must be. Because it is unquestioned, it is uncritical and perhaps unconscious. But it determines our thinking and skews our criterion of what is real.

Lonergan's favorite characterization of this imagined "body" is in the phrase "already out, there, now, real."[12] With this expression, he is trying to reconstruct the process of animal knowing. Animals have senses which can be more acute than our own. They can learn because they also have imagination and memory. They can recognize sounds, smells, know places and people, and know when it is time to eat or sleep or go for a walk. Animal behavior can be accounted for in terms of the senses, the brain, memory, imagination, and instinct, association of input and response, imitation, sensible desires, and empirical consciousness. "Already" indicates that the sense object is directly sensed as it is, and there is no process of grasping an idea in an image as in human understanding. The senses orientate consciousness outwards to what is seen, heard, tasted, smelt or touched and so we use the term "out." It is extroverted consciousness. Animals do not have epistemological problems. Their knowing is simple sense knowing of particular things. They can orientate their living in terms of space and time. In space they recognize places "there," learn to move to a place for feeding, to another place for sleeping, to another place for playing. They live in the present, a "now"; the cycle of the seasons gets embedded in their memory. They have memory and are capable of storing food for the winter and the like but predominantly live in the present moment. This "out, there, now, real," can also be called elementary knowing.

Animals do have a criterion of the "real"; what is real is what can be sensed. It is "already, out, there, now." They can also distinguish between real grass and plastic grass, real milk from pictures of milk, or real dogs from pictures of dogs on television. They do this by smelling, by seeing, by remembering, by tasting. They can know particular concrete sensible things as such. But they cannot ask questions, cannot universalize, cannot have insights, cannot define things, and cannot divide them into genera and species. Animals know "bodies" by a sensitive knowledge of the particular, the

---

12. Lonergan, *Insight*, 275–79.

concrete, the individual. However, humans as well as having this elementary knowing, also know things by knowledge of understanding and judging the universal, the abstract, the general.

There are then two kinds of knowledge operating in the human. There is the elementary knowledge of sense, which tends to be immediate, direct, single, simple, and it characteristically is knowledge of extroversion, of what can be called the "already, out, there, now, real." But as well as that, the human person can ask intelligent questions, seek ideas to answer the question, formulate appropriate solutions, create experiments to check the hypotheses, judge the sufficiency of the evidence for a particular solution and then reach a critical affirmation. This knowledge is intellectual knowledge; it is discursive, mediated, indirect, painstaking, slow, partial, both receptive and active. It is human intellectual knowing in science, philosophy, common sense, etc. The difficulty is that merely sense knowledge tends to be confused with fully human knowing, and the imaginative assumptions of the former are foisted on the latter. Then we have endless confusion. The point is to distinguish critically these two forms of knowledge, not to eliminate one or the other.

We have opted for discursive, intellectual, critical knowing as giving verifiable knowledge of reality. Hence, we know things, substances, not only by sense experience but by direct understanding of possibility and reflective understanding of reality: theories verified in instances that have been experienced. Our advancing studies are constantly improving our knowledge of things. Scientists once thought that earth, air, fire and water were the basic elements, but now we know that the periodic table of the hundred plus elements of Mendeleyev is correct. We thought air was one thing but now it is known to be a mixture. We thought fire was a substance; now we know that it is a by-product of a chemical reaction called oxidation. We thought water was elemental but now we know it is hydrogen and oxygen combined. We thought space was a substance called "ether" but now we realize it is a space-time continuum.

Identifying and Defining Things

Aristotle approached this question of substance and accidents by looking at examples of substances and accidents and generalizing from their characteristics. It was and is a legitimate procedure. But he had great difficulty laying out these characteristics and realized in the end that substance can only be defined as an essence and that essence is grasped by an act of intelligence.[13]

13. See Aristotle, *Metaphysics*, 7, 17, 1041b1–30.

Our approach is to start where he left off: to focus on the subjective cognitional side. What is the question you are asking when looking for the substance? What is the question you ask when you look for attributes? What procedures do you follow in order to answer these questions correctly? Different questions lead to two different acts of understanding, one of which is an insight into central form or substance; the other of which is into relations, accidents, properties or attributes. For want of a better terminology, I use the terms "inclusive insights" for insights into substances and "abstractive insights" for insights into accidents. In this section we focus on insights into things, and in the next section insights into properties.

Inclusive insights are insights into the unity, identity, whole of a thing. The questions you are asking in this case are: What is this thing as a whole? What is its identity? What is its name? What makes it to be one? All the data relevant to this insight is taken together. These are actually variations of the classic question for understanding: What is it? The data for answering this question comes from seeing, hearing, tasting, smelling, remembering and imagining, but the answer comes in an inclusive insight into the unity of data taken together as an individual "this." It is a dog; it is a galaxy; it is a human person; it is an electron. The evidence for these affirmations can be quite varied, complex, directly observed or discovered by using instruments; it depends on the context of the science, and the use of terms. At some point we may not have sufficient evidence to affirm what it is.

When patients began to die of an immune deficiency in the early eighties, doctors did not know whether it was caused by a virus or a bacterium. But then the evidence is found by research, experiment and observation. The cause could pass through a filter so it is very small, smaller than a living cell; therefore, it must be a virus. If you are given an unknown solution in a chemical laboratory and told to identify this substance, you follow the standard procedures, perform the tests, identify the characteristics, eliminate other possibilities, and, finally, name the substance. All the properties, attributes, characteristics are relevant to the final insight; they are preparatory to the final insight. But the final insight is not into the properties but into the unity, identity, whole which unifies the properties.

Aristotle actually used a telling example when he identified substance with essence, namely, a syllable.[14] If you write letters C-A-T on the board each letter is a thing; each letter is a whole; each is grasped in an insight and each insight has to be learned and taught laboriously to children. The letters are the units grasped by intelligence. But if you combine the letters into syllables or words then the unity shifts to the word or the syllable;

14. Aristotle, *Metaphysics*, 7, 17, 1041b10–30.

now it is "cat." Once you are grasping words or syllables as wholes, the individual letters become parts, not wholes. The individual identity of each letter is subsumed into the unity of the word or the syllable. Each letter is relevant but only as a part defining a new whole. All the parts are relevant, but the insight is into the unity of the parts in a word or syllable. What has been added to the three individual letters such that there is now a new reality, a word or syllable? What has been added is a unity, whole, identity: an essence. It is not a material element or part that is added, not another letter, not some glue sticking the letters together, but an intelligible unity immanent in the word. When Aristotle affirmed that all living things had souls, he was simply affirming the empirical fact that living things exhibit an extraordinary unity of parts, where the unity self-organizes, develops over time, reproduces itself, and eventually degenerates. To understand a lion or a cat is to understand that the parts constitute a unity.

The parts of a thing are all relevant, but sometimes parts are relevant in different ways and in different degrees. A cat can live without a tail but not without a heart. The parts can be related to the whole in degrees of importance. Intelligence is operating not just in enumerating parts, or properties, or characteristics but in identifying a thing as a "unity, identity, whole." Let us consider some examples of how things can be defined as unity, identity and whole.

Unity. The unity of a living tree is different from the unity of a statue, a motor car, a computer, or even another tree. There are different kinds of unity. The unity of artefacts is an imposed, artificial, external, a unity from the outside. It would be a considerable mistake to put the unity of a cat on the same level as the unity of a motorcar.

Identity. What is this material? We check the color, the consistency, the weight and the like. We use our memory and imagination; we may have to run tests. We identify the material out of which it is made. We answer, wood, gold, hydrogen, water, and the like. Who is this person? We search our memories, ask our friends, look up Who's Who. Oh! It's the local doctor. What kind of a tree is this? You observe carefully, examine the leaves, check for fruit or flowers, look up an encyclopaedia. Oh! It's an oak.

Whole. There is a unity of wholeness that belongs to the universe, an army, a crowd, a motor car, a factory, a molecule, a bicycle, the solar system, a shoe, or a shirt. We all know what these words mean and what constitutes a member of the class and what does not. We usually understand the difference between wholes and parts. They are unities in a loose sense or wholes but the wholeness differs from that of a living thing. But we can still call them substances even though the unity is that of an aggregate, extrinsic, transient, but still intelligible and useful and verifiable.

We have identified an elementary knowing of things dominated by sense and imagination, as the already out there now real. We have now identified an explanatory knowing of things by way of asking questions, searching for data, gathering information, assembling evidence, doing some research, asking for help, and coming to a correct answer. Elementary knowing and the imaginative schema of in here and out there tends to perdure but it is an imaginative illusion. We know things by asking intelligent questions, experiencing data, understanding explanations, checking the sufficiency of the evidence and affirming a correct answer.

Properties

Having discussed inclusive insights into substances, let us consider abstractive insights into properties or accidents. The question being asked here is different. It is not a question into the unity, identity, wholeness of the thing, but a question into its characteristics, its size and shape, its color or smell, its being subject to the laws of physics and chemistry, etc. Aristotle enumerated nine such as quantity, quality, relation, somewhere, at some time, being in a position, possessing, or acting or being acted upon. From the point of view of common sense, we think of properties, as color, weight, shape, size, smell, feel, and other sensible characteristics.

In the explanatory context of the sciences conjugate forms are usually in the form of laws, regularities, systems and causes, proper to each specialization. For example, when considering how things move, Galileo sought a formula to define acceleration. He experimented with falling bodies. The relation between time and distance became the focus of attention. What the falling bodies were made of was not immediately relevant. He was looking for the laws of motion, gathering data from pendulums, projectiles, planets, comets and birds. He was looking for the laws which govern the movement of any and every kind of substance. He discovered that the distance a body falls is directly proportionate to the square of the time taken to fall. Laws are properties not things, conjugate forms rather than central forms. How do you distinguish between stars, and satellites, and meteorites with the naked eye? They move in different ways. They have different properties. How do you identify a bird or a fish? Describe the color, the size, the shape the structure, the characteristics; then describe how it moves. From this, a specialist could tell you what it is. Describe your symptoms and the doctor will tell you what disease you have. You know a thing by how it moves, what are its characteristics.

The most obvious thing about attributes is that they cannot exist or be operative without substance. You cannot have relations unless you have terms to be related. You cannot have color unless you have a thing that is colored. You cannot have movement unless you have something that is moving. You cannot have a law unless it is verified in some instances. You cannot have a quantity unless it is a quantity of wheat or sheep or wine, or stones, etc.

Laws, relations, motions, attributes, are grasped by insight; but it is an abstractive insight into aspects of the data usually relevant to many substances or things. Because they are understood, they are forms. Terms define relations and relations define terms. The terms are usually central forms or substances; the relations are usually conjugate forms or properties or accidents.

Things and Properties Related

One mistaken way of relating attributes to substance would be to claim that we can see the attributes and therefore they are real. But we cannot see the substance and so it is not real. This is pivotal in the empiricist tradition and also in the Kantian tradition, but it based on a false epistemology and so the conclusions are invalid. We understand substances as wholes, and therefore they are central forms. We understand attributes as characteristics, and they are conjugate forms.

A further Neo-Scholastic argument supposes that if you remove all the attributes, each of which is non-essential, you will be left with the substance. This was a kind of impoverishing abstraction and supposed that the substance was hiding behind the accidents. But if you strip away all the attributes you are in fact left with nothing.

Our focus is on two different kinds of question. One question asks, what is this as a unity, identity, whole? The correct answer will be the substance, the central form. The other question will ask, what are the attributes, or characteristics or properties of this whole? The correct answer will give you the conjugate forms. Both are forms, in other words what is correctly understood. For convenience we named these insights inclusive and abstractive. Inclusive because to identify the central form you need all the data pertaining to this particular individual thing. Abstractive because to identify the characteristics of the thing, you are focusing on some of the data and relating it to other relevant data. For instance, to classify a bird the shape of the beak may be a clue. Or in chemistry a litmus test will indicate acidity and that might help identify the substance.

These two insights are complementary. A fundamental path to progress in understanding is to pivot from one kind of insight to the other. To know what a thing is you name it, identify its properties, give a general assignment of what sort of a thing it is, proceed to investigate other properties, then you get it. The more you understand the relations, the better you understand the terms. The more you understand the parts the better you understand the whole. The more you understand the conjugate forms, the better you understand the central form. In other words, the more correct abstractive insights one has, the better one's inclusive insight is. It also works in reverse. The better you understand what a thing is, the more you can define the properties. This is an intrinsic aspect of how understanding develops. For instance, if you study the discovery that fire is combustion, you will notice how the properties of fire were noted: it consumes some part of air but not the whole of the air; there is no overall change in weight in the enclosed equipment, and it happens to all metals. You identify gasses by their properties; some promote burning and some do not. Oxygen was named and identified; the nature of fire was discovered.

This distinction between substance and accidents can be taken in a descriptive context, an explanatory context and a metaphysical context.

In the descriptive context you are considering how things appear, how they look, how they are perceived by the senses, and above all how they are known in description. Even in this general context it is necessary to distinguish things from their properties. When Aristotle spoke of the form of a building or of a table, he was actually speaking in a descriptive manner. His specification of the nine categories of accidents was descriptive; they were imprecise, but they fit in many cases. Even children know the difference between substances and accidents in this loose descriptive sense. But if you start asking precise questions about unities and relations you have to shift to an explanatory context.

In an explanatory context you are prescinding from the observer and relating things to one another by way of definition or measurement. Science moves from description to explanation and back again. The periodic table of chemical elements is a good example of explanatory terms and relations, central and conjugate forms. Evolutionary biology presents us with distinctions between classes, orders, families, genera, and species. The diagram of a typical cell presents the essential terms and relations of parts and wholes. The distinction between things and properties is crucial for scientific advance. All sciences from all the branches of physics to all the branches of the human sciences involve recourse to the notions of central form and conjugate form. Progress is achieved by pivoting from one to the other.

In a metaphysical context we are concerned only with the general identification of two different kinds of acts of understanding namely inclusive and abstractive insights, and hence two different kinds of realities, that of central form and conjugate form. To identify specific forms is the job of the scientist in the laboratory, or in the field using methods proper to his inquiry. The metaphysical distinction between substance and accidents is a heuristic; in itself it is empty. The metaphysician knows that a tree has or is a substantial form but does not know what the specific content or name of that essence; it is the botanist who will specify the precise nature of a particular species of tree and name them.

Medieval thinkers, because they could talk about the nature of a tree or its substantial form, sometimes thought that they then knew the specific essence or definition of the tree. In that they were very much mistaken. They could talk of the nature of fire, the nature of stone, the essence of lead, the soul of a human being and, being able to talk about them, they thought they knew specifically what they were. To be able to talk of natures, essences, universals, forms is to talk in general and heuristically. But this is very different from scientific knowledge identifying specific substances or forms. Perhaps this heuristic grasp of substance was a block to the emergence of scientific knowledge of the specificity of each individual species. If you can already name and know what a thing is, why investigate further?

The notions of things and properties, substances and accidents, central and conjugate forms, terms and relations, are complementary rather than opposed. The notions are common currency in all human knowing. They are the basic structure of all scientific thought and discovery. You cannot have one without the other. The misunderstandings of the meaning of substance and accidents from the time of Descartes to contemporary times is a complex comedy of errors. There is a role here for the philosopher to elaborate clear general ideas of substance and accidents. There is a role here for the scientist to specify in particular cases what are the specific properties of identified substances and verify all this in critical judgments.

The relations between the insights will be reflected in the relations between the contents known in the insights. Inclusive insights are to abstractive insights as substances are to accidents, as central forms are to conjugate forms. Structural aspects of cognition will be reflected in structural aspects of the real world.

Things and their properties do not exist in splendid isolation from one another. One way of pinning down the interrelation and interdependence of things and properties is by way of a cycle or "scheme of recurrence." The notion is relatively simple and basic. Schematically, if A causes B, and B causes C, and C causes A, you have a simple closed scheme of recurrence. This scheme of recurrence works by itself and is a process of mutual causation in action with elements that are interdependent and interrelated in a precise way. However, schemes are rarely that simple. Things can belong to more than one scheme. Whole schemes can emerge, decline, be interdependent with other schemes. Naturalists are familiar with ecological systems, where flowers are dependent on bees for pollination, where scavengers are dependent on leftovers, where a whole food chain sets the conditions for a whole marine environment, where a change in temperature upsets the balance destroying some schemes and creating new ones. Examples of schemes of recurrence are the planetary system, galaxies, the nitrogen cycle, the seasons. Within living things there are many schemes in terms of blood circulation, digestive system, muscles, and the like. Schemes are systems of interrelationships, which may be open or closed, permanent or fragile, simple or complex.

Nowadays, we talk of ecosystems and environments and ecological niches—all of which are comprised of various schemes of recurrence. A species is defined by how it fits into its niche in a particular ecosystem. The emergence of a new species or extinction of an existing one can change the environment, just as a change in the environment can endanger current species or favour a new species to emerge. Climate change studies are very complex because they involve many different schemes of recurrence, which interact with one another in complex manners.

Schemes emerge, survive, and disintegrate over time. Schemes are subject to schedules of probability for their emergence and for their survival. All central and conjugate forms in the universe are caught up in a complicated web of interrelationships, and to understand this total web we break it down into specific patterns or schemes of relationships. Schemes are not just a way of thinking but are to be verified in the causal relations really operative in the universe. Let us examine how these insights help us to understand change and emergence in our universe.

Change in Being

Parmenides could not conceive of how things could change. If something new comes into being, where does it come from, from being or from non-being? If it came from being then it already existed. But nothing comes from non-being as that is the height of nonsense. Therefore, he had to postulate that Being is one and unchanging. At the other extreme, Heraclitus was so overcome by the reality of change that he postulated that everything is changing. However, if everything is changing you have chaos, not change. Aristotle as usual chose a middle path. There is being that is in potency and being that is in act. The reality of the being of the universe is not that of static completion but of dynamic change. Change is to be understood in terms of continuity and discontinuity. This is the nature of the material world. In any change something must remain the same and something new comes into being. Change is not annihilation and re-creation, it is continuous and intelligible. We can understand the process of change and kinds of change, the causes and results of change. The philosopher approaches this with the aim of a general delineation of the nature of change. The scientist specifies what is changing into what and how and why it is changing.

Changes in properties are easy to understand in that the substance remains the same in numerical identity but the attributes can change. An oak starts as a sprouting seed, becomes a seedling, then a bush, then a sapling, then a tree, then a large tree; it gives out acorns, reproduces and eventually dies. It is the one numerical tree which undergoes many changes of size, color, shape, various chemical and biological processes happen at particular places, roots, trunk, branches and leaves. The changes follow the cycle of the seasons. Such changes are the actual realization of potencies for change within the seed and plant. It is easy to understand that the tree remains the same tree while its conjugate forms, such as height or color, can change; there is both continuity in the underlying sameness of the whole tree or plant, and discontinuity in the changing appearances and size and growth.

Substances also can change. Just as you have conjugate potency, to conjugate form, to conjugate act, you also have movement from central potency, to central form, to central act. Aristotle deals with substantial change in terms of generation and corruption. In what way is there continuity when the very substance changes? He understood this in terms of potencies and act. Living things have the potency to generate new living things. Substances exist not permanently and eternally, but come into existence and pass out of existence. But there is order and intelligibility in the process. If you burn wood, you get ashes, not stones or anything else. If you kill an animal, you are left with flesh and bones, but the animal as such ceases to exist.

Aristotle posited prime matter as the underlying subject of change. There is some principle of continuity. The physicist might identify the underlying matter in terms of subatomic particles or atoms. The chemist might identify the underlying matter as atoms and molecules. Biologists specify how living things are generated and from what they are generated; they specify conditions for living and the causes of death. What happens at death is a corruption of the unity of a living thing and a degeneration into lesser parts. There has to be some sort of continuity; there is an intelligible process of changing; change is not magic; there are limits to change. What this specific continuity is in each case is specified by the scientist; the philosopher is content to specify that there must be some central potency, form and act that falls apart, dies, decomposes into its parts and reconstitutes itself into different things.

Things within Things?

Aristotle in his search to define substance asserts clearly, "No substance is composed of substances which exist in actuality."[15] This seemed rather obvious to him and important in defining the notion of substance. He does not argue much on the issue, as it seems to have appeared too obvious. He has worked out the example of the letters and the syllable. If the syllable is considered as a substance, then at the same time and in the same respect the letters cannot be considered as substances. Either you are looking at three individual letters, each of which has an intelligibility and a unity, or you are looking at one syllable composed of three letters; but the same thing cannot be three and one, in the same respect, and at the same time. The letter and the syllable are a simple example establishing the principle for understanding more complex unities especially those of living things.

If you consider a tree as a substance, then you cannot, at the same time and in the same respect, refer to the branches, the roots, the leaves and the like, as substances. A substance is a unity of parts. A substance is a central form. An individual tree is one central form. It has a unity and identity; it is a whole. Many of the parts are detachable; many of the conjugates change over time, but as long as the tree continues to live, it maintains that unity, that identity, which is one and one only. For living things Aristotle referred to the soul as this intelligibility of the whole, its substance, which is there when the tree is alive. When the living thing is killed or dies the unity of the whole is lost and degenerates into the juxtaposition of individual parts.

From the point of view of common sense or description this position might be considered counter intuitive or even ridiculous. Surely a branch of a tree is a thing and therefore a substance! Surely the eye of an animal is a thing and therefore a substance. Surely the human heart is a thing and therefore a substance! It seems to common sense that there are things within things, substances within substances. However, this is a point where we are obliged to move into an explanatory context and use the technical terminology of central and conjugate forms. In our next chapter we will be establishing a hierarchy of genus and species. We will be establishing the real differences between atoms, molecules, cells, plants, animals, and humans. In the following chapter we will be establishing the unity of the central form of the human person as the apex of this hierarchy. What is at stake is the unity and identity of the human person as one, whole, single, individual central form.

---

15. Aristotle, *Metaphysics, Z*, 13, 1039a5.

Strictly speaking the human person is one central form and therefore one thing. It is strictly incorrect to refer to the eye or the liver or the heart as a central form. However, in common parlance it is quite acceptable and necessary to talk about the heart, the liver or the spleen as a thing. One hopes that a surgeon is intimately familiar with the distinction between these things. But then the word "thing" is being used in a descriptive sense and not in a full philosophical and strict sense. Parts cannot be wholes. Wholes cannot be made up of smaller wholes and cannot be without parts. It is important to get the balance right because that is how our minds work and that is how the real world works.

Lonergan, using his own terminology and approach, affirms the Aristotelian position that there are no things within things. In the full explanatory position, if something is affirmed to be one central form, then within that central form there cannot be other lesser, smaller, central forms, but only conjugate forms. Central forms are affirmed by appealing to all the data pertaining to that unity; the same data cannot be used to affirm further central forms; substances cannot be made up of substances. The human person is affirmed to be one central form, because all the data regarding limbs, organs, senses, mind, consciousness, knowing, willing and loving, and all the rest of it, constitute one unity, of one person, called John. John is the whole, the central form. The heart, the eye, the brain, the blood, the intellect, the will are parts of the whole, conjugate forms. We know by understanding correctly. One kind of question and insight (what is it?) gives us the central form. Another kind of question (what are its attributes or parts?) gives us conjugate forms. This represents a rejection of the extremes of reductionism, holism and process philosophy.

Our position is that there are two kinds of questions. One question asks, what is the unity identity, whole, of this particular data, and so seeks a central form. The other question asks, what are the characteristics and laws that apply to this particular thing, and so seeks conjugate forms. Both central forms and conjugate forms are to be understood and verified. Aristotle had a valid point is saying that one substance cannot contain actual substances within itself. Even though it is surprising at first, we reject things within things, or substances within substances, or central forms within central forms. There is no profit in neglecting important distinctions and intelligent questions. We challenge the simplifications of reductionism because it ignores unities, identities, wholes. We reject the exaggerations of holism when it goes beyond the evidence and imagines unities that do not exist. We question process philosophy because central forms are experienced, understood and verified to exist.

Summary

What kind of a universe are we living in? We saw in part 2 that our universe is constantly changing in terms of potencies being realized in forms and forms struggling to exist and to continue to exist, and that it is largely good. This is the universal nature or composition of our universe. In this chapter we have seen that there are two fundamentally different types of forms, the forms of things or substances, and the forms of attributes or properties. Forms are what is understood, the intelligibilities. These emerge from potencies and realize themselves in actuality. The forms of things emerge from corresponding potencies and realize themselves in corresponding existence. The forms of properties emerge from corresponding potentialities and realize themselves in corresponding events, occasions, or existence. The traditional terminology starting from Aristotle has been substance and accidents. Accidents can also be called attributes, predicates, qualities or quantities. Lonergan uses the terminology of central and conjugate potencies, forms and acts.

This distinction is of universal relevance as it encompasses all areas of human knowing, from common sense, to science, to the human sciences, to philosophy and even theology. It is a fundamental characteristic of the way we think, and also of the way the universe is. We think in terms of identifying characteristics which, taken together, will identify the substance. If we know the substance, that helps us to further specify or study other attributes. In our intellectual development we pivot from things to properties and back again. Properties can only exist in things; things can only exist with properties; they are mutually dependent and complementary.

The notion of things and properties is not an invention of philosophy but is a fundamental construct of scientific thought. It is essential to grasping the notion of change; something changes but something remains the same. Change is not annihilation and creation, not magical appearing and disappearing. Similarly, the transition from description to explanation can only be negotiated on the basis of the intellectual grasp of the same thing, which has certain properties from the point of view of description and other properties from the point of view of explanation. You can have descriptive or explanatory notions of things. Our notion is very flexible and general, useful and necessary.

11

Kinds of Things: Genus and Species

Hence, the greater one's familiarity with human intelligence and its properties, the clearer it becomes that our development of the notion of higher viewpoint into a theory of explanatory genera and species has exploited the basic and permanent factors that will hold their ground in subsequent modifications and improvements.[1]

The greatest enterprise of the mind has always been and always will be the attempted linkage of the sciences and humanities. The ongoing fragmentation of knowledge and resulting chaos in philosophy are not reflections of the real world but artifacts of scholarship.[2]

The overlaps and interdependence of the sciences, the patterns and hierarchies of the discoveries in different fields, the underlying order that they are gradually uncovering, is without question one of the most enthralling aspects—perhaps the most enthralling aspect—of modern science.[3]

Science is invading—and bringing order to—philosophy, to morality, to history, to culture in general, and even to politics.[4]

1. Lonergan, *Insight*, 466.
2. Wilson, *Consilience*, 6.
3. Watson, *Convergence*, xxv.
4. Watson, *Convergence*, xxvii.

Diagram Three: Hierarchy of Central Forms
based on Successive Higher Viewpoints

Descriptive: Example	Sciences: Explanatory	Central Forms: Genera	Central Forms: Species	Conjugate Forms: Processes, Parts
Books	Anthropology	Human Persons	One Species Only	Two-legged, sensing, questioning, thinking, deciding, loving, laughing, and so on.
Chapters	Zoology	Animals	Mammals, Fishes, Insects, Snakes, Snails, Primates, Crustaceans, and so on.	Seeing, hearing, eating, moving, organs, processes, reproduction, flying, remembering, and so on.
Paragraphs	Botany	Plants	Trees, Bushes, Flowers Vegetables, Bananas, Tubers, Geraniums, Roses, and so on.	Growing, reproducing, seeds, leaves, roots photosynthesis, xylem, phloem, and so on.
Sentences	Biology	Simple Cells	Procaryotes, Eukaryotes, Parasites, Bacteria, Stromatolites, Archaea, Sponges, and the like.	Mitosis, meiosis, growth, cytokinesis, digestion, metabolism, Golgi apparatus, and so on.
Words	Chemistry	Molecules	Pills, Salt, Sugar, Sulphuric Acid, Artificial Fertilizers, forms of carbon, gasses, and so on.	Acidic, alkaline, liquid, solid, cold, hot, poisonous, explosive, stable, oxidize, and so on.
Letters	Physics	Basic Elements	Hydrogen, Nitrogen, Oxygen, Lead, Gold, Sulphur, Silicon, Iron, Uranium, and so on.	Positive/negative charge, spin, mass, waves, laws, antimatter, light, heat, radiation, and so on.

Introduction (Diagram 3)

THE SECOND LAW OF thermodynamics states that entropy always increases with time. Popularizers of science like to interpret this as saying that disorder, chaos, and randomness within a system always increases. However, if you look even cursorily at the history of our universe and of our solar system what is astonishing is the amount of order that has emerged. We understand the functioning of the principle of finality and so are not surprised. We continue in this chapter to identify aspects of this emergent order. Now that we have distinguished between central and conjugate forms, substance and accidents, we can ask how the central forms in this universe are distributed or ordered. Are they organized into classes or groups or are they chaotic? Can they be divided into genera and species and what is the basis for this distinction? As a parallel, how is human knowing of the universe organized? Is it a chaos of knowledge about disparate things or do the sciences relate to one another in a systematic way? Is there an integrating framework? We have described the function of metaphysics as the department of human knowing that underpins, penetrates, unifies and transforms all other departments. Now we have another chance to show how this might work. Remembering that we are using the method of isomorphism, we will start with cognitional experience and take simple examples from everyday knowing, which will reveal the notion of successive higher viewpoints, which is our clue to the hierarchy of the sciences and the hierarchy of central forms. We will then be in a position to discuss the appropriate relations between the levels and some pedagogical principles following from this. The quotations above point to various ideas and terminologies that attempt to unify all our knowledge. "Consilience," "convergence," and "supervenience" have been suggested by various authors as keys to unification. There is a strong tendency to unify all knowledge by reducing it to physics and chemistry. We have found that unsatisfactory and established the notions of central and conjugate forms which will enable us to establish an ordered hierarchy of forms. Please refer to diagram 3, which presents the notion of successive higher viewpoints isomorphic with a hierarchy of genera and species.

Descriptive Examples of Successive Higher Viewpoints

A horizon is the limit of our vision from a certain given height. But if we climb to a higher point, our horizon expands, and we can see farther. We use this metaphor for acts of understanding that represent lower or higher viewpoints. We have already identified the characteristics and unfolding of individual insights. We are thus far familiar with insights that are descriptive and explanatory, inclusive and abstractive, direct and reflective and deliberative, as well as inverse insights. The higher viewpoint occurs when the content of a series of previous individual insights becomes the data for the further act of organizing intelligence leading to a higher viewpoint. The easiest way to explain this is to take a simple example, so let us imagine the progress of the human mind in learning how to read.

The first step, fairly obviously and inevitably, is to learn the letters of the alphabet. Each letter has to be learned individually. Each has to be written down, recognized, associated with a sound and remembered. Each grasp of each letter is an act of understanding into how images of sight and sound are related intelligently. It takes time to learn each letter, perhaps a year for the whole alphabet. As you proceed through the letters, you have to do constant revision to keep previous insights fresh in the mind. Intelligence is operating but it is operating on the same level—learning individual letters and finally knowing all the letters in capital and lowercase formats. But is the student who recognizes all the letters able to read? True they can recognize every individual letter in a book from start to finish. But is that reading? To learn to read something, more is required than understanding the individual letters.

The first jump to a higher viewpoint is from the individual letters to words. It is all very well to be able to identify the individual letters but a jump in understanding is required to recognize sequences of letters as the unit of meaning—incorporating the letters but going beyond them. It is one thing to recognize the three letters, "d" "o" "g"; it is quite another to understand "dog." Each word is a unit of meaning. Each word incorporates the letters but goes beyond the letters to a new meaning. It is a higher viewpoint. The units of previous understanding are now the data for a new and higher insight. Words presuppose the understanding of the letters, but understanding the individual letters is not enough. In reading words, you are focusing on a higher meaning contained in combinations of letters. This is an intellectual jump, not a logical transition. Helen Keller's moment of revelation and liberation came when she recognized that the letters spelt in her hand meant the word "water" and referred to the reality of water streaming over her other hand. She had already learned the individual letters, but they meant little to her. To those who cannot read, reading is a kind of magic. But to be able to understand words is to realize that it is not magic but intelligence developing and operating according to its proper mode of understanding higher viewpoints.

But is the person who can read words able to read a book? Is reading only about recognizing words? A dictionary contains thousands of words, with each word's meaning explained, but it is all a tiny bit disconnected. Words need to be combined into sentences. The sentences are composed of words. Each word has to be understood. But the understanding of the whole goes beyond the understanding of each part. A further jump in understanding is required to focus on the sentence as the unit of meaning, going beyond but incorporating the individual words, which themselves include and go beyond letters. Helen Keller describes the moment three months later when she grasped the meaning of a sentence. A sentence is a new unit of meaning that incorporates the words but goes beyond the meaning of the individual words. This whole new unit of intelligibility is grasped in a higher viewpoint. It takes a learning process to understand the individual words and a new learning process to understand the sentence as the unit of meaning.

A further development on the same lines takes place when you formulate paragraphs, chapters and write articles and books. Each paragraph is supposed to be a unity of meaning, as is each chapter, and each book as a whole in its own way has a unitary theme. The focus shifts from the letters, to the words, to the sentences, to the paragraphs, to the chapters, to the book as a whole. In a descriptive way these are examples of higher viewpoints. The higher presupposes the lower. You cannot read a book without recognizing letters and words. But the meaning of the chapters and the book as a whole goes beyond individual words, sentences and paragraphs.

The same kind of process can be traced in mathematics. You have to start with the numbers representing quantities, learning to count from one to ten and beyond. You proceed by way of simple operations of adding and subtracting. You continue by generalizing such operations in terms of multiplying and dividing. Fractions arise and you learn how to deal with them, then negative numbers, surds, roots, decimals, and the like. Arithmetic moves on to algebra, which is a further generalization of rules, operations and results. You can then move on to calculus, trigonometry, probabilities, permutations and combinations. It is a process of successive higher viewpoints, with the higher presupposing the lower, the lower preparing the way for the higher, the lower becoming the material about which questions are asked and general understanding is formulated. It is a process of increasing differentiation, sophistication, and higher understanding. It is a series of successive higher viewpoints.

The same kind of progress can be noted in learning to become a doctor, an engineer, or a philosopher. You study the parts, the history, various areas of interest, various tools of the trade; you do the theory and the practice. The first year is all confusion as everything is new, and difficult and expanding your horizon in every direction. It is hard to see how it all fits together. The second year continues that expansion of horizon, but you begin to experience interconnectedness of the courses, areas, principles, and results. In the third year everything begins to fit together. Finally, you think like a doctor, engineer or philosopher: you become a doctor, an engineer or a philosopher. You have reached a higher viewpoint. The highest viewpoint that we aspire to is that of the philosopher who seeks a comprehensive, ordered wisdom. She is not expected to know all the details but is expected to have a correct, comprehensive, differentiated view of the whole and the principles by which everything works and forms an ordered unity. A comprehensive exam does not usually test one's knowledge of details but one's grasp of principle, of interconnectedness, whether you think like a doctor, or engineer or a philosopher. These are further examples of the development of intelligence by way of successive higher viewpoints.

Ordering the Sciences

The phenomenon of intellectual development by way of successive higher viewpoints is a structural element in the development of understanding. Is it possible that this could be used to establish the proper relationship between the various sciences, including the human sciences? It would seem a bit strange if all the sciences were related haphazardly or at random. If such were the case then we would have to admit that our knowledge would be structurally haphazard, chaotic or random. But that does not seem to be the case: discoveries in one science can open doors in other sciences, some sciences seem to depend on others, and some seem to be more comprehensive than others. This points to relationships of succession, dependence, and higher viewpoints. It would seem to fall to philosophers to explore the relationships between the sciences. They can only do this by grasping the interconnectedness of parts of knowledge and see how various departments are interrelated and interdependent, parts within a whole. Our hypothesis is that the experience of successive higher viewpoints gives us the model for the unity of the sciences and solves the problem of how they are systematically related. In relating the sciences, we are continuing to use our method of isomorphism using the structure of knowing to point to the structure of the known.

I suggest Diagram 3 as a simple structural presentation of how the sciences are related on the basis of successive higher viewpoints. Physics represents the lowest, most universal viewpoint. Chemistry represents a

higher viewpoint, going beyond the matter of physics to a better understanding of a new reality. Biology represents a higher viewpoint including
living things, the phenomenon of life, the intelligibility and laws proper to
living things. Botany studies complex, multicellular organisms called plants
and the different kinds of and characteristics of this living form. Zoology
goes further to study animals, their genera and species, sensation, feelings,
brain, evolution, interconnectedness, disease, eating habits, mating habits,
stages of development and the like. Anthropology studies the human in all
its many aspects and includes all the human sciences, history, economics,
politics, sociology, psychology, medicine, literature, language, art, and philosophy. Of course, there are many specializations and sub-specialization
into which these five could be further divided. I am using these terms to
reveal the structure of interdependence between the basic sciences using the
model of successive higher viewpoints.

Physics is the most universal of all the sciences in the sense that its laws
apply to every material thing of whatever kind. Physics studies light, electricity, magnetism, motion, shape, quantity, vibrations, momentum, speed
of light, gravity, energy, space and time, and so on. It pivots from studying
central forms, such as atoms and subatomic particles, to conjugate forms
such as laws of motion, laws of optics, and the like. It includes the laws of
acceleration, of thermodynamics, electromagnetism, and forms of energy,
the strong and weak atomic forces, gravity and electromagnetic radiation.
Physics encompasses the specializations of astronomy, cosmology, geology,
nuclear physics, particle physics, and the like. It studies all this data from
the point of view of their material characteristics. What are the individual
atoms? What are the subatomic particles? What are the forces that hold
them together and that can be used to break them apart? It reveals the
causes of changes in the weather, the history of the solar system, why bodies fall, how engines work, how to send a human into space. All material
things including plants, animals, and humans are subject to the laws of
physics, in so far as they are material things. The laws of motion apply
equally to atoms, to billiard balls and to a rugby scrum.

But there is a range of data that is incidental to the physicist. The physicist is indifferent to living things as living, intelligent beings as intelligent,
or even atoms as complicated molecules. Those are the further purviews of
chemistry, biology, psychology, and other sciences. There is a whole range
of data to which the physicist as a physicist is indifferent. You could call
that data a coincidental manifold from the point of view of the physicist.
It is there, it is acknowledged, but it does not fit the job description of the
physicist to deal with it. The laws of motion apply indifferently to atoms,

water, bacteria, acorns, lions or humans. The physicist is equally indifferent to differences between water, bacteria, acorns, and humans. These present the possibility that there might be a science or sciences proper to the study of these matters which are beyond the sphere of the physicist.

Chemistry. There is a necessity for a science called chemistry to deal with the intelligibility of elements and their relations with one another in compound molecules. Physics is interested in the physical properties of water, but the chemist is interested in water as a compound of hydrogen and oxygen. How do these molecules come about, what are their chemical properties, and what other compounds are possible? Chemistry formulates the laws proper to such mixtures and compounds of the basic chemical elements of the periodic table. It asks how and why elements combine in this way. Again, we notice the pivoting from central forms such as the elements of the periodic table plus the millions of compounds they can form, and the conjugate forms, properties, characteristics of classes of compounds. Organic chemistry and biochemistry continue into the complicated chemical mixtures and processes that prepare the way for living things. Medicines, insecticides, fertilizers, artificial additives, environmental studies are all fertile fields for the chemist.

Chemistry takes the laws and discoveries of physics for granted; that is not its area. The laws of physics continue to operate and are presupposed. But water is not just a mixture of hydrogen and oxygen; it is a new substance, a new reality, a molecule, a higher central form, to be grasped in a higher viewpoint. There is nothing in hydrogen or oxygen taken singly to suggest the possibility of water, its characteristics, its versatility, its stability, and its importance. The laws of chemistry apply wherever there are combinations of elements and molecules. It is an autonomous science with its own data, its own questions, its own field of operations and its own laws, procedures and results.

However, there is still a vast field of sense data on which chemistry has little to say. If things move of themselves, grow, give birth, die, then there is a phenomenon of living things and the chemist as a chemist cannot explain why or how this happens. By all means, the chemist can study the chemistry of living things but living things as living things call for a higher science which we are calling biology, the science of life. From the point of view of chemistry, the data on living things is a coincidental aggregate. It is there; but it is not the task of chemistry to systematize it. This is a call for a higher viewpoint, a higher science, and a new reality of living things to be grasped explanatorily in a science.

Biology is this higher science that studies living things as living, the cell as the basic unit of living things, the definition of life, the intelligibility immanent in living things. It is a higher viewpoint, a jump in understanding. To understand living things, you are focusing on something that is dynamic, that is generated, moves of itself, grows through stages, survives but changes over time, reproduces, ages and dies. It is a more complicated subject matter than physics or chemistry, and a more complex insight is required to grasp the unity behind all the changes. It is a new science. It is not just a complicated chemistry but a new set of insights into a new kind of reality. Biology is an autonomous science, presupposing the contributions of physics and chemistry but going beyond them to grasp the intelligibility of living things.

There is a jump from physics and chemistry to biology; it is not an extrapolation, a deduction or a logical necessity. There is nothing in physics and chemistry to suggest the possibility of living things. There is a clear dividing line between non-living and living. It is a new reality, demanding a new method, new concepts, new understanding, and a higher viewpoint. Different kinds of laws will be formulated in biology and different processes, unities, structures and functions identified. All these new laws presuppose and depend on the laws and principles of physics and chemistry. All with a view to understanding living things and their uniqueness, their new reality as living things.

Biochemistry can help biology to reveal the chemical processes incorporated in living things. Chemistry retains its own validity and autonomy when dealing with its proper material. But the biologist too is autonomous in dealing with his own proper material and that includes all that is living, the phenomenon of life. It would be a big mistake to think that biology was just more complicated chemistry. So, biology studies cells, the parts of cells, the biochemistry of life processes, multicellular organisms, the kinds of cells and organisms, their origin, their characteristics, their laws, reproduction, degeneration, the systems and subsystems that sustain life. It encompasses central and conjugate forms. It classifies living things in terms of classes, orders, families, genera, species, subspecies and varieties and perhaps more.

Botany takes physics and chemistry and basic biology for granted. The laws of physics, chemistry, and biology continue to apply to the vegetative kingdom. But there is a new reality studied, which we name plants, which exploit the energy from the sun in photosynthesis. They incorporate many chemical and physical processes but go beyond them. The laws of botany are needed to systematize this coincidental manifold, which lower sciences cannot deal with adequately. It is a new, higher reality that calls for a new, higher viewpoint in a new, higher science. The explanatory definition of a particular species of tree will take a botanist a book to elaborate adequately. But all the details of the book are answering the simple question, what is a Eucalyptus tree? A range of living organisms have emerged with distinctive characteristics that we call vegetable life or plants. They use photosynthesis; they absorb carbon dioxide and give out oxygen. They absorb materials from the earth. They have highly complex specialization of cells devoted to specific tasks. Yet they constitute a unity of many parts. A tree has a unity of a living thing characteristic of plant life. This unity is grasped by understanding. The specialized functions of the parts work for the good of the whole.

Zoology. A different form of life emerges where the basic metabolism is different from that of plants. In general, we usually call it zoology, the study of the animal kingdom, a development in living things where energy is taken from food and metabolism. There is a specialization in sensation, nerves, brains, mobility, food and habitat. It includes a vast range of species, kingdoms, variations and subspecies. Every environmental niche seems to be occupied by living things appropriate to that environment. A new range of data is systematized which from the viewpoint of previous sciences is a coincidental manifold. The new range of data calls for systematization in a higher viewpoint, in this case the science of zoology.

Basic laws of physics continue to apply. Movement of animals, fish, birds, insects involve the laws of motion, fulcrum, energy, contraction, expansion, friction, density, specific weight, center of gravity, and the like. Basic laws of chemistry continue to apply to the systems that sustain life, the brain, the heart, the muscles, the blood, the lungs, and all the other life-sustaining processes. The cell continues to be the fundamental unit but now there are different kinds of cells, a new unity of function between the cells, a new specialization and integration between the cells. It is a new, more integrated, and differentiated reality to be grasped by a new higher viewpoint. Zoology takes for granted the previous sciences that we have named but goes beyond them as a new explanatory science. The units studied are more complex and require multitudes of insights simply to answer the questions like, what is a lion? Chemistry can answer the question, "What is water?" in a simple assertion that it is H_2O. To define a lion would take at least a book.

Anthropology. Finally, there is a range of data that is beyond zoology, is incidental to zoology, and is a further coincidental manifold from the point of view of zoology. There are animals that talk to one another, grow their own food, build houses and roads and cities, invent science, write books, formulate laws, distinguish between moral and immoral, and worship God. This calls forth specializations and sciences to deal with the data of intelligent life, human culture, human beings as talking, thinking, judging, valuing and relating to divinity. In general, we call these studies the human sciences, anthropology, or the humanities. Here the one studying is also the one being studied. Here we find there is one central form, the human person. The various human sciences study the potencies, needs, the history, the social, economic, cultural, moral, and religious behavior of that human person. We will tackle this in detail in our chapter on the human person.

We seem to have found a principle by which the sciences can be systematically organized to deal with all the kinds of genera and species found in our universe. This explanation will help us to relate the sciences to one another and to see that there is a unity to the division of the sciences. It is an explanatory account based on the reality of the phenomenon of successive higher viewpoints and the reality of the central and conjugate forms affirmed and verified in these viewpoints. The philosopher is suggesting a heuristic framework within which the hierarchy of the sciences can be related intelligibly. We have focused on a simplistic characterization of the sciences as physics, chemistry, biology, botany, zoology and the human sciences. Real life is more complicated, and sciences proliferate, cross boundaries, specialize, and subdivide endlessly. However, despite all the diversity there is an underlying ground for a unity within a general hierarchy of sciences.

Hierarchy of Genera and Species

Our approach has been heuristic and based on the principle of isomorphism. If there is a phenomenon of successive higher viewpoints in the development of human intelligence, it might be because there is a parallel succession of higher integrations of central forms in the real world. We have already explained the notion of higher viewpoints in the development of human intelligence and how it grounds an explanatory hierarchy of the sciences. Now we want to affirm and explain that the hierarchy of the sciences suggests a real hierarchy of genera and species existing in the real world. Please refer to column three in our diagram 3. Again, we are simplifying in order to bring out the broad picture which is after all the task of the philosopher.

The central forms dealt with in physics are atoms and subatomic particles. The conjugate forms are the laws of light, of energy, of heat, of motion, of electricity and magnetism, of radiation and the technologies based on these. Atoms are the material from which everything else in the universe emerges. At first there was hydrogen, then helium, then the other elements emerged when conditions became favorable. This is the basic potency from which higher forms emerge to survive or to become extinct. There is a certain fascination with finding the smallest and the most basic particle out of which everything else is made. We thought it was the atom but then discovered subatomic particles. At first, there were four subatomic particles and now there are about sixty in the standard particle model. And still we seek the common matter out of which these are made, whether they be quarks, or waves, or particles, or energy, or strings.

However, as well as the question, what is the atom made out of, there is the more fundamental question, what is an atom? It is certainly a unity of parts; it has an identity, as you can distinguish hydrogen from helium, and so on. The atom is a central form. It comes into existence when subatomic particles combine to form the atom, and it can go out of existence, if the nucleus is broken apart in nuclear fission. It has stability but not an eternal permanence. Each atom is numerically different from the next. There is potency for higher things, but they become known only in the emergence of those higher things. There is an interchangeability of mass and energy according to Einstein's famous equation of $E=Mc^2$. Matter can be changed into energy and energy can be changed into mass according to this formula in those proportions.

There are different kinds of atoms building up in mass and complexity until you have the periodic table of over one hundred elements. The elements are the terms related systematically to one another in the periodic table. The periodic table is a good example of explanatory system where terms define relations and relations define terms. Each element is a central form or substance, distinguishable from one another by atomic weight and other conjugate forms. These are the central forms studied in chemistry.

But that is only the beginning. Chemistry has to discover what happens when elements combine to form complex mixtures or compounds. There is no way of predicting that hydrogen and oxygen will combine to form water. That they do so becomes intelligible when the laws of combination and valence are formulated. You can have a mixture of hydrogen and oxygen but that is not water; they are both gasses at normal temperatures. But when combustion takes place, they become a compound called water. A new substance has been generated; its properties need to be investigated, and so on.

You can have millions of compounds formed by reactions and combinations of elements with one another. They are new, more complicated, differentiated central forms or substances. They can build up in complexity. There are rules of what can combine with what and how. It is the task of chemistry to understand these classes of compounds, how they combine, what are their properties, what are the processes involved, where are the elements and compounds found, what can they be used for. Biochemistry deals with the chemistry involved in life processes involving proteins, amino acids, organic chemicals, chemistry of metabolism, etc.

Then we have the central forms of biology: living cells, which represent a new kind of central form or substance that emerges from the potencies of the lower orders and form new, stable, unities, identities, wholes. The same process of emergence is operative: new things are emerging from the old ones, and they are genuinely new central forms even though they include and go beyond the old ones. They are grasped not by seeing but by understanding. As this is a particularly difficult topic, we deal with it in our next chapter on, what is life?

Next in our hierarchy of central forms are plants and animals studied in the sciences of botany and zoology respectively with all their subdivisions and specializations. Plants and animals differentiate enormously in relation to sources of energy, of food, of habitat, of climate. These central forms are organized in terms of evolving from one another, a tree of life, a history of differentiation and integration. It is the tasks of botany and zoology to identify and relate all the various genera and species of the plant and animal world.

Finally, human persons represent a new unique central form presupposing all the others but going beyond them in ways that we have yet to explore. We postpone a detailed consideration of this, highest central form until the chapter on the human person.

The hypothesis suggested by the phenomenon of successive higher viewpoints seems to be confirmed, when we verify a parallel succession of higher integrations of central forms in the universe: subatomic particles, atoms, chemicals, cells, plants, animals, humans. There is a really generically distinct hierarchy of successive higher viewpoints, that is confirmed and verified in the corresponding hierarchy of empirical sciences and the relevant central forms studied in these sciences.

Relations between Levels—Sublation

We have distinguished six levels of successive higher viewpoints, which we have identified as the basic explanatory sciences: physics, chemistry, biology, botany, zoology and anthropology. As a parallel in the real world, we have identified six levels of successive higher integrations which we have identified with atoms, molecules, cells, plants, animals and humans. This is a bare skeleton to illustrate the hierarchy and there is a multitude of detail, complexity and elaboration that could be added to this schema. Each can be divided and subdivided into specializations of various kinds, on various bases. However, our question here is simply to establish some heuristic principles by which these six levels are related to one another. In considering the relationships between the levels, we are still looking for an overall view of everything and trusting the empirical sciences to fill in the details.

We use the term "sublation" to express the relationship between the levels of central forms. We have invoked this principle earlier to relate the four levels of cognitional structure to one another, and, in parallel, how the four metaphysical elements relate to one another. We saw how experience was sublated by understanding, how experience and understanding were sublated by judgment of fact, and how experience, understanding and judgment of fact by judgment of value. We then saw how potency was sublated by form, potency and form by act, and potency, form, and act by the good.

Now we use sublation to relate the series of central forms, which seem to form an order or hierarchy. By sublation we mean four principles governing the relationship between the levels of central forms with their corresponding sciences.

Firstly, *something genuinely new emerges* when a higher viewpoint systematizes the insights that have occurred at a lower level. It is not simply another insight at the same level. It is not simply a horizontal development but a vertical jump to something new. It is a new start, not just more of the same. Just as insight into a word is something new and beyond the insight into the letters, the insights of biology trump those of physics; they are new insights, higher viewpoints.

In parallel, the higher integrations represent something new, a new kind of central form. It is not just more complex, or bigger, but a new principle of integration, a new level of intelligibility, a new reality. It also represents a vertical jump. A cell is not just chemical processes but is a new integration, a new reality, which requires a new way of thinking to develop the new science of biology. The emergence of these higher integrations is not predictable or logical, or even expected; it comes as a surprise.

Secondly, *the higher viewpoint always leaves intact the insights and laws that operate on the lower level.* The higher sciences do not replace or absorb or nullify or denigrate or devalue the lower sciences in the hierarchy. Each science is autonomous and independent in that limited sense of having their own proper mode of operation, their own proper object, their own proper place in the hierarchy, their own proper methods, procedures, and techniques.

The higher integration also leaves intact the central and conjugate forms proper to the lower sciences. The molecules of chemistry do not mean that the atoms and conjugate forms proper to physics are not valid at their own level. There are central forms and conjugate forms proper to each level of understanding and integration. The lower can exist independently of the higher existing.

Thirdly, *the higher actually enhances the value and importance of the lower*. We have tried to use the terms higher and lower in a neutral sense and when we have used the term "hierarchy" we have tried to use it in a neutral non-judgmental sense. But for the higher science to operate properly it often has to have recourse to materials from the lower sciences. This makes some areas of the lower sciences of extreme importance for the operation of the higher sciences. To understand the functioning of a living cell, you must understand the chemical processes, transformations and constraints that are operating in the cell. The health of a human person can be enhanced or hindered by the presence and operation of various chemicals, medicines or poisons. Uranium becomes a valuable resource when humans discover how to use it to produce electricity or make bombs. The science of optics can help partially blind people to be able to see. The chemistry of DNA can help understand and explain inherited traits from parents to children.

Fourthly, *the higher integrations continue to depend on the proper functioning of the lower levels*. If all vegetative life were destroyed, it would be hard for herbivores to continue to survive. If weather patterns change substantially, humanity may not survive the consequences.

Principles Guiding Relations of Genera and Species

Certain conclusions follow from our analysis of the principle of successive higher viewpoints as a basis for the hierarchy of sciences and the parallel hierarchy of higher central forms in the real world. Further development and understanding depends on a proper understanding of this relationship, which should be incorporated into the study of each of the disciplines. Collaboration between disciplines requires a common framework within which everybody is working so that everybody can get maximum profit out of their own discipline and make a genuine contribution to the advancement of our true understanding of the universe. This chapter is attempting to elaborate such a framework. Specialists need to know where they fit in the overall picture in order to make their correct, appropriate and proper contribution to the advancement of science. The occupational hazard of every specialization is to think that they are the one and only source of knowledge. We have carefully distinguished the overall wisdom of philosophy and the contribution of the sciences to understanding the details of the parts. Let us specify certain principles that should govern a correct understanding of the relationship between the sciences and foster creative collaboration.

(1) Central forms of a lower integration do not continue to exist as central forms when integrated into a higher central form. Or in Aristotle's terminology, a substance is not composed of substances existing as such. Our analysis of higher viewpoint and corresponding higher integrations is at the same time a refutation of reductionism and an affirmation of a hierarchy of different kinds of things. Water is not explained by an exhaustive treatment of hydrogen and oxygen individually; it is not a mixture of hydrogen and oxygen but a compound; it is a higher integration displaying unpredictable, unique, novel properties, different from those of oxygen and hydrogen individually. Water can be said to contain hydrogen and oxygen, to be composed of hydrogen and oxygen, but if it is water, it is water, and it cannot at the same time and in the same respect be called simply hydrogen and oxygen. A living cell is not fully explained by an exhaustive treatment of the chemistry of each of its parts. It is the new identity or whole that has to be explained, that is unique and that is the proper subject of biology. A human person is not to be explained by an exhaustive treatment of physics, chemistry, biology, zoology and sensitive psychology, but rather a study of a new, intelligent, rational, moral person as a new higher integration of previous potencies. If a human person is one central form, then the parts of a human being cannot, at the same time and in the same respect, be called central forms.

We have already given a brief treatment of things within things. From the strictly explanatory point of view, if the whole is a substance, then the parts cannot at the same time, in the same respect, be substances. If an animal is one central form, then in the same respect and at the same time you cannot affirm that the organs are central forms. We are discoursing in an explanatory context. This poses many problems for the imagination, but our criterion of truth is not imagination but critical judgment.

(2) Conjugate forms, which operate at lower levels, continue to operate at higher levels, all else being equal. The physical laws of motion apply equally to stones, to sugar, to cells, to trees, to lions, to humans. A golf swing is just pure physics of momentum, contraction, expansion, rhythm, timing, speed, arc, elasticity, angles, momentum, weight, and the like. Digestion is mostly chemistry of enzymes and proteins. All the laws of physics, chemistry, biology, botany and zoology in principle apply to the human person. Economics is a human science that formulates its own definitions, relations and laws pertaining to human economic behavior, production, inflation, and all the

rest of it. The laws of physics, chemistry, biology, etc. must be taken into account by good economists, but they also add new conjugate forms. Economic laws have meaning at the level of human persons and society; they only emerge when humans engage in economic activity.

(3) The higher central forms depend on the lower. The higher integrations only become possible with the preexistence of the lower integrations. Chemical compounds presuppose the preexistence of atoms and elements. The emergence of life requires a certain combination of chemical compounds. Human intelligence depends on the preexistence of a developed sensitivity. The nerves, senses, brains, memory and imagination, coordination, of animals prepare the way for the emergence of intelligence. We have presented a detailed analysis of the process of emergence in chapter 9. New forms depend on the materials from which they have emerged.

In the process of human learning there is a dependence of higher viewpoints on lower viewpoints. You cannot reach the higher without passing through the lower. If you want to become a chess grandmaster, you have to start at the beginning with the rules, the pieces, the aims and the tactics. You proceed to an understanding of basic strategy, theory, memory, style, techniques, endgames, and become an average club player. Master and grandmaster make moves that are unintelligible to the average club player; it is a new way of thinking about how to win. A good biologist must have some understanding of basic physics and chemistry. A full understanding of the human person would include an understanding of how the laws of physics and chemistry apply to the human person. Higher integrations can only occur where lower integrations have already occurred. Hence you have an increasing contraction of the space where certain things can happen. If there is no hydrogen you cannot have helium. If the organic chemicals are not there, then there cannot be life. If the animals are not there, then there cannot be human life. Humans can only emerge where all the preexisting conditions have been met, which is very limited sphere in time and space.

The lower precede the higher in time, both in developing understanding and in emerging higher integrations of central forms. In its most basic pattern, potency precedes form and forms may or may not continue to survive. Development is from the undifferentiated to the differentiated, from simple to compound, from static to dynamic, from incomplete to complete.

(4) The specific contribution of any science at any level is an understanding of the particular integration proper to that level. Conrad Lorenz is said to have been given a Nobel Prize for discovering that ducks are animals. He studied not the biochemistry of ducks, but ducks as ducks, how and

where they emerged, what makes them adapted to survive, how they behave as ducks as distinct from geese, what are their proper behavior as ducks. Knowledge of lower sciences might be a help but does not belong to the specific difference of the particular discipline. If you want to study human beings as humans, study what makes them different from animals, namely intelligence, rationality, valuing, relating to God and freedom, and not what they have in common with animals.

It is important to find out what a thing is made of, its material substrate, but this does not exhaust what a thing is in itself. If you want to understand human intelligence, by all means study human brains, but remember that that is only the material substrate for human intelligence. To understand human intelligence, one must study human intelligence itself, namely, the operations of human intelligence in its acts of understanding, reasoning, judging, and valuing, as well as how these are interrelated and interdependent in the human mind.

(5) The higher central forms in the hierarchy of forms are more difficult to understand than the lower. We continually make the mistake of applying the thinking appropriate to lower sciences to the higher sciences. We continually try to explain life in terms of physics and chemistry. We continually try to explain human intelligence in terms of animal sensitivity. What is required is a higher viewpoint by which we grasp the unity of a higher integration. It is very difficult to understand the human person because all the insights of physics, chemistry, biology, botany, and zoology are merely preparatory steps leading to what is specifically human. To grasp the full range of human intelligence, rationality, responsibility, and freedom in one viewpoint is the work of wisdom, a philosopher, to which we aspire but never attain, at least not comprehensively. Aristotle spoke of the soul of a living thing, but this means nothing to this generation because we have lost the sense of the unity and integration and intelligibility proper to living things. We tend to explain living things in terms of chemistry and DNA. What is a human person, is a simple direct question. But all the libraries in the world and more would be included in the total answer. So many efforts are made to explain consciousness in terms of chemistry. This would be fine if chemical molecules were conscious, but they do not seem to be. There is a chemical component that prepares the way for consciousness, but if you want to understand consciousness, study consciousness: where and when and how it occurs in animals and humans. Study it for what it is, and not merely the material preconditions for its occurrence.

(6) Things can go wrong at any level of operation, and this can affect the whole. The proper functioning of higher levels presupposes the proper functioning of the lower levels. An ancient adage recommends, "first live and then philosophize." To be able to philosophize presupposes a healthy mind and body and all that that entails. Cerebral malaria is not a favorable condition for doing philosophy. Philosophy is hard work on an empty stomach.

Problems can arise at any level. Depression in a human being can be caused by lack of chemicals, by repressed guilt, by a malfunctioning pineal gland, or by an awareness of the tragic side of life. Problems are solved at the level at which they arise. Depression might be cured by pills, or by counseling, or by brain surgery, or by seeing that life is not just all tragedy but tragic-comic.

There are a number of explanations at different levels of why a football team keeps getting bad results. Firstly, they may be unfit and incapable physically of playing for ninety minutes. Or secondly, they may be eating the wrong foods and drink before the match and their bodies are lacking sugar for the muscles. Or thirdly, they may have a collective inferiority complex, lack confidence and do not believe they can win. Or fourthly, they may be using inappropriate tactics or strategy.

Hence, it is important to diagnose problems correctly, to grasp at what level the problem occurs and what the appropriate solution is.

(7) The proper functioning of one level promotes the proper functioning of other levels. Healthy biological functions will foster precise mental functions. The proper functioning of senses, imagination, and memory promotes proper functioning of questioning, observing, relating, criticizing and concluding. Sophisticated, clear, perceptive understanding in any of the sciences makes it possible for epistemologists to identify the methods, procedures, mental operations involved in knowing and evaluating.

(8) Causes can operate from lower to higher and from higher to lower levels. If cells turn cancerous, then the whole is in mortal danger. If the body is lacking iron, then trouble is brewing on chemical, biological, and psychological levels. It is hard to type, write, or otherwise function as a scholar with a broken arm. Too much carbon dioxide in the air can change the climate and kill people

On the other hand, the higher can affect the lower levels. There is some truth to the phrase, "mind over matter." A positive attitude to life can aid recovery from sickness. The practice of mindfulness can decrease blood pressure. Worry can cause indigestion. It is possible to be celibate and fully human.

(9) We are putting forward the idea of a harmonious functioning of all levels in one operating whole. Descartes had a problem of how mind could interact with body, what became known as the "problem of interaction." Various solutions to this so-called problem were presented in occasionalism or pre-established harmony or psychophysical parallelism, or in the denial of mind altogether. This is still a problem for some in our day. But it is a problem posed by the imagination and not by intelligence. If you imagine matter as that which is sensible and visible and tangible and obviously extended in space and time, and you imagine spirit as that which is invisible, intangible, and obviously not extended in space or time, then there is an obvious difficulty of imagining how something extended in space and time can touch or be in contact with something that is not extended in space and time.

But if you think in terms of central and conjugate forms and in terms of higher and lower integrations of forms, then it is not difficult to distinguish central forms which are sensitive, namely, operate at the level of sensation, and central forms which as well as being sensitive, are also intelligent, rational, moral, religious and free. When put in these terms it is a question of understanding and relating intelligently and not of imagining a ghost operating in a machine.

(10) The human person is the highest central form that we know of in this universe. The human being emerges from the universe and is the peak achievement of the universe. We may not be in the geographical center of the universe as was thought in the geocentric view of Ptolemy; there may not be anything special about the position of our solar system or galaxy. But we are the highest known achievement in the natural development of our universe.

All the laws of all the sciences are relevant to the understanding of the proper functioning and flourishing of the human being. We go beyond other animals in being intelligent, rational, moral and religious and performing our activities freely. It is of some importance to get this perspective right. A BBC naturalist asks, "Aren't whales just as important as human beings," addressing the question to a little girl in a class. Of course, the politically correct answer is "yes," which the little girl duly gave. But it is not the correct answer. It is very important to preserve endangered species and to save the planet. But nothing should confuse the principle that human beings are special in the animal kingdom because they are different and more valuable; they are really intelligent, rational and moral, a higher integration embodying a new reality and incorporating higher conjugate forms in a new genus of being. It is a higher reality and a higher value.

Some scientist imagined trying to reproduce a human being in the laboratory starting from scratch; he thought it would soon be possible.[5] I would say that to reproduce a human person artificially in the laboratory you would have to start from the Big Bang and allow the universe to unfold in all its dimensions over billions of years to reproduce the richness and diversity, complexity and intelligence of the universe and the human person who has emerged from that matrix.

(11) How do we account for the emergence of diversity of genera and species? Darwin of course appealed to the principle of natural selection, namely, chance mutations do occur in reproduction, unhelpful mutations will die out naturally, and favorable mutations will give the organism a better chance of surviving and thriving and reproducing; hence, these traits are selected and propagated. There is no problem with that, except that it is not the whole picture. Our vision is of a total universe that is emergent and developing. Physics studies the emergence of form from potency, matter from energy, atoms from subatomic particles, and all the processes involved. Chemistry studies the emergence of a diversity of complicated compounds from the basic hundred or so basic elements. Biology studies the emergence of life, the workings of a simple single cell, the emergence of multicellular organisms, and the division into plant and animal life. Zoology studies the emergence of a diversity of living sensate animals in all their diversity. Anthropology studies the emergence of hominoid species and finally homo sapiens. We posit a principle of emergence of successive higher integrations, some of which survive, and some die out. This happens in terms of effective probabilities, not in term of determinism or deduction. There is an element of chance operating across the whole range of our universe and that allows for novelty and new higher integrations. The tendency to disorder has to be complemented by a principle of finality according to which higher forms emerge. This has been elaborated in great detail in chapter 9.

Conclusion

We can all appreciate the awesome diversity and richness of our universe with its countless individuals of all kinds. We marvel at the number and variety of particles, atoms, molecules, cells, plants, animals and humans. Far from being a chaos, we discover that these are ordered in a hierarchy of central forms and that this provides a basis for the distinction and

---

5. Potter, *How to Make a Human Being.*

relation of all the sciences. Scientists explore the specifics of each of these individual central forms.

Our task is the metaphysical project of grasping the overall picture, the integrating framework, the principle of unity behind this diversity. We found it in the clue of successive higher viewpoints by which our understanding develops. We used this as a basis for showing how the sciences are related in terms of a hierarchy of higher viewpoints and similarly that things studied in each of the sciences are related in terms of a hierarchy of higher integrations. Our heuristic anticipation seems to mesh perfectly with the wealth of understanding of the specific sciences themselves.

Collaboration between disciplines presupposes a common framework in which everybody operates. Such an understanding of the whole picture and the interrelations between the parts should help scientists to understand their place in the overall picture, their specific contribution to the whole, and their dependence on other sciences. It should help them to ask the right questions and seek the intelligibility proper to their discipline, whether physics, chemistry, biology, botany, zoology, or a human science.

12

Understanding Living Things

First, then, in any plant, animal, or man, there is to be affirmed an individual, existing unity. By central potency it is individual; by central form it is a unity, identity, whole; by central act it is existent.

Secondly, besides central potency, form, and act, there are conjugate potencies, forms, and acts. Moreover, the central potency, form, and act are constants throughout the development; it is the same individual and existing unity that develops organically, psychically, intellectually; and so development is to be formulated in terms of conjugate potency, form, and act.[1]

The surest way to grasp complexity in the brain, as in any other biological system, is to think of it as an engineering problem. What are the broad principles needed to create a brain from scratch?[2]

The principle of Biological Relativity is best stated as the theory that all levels in organisms have causal efficacy. There is no privileged level from which all the others may be derived. The principle Does not, however, mean that all levels are equivalent. The nature of causal influence of each level on the others may differ.[3]

Introduction

WE HAVE OUTLINED A hierarchy of successive higher viewpoints, a hierarchy of sciences, and a hierarchy of central forms proper to those sciences. It might be profitable to consider the jump from non-living to living things in greater detail. It is obviously a key feature of our world-

1. Lonergan, *Insight*, 484.
2. Wilson, *Consilience*, 112.
3. Noble, *Dance to the Tune of Life*, 181.

view and is open to many confusions and misunderstandings. We remind ourselves that we are metaphysicians and not biologists. Our aim is not to give specific answers to particular questions but to provide an integrating structure into which our scientific findings will find their proper context, as we have explained in detail in chapter 3. The biologist is particularly prone to philosophical presuppositions which skew the research and in the end are found to be wrong and harmful. With clear and correct background presuppositions the biologist is better prepared to ask and answer the most fruitful and pertinent of questions. Therefore, our aim in this chapter will be simply to supply the correct integrating structure for the fruitful pursuit of understanding living things.

We will start with Aristotle, whose philosophical presuppositions were largely correct and fruitful, but whose empirical studies was very limited and often wrong. We will proceed to deal with two common but wrong ways of understanding biology, vitalism, and mechanism. We will then try to show how understanding living things involves a new science, a new understanding, a new method, and a new reality—something beyond physics and chemistry. The key here is to understand development and to do that we need to formulate a genetic method to complement what we have already said about classical and statistical method. This will help to suggest some principles in doing biology and how we can then move on to the higher viewpoints of botany, zoology and the human sciences.

Aristotle on the Soul

Aristotle dealt with the question of what life is in terms of his definition of the soul, the notions of substance and accidents, matter and form, potency and act. It is in this metaphysical context that his dealing with the soul is to be interpreted. It seems that the *De Anima* was written after the *Metaphysics* and belonged to his later writings.

In the *De Anima*, Aristotle admits the difficulty of the topic. It is hard to figure out the substance of the soul, to discover the method of the biological sciences, and to find the correct starting point. He starts with his customary musings on the possibilities and difficulties and considers the various contributions of his predecessors and contemporaries to the discussion on the definition of the soul. He rejects the Platonist idea of the soul as a subsistent substance; he rejects the idea of the soul as a number; he rejects the notion that it is a material element or a part, and he rejects the idea that the intellect is the soul. In book B, he gives us two formulations of a definition of the soul:

Accordingly, the soul must be a substance as the form of a natural body potential with life, and (such) substance is an actuality.
So the soul is the actuality of such a body.[4]

If, then, there is something common to be said about every
(kind of) soul, this would be: "the first actuality of a natural
body which has organs."[5]

What on earth does this mean? Aristotle is taking for granted his basic
principle of matter and form. Form is immanent in matter; matter is potentiality to form; matter is unknowable except in relation to form. Form
is what is understood when we correctly define a universal. Forms are real,
not in the sense of existing as subsistent, but in the sense of belonging to
the intelligibility of the real world.

He realizes that the forms of living things are a special category of
form. They are a different kind of intelligibility because living things move
of themselves, grow over time, come into existence, go out of existence,
and reproduce themselves. Hence, he used the term "soul" simply meaning
the form of a living body. As form is to matter, so soul is to body. He does
not think of soul and body as two distinct things, he thinks of them as
two principles inextricably linked, as the formal and material causes of the
living creature. One cannot exist without the other. They are principles or
causes and not things in themselves.

One individual substance is constituted by the principles of matter
and form. His prime example of substance is actually the soul of an individual person, or an individual horse. Again, he is taking for granted his
distinction between the first category of substance and the nine categories
of accidents. Again, the substance is not apart from the accidents but is
grasped as the substrate, the underlying subject, the essence, that constitutes the unity of the living thing.

Aristotle's method is an empirical method. His definition of soul is
empirically verifiable. The schema he is working on is that living things
display distinct activities; he is thinking of growth, taking in food, local motion, seeing, hearing, smelling, desiring, imagining and remembering and
thinking and deciding. These activities are observable, verifiable, they are
either present or not present.

The activities are directed to objects. Seeing is in relation to light and
color and shape. Hearing is in relation to sound, noise, vibration, tone.
Desiring is in relation to food, or satisfaction or building a home, or some

4. Aristotle, *De Anima*, B, 1, 412a20.
5. Aristotle, *De Anima*, B, 1, 412b5.

object known. Thus, he discusses the various faculties of sensation in terms of their objects, both of which are empirically verifiable and part of the science of biology and botany.

Thus, if an animal displays the activity of seeing, then it has the power or potency to see. The nature of things is revealed in their activities and potencies. A horse need not be actually seeing for the statement to be true that horses see. They can still see when they are asleep or not actually seeing, they have the power or the potency to see. Similarly, if an animal displays the activity of remembering or growing or moving, then they have the power to remember, to grow or to move. This is simply grasping the capacity underlying the acts.

Each living thing then has many powers. How do they operate? Is it the powers that operate or is it the soul that operates using the powers? Aristotle notices that each living thing is a unity with many powers. The soul acts as the unifying principle of the activities of many powers. It is not the intellect that thinks but the person who thinks using the intellect. It is not the eye that sees but the animal that sees using the eye. When the leg is hurt, it is the animal that feels the pain not the leg. Soul is the principle that justifies us saying the animal acts as a whole, as a unity. When the animal reproduces, it is not the reproductive organs that reproduce but the animal using the reproductive organs. There is a verifiable meaning to the term "soul." It results from a correct understanding of the activities specific to living plants or animals.

Using these principles, Aristotle distinguished three kinds of soul: the vegetative, the animal, and the intellectual—each differentiated according to its respective activities. Nutrition and growth, without local motion or sensation, are the characteristic activities of plants. Animals add to these the activities of sensing and local motion. Humans add to these the activities of understanding, knowing and willing. It is one soul that is the source of principle of all these activities. It is not that the human has three souls, but one soul which is the principle of all nutritive, growth, local motion, sensation and intellection.

Aristotle correctly understood the notion of soul. He had a correct notion of one substance perduring over time while the accidents changed. With the notion of potency and act he was able to deal in a general way with the development of the organism from birth, through growth and reproduction, to death. He had a correct understanding of the overall picture, the metaphysics, even though compared to today, he was deficient in details of biological functioning. Aristotle was a man of his time. He knew nothing of the chemistry of the cell. He knew nothing of cells producing cells. He accepted the notion of spontaneous generation of living things; it seemed that you could see this happen. His knowledge of internal organs was limited, and his knowledge of species was not extensive. Big gaps remain in his treatment of reproduction or the function of organs or the taxonomy of plants and animals. Nor did he have any notion of evolution. His was a static universe, where each species reproduces itself and is not linked to others in an evolutionary sequence. However, for whatever defects of details he suffered from, he had a healthier grasp of the wholeness of living things than many contemporary biologists.

This correct metaphysics along with defective details passed into the theology and philosophy of the medieval period. Unfortunately, in the period of decline of Scholastic philosophy and in the modern philosophies of Descartes, Hume, Kant, Ryle, and the like, this notion of soul is quite lost. It is unfortunate that in popular culture and in the life sciences the term "soul" is rarely used and, if used, is invariably incorrectly used. Lonergan does not use the term in *Insight* and is content with applying the notion of central form to living things. I think his attitude would be that he does not wish to waste time trying to rehabilitate the term "soul." But what he means by central form is totally consonant with Aristotle's notion of soul. Whatever about the term "soul," it is vital to rehabilitate its meaning as central form. We cannot understand living things if we have no concept of the unity and wholeness of a living thing, which we refer to as central form, and the constant changes and developments, which we refer to as conjugate forms.

Vitalism and Mechanism

There are two extremes to be avoided in seeking a correct understanding of living things: vitalism and mechanism. These positions attempt to explain living things in what is considered to be an obvious answer. Vitalism is not so common, but mechanism seems to be the default position of most modern biologists. It might help if we consider these extreme positions first, so that we can aim at somewhere in the middle ground.

(1) *Vitalism.* When we think of the soul, we very often try to *imagine* the soul rather than trying to define it. So, we imagine it as a kind of ghost, invisible, intangible, spooky, insensible, ethereal, but somehow real. We imagine these as added on to the molecules, atoms and subatomic particles of physics and chemistry. We imagine that the soul is not material and is separate from material things; yet it is real. It is like a breath that is breathed into a body and gives it life; and when the breath leaves the body, it is dead. We imagine where the soul is, how many souls there are, we imagine it as separate

from the body. We tend to think of two *things*, the body and the soul. We tend to imagine the soul as superior to the body or imprisoned in the body. We imagine it as a vital force making the body alive. We wonder where the souls of animals go when they die. We readily succumb to Cartesian dualism, imagining the soul as the ghost in the machine. This is a prime example of where imagination takes over from intelligence. Although we are obliged to imagine when we wish to understand something, unfortunately, we sometimes force the intelligence to fall in line with the demands of imagination and not vice versa. Aristotle was not a vitalist, in the sense of imagining a ghost in a machine, but he had a correct understanding of the notions of soul and body as principles and causes to be grasped by intelligence, rather than separate things to be imagined. Vitalism is an extreme in that it reifies the soul, and makes it a separate thing, independent of the body.

(2) Mechanism. The opposite extreme is to affirm that besides the obvious existence of molecules, atoms and subatomic particles, there is absolutely nothing more to be added to the living thing. There is no ghost, no element, no mysterious reality, no spooky entity—nothing other than matter is needed to explain life. Life is just the sum total of all the physical and chemical processes and elements that can be discerned by physics and chemistry. The parts are added together, and they are supposed to make a whole. The whole is nothing more than the sum total of the parts. Once you understand all the parts in all their details in physics and chemistry, you will have understood the whole; there is nothing more. Living things are no different from non-living things, except that they are much more complex, but in principle they are the same—they are purely mechanical. Hence, they are to be explained in terms of the same physical and chemical laws and principles and processes. Hence, there is no need for an autonomous science of biology which is just complicated physics and chemistry. As James Watson puts it: "Life, as we now know, is nothing but a vast array of coordinated chemical reactions. The 'secret' to that coordination is the breathtakingly complex set of instructions inscribed, again chemically, in our DNA."[6]

Most modern biology seems to be based on a mechanist, physicalist, materialist, reductionist philosophy. Biology can go into incredible detail about the molecules, the systems, the parts, the processes, the biochemistry, the organs, and the like, and think it has explained everything. But unfortunately, it has left out everything that is distinctive of a living being as a unity identity whole, that moves of itself, grows, reproduces, is conscious, has a past a present and a future, and acts as a coordinated whole.

6. Watson, *DNA*, 420.

Genetic Method

Classical methods of science anticipate a mathematical correlation expressing a direct intelligibility on which the concrete will converge. Statistical method expresses a law or generalization from which the concrete diverges non-systematically. However, neither of these methods are adequate for the study of living things, so we have to develop a new method appropriate for the study of things that are alive, that are born and die, that grow, that possess their existence over time and space, that are examples of living higher integrations. We need a new heuristic structure to formulate the expectations of insight and guide research for the understanding of living things. We call it a genetic method because it will deal with the genesis or development of things that are dynamic and alive, that exist and change over time. Perhaps the easiest way to present this is to posit a definition of development, which is the heuristic structure underlying genetic method:

> A development may be defined as a flexible, linked sequence of dynamic and increasingly differentiated higher integrations that meet the tension of successively transformed underlying manifolds through successive applications of the principles of correspondence and emergence.[7]

Growth is a linked sequence. It is a sequence because one thing follows another, and the latter is usually dependent on the occurrence of the former. The living thing goes through a sequence of developments which can be traced in great detail in biology textbooks. Each organ or part emerges at its particular moment. It is a linked sequence because the later developments are dependent on successful completion of the earlier developments. The order can rarely be reversed. If something goes wrong at any particular stage, it can have grave consequences for the emergence of later stages. Understanding a chemical formula is one simple direct insight, but grasping a sequence involves the past, the present and the future state of the living thing. It is enormously more complicated and difficult.

The development of a living being is flexible. In the world of biology, you do not expect the same exactitude that is found in physics and chemistry. There is flexibility in terms of size and shape and color; there is flexibility in terms of stages of development and how quickly or slowly they are reached. Snow crystals can be very complicated, but they are usually in geometrical form; the branches of a tree, however, even though they conform to a general shape, will all be different and will not follow straight lines, triangles or fixed geometrical patterns.

7. Lonergan, *Insight*, 479.

The direction of development is towards dynamic and increasingly differentiated higher integrations. The direction of development is from undifferentiated to differentiated. Stem cells are generic and undifferentiated: they can become any specialized kind of cell. But once they have become differentiated there is no turning back. The human fertilized ovum is just one cell. But as it duplicates, each cell becomes more and more differentiated. The adult is made up of billions of cells each with its specific function, in its specific place, doing its specific job in relation to the integrated whole. Development is a process of increasing differentiation and integration. The parts become more different from one another. However, the whole is the integration of all the parts into one developing subject. The integrations are constantly on the move through development or decline. It is a dynamic process. Such a process of developing hierarchies of interdependent integrations is precisely what is studied by genetic method.

The principle of correspondence is the requirement that the higher integration is limited by the underlying manifolds that it integrates. Living forms that emerge in water, sunlight and oxygen are different from living forms that emerge in high temperature, under-water, or volcanic, sulphur-based forms of life. It is true the same environment can produce different forms of life, but there continues to be a dependence of the higher integration on the materials that it integrates. An insight integrates data and images; the insight must correspond to the materials that it integrates.

The principle of emergence is the expression of the principle of finality operating in the universe of proportionate being. The prime example is how insights emerge from images and sense data. Living forms can only emerge in an environment where the temperature, the chemicals, the water, oxygen and sunlight have already prepared the way. Mammals can only emerge in an environment that is suitable and confers an advantage. Intelligence can only emerge when sensibility has reached a high degree of sophistication. Emerging forms depend on the material out of which they emerge. But the forms confer a new unity, a new integration, a new reality on the materials. Each successive stage in the growth of an organism can only emerge when the material conditions are ripe. Intelligence is only possible when the brain is sufficiently organized and differentiated. A genetic method is needed to understand that linked sequence of emergences in one insight.

In living, growing things there is always a tension between what was, is, and is to be. A living being possesses its reality over time and changes over time. Previous stages are being outgrown; the organism is moving forward to the future. The present is a tension between what was and is and what is to become.

A prime example for us of development is the development of human intelligence. This has been our starting point and template for understanding the structure of the universe. Now we can use it as an example for understanding development. Human intelligence develops under the dynamic of the desire to know. It moves dynamically through a sequence of stages, from experiencing, to understanding, to judging and evaluating. When the images and data are disposed the insight emerges. Understanding seeks higher viewpoints. A variety of insights invite integration into a coherent system. Description leads to explanation which leads to interiority. It is one single human intelligence which realizes itself in a sequence of stages which are flexible depending on particular teachers, data, books, and other circumstances. Later stages depend on the completion of earlier stages. Our familiarity with each of these elements of intellectual development means that we can use it as a template for other kinds of development. However, intellectual development is more flexible and creative than other kinds of development; it can understand its own development.

The insight into what is a living thing is a single insight into a central form; it is the central form, which subsists through all the sequences of stages and is the principle of operation from which changes emanate. The conjugate forms are the multiple properties, characteristics, systems, organs, parts, processes, insights into central forms as they subsist and conjugate forms as they change.

Central Form of Living Things

There is a real jump in complexity when we move from the non-living to the living. But it does not seem to be simply a matter of complexity but a different kind of intelligibility. We are looking for an insight into the unity, identity and whole of any living thing, whether a cell, a worm, a lion, or a person. This is one insight into one central form, but the data is enormously complex and the interrelations between aspects of data are also complex. Our position is that this is a higher viewpoint, requiring a new science beyond physics and chemistry because new and different central forms are being studied. Let us take our bearings and remind ourselves of some positions we have already reached.

We write as philosophers not biologists. We are formulating what should be the implicit philosophical presuppositions of the biologist. What is the worldview of the biologist, his criterion of what is real, what framework is guiding and interpreting his work? We are using a method of isomorphism which suggests a fruitful parallel between the process of knowing and the emergence in the known.

In chapter 10 we distinguished between an inclusive insight into the central form or substance (which grasps the unity-identity-whole of the thing) and an abstractive insight (which grasps the conjugate forms or properties which are common to many things and often change). In that chapter we use this distinction to differentiate central and conjugate forms as applied to inanimate things. In chapter 11 we used the cognitional experience of successive higher viewpoints as the ground for the distinction between levels of being, namely, atoms, molecules, cells, organisms, plants, animals and humans. Now, we use this cognitional experience to identify the jump from understanding inanimate things, to grasping the central form of living cells, plants, animals and humans.

Let us try to evoke this act of understanding the essence of living things by presenting some of the evident differences which can only be grasped by a special kind of insight using a genetic method. What are the basic characteristics of living things as opposed to non-living? Let us observe and try to describe what we find. This is very elementary but just an indication of the difficulties specific to biology and the need for new methods and concepts. The principle we are using here is that you know a living thing by how it moves, that is, how it *changes*. We are looking to understand the central form of a living being, namely, the unity-identity-wholeness of a living substance and how it differs from that of an inanimate object. The key to understanding the central form of a living thing is to observe how it changes.

(1) What is the difference between a real, healthy, living frog and a mechanical toy frog, batteries included? I think everyone will admit that there is a substantial difference but how do you express that difference. We have to say that living things have some principle of self-organization or self-movement and that non-living things do not. The movement of living things comes from *within* and not from without. Once the fertilized egg is laid, there is a long process of hatching, growing, maturing, living, and dying—and it all comes from the *inside*. Certain conditions of temperature, humidity, protection from extremes, have to be met. But the egg has the potential, given the necessary conditions, of becoming a chicken or a duck or whatever. The toy frog may well move or croak, but it has to be turned on and off from the outside and the batteries have to be replaced periodically. It is not in control of its own motion. A mechanical toy can easily be divided into parts and the parts put together again to form the whole. This cannot be done with a living thing; the unity is too integrated and interdependent for that to happen.

(2) All living things, from cells to plants to animals to humans *are generated, grow to maturity, grow old and die.* The living thing possesses its being not statically but dynamically; not wholly at one time and place but spread out in time and place. The one thing has its being not in the present but in *stages* over time. The toy frog remains basically the same, with minor changes such as slowly rusting or the battery running down.

(3) Living things grow and become more and more complicated, in a process of *differentiation and integration.* It differentiates as cells multiply and divide, become more specialized, organs develop and function, movement becomes easier, capacities are realized. The process continues to maturity of the living thing. Parallel with the process of differentiation is a process of integration. The more specialized the living thing becomes, the more centralization of a nervous system and brain are necessary: the parts must act for the whole, and the whole exercises control over the parts. A tadpole who loses its tail and develops legs must adapt and integrate this change into his way of surviving. The toy frog gets older, rusts, breaks down and is thrown away; there is no process of growth or development.

(4) There is *continuity over time in the central form of a living being.* The unity or wholeness of a living thing is different from that of a toy frog or a computer or any mechanical device. If you are given a puppy dog called Fido, and you keep him for fourteen years, he changes in size, shape, habits, abilities, affections, skills, and the like, but he always remains the same Fido. You yourself are the same human being who was born, fed, learned to walk, to talk, to read, to relate, to grow, to play, to study, to understand, to develop understanding, to be good or to try to be good. A vast accumulation of memories and experiences bolster this sense of identity. It is difficult for a reductionist, or a nominalist, or even a postmodern philosopher to deny the continuity and sameness of a living thing over the stages of life from birth to death. The central form remains the same, the conjugate forms change in sequence. Apparently, the particular physical material atoms and molecules of a human body are replaced entirely over the course of about seven years, but the person remains the same person, if a bit older.

(5) The *integral unity* of a living thing is vastly different from the mechanical, accidental unity of a toy frog. The animal acts as a whole; there is a centre of control; all the parts work for the whole. It is the animal that sees and not the eye, the animal that runs and not the legs, the animal that feels pain and not the stomach, the animal that is hungry and not the digestive tract. It is the animal that reacts. It is the animal that coordinates seeing

and hearing and smelling, along with reacting, pouncing, and barking. In the living thing, if a part is damaged, it is the whole that suffers. It is the whole that lives or dies and not the part.

The parts are related to the whole in varying degrees of integration and importance. Some parts can be cut off and the animal survives; some parts can be grown again. Transplants are possible in some cases not in others. Hip and knees can be replaced, but not brains. For the human being we refer to the centre of control as the self or the person or the subject, and the brain is the physical, chemical biological centre of control. Animals can be conscious and so must have some elementary sense of self as the centre of operations.

The individual cell is the smallest unit of all living things. The single-celled bacterium is itself a living unity of integrated parts. It has its own complex structures, its own way of being generated and corrupted, its own way of growing, ingesting, processing, surviving, unifying many different processes and activities, reproducing. But in a multicellular organism, the single cell is subordinate to the whole; each cell is assigned a place and a task; it is not free to do its own thing; it is part of the whole.

By way of contrast, the toy frog can be taken apart and put together again. It is a mechanical unity, produced in a factory, is moved by a battery, does not feel pain, can be dropped, stood upon, taken apart and glued together again with superglue.

(6) Living things have a way of *producing their own energy* needs. They have a form of metabolism, from the cell, to the plant, to the animal, to the human. For plants the energy mostly comes from the sun by a process of photosynthesis, though nutrients from the earth are also absorbed into the growing plant. For animals, food is combined with oxygen to provide energy, and carbon dioxide is given off. Materials not needed are cast off or excreted. Our toy frog cannot replace a depleted battery.

(7) Living things have *sensitivity*. Even the simplest cell is sensitive to temperature, light and moisture. Living things can only survive in certain defined ranges of temperature, light and moisture. Energy comes from the environment, so this is not surprising. This is a rather elementary sensitivity.

Plants develop this sensitivity in relation to sunlight as its source of energy but also hot and cold, and the presence or nutrients and whatever else is required for plant life. Certain plants will thrive in a certain environment; others will not. Plants fit in with their environment. Plants turn towards the sun; root systems concentrate on areas containing nutrients or moisture.

Animals exploit sensitivity to the full, developing senses of seeing, hearing, tasting, smelling and touching to the full. They develop the ability to move around, and to be more adaptable in coping with the environment. They develop brains and nerves to operate the senses, to coordinate input and response. There is increasing centralized control in terms of differentiation and integration. Humans develop beyond sensation to intelligence, reason, moral sensitivity, religious awareness, and freedom.

(8) Living things *reproduce themselves.* Every living thing has a way of reproduction. This is one of the most fundamental and necessary characteristics of living things; otherwise, they would all be extinct. The simplest and earliest form of reproduction is by cell division. The emergence of sexual reproduction adds enormously to diversity and differentiation. There is great diversity of ways of reproduction in plant life and animal life. There is a struggle to survive, to reproduce, to produce enough seeds or births to ensure the propagation of the species. This is perhaps the key activity of living things, and the most intricate biochemistry is involved in explaining how this happens.

(9) Living things have developed *coping and survival mechanisms,* complex immune systems, defensive systems, survival techniques. Living things have learned how to deal with many challenges, sicknesses or diseases or droughts, or cold, or fire. The have learned how to adapt to changes. Our toy frog is at the mercy of recalcitrant children.

(10) Significantly, living cells *have never been synthesized* in a laboratory. Technicians can split genes, arrange in vitro fertilization, perform miracles of surgery, clone sheep, remove brain tumors, but they cannot produce a living cell from chemicals. It seems that life emerged once in the history of our planet; we know approximately when, but not how or where this happened. But we cannot replicate it. There is a really big jump from inanimate to animate. They are quite different genus of things operating at different levels.

(11) Living things can be *classified in a complicated system of relationships,* a tree of life mapping this diversity and interdependence. Biologists, botanists and zoologists spend much of their time classifying their specimens. New specimens from the field have to be fitted into their appropriate place in the tree of life. We understand that cells, and plants and animals are distinguished into genus and species in a complicated network of kingdoms, classes, orders, families, and the like. We consider that we have answered the question, what is this specimen, when we can correctly assign it a place in our classifications. We correctly assume that there is a real difference

between species of plants and animals. These classifications are not based on the size, or the color or the shape but on the whole of the characteristics of the specimen, on its central form. Taxonomy and classification are proofs that we recognize a real, verifiable, difference between genera and species. In practice we recognize the difference between central forms and conjugate forms. We classify according to the central form, the whole, the living thing assigned its place in the tree of life. We recognize where it belongs because we put together all of the particular conjugate forms and recognize they together constitute a specific central form.

(12) Explaining the central form of living things is the complicated task of biology. Biology moves from observing what can be seen of living things, to explaining what is a living thing. To answer in explanatory terms, it will relate things to one another. Measurement makes a contribution in blood tests, blood pressure, sugar levels, temperature, efficacy of the lungs and the like. More important will be moving to a technical vocabulary where words have a special defined explanatory meaning. It is evident that I am not a biologist, but a science of biology will talk about systems, such as circulation, respiration, digestion, skeletal, muscular, vascular, neurological, and the like. It will talk about processes such as metabolism, photosynthesis, adaptation, mutation, sensation, and the like. It will study the very smallest parts of cells, chromosomes, membranes, Golgi apparatus, prokaryotes, and eukaryotes, replication, translation and transcription, and the like. It will study larger organs as brain, heart, limbs, eyes, ears, and the like as well as limbs, muscles and tissues. It will study the chemistry of amino acids, proteins, bacteria, amoeba, infection, inflammation, indigestion, and the like. The field of biology will be split into specializations, as genetics, haematology, cellular and molecular biology, physiology, anatomy, forensics, evolution, and the like.

I have made the above twelve points to justify the claim that the central forms studied in biology are higher forms than the forms of physics and chemistry; that biology sublates physics and chemistry; that the science of biology cannot be reduced to the sciences of physics and chemistry. I hope the comparison between the living frog and the toy frog has helped us to identify what biology is studying, namely, the unity, wholeness, activity and identity of living things. The important thing is to understand, but unfortunately our imagination is more active and dominant than out intelligence, and so we try to imagine what this central form looks like. We imagine a ghost, a "soul," a spooky entity, a "spirit." Of course, we need our imaginations to think, but images are the servants of intelligence and not the masters. Imagination is not the criterion of the real but critical intelligence.

An act of understanding grasps an idea or form or intelligibility present in data. There is an isomorphism between the idea grasped by the mind and the form immanent in the thing. Understanding in mathematics or physics or chemistry is relatively easily grasped and can be expressed in very precise equations and laws and quantities. In biology the insight into the central form of a living thing is a complex insight deriving from a multitude of data as enumerated above. It is easy at the level of description to know the difference between living and non-living. But it is very difficult to articulate this, especially when you try to do it at an explanatory level. The history of the word "substance" is a cautionary tale as to how this can easily be misunderstood. We have shifted to the terminology of central and conjugate form, rather than soul and body, to avoid those pitfalls. The central form is the intelligibility of the living thing as a whole, as an existing individual thing, including all the data relevant to understanding that thing as a unity or whole. It is not to be imagined as ghost or spooky entity; it is to be understood as the intelligibility or essence of a living thing.

We hold that biology is related to physics and chemistry by way of sublation and not by way of reductionism or mechanism. Sublation means that: (1) new realities emerge, (2) previous realities and sciences retain their validity, (3) lower sciences are in fact enhanced in their value and contribution to the higher science, (4) living things continue to depend on proper functioning of laws of physics and chemistry. This schema can be applied and verified in the above comparison between the insight into a toy frog and the insight into a living frog.

Conclusion

Why all the intellectual effort to understand the central form of living things correctly? Largely because this grasp of the correct meaning of soul will be the basis for our understanding of the unity of the human person, which we discuss in our next chapter. A mechanist materialist understanding reduces the human person to atoms, molecules and cells which have evolved randomly to produce a very complicated machine to which is attached no special value other than any other machine or animal. A vitalist understanding sunders the unity of the human person into a ghost inhabiting a body. I hope a correct understanding of the central form of a living thing, in the order and diversity of genera and species, gives us a basic understanding of the unity of the human person, who emerges from the animal kingdom, but incorporates capacities for asking questions, understanding ideas, affirming truths and values, deciding responsibly and freely, loving deeply, and relating to God. Mistaken presuppositions of materialism, vitalism, determinism, indeterminism, empiricism, and reductionism, distort the research, the interpretation and presentation of results of biology and do nothing to foster the progress of real correct understanding.

13

Understanding the Human Person

Only a critical metaphysics that envisages at once positions and counterpositions can hope to present successfully the complex alternatives that arise in the pursuit of the human sciences, in which both the men under inquiry and the men that are inquiring may or may not be involved in the ever possible and ever varied aberrations of polymorphic consciousness.[1]

The central idea of the consilience worldview is that all tangible phenomena, from the birth of stars to the workings of social institutions, are based on material processes that are ultimately reducible, however long and tortuous the sequences, to the laws of physics.[2]

The social sciences are good at describing and analysing human activities, cultures, institutions, social relations, and social structures. But that is not the same thing as actually understanding human beings per se, what we are, our constitution and condition.[3]

This notion of humans as the most dominant, intelligent, or complex seems to some biologists to be transparent anthropocentrism, an attempt to flatter ourselves, to feed human vanity, or to put a scientific gloss on the Christian notion of humans as central in the universe and, since Darwin, as central to the evolutionary process.[4]

1. Lonergan, *Insight*, 532.
2. Wilson, *Consilience*, 297.
3. Smith, *What Is a Person?*, 1.
4. Rosenberg and McShea, *Philosophy of Biology*, 142.

Diagram Four: The Human Person, diagram of Transcendental Imperatives, Levels of Consciousness, Intentional Questions, Activities and Products.

Imperatives	Levels	Questions	Activities	Products	Life Lived
Be in Love (Religious Values)	5. Religious Orientation	Ultimate Longing	Praying Worship	Faith Hope, Love	Holiness
Be Responsible (Moral Values)	4. Level of Valuing	Questions of Value	Deliberative Insights	Judgments of Value	Decisions Implement-ation
Be Reasonable (Cultural Values)	3. Level of Judgment	Questions for Reflection	Reflective Insights	Judgments of Truth	
Be Intelligent (Social Values)	2. Level of Understanding	Questions for Intelligence	Direct Insights	Formulations Expressions	
Be Attentive (Vital Values)	1. Level of Experiencing	Feelings Psyche	Imagining Remembering	Utterances Sounds	

Introduction (Diagram 4)

FINALLY, WE REACH THE apex in the process of emergence with the appearance of the human person, homo sapiens. We reach the highest degree of complexity of being and hence of difficulty in understanding. But we also reach the point of most importance. Mistakes in the physical sciences have damaging consequences, but mistakes in the human sciences lead to even more dangerous misconceptions, policies, and actions, resulting in distortion and decline. False or twisted notions of happiness, freedom, priorities in life, values, human intelligence and human dignity, lead many astray and destroy healthy community living.

We continue to respect the proper relationship between philosophy and the sciences that we established in chapter 3. Metaphysics underlies, penetrates, transforms, and unifies, in the human sciences as it does in all other departments. Philosophy presents an overall framework of the whole, derived from the self-knowledge gained by self-appropriation. This is not a treatise in psychology or sociology or any or all of the human sciences. The individual human sciences work out the myriad details, perspectives, specializations, and parts that make up the whole. There is no end to the enrichment that each particular human science can add to the basic framework presented by a correct philosophical anthropology. But sadly, in many cases the human sciences are weakest in their grasp of this basic correct framework and its parameters.

Our emphasis in this chapter shifts from isomorphism to self-appropriation and interiority. We used a method of self-appropriation to identify an invariant structure of human knowing summarized in the diagram 1 in chapter 1 on Foundations. We can use that same approach to present the *whole* picture of the human person as, mind and heart, feeling and deciding, loving and living, free and responsible, personal and social, body and soul, natural and cultural, material and spiritual—as one unified integrated human person with a multitude of potentialities and characteristics.

In appropriating a correct cognitional structure, we did refer to and learn something from the multitude of diverse epistemologies produced over the course of the history of philosophy. But we did also refer to our own experience of knowing, to check whether these theories were verified or in conflict with our own direct experience of cognitional process. Personal experience trumped the theories, the concepts, the authorities, and the traditions. In much the same way the history of philosophy presents us with a variety of theories about the human person and we can learn something from these teachings. However, the critical test is to then ask do these theories gel with your own personal experience. Which of the various approaches are true? There is a scholarship side to studying the human person in the theories, the books, the anthropologies presented by scholars. But there is the interiority side also in which we are obliged to criticize such ideas by reference to one's own personal experience. This is particularly necessary as there are so many misleading, truncated, incomplete, wrong notions of the human person pervading the human sciences. We need to broaden our notion of self-appropriation applied to cognitional process and include a subject who has a vast range of feelings and desires, who is free to decide to go forward or backwards, is tasked with implementing decisions, is living in a web of social relations, and either accepts or rejects self-transcendence and a religious orientation in life. We are moving from self-consciousness to full self-knowledge on the whole range of human potentialities in feelings, decisions, relationships, success and failure, life and death.

By the human sciences, we mean the whole range of all sciences focused on understanding aspects of being human: human behavior, human activity, human life, human knowing and loving, human art, history, language and culture. We include all that is studied in sociology, psychology, anthropology, economics, politics, literature, languages, humanities, arts, philosophy, religion, science, technology, biography, autobiography, including the history of all these subjects and the specializations and sub-specializations into which they are divided. It is an enormously wide range of studies, but all are focused in one way or another on correct understanding of the human person in his/her particular characteristics, perspectives, specializations and activities.

The comprehensive theory that is needed in the human sciences is nothing less than a critical philosophy of the human person. What we have been doing for the empirical sciences is outlining an integral heuristic structure of proportionate being. Now we need to outline an integral heuristic structure for understanding the human sciences and the human person. This heuristic anticipation will guide research; enrich our overall understanding; pick out significant topics, issues, and questions; design the kind of survey needed to answer these questions; interpret the data correctly and present the findings in an unbiased way. This philosophy of the human person has to be critical, methodical, verifiable, and comprehensive. Because it is based on the structure of human knowing verifiable by all humans, it will be a philosophy grounded in interiority. And this philosophy will in turn, provide a stable basis for the specializations of individual human sciences.

In §2, we will illustrate how the human person is the apex of the process of emergence, even though the laws and principles of previous levels also apply to the emerging person. In §3, we will describe the structure of all the capacities of the human person. In §4, we will highlight the marvel of human intelligence contrasting it with artificial and animal intelligence. In §5, we will distinguish legitimate and illegitimate forms of pluralism. In §6, we will identify the unity of the human person in its central form. In §7, we will ask in what respect is the human person material or spiritual. In §8, we will try and put it all together.

The Human Person as Apex of Emergence

Everything we have said so far about the integrating philosophical framework for a correct worldview is applicable to understanding the human person. Just as we presented an integral heuristic structure for a correct worldview of the universe, so now we present a heuristic structure for the fruitful study of the human person. This might be a good time to just run through what we have said so far and apply it to the human person as a kind of summary of where we have reached.

We have said that everything known about the universe of proportionate being will be constituted by potency, form, act, and value. By this we mean that there will be some element of sensibility, some element of intelligibility, some element of real or existence added to essence, and also an element of value. Beings in the proportionate universe emerge from potency to form, and forms manage to exist for a limited time in a specific place and can make a positive or negative contribution to the finality of the universe. The human person emerges from potency, has a specific form, exists for a short spell of time on this earth, and makes a positive or negative contribution to the good of the universe. Any correct understanding of the human person must include these four fundamental constitutive elements.

We have distinguished central and conjugate forms, in other words, substances and accidents, or things and their properties. Forms are of two basic kinds, central and conjugate. Central forms are wholes, unities, identities, integrations, for instance: trees, particles, dogs, desks, gold, bacteria, and the like. We understand them as a matrix of properties, with some permanence in place and time. We identify them in an *inclusive* act of understanding as things, unities, wholes. We recognize that the substance has certain characteristics and can perdure through certain changes of properties. By conjugate forms we mean laws, correlations, functions, properties, attributes, categories using data taken from different sources across the board. These are grasped by what I called an *abstractive* insight and can change without a change of substance. Both central and conjugate forms emerge from potency and exist or are real or happen; they represent degrees of intelligibility and degrees of goodness.

We will be claiming that the human person is one central form but experiences a succession of changes in conjugate forms during growth, maturity, decline and death. This is crucial for a correct understanding of the unity of the human person and the multitude of capacities, characteristics, properties, accidents that are also part of the unity of one human person. We have studied these in our last three chapters establishing the difference between central and conjugate forms, the context of genus and species in which that is placed, and a genetic method to grasp the unity of a developing living thing.

Central forms emerge in a hierarchy of increasing differentiation and integration. We distinguished between genera and species. We used the model of successive higher viewpoints to illustrate the emergence of higher genera from lower simpler genera and how genus differentiates into species and species differentiate into sub-species. The human person emerges at the apex of this chain of living things, the highest level of differentiation and integration that we have so far witnessed. (Please refer to our diagram 3 of successively higher forms of genera and species.) All of the laws of physics, of chemistry, of biology, of zoology, of sensitive psychology, apply to a comprehensive understanding of the human person.

Everything discovered and applied in these sciences has direct applications in understanding embodied human persons.

However, to all that has gone before it, the human person has added the capacity to ask questions, understand ideas, formulate language, distinguish true and false, good and bad, as well as to decide and act responsibly, and to be oriented to the divine. The human person represents the highest integration and differentiation of the capacities of our universe. The human person represents the apex of the process of successive higher integrations. S/he seems to have capacities that go far beyond anything else in the known universe. The human person can question, think, express, grasp truth and value, and decide responsibly. S/he can modify the environment, invent science, apply technologies, use language, build libraries and cities, investigate and understand his/her own history, habitat, and universe. There is a whole range of data, which is coincidental from the point of view of biology and zoology but now calls for a higher science or sciences, the human sciences. How are they to be organized, conceived, and conducted? What is the role of philosophy in this ordering of the human sciences?

On the one hand, we note the extraordinary complexities, the wide variety, the multitude of detail, the many parts that characterize us as human beings. On the other hand, we recognize the unity of human person, the sameness of human persons, that we are all one species. Much confusion exists precisely on the point of how much we are all the same and how much human beings differ. Is there one definition that applies to all human beings? Our recourse to clear up this controversy is to appeal to the kind of inclusive insight that grasps wholes and a kind of abstractive insight that grasps changing parts. In this chapter, we will establish a framework and parameters within which the various human sciences can give us a detailed, rich, account of the many capacities of all human persons.

In the next section, we present some hints of what the human sciences might look like when guided by a philosophy of interiority. In doing so, we maintain first philosophy's dual role organizing, unifying and transforming the human sciences, while at the same time allowing the autonomy of the human sciences in choosing their specific methods, agendas, questions, and conclusions about particular aspects of human behavior. It is only in the context of such a complementary relationship that the human sciences can become progressive and cumulative in their understanding of the human person.

Describing Characteristic Activities
of the Human Person

Aristotle had a simple but valid principle that you know what a thing is by studying its movement, its change, or its activities. If you are studying the human person, concentrate on the activities that differentiate the human from other genera of things, or plants, or animals. We study the human person as a human person and take for granted all that can be said in the other sciences of physics, chemistry, biology sensitive psychology and zoology about the embodied human person. But to know humans as humans we need to go beyond those sciences to investigate the essential, characteristic activities that differentiate a human person from a non-human animal.

We write as generalists sketching in broad strokes the invariant structure of what it is to be a human person. This could be called a basic phenomenology of the human person. We will sketch out a broad meaning for consciousness, activities, patterns of experience, differentiations of consciousness, knowing, deciding and transcending. We are seeking the invariant structure of human personhood using self-appropriation. We appeal to the evidence of the data of consciousness for these statements and invite you to do the same by paying attention to your own operations of experiencing, inquiring, understanding, and judging. Some of this has already been dealt with in previous chapters, so we will be quite brief. You might attend to diagram 4 on the Human Person which indicates the structure of these activities.

(1) Conscious Experience

We have already said something about consciousness in our first chapter on Foundations. It seemed an obvious place to start as our method is based on the premise that we are able not only to be conscious of the world around us but also to focus our awareness on the workings of our own minds. We limited ourselves to the context of understanding the sequence of activities involved in human knowing. Now we are throwing the net wider to explore our consciousness of our deciding, our implementing, our good deeds and bad deeds, our relating to others, our loving, our praying, our successes and failures, our appreciation of beauty, to the whole gamut of human conscious experience.

When we wake up in the morning, we move from being totally unconscious, to being vaguely aware of our surroundings, of the time of day, the tasks before us, and the need to get a move on. As we do set about dressing and breakfast, we become more clearly aware of the situation, planning how to get to work, what challenges work will entail, and we start to become more deliberately aware and conscious. There is a difference between being dreamlessly asleep, unconscious, or under anaesthetic, and its opposite, to be alert, awake, attentive, responsive. Being conscious in itself is a simple experience of awareness quite distinct from activities of questioning, thinking, or deciding. Normally the word is used as an adjective, a conscious feeling, a conscious thought, conscious motivation, and the like. Consciousness is an abstract noun derived from that experience. But consciousness itself is not abstract but concrete, an experience in the here and now accompanying all our thoughts, words and actions.

Consciousness is not so much an activity as a state, an awareness of the subject that is concomitant with an awareness of objects. At the same time and in the same act by which I become aware of any object I am also aware of myself as the subject of the awareness. Generally, we do not pay much attention to the self when we are performing activities such as preparing breakfast or driving a car. The self is in the background of our consciousness not in the foreground. We do not focus on our inner thoughts and feelings unless we have to. We are not focally aware of our motivation, for example, unless we have a reason to examine our consciences. But we are always implicitly aware of ourselves as the subject, source and centre of our feeling, knowing and deciding.

This consciousness is given. We wake up and behold we are conscious. We do not actively attain it as the conclusion of a process of thinking or reasoning; we do not make ourselves to be conscious, even though we can direct our consciousness by concentrating on work or suspend our consciousness by going to sleep. Hence, we can affirm ourselves as a subject, a self, the centre of the universe from our point of view. We presume that anybody reading this is conscious and therefore aware of themselves as subjects or selves.

We can shift attention to the self as the subject performing cognitional or volitional activities. However, when we do that, we are turning the subject into an object. The self becomes the object of our attention. As such we can have some experience and understanding of what it means to be a self. But still the subject as a subject eludes our direct attention.

But we can heighten our awareness of the subject as subject indirectly by raising the level of our consciousness. The tonality of our conscious awareness depends on the level of our mental activities. Our diagram of the Human Person distinguishes five levels of conscious activity, namely, experiencing, understanding, affirming truth, evaluating, and religious orientation. The activities are in a series because the later presuppose the earlier; the earlier prepare the way for the later. There is a heightening of consciousness as we move from, daydreaming, to serious thinking, to critical affirming, to responsible evaluating, and to praying.

Consciousness is not an easy topic. Primarily it is a basic experience that needs to be experienced and identified before it is defined. But precise definition and understanding is possible. It is not helpful to think of consciousness as anything and everything that goes on in the head. It is not helpful to think of consciousness as knowledge. It is not helpful to dismiss consciousness as a mystery; that is just surrendering. It is not helpful to formulate a theory of consciousness without having attended to the experience of being conscious. It can be very helpful to investigate the physical, chemical, biological and neurological substrate that makes consciousness possible. But it is a mistake to think that such explorations will explain consciousness. We have often referred to the process of sublation where lower levels prepare the way for higher levels. The neurological is the substrate that prepares the way for consciousness but does not explain it.

(2) Feelings

We are feeling animals. Feelings pervade our whole life and even enter into our dreams. They permeate our work and play, our relationships and thoughts, our hopes and dreams, our living and our dying. We think of the obvious list of feelings as desires, fears, loves, hate, pleasure and pain, satisfaction, remorse, guilt, disgust, anger, unease, dread, tension, excitement, confusion, hesitancy, rejection, loneliness, joy, happiness, and one could go on and on. Existentialists like to dwell on such feelings as boredom, absurdity, fragility, nausea, meaninglessness, contingency, anxiety, despair, interest, curiosity, intimacy, risk, authenticity, sincerity, care, ambiguity, conscience, call, uncanny, fascination, eerie, uncertainty, inferiority, nausea, absurdity, fear of death, meaninglessness, self-righteousness and the like. If we try to suppress feelings, we become heartless, listless, bored, apathetic, depressed, stoical, repressed, and so on. Feelings are operative in all areas of life. They operate in relation to work, to relations with others, to appreciation of beauty in music and art and literature, to religious experience of the holy, the fascinating, the other-worldly. They operate through symbols which can attract or repel, and they can raise us up or crush us down. Some feelings we can control, while others are more recalcitrant and overpowering and have a life of their own. Modern philosophy has done much to focus on and identify the full range of feelings and their influence on life and behavior. They are an essential aspect of what it is to be human.

Feelings are so varied, pervasive and elusive that it is hard to categorize, to classify or to formulate theories about them.[5] Feelings are not just superficial transient emotional states, but in a deeper sense they accompany our better and worst inclinations. We can do no more in this short sketch than recognize their importance and make one or two basic distinctions. Some well-known quotes might indicate the centrality and depth of feeling. Lonergan states, "Such feeling (intentional responses) gives intentional consciousness its mass, momentum, drive, power. Without these feelings our knowing and deciding would be paper thin."[6] "There are in full consciousness feelings so deep and strong, especially when deliberately reinforced, that they channel attention, shape one's horizon, direct one's life. Here the supreme illustration is loving."[7] St. Augustine, "You made us for Yourself, and our heart is restless until it finds its place of rest in You."[8]

Lonergan distinguishes between two kinds of feelings. On the one hand, feelings which respond to the satisfying or dissatisfying, the agreeable or the disagreeable, and which are ambiguous, neither good nor bad. But on the other hand, there are feeling responses to values, or persons, or beauty, or truth, or virtue, which carry us forward towards self-transcendence. I would call the first sensitive feelings and the second spiritual feelings, for want of a better terminology. *Sensitive feelings* are usually biologically based, also experienced by non-human animals, transient, but can be very powerful. In themselves they are part of what it is to be a rational animal. They usually orient us to sensible satisfactions which in themselves are natural and normally good. Moral evaluation accrues from the context of an action that might follow, from the motivation, the action itself, the intention, and the consequences. However, feelings can overcome our rational convictions; they can drag us in a direction we had not chosen; they can distort, corrupt and redirect the desire for self-transcendence in favour of more immediately satisfying desires.

By *spiritual* feelings I mean feelings that are not intrinsically conditioned by the empirical residue and are constitutive of the process of self-transcendence. (This terminology will be better explained when we consider whether the central form of the human person is material or spiritual.) I am first of all referring to the pure, detached, unrestricted, desire to know and to love. The source and first principle of Lonergan's philosophy

---

5. I wrote two chapters on feelings in *Value Ethics*: chapter 5, "Lonergan on Feelings," and chapter 6, "Self-Appropriation of Feelings and Values."

6. Lonergan, *Method in Theology*, 32.

7. Lonergan, *Method in Theology*, 33.

8. Augustine, *Confessions*, 1.3.

and theology is the desire to know. If there is no desire to know, there is no understanding, no knowing, no intellectual conversion, no moral or religious conversion. The desire to know is a constitutive part of the process of understanding and judging. The desire to know is the dynamic of the process, guides the process, is oriented to being (meaning everything), is the criterion of success in reaching truth and value. The desire is a special kind of feeling; it is deep, spiritual, pervasive, permanent; it broadens out into desire for the good, for happiness, for transcendence, into love of God and neighbor. The desire to know can be elaborated in terms of the felt obligations of the transcendental precepts, be attentive, intelligent, reasonable, responsible and in love, which we identified in chapter 1 on Foundations. By self-transcendence, Lonergan meant going beyond imagination to understanding, beyond hypotheses to truth, beyond satisfaction to value, beyond this world to natural knowledge and love of God. He identified a process of intellectual, moral and religious conversion. One crucial aspect of this process is affective, it is a feeling orientation, a desire, a felt obligation, a love that opens out to the ultimate goodness of God.

Feelings can be an important vector in the process of developing, but sadly also play a part in the spiral of decline. Aristotle emphasized the importance of training the young to do what is right regardless of their feelings. But he pointed out that once habits of good behavior are established, the actions become easy and pleasurable. However, feelings can also drag reason along their reckless path, establish vices rather than virtues, and be quite destructive of normal human living. In the mature human adult sensitive and spiritual feelings can be in conflict but can also be integrated into a harmonious and integrated affective dimension of life.

(3) Cognitional Activities

We have already outlined the sequence of activities involved in moving from a question to a correct answer. We have described the process of desiring to know, questioning, experiencing, understanding and its five characteristics, formulating, reflecting, judging, and then the process of evaluating. These activities are common to all human beings. We are then justified in asserting that all human persons are potentially intelligent, rational, reasonable, and moral beings. We explained this in sufficient detail in our first chapter on Foundations.

(4) Deciding

The more traditional terminology refers to the faculty of will, willing, willingness, will-power, training the will, and the like. The terminology of deciding, decision making, is more contemporary and encourages us to self-appropriate our own activity of deciding. Deciding can be done well, and it can be done badly. We can only sketch a position here to establish the principle of free and responsible deciding and its limits. Deciding is not the same as wishing, or wanting, or desiring, or liking. It is much the same as choice but in choice there are often clear alternatives, choose one and reject the other. To be or not to be. Decisions can be punctual in the sense of this here and now I will or will not do. Or they can be habitual in the sense of deciding to study medicine and then taking the steps necessary to fulfil this dream over seven years. They can be superficial, and one can easily change one's mind. Or they can be deep commitments lasting a lifetime.

In the normal case we think of deciding as following a judgment of value which usually takes the form of, "this is the best thing to do in this situation." Look before you leap. There is a basic truth in that. However, the activities involved in reaching the judgment of value are also free and one can allow interference and bias to enter so as to avoid a conclusion that we do not wish to reach. Rationalization in its many forms allows the mind to twist evidence or argument to justify a judgment of value which suits ones wishes or feelings.

Our decisions are free. We are not forced to think or to know or to value or to decide or to implement. We are responsible for the actions that follow. The only proof we can offer for this freedom is our own awareness that we could have decided otherwise. It is part of our social fabric that people are responsible for their actions and can be held accountable. Freedom is not arbitrary, meaning "I can do what I like." Freedom is responsible in that I am obliged to seek what is good, better, best, and to avoid what is bad, worse, worst. We are both free and responsible. We feel obliged to do what we are told, to do what is right, to make our contribution to the family and the school and the community. But the feeling of obligation can be set aside, and we choose a more personally satisfying course of action. But inevitably a sense of guilt ensues. We all have a conscience, namely, an awareness of moral obligation and whether we have fulfilled or neglected the various duties to which we are all obliged.

Lonergan distinguishes between essential and effective freedom. Essential freedom is the principle that we are free by definition and should be able to choose the right course of action. But freedom is also an achievement; we struggle to form habits of doing the right thing. But often we fall into decline and develop vicious habits, in the end succumbing to addictions and loss of effective freedom. It seems that humans are subject to a certain moral impotence, an inability for sustained development in all areas.

(5) Doing, Implementing

We use instruments, invent language, develop agriculture, build temples, pyramids, skyscrapers, bridges, invent machinery, electricity, radio, nuclear power, smart phones, manufacture, computers, data banks, medical interventions and improvements, transport, and so on. Most people are obliged to work. This seems to be true of all societies, ancient and modern, simple and complex, pre-technological and technological. It is a matter of survival. Some think of agency as a philosophical problem: how can a spiritual faculty of willing order a physical body to do something. However, that assumes an artificial Cartesian dualism. But most people do not have a problem deciding to eat a meal and then eating, deciding to cultivate a garden, and then cultivating, deciding to look at the stars, and then looking at them. Agency is only a problem when you think of the human person as two things, spirit and body, or ghost in machine.

(6) Relating to Others

We are social beings, born into a family; our primary relations are with parents and siblings, gradually expanding to friends, community, school, town, state and nation and world. We are socialized, inculturated, educated, formed, in some kind of community with its own language, customs, culture and way of doing things. Our personalities emerge by interacting with others. We form our social intelligence by such interactions. We become social beings, depending on others and making a contribution to the welfare of others. No one is an island. Psychology, economics, politics, cultural anthropology, sociology take these basic experiences as the data for an explanatory understanding of the complexities of all these relationships. We are also political beings where we decide together the direction, structure, and procedures of leadership in the community, locality, nation, continent, and world. Vastly different structures operate in various countries, and they impinge mightily on our individual way of living. Politics deals with disagreements about social order, priorities, classes, interest groups, interpretations of constitutions, rich and poor, white and black, ethnic tensions, differences about values, about the very notion of society and how we should live together. Politics tries to balance these differences, promote law and order, respect the individual rights of citizens, and balance individual freedom and the common good.

(7) Worshiping

Above and beyond questions about scientific causes or how to live, we can and do ask questions about the ultimate cause of the universe, the ultimate meaning of human life. We feel dependence on a higher cause, we are open to the divine. Every culture has had a religious dimension to it, and I would think that this is very human, very natural, and that human nature is open to know and love and be united with the divine. There is a religious dimension to our life, and we perform the activities of praying, meditating, worshiping, adoring, thanking, asking, and loving. We are *homo religiosus*. We are open to salvation, to holiness, to redemption, to grace, to eternal life, to divinization, to forgiveness, to mysticism, to a religious dimension in our lives.

(8) Experiencing Unity

Despite the fact that there is such a variety of activities performed as a matter of course by every normal human person, there is also a unity within and informing all these acts. There is an experienced self at the centre coordinating the whole orchestra. I experience myself as the centre of the activities of experiencing, understanding, judging and evaluating. I am the self who feels, loves, decides, converses with others, worships God, gets a job, fulfils obligations, eats and sleeps and goes about his business.

I am the same self who did these things yesterday, the year before that, thirty years ago, fifty years ago and maybe more. I am the self with memories of childhood, being an infant, advancing in school year by year. I faced adolescence, made decisions about my future life, worked to fulfil those ambitions, was sometimes successful, sometimes a failure, sometimes healthy and sometimes sick, sometimes good and sometimes not so good, sometimes optimistic sometimes depressed, sometimes at work and other times at play. I am the self at the centre of my particular network of relationships. But I am aware that I am that self-same subject, now older and wiser, changed but still the same, developing and declining.

The same self can be conflicted, taking sides in politics, in arguments, in decision making. The same self can be subject to nightmares, hallucinations, split personality, neurosis and psychoses, autism, schizophrenia, anxiety attacks on a grand scale, depression and other disruptions of a normal functioning sense of self. Such abnormal states occur. That does not prove that the abnormal is normal. The purpose for the treatment of such abnormalities is to restore a normal sense of self, of one who is whole, who is responsible and reasonably content.

Hume argued that the sense of self was a passing feeling, that what I have described above as continuous, unifying experience is just a sequence of individual, discrete experiences and that there is no need to posit a self as continuous, permanent, and substantial. Many have followed this line that the substantial self is an illusion. I have emphasized the experience of being a self in its different dimensions to show that it is not an illusion. This is the data of consciousness that has to be accounted for adequately, and so we will consider seriously the themes of central and conjugate forms, person and nature, material and spiritual. These considerations are based on the empirical evidence outlined briefly above. The implications need to be accounted for in adequate, contemporary, philosophical terminology.

Legitimate and Illegitimate Pluralism

Why are human persons so different, in culture, language, opinions, religions, means of production and ethical and political systems? Are these differences always a source of division and conflict, or can they be seen as a richness of complementary perspectives? This section proposes that diversity in principle is a richness and perfectly legitimate. The only illegitimate source of division arises from lack of psychic, intellectual, moral and religious conversion. Let us first explore legitimate sources of diversity in life and in philosophy, and then we will try to discern the illegitimate sources of conflict, division, war, criminality, corruption, and the like.

(1) *Pluralism of Common Sense.* Every village has its own way of dealing with human realities as experienced by them at a particular time in a specific case. There are so many different ways of cooking, of speaking, of dealing with emergencies, of reacting to strangers, of dressing, but in this particular village, at this particular time, there is only one best way. Common sense is a specialization of intelligence dealing with the concrete and particular of each unique time and place. It is descriptive in the technical sense of looking at something from a personal point of view, from a perspective limited to that time and place and person. Hence, it is relative to that time and place. The custom or behavior will vary from village to village, from one generation to the next, from one country to another. This is just part of the human condition. An African proverb states that, he who does not travel thinks his mother is the best cook in the world.

(2) Pluralism of Culture and Language. Cultures are the meanings and values shared in a society of persons. There is almost an infinite variety of possible languages that people invent for communication, for expressing feeling, for praying, for teaching. There are an amazing variety of foods to be cultivated, manners of cooking and presenting and of eating. There is a variety of ways of building houses, keeping warm, modes of production, ways of religious expression. There are many varieties of political systems, kinship relations, economic inventions, social arrangements, family structure, ways of behaving, weapons and farming implements. Embedded in the cultures will be beliefs and values proper to that group. They adapt as best they can to the times, the circumstances, the uniqueness of time and place. Who is to say that one way is better than another?

(3) Pluralism of Specializations. In contemporary society specialization is to be found everywhere. There is social specialization of groups and subgroups, in-groups and out-groups, interest groups, play groups, age groups, ethnic and religious groups. The economy demands specialization in production, distribution, retail and wholesale, money as exchange, banks, stock exchange, factories, workers, skills of every sort. Both theoreticians and practitioners are needed. Science and technology develop through more and more specialization. Historians divide their subject into fields, times, persons and events. Lonergan has conceived of doing theology according to a method of functional specialization. The legal profession becomes more and more specialized. Each specialist sees the world through the lens of his own specialty; his own specialty being the most important. Specialties are an enrichment; but the specialist must also recognize the existence of other specialists. We tend to think of our own specialty as the most important of all.

(4) Pluralism of Development. Every study and every topic must be studied in its development, in other words from the point of view of its history. Where did it come from and how did it get to be the way it is? Everything has its historical perspective, which can usually be studied in great detail. This is sometimes called the diachronic point of view. To fit the data together one needs to understand development as a linked sequence of stages; each stage has to be studied but understood as a result of past development and a stepping-stone to future developments. The human person can develop as a whole person but also physically, emotionally, intellectually, spiritually, sexually and in many other ways.

But as well there is the synchronic: the studies of the one whole at a particular stage of development. Where is this subject now? What are the terms and relations, which define this subject now? What state of development has it reached? What is the present systematic presentation of this subject? Where is the beginning, the middle and the end of this topic now?

(5) Pluralism of Differentiations of Consciousness. One can identify stages of meaning depending on education, intellectual development and state of differentiation of consciousness. One way of identifying this pluralism is to recognize three stages of meaning.

The first stage is common sense; a descriptive but intelligent grasp of how to survive, how to get things done, how to deal with the concrete and practical. The second stage is theory where terms and relations are defined in relation to one another and thinking prescinds from the observers' point of view. Every academic discipline starts with description but usually moves on to an explanatory point of view, a technical terminology, by explanatory measurement and definition. The third stage is interiority where the activities of knowing become the focus of attention; where the difference between common sense and explanation are understood; where the familiarity with the activities of knowing becomes the basis for our understanding of the known. These are three different stages of meaning where common sense cannot understand theory and interiority; explanation can understand common sense but cannot understand interiority. Interiority is able to appreciate the advantages and disadvantages of previous stages of meaning.

(6) Pluralism of Patterns of Experience. By pattern of experience is meant a set of mental activities governed by a goal and cooperating towards the achievement of that goal: a typical combinations of motor activity, feelings, sensitivity, intelligence, reason and responsibility, come to be performed with ease and flow in the various patterns. We are presently, hopefully, operating in the intellectual pattern of experience in which the goal is to understand correctly. We are driven by the desire to know, we try to exclude extraneous biases and interests, we focus on experiencing, understanding and judging the matter in hand. We are putting into effect the principle that truth is to be found by such activities as assembling evidence, getting ideas, formulating hypotheses, examining the justification for the conclusion. It is a rigorous and difficult pattern of experience, but it is the pattern of experience in which truths in philosophy and the sciences are found.

One can distinguish many other patterns of experience. In the biological pattern of experience, we focus on vital values, health, keeping fit, eating and drinking, sleeping, surviving operating at the level of sensing, imagining and remembering. Our minds are relaxed and at home in these activities. In an aesthetic pattern of experience, we focus on beauty. We enjoy listening to music, we lose ourselves in a dance, we express our feelings in a painting, we enjoy a great game of chess—a thing of real beauty. In a mystical or religious pattern of experience we pray, we experience the holy, we worship, adore and love, we are absorbed in a religious ceremony. We can also identify an artistic pattern, a practical pattern, an interpersonal pattern, an ethical pattern, and perhaps more.

Quite often these patterns overlap, mix and mingle and we move from one to the other easily and unconsciously. However, it is important to be able to distinguish them and know what we are doing. For example, it is not helpful to confuse the aesthetic appreciation of a drama or poem with the intellectual pattern of experience, which is seeking correct understanding, concepts, definitions, truth and values. It is confusing to take examples from aesthetics to prove some point in philosophy.

(7) Pluralism of Religious Traditions. There are many religions and religious traditions. We are not saying that they are all the same or of the same value, but it does mean each religion has a right to exist and that understanding other persons may involve understanding that they come from a different religious tradition.

(8) Pluralism of Philosophies? There would seem to be a legitimate pluralism of philosophies as we easily identify an African Philosophy, a Western Philosophy, an Eastern Philosophy, Greek Philosophy, Roman Philosophy, Islamic philosophy, Bantu Philosophy, and so on. There is a pluralism of philosophies, which develop in different places and in different times and respond to the political, cultural and economic conditions of their people. Philosophers do not operate in a cultural or ethical vacuum. To be relevant a philosophy must make a contribution to solving the social, cultural, philosophical, political, and ethical questions of the time and place. This is legitimate and enriching in principle. However, the obvious question arises, does that mean that philosophy is irretrievably divided and changes over time and place? In what sense is there a one correct philosophy?

In principle I would say that there is only one first philosophy, or metaphilosophy, or metaphysics, that is correct, adequate, and in the mode of interiority. There is one criterion operating in all our knowing and it is the criterion of truth. This applies to the sciences but also to philosophy which is based on the facts of human knowing. There is only one fully correct account of the process and structure of human knowing. It follows that there is only one correct account of the processes and structure of the proportionate known. There is room for a pluralism of philosophies based in different cultures, languages, contexts, differentiations of consciousness as explained above. But there can be no room in principle for pluralism based on absence of intellectual conversion, for distorted accounts of human knowing based on imagination rather than accurate reasonable and responsible self-appropriation. Philosophy is more than mere opinions because we are motivated by the desire to know what is true and what is false. A dialectical method is needed to sort out the various sources of pluralism and that is a correct worldview or first philosophy. Only such a philosophy can discern how all philosophies, however contradictory, can make a contribution to the clarification of a single goal, namely, a clear correct account of human knowing and the consequent structure of the known.

Let us now try to identify *illegitimate sources of pluralism*. An interiorly differentiated consciousness can appreciate the richness and diversity of persons, cultures, languages, methods, values and ways of doing things. The sad reality is that within that positive matrix there is often an underbelly of mistaken views, dangerous principles, unwarranted assumptions, and ethical disvalues rather than values. They are social, cultural, intellectual, moral and religious differences which are not complementary but contradictory, not enriching but impoverishing, not legitimate but illegitimate. We are fundamentally free to choose good or evil. Knowing what is right and good does not necessitate doing what is right and good. Good decision making is a skill and habit which is needed over and above knowing what is good and right. We struggle to form our willingness, to make good decisions, to think of others as well as ourselves. In this section we will try to identify the source of these illegitimate differences, which foster decline rather than progress, tear a society apart, are the source of deep conflict, and cause real harm to individuals and relationship.

In Lonergan's thought, a dialectic is a set of linked but opposed principles of change operating in the same subject or group. Anything that can be done well can be done badly. Is there a method of discerning out the good from the bad, the true from the false, the right from the wrong? Lonergan identifies a dialect operating in three kinds of conversion, intellectual, moral, and religious, and Robert Doran adds a fourth, namely, a psychic conversion.[9] Each of these represents an area where linked but opposed principles of change are in basic conflict. Human persons are free: they are not necessitated to be honest or good or true or kind; it is a struggle to do the right thing. It is a personal choice with huge consequences. Each individual must negotiate these inner conflicts for him or herself. Let us briefly identify these conflicting principles.

9. See Doran, *Subject and Psyche*, 217–21.

Psychic conversion refers to the area of affectivity where there is basic conflict between the desires for transcendence and the multitude of biological desires for satisfaction. Affectivity pushes us in a certain direction, up or down. Where affectivity is twisted, distorted, selfish, aiming at short term pleasure, it is very hard to be open, honest, integrated, aiming at the true, good and beautiful. The dynamic driving the process of knowing is the pure detached unrestricted desire to know. But besides the desire to know we have a multitude of other desires for satisfaction, for pleasure, for security, for love, for success, for fame and fortune Such psychic processes as repression, bias, denial, paranoia, homophobia, xenophobia, regression, and the like. These can stifle the desire to know, lead it in a self-serving direction, distract it in all sorts of ways, and turn towards more palpable possibilities.

Intellectual conversion identifies the conflict between sense and intellect in human knowing. This opposition can be seen between images and ideas, "body" and thing, knowing as discursive and knowing as contact, intuitive, direct, and simple. In an earlier section (chapter 2, section 5), we identified the confusion between the biological pattern of experience and the intellectual pattern of experience. Lonergan lays special stress on the danger of confusing these two patterns. The key to intellectual conversion is to acknowledge judgment as the criterion of truth and not imagination. Judgments of truth emerge from questioning, experiencing, and direct and reflective understanding, as explained in our chapter on Foundations and diagram 1. We know from our own experience that truth is found through a sequence of activities, is discursive, is not automatic, proceeds step by step, and has its own immanent and operative criteria operating, namely, be attentive, intelligent, reasonable and responsible. But it is a struggle to be at home in that conviction.

"Moral conversion changes the criterion of one's decisions and choices from satisfactions to values."[10] True values are judged not by feelings, not by convention, not by a priori concepts, but by the discursive activities of knowing truth and then value. It is found by intelligent reasonable and responsible answers to question of worth, appreciation, evaluation, and discernment of priorities. Children follow their emotions. Mature good people follow their convictions. A life of ethical living results in a morally informed conscience. The good and wise person is the best judge of goodness and wisdom in any particular situation. Moral judgment develops in stages over a lifetime.

Religious conversion is a transition from a worldly view to an other-worldly view, from proportionate being to transcendent being. It is

10. Lonergan, *Method in Theology*, 225.

responding to the best and deepest inclinations of the human heart. It represents a transformation of a philosophical worldview limited to this universe, to a view of the whole, the first cause, the first mover, the ground of all intelligibility. Although we seem to be limited in our faculty of knowing, we experience an openness to the divine, a readiness for redemption, an acceptance of the supernatural. We devote our last chapter to the religious dimension of our humanity. There are healthy religious values, a respect for transcendence, the holy, religious awe, worship, love, prayer, service, openness to the infinite, openness to salvation; to be fully human is to be more than human. There are many distortions of the religious orientation, in fundamentalism, fanaticism, obscurantism, superstition, exploitation of religious persons, hypocrisy, and immanentism. There is also a resistance to admit our dependence on an omnipotent being.

In conclusion, then, the person is a unity in tension and the tensions work themselves out in a multitude of ways. All of these tensions in human persons and communities can be studied and worked out with a dialectical method. It is no easy task in practice to distinguish legitimate and illegitimate forms of pluralism, but it is possible. Just as it is possible to work out the sequence of activities required for judgments of truth, so it is possible if more difficult to objectify the process of evaluation leading to judgments of value and good decisions.[11] Because human persons are complex beings, it is necessary to use the whole battery of empirical methods to catch relevant and essential aspects of what it means to be a human person. We are aiming for one inclusive insight into the unity of all the relevant aspects of the human person. We need to distinguish the insight into the unity, identity, whole of the human person, and the insights into the parts, the characteristics, the properties, and concrete diversities between persons.

Central and Conjugate Forms of the Human Person

In our previous sections we have mostly described the multiple and complex characteristic activities and capacities of the human person. We have already devoted chapter 10 to the distinction between central forms/substances and conjugate forms/accidents, and now we apply these distinctions in order to understand the unity of a single human person. In these sections we wish to identify philosophical foundations underpinning our descriptions.

In the mode of interiority, we will focus on the kind of question, the kind of insight, and the kind of judgment we seek when we are asking,

11. Lonergan devotes a long chapter in *Method in Theology* to objectify the details of a method of dialectic.

"What is this human person as a unity-identity-whole?" We contrast that with the kind of question, insight and judgment you require when you are asking, "What are the properties of this whole human being?" We will shift to the terminology of central and conjugate potency, form and act in order to be more explanatory and precise. We are building on the successes of the theoretical mode of thinking but adding a further perspective of interiority which gives us a reinforced but more flexible notion.

Let us start with the central form and here we are asking the question, "What is a human being as a unity-identity-whole?" All the data regarding the activities, the potencies, the faculties, the achievements, the failures, the appearances, the age, the sex, and the like are relevant to the answer. All examples of human beings from ancient times, from Africa, from Europe from all places cultures and times are relevant. All the data from all the human sciences, history anthropology, economics, politics, and the like, are directly related to answering the question. The laws of motion, light, temperature, energy, of physics are relevant. The laws of chemistry, biology, sensitive psychology, are also relevant and apply to human beings and therefore are to be included in the insight into the unity of the human being. All these partial intelligibilities are to be included and certainly cannot be excluded. We are asking one question, what is a human being? We are looking for one inclusive insight into the unity of a mass of data. What holds this data together in one insight?

To formulate a hypothesis is our next task. Traditionally the definition has been as simple as *rational animal*. This focuses on certain crucial aspect of the human being but is somewhat impoverished in that it seems to exclude so many other important characteristics. I would prefer something like the following. "A human being is one integrated whole, including embodied sensitive animal characteristics; who is conscious, experiences, feels, understands, uses language, knows truth and falsity, right and wrong; who acts freely and responsibly, relates to others, loves and hates; who is social, moral and religious; who grows through a sensitive, an intellectual, moral and religious dialectic, between progress and decline." This may sound cumbersome, but it is more informative than the minimalist "rational animal." Christian Smith in *What Is a Person*? also proposes a long and complicated definition of the human person.[12] The terminology is different, but it is consonant with the above definition. If the human person is the most complicated and developed reality in the universe, it is not surprising that the definition is also complex and differentiated even though the person is also an integrated single whole. The inclusive insight into a central form

12. Smith, *What is a Person?*, 61.

grasps the identity of the single, one, identical form, which integrates all of these characteristics. It is one insight into one individual central form. It is an act of understanding and not an imaginative presentation of a ghost or a spooky entity. It may not be a perfect formulation of a definition, but I think it is true to the data and facts presented previously.

The central form does not change over time. It is the one specific human being who is generated, is born, nurtured, grows, loves, lives, becomes independent, starts a family, reproduces, works, ages and dies. The unity and identity remain the same. It is not that a "substance" hidden behind the changing accidents that remains the same. On the contrary, it is the intelligibility, the integration of parts, the specific identity, the wholeness grasped by understanding, that remains the same. Imagination has great difficulty with changing appearances of something that remains the same. But we are not appealing to imagination but to intelligence, understanding, formulating and judging.

Aristotle cryptically remarks, there are no degrees of substance.[13] Unfortunately, he did not elaborate, or he might have formulated a bill of human rights. Humans differ in size, wealth, health, age, sex, ability, education, culture, language, skin color, and so on and so forth, but in so far as they are human beings, they are in principle all equally human beings. No one human being is more of a human being than anybody else.

Aristotle also remarked that a substance cannot be composed of other substances.[14] That is an early answer to modern reductionists. If the human being is one unity-identity-whole grasped by understanding, then she cannot be composed of other unity-identity-wholes. If you have one whole, then the parts are parts and cannot be wholes.

The conjugate forms are the answer to a different question, namely, what are the properties of this one central form? This question intends the conjugate forms and will reach a different kind of insight and judgment. Conjugate forms are forms because they are grasped by understanding. The individual elements of the above definition, taken separately, are conjugate forms. Descriptive conjugate forms would be height, weight, skin color, age, and the like. The conclusions of the human sciences of sociology, anthropology, economics, and so on would be more explanatory conjugate forms, more systematic and hopefully correct. The laws of physics, chemistry, biology and zoology insofar as they apply to human beings would also be conjugate forms. Properties can change, develop, disappear, be transformed within the continuing unity of the central form. The human being is an extraordinary

13. Aristotle, *The Categories*, 3b32–4a9.
14. Aristotle, *Metaphysics*, Z, 13, 1039a5.

example of a multiplicity of potencies, levels, characteristics, activities, feelings, all of which grow and develop individually and collectively. Properties vary in importance. Intelligence for example is a conjugate form not a central form; but it is extremely important. Skin color or size or weight are also conjugate forms but not of central importance.

The notions of central and conjugate forms are complementary, they do not exclude one another, they are not separate things. The central form is the unity, whole, identity of all of the conjugate forms taken together. The conjugate forms cannot exist unless they are integrated into a central form. The conjugate forms represent the varieties, the richness, the diversity, the details integrated into the one central form. The human mind in its search for understanding pivots between the question, what is this thing as a whole, and the question, what are the properties of this particular thing. The more you understand the central form the more you know the conjugate forms and vice versa. Similarly, in the world of nature emergence of new things often happens by gradual adaptation. Certain conjugate forms change, the change becomes embedded, perhaps the function changes and finally the botanist declares that there is a new species.

My justification for this understanding of the human being depends on what we have elaborated in chapter 10, and the account of our consciousness of unity and identity given above. There are no pure mental events that do not depend in some way on the brain, the neurons, the blood flow and a healthy body. I am very conscious of being one person, one substance, one self, with an identity and a unity stretching over seventy years. I am one person who sleeps, wakes, prays, eats, works, grows tired, studies, understands, decides, feels, and hopes. I experience myself as an embodied being. I do not inhabit a body, but I am an embodied substance.

The human sciences need that kind of an understanding of the unity of sameness within the diversity of properties of human beings. Anthropologist will often go on and on about the diversity of human cultures, peoples, and traits and eschew any attempt to grasp what is common across cultures, times, and places. Variety can be seen as a richness when it is linked with an underlying appreciation of the sameness of all human beings. Without that unifying notion, the diversity becomes a chaos of unrelated and fragmented traits. Some measure of sameness does not mean uniformity.

Material and Spiritual

Our concern now is in what respect and in what aspects the human being is material and/or spiritual. It is of some importance for philosophical anthropology to be clear on this distinction because it is crucial in our understanding of the human person. But we have to determine explanatory definitions of material and spiritual and to determine precisely in what respect the human person is material and to what respect spiritual. Fortunately, we have laid the groundwork for this distinction in part 2 and it should not be too difficult.

(1) The Material. Let us summarize the conclusions we reached in chapter 5 on Material/Potency. (1) We are not materialists who hold that the material and only the material exists. This position is based on an impoverished epistemology and a gratuitous assumption that only material exists. (2) We considered matter as potency to be one of the four metaphysical elements that are constitutive of our world of proportionate being. Just as our knowing is constituted by four activities of experiencing, understanding, knowing truth and value, so all areas of our universe are constituted by the elements of potency, form, existence, and value. (3) There is no problem identifying individual composite material things, which can be experienced and also directly understood and known, such as gold, living cells, trees, stars, and so on. (4) We have reached basic terms about knowing and the known and we cannot continue to ask, what is matter and to give an answer in terms such as potency, form and act. We must have recourse to an inverse insight, to grasp the absence of an expected intelligibility. We can only grasp matter as such, indirectly, as what is left behind, what is irrelevant, what lacks meaning or intelligibility, what belongs to the empirical residue. (5) Potency is the component of proportionate being to be known by an intellectually patterned experience of the empirical residue. (6) But we also find data which is irrelevant, unimportant, and is left behind, and we call that matter or more precisely, the empirical residue. The empirical residue has three characteristics, it is positive data, it lacks immanent intelligibility of its own, but is related to a compensating higher intelligibility. (7) Individuality is an example of the empirical residue, because it is positive data, you can point to a multitude of individual things. It lacks immanent intelligibility because there is no reason or principle why this is this and that is that. It is related to a compensating higher intelligibility whereby we can abstract from individuality and generalize, abstract, understand and affirm laws and definitions. (8) Other examples of the empirical residue are probability, inertia, particular times and places, and the continuum. (9) We can define matter as whatever is constituted by or intrinsically conditioned by the empirical residue.

(2) The Spiritual. We are looking for a technical, philosophical, correct definition of the spiritual. We are not appealing to religion or to the supernatural or to vague, spooky entities. Spiritual can be used as a noun or as an adjective, so it may be a central form or a conjugate form (a substance of an accident). Our only direct experience of what might be called spiritual is the activity of human intelligence, human knowing and evaluating and consequent decisions and implementation. Fortunately, we should be fairly familiar with those activity by now. We define the spiritual in positive terms as to its capacities and activities and therefore can affirm what it is.

Our first approach would be to suggest that just as the material is intelligible but not intelligent, the spiritual is what is intelligible and also intelligent. The material is intelligible, simply meaning that it can be understood. We have written a chapter to demonstrate how that is so and given a summary above. We know what we mean when we say, we understand that something is material. But the material is not intelligent; it does not perform cognitional acts of questioning, understanding, knowing and evaluating.

The spiritual is both intelligible and intelligent. We can understand our own acts of intelligence. The mind is not a black box, it is not a mystery, nor is it inaccessible to our attention and understanding. Just as we can study the activity of frogs, we can also study how the mind performs a series of activities which constitute the activity of knowing. As well as being intelligible, the spiritual performs acts of intelligence, is intelligent. We should be very familiar with these activities of questioning, thinking, understanding, getting ideas, formulating hypotheses, checking them against evidence, and finally concluding they are true or false. We can include also the acts of deciding or willing that proceed from knowing true values. We call these activities spiritual and now we need to define explanatorily what we mean by spiritual.

In contrast to our definition of matter, we can now define the spiritual as whatever is not constituted, or intrinsically conditioned by the empirical residue. The empirical residue we remember is data that is left over after understanding and judging; examples are, individuality as such, particular times and places, or actual frequencies as they diverge unsystematically from the ideal. It is clear that being intelligent is not *constituted* by the empirical residue, but in what sense is it *conditioned* by the empirical residue? Can understanding occur without individual events or things, without consideration of time and place? Our position is that human intelligence is conditioned by the empirical residue, but it is an extrinsic not an intrinsic dependence.

We have insisted from the beginning that understanding depends on experiencing, that ideas emerge from images, that verification takes place by reference back to instances, that all human knowing begins in the senses. Similarly, we have insisted that the chemical emerged from the physical, that the biological emerged from chemical, that the sentient emerged from the biological, that intelligence emerged from the sentient. The emergent is new but integrates and depends on previous levels. Mind depends on proper functioning of brain. But is this dependence extrinsic or intrinsic?

What is the function of intelligence or understanding? It is to abstract from material conditions, it is to grasp an idea which is immanent in the data, it is to leave behind the sensible that is not intelligible, to leave behind individuality, and particular times and places. Intelligence abstracts from the empirical residue. It grasps ideas and definitions which are universal. It grasps the connection between sufficiency of data and reasoned conclusions. The proper object of intelligence is ideas, relations, classifications, generalizations, propositions, and conclusions. Intelligence grasps the idea of truth and of value. More and more as intelligence develops does it become more independent of the empirical residue and hence it would seem that its dependence is extrinsic rather than intrinsic. Moreover, if one asserts that intelligence depends intrinsically on materiality this would seem to be a gratuitous principle and that it would exclude a priori an intelligent God.

(3) *The Human Central Form: Material or Spiritual?* Now that we have these distinctions under our belt let us apply them to the human being. In what way precisely is the human being material and/or spiritual?

It is clear that some conjugate acts of the human are material. It is obvious that we are conditioned by space and time, that our senses operate on the sensible, that we are subject to physical, chemical, biological, and organic laws. However, we also ask questions, understand ideas, judge and evaluate propositions and these are spiritual conjugate forms.

So far there is no problem asserting that some activities of the human person are spiritual, and some are material. The crunch comes when we ask whether the central form of the human being is material or spiritual. We have already seen that the human being is one even though s/he performs many activities at various levels. If s/he is one, then s/he has one central form—we cannot fudge here. A thing can have just one central form, not be two or three central forms; a substance cannot be composed of substances. And if there is one central form it must be either spiritual or material. It cannot be half-half or else it would not be one.

If we say that the central form of the human person is material, then it is difficult to see how s/he can perform activities that are spiritual. Animals cannot ask questions and get universal ideas. If human beings are intelligent and perform the activities which we define as spiritual, then they are not at the same level as animals. The central form of the animal is material. But a material central form cannot be the foundation for spiritual activities.

On the other hand, if we assert that the central form of the human is spiritual, then there is no problem accounting for the spiritual activities of understanding. Neither is there any difficulty in asserting that a spiritual central form can be the basis for material activities and conjugates. The higher levels can in some ways govern the lower: chemical compounds obey the laws of physics, have physical attributes. Living things embody many chemical compounds and reactions and processes. So intelligent beings can also have material conjugates.

The human person then, as a central form, as a substance, as a unity-identity-whole, is spiritual, by which we mean not intrinsically dependent for its existence or activity on the empirical residue; it is intelligent as well as being intelligible. Some conjugate forms of the human person are spiritual, some are material. The human person is unique in that h/she performs activities of understanding and judging, deciding and loving and acting; as well as activities of eating and drinking, seeing and hearing, being born, growing, learning, aging and dying. It is the one embodied, incarnate person who is the source and centre of these activities, and that central form must be spiritual in the precise technical philosophical sense that I have explained.

Nature and Person

Now, we come to the distinction between nature and person. What does the notion of human person add to the notion of human being? These two words are often used interchangeably as human nature or human person, as if they were the same thing. Sometimes they are and sometimes they are not. We will give a very precise distinction and definition, which has its own importance for metaphysics, for ethics, and for theology. We will start with nature and just specify two related meanings.

(1) Nature as principle of change: Aristotle distinguishes different meanings for nature in his *Metaphysics* but the main meaning for him is nature as the principle of motion, the source from which comes change. It is a common idea in Aristotle that you know what the nature of a thing is from its motion or change or activity. You distinguish the heavenly bodies according to their motion, the sun has a daily motion, the moon a daily and monthly motion, the fixed stars have a daily and a yearly motion, the wandering stars have a daily motion but after that seem to wander all over the place. If they

have different motions then they are different classes of things, they have a different nature. The nature of the vegetative soul is revealed in the motions of growth, reproduction, taking in and giving out, living and dying. The nature of the sensitive soul is revealed in range of movement, ability to see, hear, and sense, to coordinate input and response, to breed and reproduce. Human nature is revealed in activities of rational animal, thinking, talking, reasoning and concluding and willing.

(2) Nature as universal essence: When we use the expression "human nature," we are usually referring to the universal, what belongs to the essence or substance of being human, the basic characteristics or definition which all individuals must satisfy. These are not subsistent universals but universal as opposed to particular. We can also talk of divine nature, animal nature, chemical nature, etc. It was presumed that everything had a nature and so could be divided into genera and species.

Let us now concentrate on the notion of person and distinguish its use in psychology and in philosophy. Person has a meaning in psychology associated with personality, theories of personality, personality development, personality disorders etc. We might refer to this as the psychological person, but we are more interested in the philosophical person. To explain nature is relatively easy; to explain person is much more difficult. Historically we must note that the Greek and early Roman philosophers did not have a term corresponding to "person." Aristotle had the terms, nature, substance, essence, form, etc., but he did not have a word for person. He sometimes talked about the self and seemed to consider that the self was very close to the intellect.

The word was first used in a colloquial sense for the masks used by actors on the stage. The word took on a technical meaning in a theological context and then passed into philosophy and other disciplines. In the context of Christian theology, it was very important to distinguish nature and person for an understanding of who Jesus was, and how to understand the trinity. Centuries of controversy and misunderstandings followed. Boethius gave the classical definition of person as, "an individual substance of a rational nature." It is only rational beings, who can be persons. Aquinas seemed to be satisfied with Boethius' definition but simplified it to "a rational subsistent," meaning capable of existence on its own or possessing the act of existence. The word soon passed into the vocabulary of philosophy, psychology, law, education, politics and common sense.

I think our best approach is to delineate some essential characteristics of the notion of person from a philosophical point of view. The word has acquired great importance in contemporary times where we assert human rights, personal rights, the dignity of the human person, equality of persons, and personal obligations. What is the import of the notion of person used in that context?

(1) I think the essential notion of person is in view of personal *relations with others*. The key would seem to be in the different questions, what? and who? Everybody makes this distinction; everybody understands this distinction; everyone recognizes what constitutes a correct answer to the respective questions. "What?" aims at a something, a nature. "Who?" intends a somebody, a person. A person would then seem to be, "the term of possible relations with others."

I use the word "term" or "centre" to indicate that the activity of relating to others springs from a beginning, a source, a term. I could use the word "subject" or "self," but these are often used in a psychological sense with no philosophical implications. We are looking for a notion of person that will satisfy the philosophical requirements while also conforming with psychological experience. Nothing that has been said about nature indicates this as a term of personal relations. Yet to be a human being is to be a human person and that seems to imply at least the possibility of personal relations. We are rational animals but also social animals. We are relational by essence. No one gave birth to themselves. An infant would not survive more than a day without being fed, held, wiped, round the clock for months. We do not teach ourselves language or logic. We desire not only knowledge, but love. Most of the ways we define ourselves are from our relationships with other persons: son, daughter, brother, sister, mother, father, grandparent, uncle, aunt, friend, teacher, student, etc.

(2) We need to insist that personhood belongs to the central form of the human being: if it is a human being it is a human person. Some argue that the baby in the womb is a human being but not a human person. They claim that person along with personality only emerge with birth, growth, activities, language, choice and intelligence. I concede that personality is something that emerges but personhood which belongs to the central form (or substance) is there from the beginning. There are no degrees of personhood, there are no degrees of substance, there are no degrees of central form. It is the same person in the womb, in infancy, in childhood, adulthood and old age. That is why the philosophical notion of person is different from the psychological notion of personality. We can call this the ontological dimension; by that I mean that there is a real difference between a person and a non-person, or impersonal force. If you are a human being

then you are a human person. Person is something that belongs to human nature even though it is a distinct aspect of human nature.

Personhood is a spiritual characteristic belonging to a spiritual central form; but in human persons it is an embodied person, subject to the limitations of space and time. We have shown how the central form of the human being is spiritual in a very clearly defined philosophical sense. We can now assert that the human person as person is also spiritual. The activities of, questioning, understanding, judging truth and value are spiritual activities. But it is the person who questions, who understands, who thinks and knows.

(3) A person performs *conscious activities* of experiencing, understanding, judging, deciding and loving. Boethius speaks of rational nature; that surely means understanding; but understanding cannot occur without somebody understanding; understanding does not occur in a vacuum; it would seem to entail a person performing the act of understanding an object. In human knowing there is a distinction between the subject knowing, the activity of knowing and the object known. Boethius rightly limits person to rational creatures. We do not consider dogs or cats to be persons even though we sometimes give them names and treat them as pets and even have a relationship with them! They are not persons because they have no rationality, no action of understanding and loving in the spiritual sense. Personhood is reserved to humans, angels and God.

A person is a *single* subject of multiple conscious activities. It is the person who acts, not the will; it is the person who thinks, not the intellect or brain; it is the person who speaks, not the vocal cords; it is the person who loves not the heart; it is the person who walks not the legs. The person uses the eyes to see, the brain to think, the legs to walk. The person is the coordinator, the source, the integrator, the operator of all human operations. This is what gives unity to the human being. The person is the subject of every conscious action.

(4) Personhood is *universal* while persons are *particular, concrete individuals*. It is sometimes said that the Greeks were only interested in the universal, the ideal and the abstract. That it was the Christians who discovered the inestimable value of the singular, the individual and the concrete. That is why person was a discovery of the Christians and not of the Greeks. Hence the essential characteristic of the person would be precisely individuality. This would seem also to be the position of Boethius in his definition. However, I do not think this is the full story.

It is hard to think of the defining characteristic of personhood as being individuality. The distinction between universal and individual is applicable to table, cat, water, tree, house, dog, in the same way that it is applicable to human nature or human person. You can think of human nature as an abstract universal or you can think of this concrete individual human being sitting here in front of you. Similarly, you can think of personhood, person in general, defining characteristics of the person or you can think of this individual person here in front of you. Human persons are individuals, but it is not individuality that makes them persons. Angels are individuals but that does not make them persons. Even God is an individual, but he is not a person just because he is an individual.

However, it is right to stress that the human person is an individual, and that each is unrepeatable and unique. That we cannot become another person; nor another person assume our identity. There is something special about the spiritual human person here. This is indicated by the fact that we refer to humans by name, Pat, John, Mary, Matilda, etc. The name is thought to refer to this concrete individual person in all her wholeness and in her personhood. Person is at once the source of all the activities which define the human and is to be grasped as the subject of this totality of human actions, parts and appearances.

(5) Personhood is more than personality. The psychological person is the one that emerges through interaction with the mother, through being able to act, to walk, to decide, to name and to think. Mothers refer to a good baby, a quiet baby, a troublesome baby etc. Similarly, in infancy and childhood aspects of personality become more pronounced. So, psychologists distinguish structures of personality, types of personality (Enneagram and Myers-Briggs), personality disorders, growth in personality, etc. This is the subject consciously choosing, thinking and doing and making himself by these actions. This is the conscious person, who can be studied through the data of consciousness. This is usually the limit of what the psychologists consider to be a person. In this sense, they are in fact going back to the rather superficial usage of the term "persona" as a mask for behavior as used by the ancient Greeks and Romans.

(6) Persons have an *absolute value* that comes from their spirituality and incommunicability. It is also based on Aristotle's principle that there are no degrees of substance. If it is a person then it is a person, equally with everybody else. The person may be a foetus, an African, a president, a dying Aids patient, the richest man in the world, an Alzheimer's patient who has

forgotten his name. In principle, these are all equally persons with the same dynamics, same nature, same value as persons.

(7) Persons are the ground of *moral or ethical responsibilities*. Person is very much associated with the fourth level of human consciousness, and moral and personal are sometimes used interchangeably. The moral has to do with what choices you make in terms of the tension between satisfactions and true values. By these choices you constitute yourself to be a good person or a selfish person. You do this in the context of a group, community or society and your actions benefit or harm the group or community. We become subjects in relations to others.

It is the person who decides and not the will; it is the person who is responsible for his/her decisions and not the will or the intellect or the brain. Personal decisions can be individual concrete instances of deciding for this or that; or they can be habitual orientations built up over years to regularly seek the good. It is the person who is the originator of such decisions and the person who is characterized as good or evil, virtuous or vicious, kind or impatient. The person is the integrator of the whole moral person in that sense. The person deciding is the dynamic motivated and guided by the desire to know and the transcendental precepts. The person that loves is the dynamic that transforms the processes of experiencing understanding and judging and deciding. The person as the responsible decision-maker points the whole person either in the direction of personal satisfactions, or towards true values and self-transcendence.

Conclusions

Our aim as metaphysicians has been to outline a heuristic structure for the fruitful understanding of the human person. We saw how all our previous notions regarding proportionate being apply to the human person. Yet the human person performs activities beyond the capacities of other animals and must be regarded as a species unto herself. We outlined these activities, and found that they were, feeling, questioning, understanding, knowing truth and value, relating to others, religious openness, deciding freely, and implementing faithfully. We further examined the conflicts peculiar to human beings and traced the roots of this to a dialectical tension between immanence and transcendence. We discussed the nature of the human central form as spiritual and personal.

An empirical method will always involve two elements, symbolized in the image of a scissors with an upper blade and a lower blade. The upper blade is the assumption, the hypothesis, the heuristic, the anticipation of what is to be understood. The lower blade is the collection of data relevant to answering specific detailed further questions. This chapter has outlined a heuristic about the human person expecting that the details will be provided by each and every human science building up a composite picture of the infinite variety, diversity, richness, worth and flexibility of human persons. Our sketch is minimal, a scaffolding, a framework to be filled out and enriched endlessly by specific human sciences. The importance of our framework is that it makes explicit the assumptions behind the work of the human sciences; it makes sure that this framework is correct; it warns against deviations and false assumptions; it suggests fruitful questions; it suggests how data are to be correctly interpreted and presented. We outlined in chapter 3 how important assumptions are for the fruitful development of the sciences in general. This chapter formulates a heuristic structure for the fruitful development of the human sciences.

Part 3 of this work is entitled "An Emergent, Diverse, Ordered Universe." In conclusion, let us sum up a worldview that will serve as an upper blade or hypothesis for all the other sciences. In short, we described our universe as operating in the framework of a generalized emergent probability. It is one universe, and it seems that the fundamental laws of physics and chemistry, operate universally across the world of proportionate being. In all cases, potency, form, actuality, and value are to be discerned in any true theory or explanation or law. In some places, life has emerged and called forth biology, and the study of plants, animals and humans. The universe is emergent in that it has a history where new realities are emerging in all areas. These emerge not following a deterministic or deductive pattern but with an element of chance and hence novelty operating. Across the board, at all levels, we discern central and conjugate forms constituting the basic intelligibility of the universe based on an isomorphism with two kinds of insights, inclusive and abstractive. These intelligibilities are not random but form a series of ordered genera and species in all of the levels of scientific investigation. From this complex, differentiated, flexible, matrix human beings emerged. The universe continues into the Anthropocene with the same characteristics operating, with the human person subject to all these contingencies and trying to promote progress and reverse decline.

Now we have finished the easy part. Let us gird our loins to tackle the really hard questions as to where this immense, ordered, universe with its diverse population of plants, animals, and humans came from.

14

Ultimate Longing

God is the unrestricted act of understanding, the eternal rapture
glimpsed in every Archimedean cry of Eureka.[1]

It may be that inner religious and outer sociocultural factors come
together to constitute a new religious consciousness inasmuch as
(1) the inner religious factor resembles an infrastructure while (2)
the outer sociocultural factor makes possible, or begins to counte-
nance, or expresses, or interprets the religious experience.[2]

. . . to be just a man is what man cannot be. . . . But if he would be
only a man, he has to be less.[3]

Energy leaks out of the vacuum for no reason at all except random-
ness and the pressure exerted by a sink of infinite negative energy.
Overall the universe is nothing at all.[4]

Introduction

So far, we have confined our attention to the universe of proportionate being, namely, the whole scope of what can be known through direct
experience, understanding in all its varieties and correct affirmations of
truth and value. Thus far we have outlined a worldview of a universe that
is sensible, intelligible, real and good; which has a history of development
from plasma to subatomic particles, to atoms, to molecules, to living cells,
to plants and animals, and finally to the emergence of human persons

1. Lonergan, *Insight*, 706.
2. Lonergan, *A Third Collection*, 55.
3. Lonergan, *Insight*, 750.
4. Potter, *How to Make a Human Being*, 18.

and societies. We have discovered a universe rich in diversity, incredibly complicated, beautiful to behold, with every new discovery leading to further questions and showing how superficial and feeble is our present understanding. We have stressed that the components of our knowing are proportionate to the elements known. We concluded to a world view of generalized emergent probability.

A series of further specific questions of detail arise in all the disciplines to illuminate and fill out our scientific and practical understanding of our planet. But questions also arise in another direction. Is this scientific and philosophical account of our universe our ultimate boundary or horizon? Have we reached the limit of what we can say? Is there not a wider horizon to be considered? If all scientific disciplines answered all their particular questions, would we be satisfied? Is there not another ultimate question, the answer to ultimate longing? I feel we are obliged to make a jump to a kind of knowledge of transcendence; is there something more to the understanding of our worldview than the knowledge built on direct experience of the sensible?

Being is the objective of the pure desire to know. To know, as humans, we have emphasized is to experience, understand, and judge truth and value. But is our human knowing intrinsically limited to what we can directly sense and experience? Can we not move to ultimate questions and ultimate answers? Can we not ask questions about where the universe came from? What was there before the Big Bang? What is the ultimate cause and reason for the existence of the universe, for you and for me? Can we extrapolate from scientific accounts of all the details of our experience to such general questions? I hope to show that knowing is understanding correctly, and its dependence on direct sensible experience is actually extrinsic. We can and do ask questions about what cannot be seen or heard or sensed, and sometimes we can answer them.

In this last chapter, we will show that such questions arise naturally and legitimately and can be correctly affirmed or denied. We are now raising the final and ultimate question about the meaning of the universe, the question of the ultimate intelligibility of the universe. We will approach this in two ways. Firstly, from the point of view of the intellectual pattern of experience, we will ask philosophical questions and attempt an intellectual grasp of a correct answer (§§2–5). We will be following the arguments of chapter 19 of *Insight*, which is complicated, detailed, and technical. Lonergan wrote it in this way to leave no loop hold for objections or counter arguments. I will present what I consider the central notions and arguments as clearly and correctly as I can. Secondly, from the point of view of a religious pattern of experience, we will investigate whether to be fully human is to more than human; whether within us there is a desire for transcendence, an openness to the divine, an ultimate longing, a fifth level of consciousness (§6).

Libraries overflow with books on this topic. World religions express answers to these questions according to their culture, in their own ways. In one chapter, I attempt to sketch out our position on this issue and so complete our worldview of everything. It is as important as it is difficult. I try to be simple and succinct, but sufficiently clear to identify and affirm a specific position.

The Question of God Arises Spontaneously and Necessarily

We have been motivated in metaphysics by the desire to know, operating in the intellectual pattern of experience, paying attention to the evidence, searching for explanations, ideas and understanding, working from the evidence to the conclusion by induction or deduction or any other appropriate method, and motivated simply by the search for truth and value. The desire to know is in principle unrestricted. There is no limit to the range of the questions we ask. To what extent we can answer these questions remains to be seen, but the normal expansion of human questioning will eventually lead to questions of the ultimate cause, the first being, the ultimate explanation, the unmoved mover, or whatever terminology you prefer. It would be obscurantism to brush such questions aside. The question of the existence of God arises quite naturally, spontaneously, and necessarily.

When we can ask about truth, the ground of truth, and the ultimate foundation or source of truth and we are asking about the ultimate and hence about God. When we can ask about value, about ultimate value, about the source and guarantee of value, we are asking about God. When we ask about religious experience, about its universality, its source, its authenticity or inauthenticity, we are asking about God. When we ask about the ultimate cause of the existence of the universe, the first cause, we are asking about God. Proximate causes within the universe of proportionate being are reached by common sense, the sciences, the humanities, by an epistemology and metaphysics to integrate, transform and unify that knowledge. When we start looking for ultimate causes, we are going beyond the horizon of proportionate being to its origin, its intelligibility as a whole, to its transcendent source.

Such questions are not meaningless. To assert that there is no ultimate meaning to the universe, that there is no first cause, that it all happened by chance, is a worldview which casts a dark shadow on everything else that we supposedly know. If the universe as a whole does not make sense, then the parts do not make sense either. On the other hand, if there is an ultimate intelligibility to the universe as a whole then all the intelligible parts fit into the one picture and do make sense. Questions set the criteria and conditions for producing an appropriate correct answer. The first stage in coming to know something is to give it a name. Here we are calling the ultimate cause of the universe by the name "God." For the moment it is a nominal definition of the word, namely, how to use the word correctly.

To transcend simply means to go beyond. In asking about something beyond the universe of proportionate being, we are asking about the transcendent. This is possible and justified because sense experiencing is not intrinsic to the process of human knowing. For the knowledge of empirical science, and for the knowledge of this proportionate universe, it is necessary that theories should be verified in sensible experiences. But knowing is intrinsically understanding and judging; truth is the correct understanding and grasp of the virtually unconditioned; understanding abstracts from the empirical residue; human intellectual knowledge is properly knowledge of the intelligible rather than the sensible. Let me defend this position by the following arguments.

1. In our previous chapter we argued that the central form of the human person is spiritual. One of the definitions of spiritual that we used was that it is both intelligible and intelligent. The activity of understanding, being intelligent, is a spiritual activity because it abstracts ideas, affirms truth, and judges values. Ideas are not necessarily subsistent ideas, but all ideas are intelligible, abstract and general; they are distinct from images which are sensible, concrete and particular. Ideas are intelligible and spiritual such that they can only be dealt with by a being which is intelligent. Intelligibility in the world of proportionate being is dependent on sensible evidence, images and experience. Human knowing in common sense and the sciences is dependent on experience. But intelligence itself is immaterial and spiritual, its proportionate object is the intelligible and so is not intrinsically bound by direct experiencing.

2. The structure of human knowing of common sense and of science is a contingent structure; it could have been different. It is not necessarily the case that intelligence can only know through the sensible. It would seem ridiculous to bind intelligence intrinsically to material conditions. Such a position would deny God the possibility of knowing as God does not experience the sensible. Our human knowing of the universe is of the material, the formal, the real, and the good, and

is constituted by experiencing, understanding, judging and evaluating. But the dependence of human knowing on experiencing is extrinsic rather than intrinsic.

3. Our arguments for the existence of God will be cosmological rather than ontological. We start from the cosmos rather than from ideas and definitions. We start from the causality, which is very evident and verifiable in our universe, but we move from proximate causes to ultimate causes. We are arguing not from cause to effect but from effect to cause. What is the proportionate cause of the universe and all that is in it? The ultimate cause is of a different order than the causes uncovered by a science or a philosophy of the universe of proportionate being, as we shall see. When we ask about a transcendent cause we are taking the universe as a whole and asking, what is its ultimate cause, and why does it exist. We do not expect the cause to be sensible or visible or to be experienced through the senses. In this case, the cause transcends the effects. Our argument proceeds from effects to the adequate cause of those effects. It is a question not for science but for philosophy.

4. We show that knowing a transcendent being is possible by engaging in the process. Kant and others approach the problem of human knowing by asking for the *a priori* conditions for the possibility of human knowing, namely, to what extent is human knowing possible. But one is already engaged in the project of human knowing when one asks that question, which would seem to present a methodological problem. Our approach to knowing has been *a posteriori* rather than *a priori*. Fact proves possibility. Our human knowing is a fact; the way it works is a fact; the limits and conditions are factual and verifiable; human knowing could have been different, but it is what it is. Instead of asking, is knowledge possible, perhaps a more fruitful approach would be to engage in the process, and then to ask what mental activities constitute full human knowing, how do we distinguish subjectivity and objectivity, how do we distinguish real from illusory, how do we verify our conclusions. In this way, we show that knowledge of the transcendent is possible by engaging in the process and seeing how and to what extent we can attain true knowledge of the transcendent.

5. The question of the ultimate cause or explanation of the existence of the universe is the most important question one can ask. The answer does make a difference. What we know about the proportionate universe is incomplete until we ask and answer this question. Theism or atheism changes the whole perspective of our view of the universe of proportionate being and of course the place of human persons in that universe. We

are beyond the integral heuristic structure of proportionate being here. But it is still metaphysics as we have to ask, is proportionate being as a whole, caused or uncaused, intelligible or unintelligible, designed or a cosmic accident. Lonergan's approach is to extrapolate from something that we can understand and are very familiar with, namely, restricted human understanding to an unrestricted act of understanding which is transcendent. He regards this as the culmination of his whole project, where he was heading to from the very beginning. It presupposes all that goes before it but goes one step further.

Formulating a Notion of a Transcendent Being

Before passing a judgment, it is normal to have a clear idea about the content, implications and scope of your prospective judgment. Hence, in this section we are simply clarifying our ideas about a transcendent being and postponing an affirmation of its existence in reality until the next section. Aristotle wondered about the Unmoved Mover and what it might be doing to pass the time of day, in this case eternity. His answer was, "It is in this manner that Thinking is the Thinking of Himself through all eternity."[5] Also, "It is of Himself, then, that The Intellect is thinking, if He is the most excellent of things and so thinking is the thinking of Thinking."[6] This may sound very mysterious but Aristotle, as usual, was on the right path. The Unmoved Mover, the Intellect, must be knowing and in the highest degree, and since it itself is the highest reality, it must be thinking of itself. Unfortunately, he did not have a clear formulated notion of human knowing in terms of experiencing, understanding, judging and evaluating and so was using a general term "thinking" to define the activity of the Unmoved Mover. Hopefully, we have a differentiated and correct appreciation of human knowing and also of its objective counterpart in the world of proportionate being. We are going to use this base from which to extrapolate to an understanding, and later an affirmation, of the existence of an ultimate cause of our universe.

Let us provisionally define this being as an unrestricted act of understanding. The content of an act of understanding is an idea, in this case, the idea of being, for that is what would be required to know everything about everything, comprehensively and in detail. We are going beyond our limited acts of understanding to formulate what an unrestricted act of understanding would be like. How would an unrestricted act of understanding satisfy

5. Aristotle, *Metaphysics*, 12, 9, 1075a10.
6. Aristotle, *Metaphysics*, 12, 9, 1074b34.

the criteria set by the question of the ultimate cause of the universe? We cannot hope to possibly grasp an adequate concept or definition of God; but we can point in the direction and lay down certain conditions that a correct answer must satisfy. By way of extrapolation, we can name the transcendent, assign characteristics, define; even though we do not and cannot comprehend the full meaning of what we intend.

We should be very familiar with human restricted acts of understanding and our experience is normally focused on such restricted knowledge. However, we can speculate as to what an unrestricted act of understanding might be. We can extrapolate from our experience of restricted acts of understanding to an unrestricted act of understanding. The primary component of an unrestricted act of understanding would be its understanding of itself. It must understand itself otherwise it would not be unrestricted. It would be the most appropriate object of thought as it would be transcendent. It would be intelligence in its pure sense grasping intelligence. Not two things but one by identity. In the unfolding act of understanding there is a moment of identity when the definition or idea in the mind is identical with the particular essence that is known. Human knowing is partly by identity and so we can understand that the transcendent being knowing itself is by identity only one thing, not two. For humans, self-knowledge comes at the end of a long process of conscious knowing of other things and reflection on the unfolding of knowing. The transcendent knowing is primarily a knowledge of itself.

Secondarily an unrestricted act of understanding would understand everything else because it understands itself. To understand from a human point of view is to grasp an idea from an image. We have a notion of being which is a heuristic, the objective of a desire to know. But we do not have an actual grasp of everything about everything. An unrestricted act of understanding would grasp the idea of being, which would include everything without restriction, both proportionate being and transcendent being. The intelligibility of the universe of proportionate being is derivative, it derives from the supreme being because it understood itself. An unrestricted act of understanding would understand everything about everything, and hence would possess as content the idea of being.

We devoted a chapter to our human limited heuristic notion of being, not daring to use the term "idea" of being. An idea is a grasp of the intelligible in the sensible. You get the idea of specific weight when you understand that the relation of weight to volume determines whether an object will float or not; it is of universal relevance. It is an idea, a definition, a relation, a grasp of an essence. Our notion of being simply asserted that being is the objective of human desire to understand. Whatever is experienced, understood and known will be a being. In no way did we claim to have an idea of being, to grasp in a positive way the essence of everything about everything. Our knowing is restricted. An unrestricted act of understanding would understand everything about everything in one single, if magnificent, act of understanding, and hence would have an idea of being.

An idea of being would include everything about everything, including both the primary being and secondary beings. That is very difficult for us to visualize as we instinctively think of intelligence as human intelligence. We must distinguish two senses of the word intelligible. There is the ordinary human sense of grasping the intelligible in the sensible, the form in the matter, the general law underlying many instances, as is typical of human understanding. When we refer to the secondary intelligible, we are referring to the intelligibility of the universe, the intelligible in the sensible, form in matter. But there is also a special sense in which the word intelligible refers to intelligence in itself, the ground and root of intelligibility, pure intelligence. When we refer to the primary component, we are referring to this special sense, intelligibility in itself, the essence of intelligence. Thus, we can distinguish between the primary intelligible and the secondary intelligible. The primary component of the idea of being is one spiritual act by which the unrestricted act of understanding understands itself. It is the special sense of the meaning of intelligence, pure intelligence. The secondary component of the idea of being is the intelligibility of the universe of proportionate being which is known through the unrestricted act of understanding.

We can extrapolate from the side of the subject, from our restricted acts of understanding grasping aspects of being to an unrestricted act of understanding grasping everything about everything. We can extrapolate from the side of the object from the universe of proportionate being to the idea of being, transcendent knowledge including the ultimate cause of the universe.

This being would not be like any other being that we know. All the beings we know in this universe are contingent beings; they are potency, form and act; they could have been different; they are not necessary; they are in fact but could have been otherwise. This cannot be said about transcendent being who must be a necessary being; a being who exists necessarily, who exists of his very nature; for which you cannot assign a cause of existence outside itself. For all contingent beings it is legitimate to ask what caused them or where did they come from. For transcendent being you cannot ask this question because it is the ultimate cause and explanation of everything. To ask who made God is to imply that God is a contingent being like any other creature. Science continuously asks for causes, for further understanding, to go deeper and farther. As God is the ultimate answer to the ultimate question, further questioning is ruled out. In God, essence is identical with existence; his existence did not come from outside, from some other thing; he exists necessarily, eternally, perfectly, completely. He could be called the Uncaused Cause, the Unmoved Mover, the First Cause. Let us formulate some other characteristics of this unrestricted act of understanding.

A first thing we can say is that if God exists there can be only one such being. If God is the ultimate cause and explanation and source of all that is, then he must be one and only one. If there were two or more then this would in turn have to be explained and so you have not reached the ultimate explanation.

The transcendent being must be a spiritual being, intelligent in the pure primary sense and intelligible, outside and beyond conditioning by space and time. Any material thing is intrinsically conditioned or constituted by space and time. God is outside space and time and is not so constituted or conditioned. Hence, God would be eternal, spiritual, unchanging, but real. This being would have to be simple, undivided, unique, to be the cause of all that is, as well as the uncaused cause. The one transcendent being can understand the many, the immaterial can grasp the material, the eternal can grasp the temporal, the non-spatial can grasp the spatial.

The transcendent being would be a person, personal, because intelligent and reasonable. It is only subjects, persons, who can know and love and decide. Gender is not an attribute of God. Our English pronouns force us to imply that the person is either male or female. I use the pronoun "he" with no suggestion of male superiority or of assigning a gender to God.

God would have to be a Creator God, the proportionate cause of the existence of the universe. To be the ultimate explanation of the universe God would have to be the creator cause, the one who brought it out of nothingness and made it to exist, gave it existence. On the one hand, you have the Creator God who is uncaused cause, who exists of his very nature. On the other hand, you have creation, the created universe, the universe of proportionate being, which has been given existence from outside and made to exist. God creates out of nothing; meaning that no pre-existing material existed out of which the universe was created.

God would also be conserver in existence. No creature exists of its nature. The creative act of God is continuously operative. God's power continues to conserve things in existence according to the laws and principles of this creation. Hence God is present in every part of the universe to conserve it in existence; he is present not in virtue of his substance but in virtue of his power of conserving. God is the ultimate cause of all the particular instances of causes in the universe.

God would be omniscient. He knows everything about his creation, past, present and future in one eternal act of understanding and willing into existence. Just as we know one in many, one law that applies to many instances, so God knows everything about everything not in multiple acts of understanding but in a single unrestricted act of understanding. God knows the past the present and the future, knows every detail of every event and thing and attribute, God knows what every person will freely choose to do without interfering with that freedom.

God would be omnipotent. As he brought the universe of proportionate being into existence by an act of willing, with all its potencies, forms, acts and value, central and conjugate forms, hierarchy of genera and species, principle of finality, living things, human persons, so God can change any of the things, or laws, as long as they do not involve a contradiction.

God would be good. God is the cause of the goodness of the universe and hence would be the primary source of goodness. The good goes along with the intelligible. The primary intelligible would also be the primary good. The secondary intelligible would be the secondary good.

God creates the universe but is in no way changed by this creation; you cannot distinguish in God a time before and a time after creation. God is eternal and unchanging. Here we need to apply the distinction between primary intelligible and secondary intelligible. God knowing himself would be the primary intelligible, an act of unrestricted understanding, Being in all its infinity and richness and unity. Secondary intelligible would be the intelligible content of God's creating act, the universe of proportionate being including ourselves. In and through himself he would know all things in the universe is one single act of understanding.

Our purpose in this section is to formulate a notion of God so that we can be in a position to affirm or deny his existence. We specified some of the characteristics which must be found if God is to be the cause and explanation of the existence of our universe, the ground of the intelligibility of the universe, and the meaning of our existence. We can have an inadequate, nominal, analogous, heuristic notion of the meaning of an unrestricted act of understanding, that understands itself, and through that understands everything else.

Now we face the issue, does this Being really exist, can we know that he exists; can we reasonably affirm the existence of God? We will try to do this in our next section and will considers objections and difficulties in the subsequent section.

Affirming the Existence of a Transcendent Being

Many specific proofs of the existence of God have been given in the history of philosophy. Aristotle argued in terms of the cause of motion; every mover is caused to move by another; but that in turn is moved by another; an infinite series is repugnant; so there much be a first mover that did move himself, an Unmoved Mover. Aquinas in his famous five proofs argued from motion, from causality, from contingency, from grades of perfection, and from finality. All of the proofs boil down in essence to the proof we are presenting, the complete intelligibility of the universe. The five proofs are taking specific instances of intelligibility which require a proportionate cause. We are taking the complete intelligibility of the universe, which calls out for a proportionate cause.

Presenting a proof for the existence of God is not on the same plane as presenting a proof for Pythagoras' theorem on the right-angled triangle. It is more complicated in that more evidence, thinking and arguments are involved. It is more existential in that the person is more personally involved; personal values and inherited beliefs and practices may be challenged one way or the other. The argument for the existence of God involves understanding the transcendent, which is certainly more difficult than understanding theorems in geometry where you can at least draw a triangle and construct a helpful image. But the two arguments are similar in that they are both asking questions, combining knowns and unknowns, assembling evidence and clear definitions, and grasping the necessity of the truth of the conclusion.

Step One

We have defined being as the objective of the pure, unrestricted desire to know. Apart from being there is only non-being, nothing. Becoming is a being, properties are beings, ideas in the head are beings, mythological figures are beings, nightmares are beings, buttons are beings. They are all beings in different senses. They all can be known as belonging to their realm of being. If something is knowable then it must intelligible. The pure desire to know is a desire of intellect to grasp correctly what is intelligible. As humans that knowledge of proportionate being will always be in the form of asking questions, about what we experience, in order to understand correctly. The objective of the desire to know then must be intelligible.

Apart from being there is only non-being, namely, nothing. Humans know by understanding. You can only understand what is intelligible. Apart from what is intelligible there is nothing. The unintelligible as such cannot be real, cannot exist, cannot be understood or known. Lonergan refers to such things as "mere matters of fact," without explanation, or justification, or cause, or meaning, or intelligibility. Perhaps a better description would be a mere nonsense, or total chaos.

This is not just some piece of clever logic or an intellectual trick. It is verifiable and real in our own experience of how our minds work. Logic appeals to the Principle of Sufficient reason, but this is not merely a logical or arbitrary principle but a principle by which the human mind operates. It asserts that we spontaneously know that if something happens then there must be a cause, or explanation or reason. Nothing that happens is totally random; there is always some intelligibility to be grasped even if it is by an inverse insight. At the heart of every scientific enterprise is the desire to know. It is not enough to know that the moon has phases, we want to know why the moon has phases. It is not enough to know that different elements have different spectral lines, we want to know why they have different spectral lines. Science presumes that there are causes operating; we may or may not be able to identify the causes, but we work on the principle of sufficient reason which holds that there must be causes. We assume that there is a reason for the discrepancy in the perihelion of Mercury. We presume there is a reason why petrol burns, boats float, planes fly, plants grow, diseases spread. We presume that climate is a complex scheme of recurrence which we can study and understand; that if there are cycles of climate change there must be a reason for that; that it is possible that human use of carbon fuels is increasing the amount of carbon dioxide in the atmosphere and perhaps causing increase in temperature. We do not accept that climate changes at random or for no reason at all. We do not expect chemical elements to behave in a random manner. Even in chaos theory we are looking for formulae, theories, explanations for why things behave as they do. An aeroplane crash is usually followed by an inquiry into the cause; was it human error, mechanical failure, or a design defect? Few would be satisfied if the inquiry concluded that it was just an accident!

We can only know the intelligible. It follows that we cannot know what is totally unintelligible, or total nonsense, or totally random. Once you start naming, identifying, characterizing, describing, and so on, you are in the early stages of knowing. Ask yourself, is there anything that you know that is totally unintelligible?

Step Two

Our argument will hinge on the proposition that the universe is completely intelligible. We are required to explain clearly what we mean by completely intelligible and why that would require the existence of a Primary Intelligible or Creator God. Let us start by making some clarifications about what we mean by saying the universe is completely intelligible.

In the ordinary meaning of intelligible we claim that the universe is completely intelligible in the sense that it can be known by human common sense, the hard sciences, the humanities, philosophy and any other disciplines or skills. It is known by the invariant structure of human knowing, namely, experiencing, understanding, judging and evaluating correctly. The universe as a whole is intelligible as a generalized emergent probability. It is a dynamic universe, on the move, changing. At its root is the move from potency, to form, to act, to value. This is parallel to the dynamism of human knowing which proceeds from questioning, to experiencing, to understanding, to judging and evaluating. In every scientific field there is a presumption that you understand things and events in terms of their history. There is a principle of finality operating in this universe as the undeveloped develops, the undifferentiated becomes differentiated, the imperfect heads towards perfection, the incomplete tends towards the complete. There is a direction of development towards higher, more complex, more differentiated, more diverse things and events.

Emergence is the key term to describe this process. The prime example of emergence is in the human mind where ideas emerge from data and images under the influence of questioning; truth emerges from possibilities, hypotheses, under the influence of reflective criticism; and knowledge of values emerges under the influence of the value question through a deliberative insight. There is a parallel process of emergence in the real world, from subatomic particles, to atoms, to molecules, to living cells, to plants, to animals, to humans. In each of these fields there are further emergences of genus and species, of groups and subgroups adding to the rich tapestry of things and happenings. This happens not according to a determinist or deductivist design, nor is it totally haphazard, but happens according to schedules of probabilities of occurrence and survival. There is an element of chance operating which allows for novelty, for emergence and for decline. The general scheme allows for breakdowns, stagnation, sterility, collapse, and decline. Both classical and statistical methods are needed to understand this schema of emergence which generally aims in the direction of further development and progress.

Into this kind of universe, we humans have emerged, survived, developed, learned to read and write, to cultivate and build, to organize our
society and economy and technology to build schools and universities, to
discover moral imperatives, and even to worship God. Thus, we reflect on
the kind of universe in which we find ourselves and find it is very good.
Such a universe makes total sense; it is completely intelligible, incredibly
vast, highly diversified, from the microcosm to the macrocosm, it is wonderful to behold.

There are particular areas where one might challenge the claim to
complete intelligibility so let us recall these examples. We dealt with this
in detail in chapter 6 on the various meanings of the sensible, the material,
and potency.

1. There are degrees of intelligibility. Surds and irrational numbers
   and negative numbers are less intelligible than simple addition and
   subtraction of whole numbers. The human sciences are less exact
   sciences than physics or chemistry. It is harder to predict weather
   patterns than the movements of the planets. Explanatory knowing
   is more precise and objective than personal descriptions from one's
   own perspective. A sequence of numbers generated by a formula are
   more intelligible than a random sequence of numbers. But in all cases
   a certain intelligibility is reached.

2. Intelligibility can be potential, formal or actual. The data from a survey is potentially intelligible when the data has been gathered. It is
   formally intelligible when the decoder formulates hypotheses as to
   the results. It is actually intelligible when the results are tallied and
   correlated and checked. A crime scene is potentially intelligible when
   it is sealed off, formally intelligible when the forensic detective has a
   hunch, and actually intelligible when a fingerprint confirms the suspicion. The structure of DNA was potentially intelligible as soon as it
   was identified as a chemical; it was formally intelligible when various
   structures were proposed; it was actually intelligible when the double
   helix was confirmed as its actual structure. Understanding is discursive, it takes time, it is a process from potential, to formal, to actual.

3. We have stated that the empirical residue lacks immanent intelligibility. We discussed five examples of the empirical residue, namely, individuality, space/time continuum, particular times and places, constant
   velocity, and probability.[7] The empirical residue may lack immanent
   intelligibility, but it is of enormous consequence when it comes to our

---

7. Please refer to chapter 5, section 5 above.

human knowing of the universe of proportionate being. The universe is only intelligible to us because of the potentiality of the empirical residue. In the grand scheme of things, the empirical residue plays a crucial role; there is no universe of proportionate being without the empirical residue. The empirical residue lacks immanent intelligibility but does not lack transcendent intelligibility. The idea of being grasped by an unrestricted act of understanding includes every instance, every particular, every individual, every anomaly, every event, every detail of the working out of a universe of generalized emergent probability.

4. Evil can also be understood and so is intelligible by an inverse insight. Basic human evil can be understood as not doing what you know to be right, or deliberately doing what you know to be wrong. Personal evil is the source of enormous consequences for the person and for the family, group and society to which he or she belongs. There is also physical evil in the nature of our universe of proportionate being which we have understood as a generalized emergent probability. The universe is changing, developing, undeveloped to developed, from potency to form to act—it is an emerging universe. However, evil can be understood as a privation, a lack of expected intelligibility and also as a challenge to overcome evil by doing good.

That then is the sense of the statement that this universe is completely intelligible. As a whole, putting all the parts and aspects together it is a rich tapestry of overlapping, diverse, and interconnected intelligibilities. From the human scientific or philosophic point of view this is what we mean by claiming that the proportionate universe is completely intelligible.

Step Three

Now that we have outlined the complete intelligibility of the universe from the point of view of science and philosophy, we must move on to a further question and a different kind of ultimate intelligibility. Now we have a universe that is completely intelligible, and we ask is there a cause, a reason, a ground, an intelligible explanation of the existence of that universe. It is natural and spontaneous that such a question would arise. It does not seem to make sense to say that an intelligible universe exists without asking, why, how, and who.

We recall what we said about being and non-being. Being we said is the objective of the pure desire to know. Being then is intelligible because we can understand and know what is intelligible. The converse of this is that the non-intelligible cannot be known because it is not being, is a non-being, a nothing, a nonsense, a non-existent. And so we ask whether the proximate, ordinary, complete intelligibility of the universe has an ultimate, transcendent, intelligible ground?

Intelligibility is usually in the form of assigning causes. Intrinsic causes are formal and material. Extrinsic causes are final and efficient, and exemplary. A cause must always be proportionate to its effect. There must be an intelligible connection between the cause and the effect. In science there must be some explanation, some intelligible cause, some proportion between the cause and the effect. Magic allows for appearing and disappearing at random without explanation. The hat was empty and now it contains a rabbit. Where did the rabbit come from? Children are quite happy with the idea that it appeared from nowhere. Gullible, uneducated, uncritical persons might find it difficult to find an explanation and attribute it to the power of the magician. Most adults, however, would wonder, how did he do it. Our desire to know is a desire to understand; to understand is to assign a reason, a cause, an explanation, a rule, a universal, a law, a regularity, and the like. There is no room for obscurantism here. Obscurantists would say that we cannot ask or should not ask or do not bother to ask or refuse to ask or presume that there is no intelligible answer.

Our question then is, can you have a completely intelligible universe, as explained above, without a transcendent cause or explanation or source of that intelligibility? There seem to be three possible answers; either the universe is completely unintelligible; or the universe is partly intelligible and partly unintelligible; or the universe is completely intelligible in having a primary intelligible as its cause.

It is hard to claim that the universe is completely unintelligible; we can understand many things about it; we have sciences, books, common sense, limited knowledge; there are regularities, systems, laws operating, causes, distinctions, classifications that are intelligible. We understand one another, we teach one another, we often claim that we understand calculus, or chess, or sudoku, or Chinese.

Can we say that the universe is partly intelligible and partly unintelligible? That seems to be the most attractive option. One might be tempted to claim that the complete understanding of our universe in terms of science and philosophy is the end of the story. But the desire to know forces us to ask the further question about the ultimate cause of an intelligible universe. If there is no such ultimate primary cause of the universe then the universe is a nonsense, a nonbeing, a mere nothing.

Is it coherent to consider the universe as intelligible according to science and philosophy but without a primary cause or transcendent intelligible source? Our reasoning about the complete intelligibility of the universe is not the end but the beginning of a new series of questions about the totality of the universe operating on the principles of a generalized probability. Where did it come from, what is its purpose, what caused it to be, to exist? If we cannot assign a proportionate cause for the existence of the totality of the universe then it becomes fundamentally unintelligible and therefor a nonsense, a mere matter of fact, a mere nothing or non-being. To say that the universe happened purely by chance is to admit that the universe is a nonsense. To refuse to ask the question or consider the matter of the ultimate cause of the universe is pure obscurantism. We must to face the issue difficult though it is. We can ask about the ultimate and we can argue to a true answer.

When we look for an adequate cause, we are looking for something that can produce such an effect. Bringing something into existence that did not exist before and for which there was no pre-existing matter, is significantly different from what happens in a chemistry lab where mixing some substances produces a reaction to produce other substances. When we are talking of the coming into existence of the whole universe, its billions of galaxies, its thirteen billion year history, its diversity of genera and species, we are talking of significant power. The existence of the universe is intelligible only if we can assign a transcendent primary cause. It is unintelligible to say that the universe came from nothing, or that it happened by accident, or that it arose from a random fluctuation of the space-time quantum field of force.

We can now revert to our notion of God as an unrestricted act of understanding and add a few clarifications. When we affirm that an ultimate cause of the universe exists, we find that it is identical with the notion of an unrestricted act of understanding grasping the idea of being in our previous section. Aristotle visualized the Unmoved Mover as thinking thought thinking itself. Aquinas referred to God as *Ipsum Esse*, act of existence itself. It is not totally novel to formulate a notion of God as an unrestricted act of understanding grasping the idea of being. Primarily, God knows himself in a single act of understanding and secondarily knows the universe through his self-understanding. The universe as we know it has an ultimate ground in the idea of being understood and created by God.

God is the answer to all our questioning, and we cannot continue to ask what caused God. God is uncaused cause, the fullness of intelligibility, an absolutely necessary being, a being in which essences and existence are not really distinct. Spontaneously in science or commonsense knowledge we tend to go back as far as we can in seeking causes. But an infinite series of causes is not intelligible because that merely shifts the question without providing any answer. There must be a primary, ultimate, first cause.

We can affirm with confidence that God exists. But we are not claiming a knowledge or comprehension of the nature of God. Our understanding of what God is will always be analogical, imperfect, beyond our comprehension. We extrapolate from a restricted act of understanding to an unrestricted act of understanding; we move from proportionate being to transcendent being, from proximate causes to the ultimate cause, from a secondary intelligible to a primary intelligible.

Difficulties and Objections

Scientific Objections

Most of the challenges to the existence of God in contemporary times come from scientists. But scientists need to operate in a correct context of epistemology and metaphysics as we argued in chapter 3. Let us specify some of the arguments that arise mostly from mistaken presuppositions and implications.

(1) Let us examine the notion that science explains everything: that there is no knowledge beyond scientific knowledge. Physics studies the sensible properties of all matter in the universe; electricity and magnetism; space and time; gravity and motion; energy and mass; light and sound; measures everything, correlates everything; applies mathematical concepts to everything. It has made enormous progress in our understanding and in technological advances. Often this is presented as the whole of knowledge, that there is nothing more to be said, that they have the final answer to why the universe exists, the meaning of human life and death.

However, the claim that there are material beings and only material beings is an extra-scientific assertion. This statement cannot be verified using scientific method. It is a cultural assumption. Besides the data of sense, there is also the data of consciousness. Science usually concentrates on the former and ignores the latter. Philosophy begins with describing the process of human knowing and valuing, and realizes that knowing operates by experiencing, understanding, and judging which gives you an epistemology. An examination of the process of evaluating, asking the question of the right thing to do, understanding that some actions are right and some wrong, examining how we decide and implement our knowing gives you an ethics. Examining the content of all our judgments about the real world gives you a metaphysics. Asking about the cause of everything gives you a philosophy of God. In chapter 3 we examined the complex relationship between philosophy and science. In chapter 2 we examined the philosophy of materialism.

It is sad that good scientific work is distorted by false assumptions about knowing and the structure of the known.

(2) Let us examine the notion that something can come from nothing. The Big Bang is often referred to as the moment of creation. However, in that context the word "creation" is not being used in its classical religious and philosophical sense of a creator God, creating the universe out of nothing. In the philosophical meaning of creation there is a proportion between the cause and the effect; between a creator and creation; one can assign a sufficient reason for the emergence of something from nothing; it is a rational process, a reasonable explanation and an intelligible answer to an important question. In the scientific parlance "creation" is left in a limbo world where you are not meant to ask too explicitly about what is meant. It seems to mean that at that moment the whole universe of energy and nascent particles emerged out of nothing for no apparent reason. This flies in the face of every principle of empirical science, which holds rigorously in every area to the law of conservation of matter and energy. In science things do not appear and disappear at random; they must always be a reason, an explanation, a cause; if something is missing it must be accounted for. Something coming from nothing for no reason at all is the antithesis of science and is in fact a good definition of magic. Others try to give pseudo-scientific explanations of how things emerge from "quantum bubbles in the field of spacetime" and the like. But that simply does not make sense as an ultimate explanation.

(3) What was there before the Big Bang? Some refuse to entertain such questions and simply assert that something came from nothing and that is the end of the matter. Others try to claim that there was a time before the Big Bang when the universe alternated between expanding and contracting and we are in the phase of expanding. In other words, the universe always existed, contracting and expanding, and it does not require any further explanation or cause. This is a form of the infinite regress argument which Aquinas rejected in his five proofs for the existence of God. He argued that if there is not a first, there cannot be a second, or a third or anything else. That sounds reasonable. I find it hard to think of any material thing being infinite either in time or space.

(4) We have discovered extraordinary realities in the interaction of small particles and in quantum physics. Is it possible that physics will eventually be able to explain how energy and particles came to exist in the first place? However, science will always be science; every scientific explanation must

abide by the principle of sufficient reason and their own laws of conservation of mass and energy. Science will continue to understand and learn more and more about energy and particles, matter and anti-matter, quanta and waves, space and time, but by definition they will all be contingent explanations. Any ultimate explanation will inevitably involve a jump from science to philosophy or religion. Philosophy will continue to demand a sufficient reason and something coming from nothing for no apparent reason will never make sense.

(5) Did the universe evolve by chance; are we a cosmic accident? We have a assigned a very precise notion of chance in the context of statistical method and probabilities. There is an element of chance and probability in our existence, our conception, our birth, our education, our career choices, things that happen to us, earthquakes, floods, cancers, accidents and the like. But that is precisely what calls for understanding, for an explanation, and demands a statistical explanation. To shrug one's shoulders and assert that it all happened by chance is to give up on trying to understand; it is obscurantism. The element of chance is circumscribed by multitudes of classical laws defining systems, regularities, laws, causes, and relations. It is also limited by the notion of effective probability. There is no such thing as something that happens totally by chance, there are always degrees of probability.

(6) It is sometimes argued that the universe is so great and we are so insignificantly small, that we must be just cosmic accidents of no account and of no value. But is it harder for God to create a big universe than a small one? Is it harder for God to make a universe with a history of billions of years rather than one of a few thousand years? Why such a complex universe? Geographically, in time and space we are insignificant, but we are the only beings who have emerged with the ability to reflect on our situation, understand our universe, and ask about its ultimate cause. Emergence takes time and works on probabilities of emergence. Effective probability is the notion that even if there is only a small probability, if there are enough occasions in time and place, it will happen. Perhaps the size of the universe, the age of the universe and the number of planets in the universe is to ensure that intelligent humans will eventually emerge!

(7) Linguistic Analysts would claim that it is meaningless to affirm or deny the existence of God because there are no empirically verifiable consequences one way or the other. That position makes experiencing the pivot of meaning whereas for us our knowledge of the universe depends extrinsically on experience but knowing is essentially understanding and

judging. Meaning accrues to data through understanding and judging. In our view we are participants in the ongoing drama of a generalized emergent probability. God is present as the first cause of every cause, the giver of existence to every contingent thing or property, the final end of all our questioning. Theism is an enriching experience, a transformation of a narrow view of the universe to see it for its real meaning and significance. It confers meaning and value to every human life. It opens the mind to transcendent reality and encourages every attempt to understand and go beyond the sensible universe. By comparison the atheistic view is truncated, flat earth vision, impoverishing and limited.

(8) Psychological Projection. It was probably Freud who popularized the notion of God as a projection of a Father figure with all sorts of other psychological factors moving us to invent God, religion, conscience, punishment, commandments, and the like. For Marx it was an ideology of religion as the opium of the people. For Nietzsche God is the protector of the morality of the master and slave and helps to keep humans subservient. It has become part of popular culture that we need religion and so have invented it; it is a kind of wish fulfilment; when we are responsible and mature, we will be able to survive without belief in God. The trouble with such arguments is that they can easily be turned against those who propose them. If theism is a projection, can we not accuse atheists of repression or obscurantism or denial? Nietzsche was not noted for his mental stability. If Marx accuses traditional philosophy as an ideology of class consciousness, can we not interpret his own position as an ideology of his supposed freedom from class consciousness. Deconstruction is a rather arbitrary affair and can be turned on itself just as easily as it used to deconstruct theism.

(9) The ontological argument does not work. The argument that we have used is called a cosmological argument in the sense that it starts from the cosmos, the universe and argues from there. There is also an ontological argument, attributed firstly to St. Anselm, which argues from ideas alone and does not appeal to the existence or cause of the universe. Putting it in my own words the argument is the following:

1. God is a being than which no greater can be thought.

2. A being that actually exists is greater than a being which only exists in thought.

3. Therefore, the idea of God must include the existence of God.

4. Therefore, God must exist.

The problem with this argument is that the first three premises as I have presented them are definitions, concepts, and are consistent, but not verified as factually true statements. The conclusion however is a fact about the real actual world, an important fact. But you cannot argue from three definitions to a true fact about the real world. The argument has a long history and is controversial, but I would hold that it is not a valid argument.

Our contemporary culture is the first to propagate atheism and to attempt to eliminate religious beliefs. The scientific mentality is thought to have done away with the need for religion and God. We are after all self-sufficient, the dominant species, and with science and technology we can do anything. This is a sad misunderstanding of science, of philosophy and of religious beliefs. Good science, true philosophy and authentic religious beliefs are totally complementary and not contradictory.

Admittedly it is difficult to think your way clearly in philosophy to knowledge of the transcendent. But there is another way, and it is through religious experience.

Religious Experience: Transcendence

Not many persons are converted by syllogisms. You may not be impressed by the deep reasoning of the previous sections. Philosophy at its best can reach a theist position of a rational affirmation of the existence of God. That may satisfy purely intellectual questions but perhaps there are more things in heaven and earth than are dreamt of in philosophy. Arguments for the existence of God presuppose being in the intellectual pattern of experience, but few are at home in that pattern. There is quite a transition from a theoretical theism to religious experience and belief. Religious beliefs involve a major shift in the worldview of the theist and so a worldview of everything must include the possibility of a religious experience and orientation. This section will try to show how a religious dimension widens considerably the worldview that we have so far reached. We show how this represents a fifth level of consciousness in our diagram of the full human person. We show how important a religious orientation has been in most societies from the beginning until today. We examine religions to identify common characteristics of all that is called "religious." Finally, we will claim that religious experience is as natural to the human person as is experiencing, understanding, judging, and deciding. What does it mean then to say that to be fully human is to be more than human?

(1) Knowledge and Belief: Reason and Faith

Strictly speaking when we use the term knowledge, we are referring to immanently generated knowledge, namely, knowledge that we have personally attained by asking questions, doing research and observation, understanding patterns and relations that emerge, and finally after a critical review, presenting a correct explanation for these. It is knowledge that you have personally acquired on the basis of your own experience, understanding and judging. Your conclusions might be certain, beyond reasonable doubt, or affirmed with various degrees of probability. Our presentation of the argument for the existence of God above is an example of seeking correct understanding on the basis of critical reason alone.

Belief has a different structure in that some information is accepted as true because it comes from a trustworthy source. We accept something as true because we trust our friends, our teachers, our television channel, our textbooks, or our tradition. Belief is based on the trustworthiness of the source of the communication. The content believed can be certain, probable, or merely possible depending on the context. Belief plays an enormous role in our education and acquisition of truth. At a guess I would say that ninety percent of what we hold to be true is, strictly speaking, based on belief rather than immanently generated knowledge. Do your own survey of how much you have learned in college or university that is based on belief in the teacher and textbook, and how much is experienced and judged for yourself. The sciences are no exception as no student is required to repeat all the experiments and discoveries of the past, to check his slide rule to make sure it is calibrated properly, or to work out log tables for himself, or repeat all previous observations of astronomists, doctors, biologists, and so on.

Immanently generated knowledge is hard to attain. Belief however is simply communicated and passed on as true. There would be very little progress in any field of inquiry if we could not trust the texts and the discoveries of the past. By belief we collaborate with others in the search for further discoveries and truths and values. Knowing and believing are intimately intertwined in every field of learning in a collaborative effort.

There is a critique operative in both knowing and believing. In knowing it is reflective insight into the sufficiency of the evidence to entail the conclusion. In belief it is a critique of the source, the communication, and the credibility of the content. It is reasonable to believe what you read in textbooks, but your critical faculty should always be alert.

Belief is not irrational, it is not an abandonment of reasonable criticism, nor an embrace of an alternative worldview. In the context of religion, belief is often called faith. Religious traditions are usually based on revelations or traditions handed on from generation to generation. This is not blind faith, rather faith always seeking understanding—the classic definition of theology.

(2) Openness to Religious Experience

We need a metaphysics because from epistemology and the sciences questions arise as to the whole, as to everything, as to the relation between the sciences and common sense, as to how to put all the parts together in a single, coherent, correct worldview. We need religion because there are many aspects of human life that are not included in the worldview of science or metaphysics. These issues cannot be answered within a philosophical framework and philosophers generally ignore them or sweep them under the carpet. I want to show how the human spirit is open to this widening of perspective and in fact spontaneously enters into a religious framework, in order to face these challenges in a comprehensive worldview. Let me just list some of these challenges:

1. There is human suffering, physical pain, loss of loved ones, betrayal by friends, sickness, loneliness, failure, rejection, depression, anxiety, grief, regret, aging and death.

2. There is evil that is hard to avoid, hatred, corruption, discrimination, persecution, injustice, criminality, stupidity, harassment, exclusion, and the like. We should be able to progress regularly in all areas, but moral impotence spoils the show.

3. There are dimensions of guilt, sin, forgiveness, redemption, addiction, conversion, salvation, grace, mercy, sacrifice, holiness, fascination, awe, which everybody at some time will experience.

4. There are many religious activities such as praying, worshiping, meditating, fasting, contemplating, loving, believing, hoping that can be very much a part of authentic human life.

5. Deep in the heart of every person there are aspirations to a kind of happiness that the world does not give: hoping for eternal life, for life after death, loving relationships with others and with God, an ultimate longing for complete fulfilment of love and understanding.

6. Humans experience a feeling of dependence; the farmer depends on the weather, the businessman depends on the markets, the player depends on his team, the children depend on their parents, the citizens depend on their government, the sick depend on doctors. We

are not self-sufficient; we depend on others and ultimately on the providence of God.

The scientist sometimes considers his particular scientific worldview to be all there is to know and ignores philosophy and religion to the detriment of his own life and work. The philosopher may think that he has reached an understanding of everything, but genuine questions and aspirations to a wider viewpoint are stifled by the limits of his worldview. The human spirit is open to a further religious point of view in which the above questions are faced, the aspirations are fulfilled, and the feelings recognized. The human condition presents a definitive choice between a religious or a non-religious point of view. I claim that the final fulfilment of human aspirations, questions, and longings, is to be found in a religious dimension of life.

(3) Fifth Level of Consciousness

(Please refer to the diagram on The Human Person.) We have used the image of levels of consciousness to differentiate the sequence of intentionalities and activities proper to each level. Higher levels of consciousness emerge from lower but continue to depend on the proper functioning of lower levels. So far, we have confined our attention to the first four levels of consciousness. We have described these activities in detail in chapter 1 and built our whole metaphysics on the intentionality of these four activities. Now we ask, is this the end? Do we close our worldview with such rational and ethical considerations?

I am proposing that there is a fifth level of consciousness, a religious pattern of experience. I think it is important to differentiate this dimension from philosophical and ethical systems because it is quite different and new. It is important in the lives of many people, but it is not often that the religious dimension is clearly identified and distinguished from human speculation. We used the notion of sublation to show the relationships between the other levels of consciousness. Let us use the same principle to propose that the religious dimension incorporates something quite new; that it arises out of and depends on previous levels which remain intact; that it enhances the value of these previous levels and transforms them.

Something new arises. A religious dimension is new because it is something that is not the result of human thinking or knowing or evaluating. Religious conversion cannot be produced by human effort. We are not in control when it comes to religious experience, we are depending on an intervention from above. Conversions to a religious worldview happen and we are not the cause of this happening. We can provide the conditions for this happening, we can cooperate with these inspirations, but in some way, it is God who is responsible for this happening. In the Christian religious understanding it is God's grace from above that floods the human heart with unconditional love and the person is changed forever. Grace is understood as a free gift that is not earned, merited, or deserved; it is a gratuitous gift from God for that is what grace means. That is why the religious pattern of experience is new and different, because it involves God's intervention in our lives. This comes from above and not from below; it does not arise from experiencing, understanding and judging; it is not a product or a projection of the human mind. I am using the terminology of Christian theology because one is obliged to use some terminology from some tradition. But there are clear parallels in Islam and Jewish and other religious traditions.

In the early Middle Ages, a clear distinction was introduced between the natural and the supernatural. The context was a theoretical differentiation between what the human mind could do, and what only God could do. We have now moved from a theoretical to an interiority approach to consciousness. We try to identify in experience the point that human striving can reach and the manner and experience of God's intervention. For us what is natural means what the human mind and heart can achieve by itself, and supernatural means where God's grace takes over and transforms our worldview.

Conversion is a turning from one point of view to something new and different. It is a vertical jump rather than a continuous development in a horizontal line. We have described a intellectual moral and religious conversion in our account of activities characteristic of the human person. Accepting a religious dimension enormously expands one's horizons and worldview and consequently has a transforming effect on the other levels of consciousness.

Accepting a religious dimension to your life leaves other faculties of knowing intact. Acts of faith and belief are built on intelligence and reasonableness. Theology involves experiencing, understanding, judging truth and evaluating possible actions. It is nonsensical to claim that religious belief is irrational. Faith comes from hearing, from understanding and from judging and believing. Theology is critical, refutes contradictions, and seeks coherence and depth. Faith seeking understanding is a standard definition of what theology does. Faith actually continues to depend on the proper functioning of human faculties of intelligence and reason. Lonergan's method in theology builds on the structure of experiencing, understanding, judging and deciding each of which becomes a functional specialty on the way up and on the way down.

Faith actually enhances the value of the human faculties of understanding. From a faith perspective the sciences and philosophy are a preparation for the gospel. That is their ultimate purpose. Scriptural studies and historical research are needed more than ever to preserve the authenticity of the tradition. Intelligence is needed to express the contents of faith, to interpret correctly, to preserve and develop the tradition. In general, theology benefits and is enhanced by the intelligence, scholarship and holiness of theologians. It depends on the proper functioning of the human mind.

(4) Explaining the Diagram

In diagram 4, I have tried to find a parallel between the processes on the fifth level of consciousness with the other four levels. There is a fairly clear and helpful parallel between the second, third and fourth levels. How the fifth level fits in is not so clear but the following is the best I can do.

Imperatives. Just as it is natural for the development of the human person to attend, to understand, to judge truth and value in a human philosophy, so I feel it is natural and necessary that this leads into questions of a religious dimension. I would hold that the desire for a religious dimension is implicit in all our questioning, knowing and loving, and these should become explicit, should be expressed in words, should be named and allowed to grow. Unconditional love is the Christian way of expressing the religious imperative, our ultimate aspirations to happiness and God.

Levels. We should not take the image of levels too literally, but it does help to distinguish operations and products that are in principle quite distinct. Once we have distinguished them we can relate them to one another. There is in principle a dependence of higher levels on proper functioning of lower levels. There is a way up by which we climb from lower levels to higher levels. But there also is a way down by which there is a feed-back of the higher on the lower levels. An image of concentric circles is a possible alternative to the boxes of our diagram but computers and typewriters like straight rather than curved lines.

Questions. We appealed to the desire to know as the motivating principle driving the first four levels of consciousness. But there are further religious questions which emerge in existential situations of death and disaster, in experiences of enlightenment or depression, in unexpected moments. More technical questions are explicitly posed in theological studies. The primary religious impulse is an aspiration for ultimate total human understanding and love which can only be found in God who is infinite love and peace. Only god can save us.

Activities. There are multitudes of activities proper to the religious pattern of experience: praying, praising, thanking, worship, ritual, meditation, and the like. For a religious person all human activity is done in the context of a religious worldview.

Products. Faith seeking understanding will write books and formulate doctrines and teaching and be expressed in a trusting relationship with God. Hope spurs us on towards further development and the satisfaction of ultimate longing. Love of God, God's love for us, love of neighbor, is the summation of all laws, theology, teaching, and words.

Actions. Holiness is the word chosen by Rudolf Otto to express the common element of all religious experiences. It does take many forms; it can be misunderstood; it is a worthy goal to which you might devote your life. All the other levels of cognitional operations suppose a free implementation of understanding and judgments in a life well lived. The religious perspective adds the dimension of holiness to this freely chosen lifestyle.

(5) What Religions Have in Common

The majority of people throughout history have operated within a religious view of the world and still do. Traditional societies were dominated by religious beliefs leading to the building of temples and pyramids at the expense of improving standards of human living. Much is made of the secularizing of the contemporary world but still the majority of humans profess religious beliefs.

Efforts have been made to identify and define what are the characteristics common to all religious traditions; what makes them "religious." Many of these attempts have concentrated on externals, on rituals and stated beliefs and practices. I think it is more fruitful to identify the religious impulse from within, from psychology, from religious experience, from interiority.

A classic in this field is Rudolf Otto, *The Idea of the Holy*. He starts by criticizing Schleiermacher's claim to describe the core religious feeling as absolute dependence on God. Otto finds this too ambiguous and too narrow. He develops his own terminology and examples to try to pin down the experience at the core of all religious experience. He coins the term "numinous" from the Latin "numen." It could be translated as divine presence or divine spirit. He is looking for the core religious experience which is different from every other feeling and is difficult to define. As elements of the numinous he identifies, awe, majesty, and urgency. He suggests that awe or awesome evoke something of that feeling. This appears in the Bible as fear of the Lord or reverence. It might include dependence. It has an element of dread, uncanny, eerie, weird. Majesty or overpoweringness express the absolute unapproachability of God. A characteristic of mysticism is this self-depreciation in the face of the majesty of God. This inspires Energy or Urgency which he describes as vitality, passion, emotional temper, will, force, movement, excitement, activity, and impetus. The emphasis is on a living God and goes far beyond philosophical speculation on God. He identifies this in the Old and New Testaments, in Luther, and in how it manifests itself in different religions.

Bernard Lonergan uses the work of Friedrich Heiler to identify seven characteristics common to world religions: "that there is a transcendent reality; that he is immanent in human hearts; that he is supreme beauty, truth, righteousness, goodness; that he is love, mercy, compassion; that the way to him is repentance, self-denial, prayer; that the way is love of one's neighbor, even of one's enemies; that the way is love of God, so that bliss is conceived as knowledge of God, union with him, or dissolution into him."[8] He shows how this is verified in the Christian tradition which centres on being in love in an unrestricted manner.

Religious experience can the considered from the point of view of infrastructure and suprastructure.[9] Infrastructure regards the deep feelings, aspirations, intentions, and attitudes that are common to all religions. From these arise the suprastructure, namely, the teaching, doctrine, ritual, beliefs, customs, and external practices of each particular religious group. When this distinction is recognized, it is possible for different religious groups to cooperate; they recognize that beneath the very visible differences in teaching and practice, there is a common belief in a religious dimension to life. In the Christian viewpoint, Lonergan would recognize the work of the Holy Spirit as operative in all human hearts as the invisible, common dimension to all religions. The visible, historical, particular teaching of the Christian church comes from the incarnation and revelation in the Old and New Testament.

My contention, then, is that all human persons are naturally religious—*Homo Religiosus*. In the same way as it is natural for humans to see and hear, to ask questions and understand and judge; to evaluate and decide; it is also natural to be open to a religious dimension to life and

8. Lonergan, *Method in Theology*, 105.

9. Lonergan began to use the terminology of infrastructure and suprastructure in *A Third Collection*. It was intended to distinguish undifferentiated experience from the concepts and structures emerging from such experiences. It has wide applications, to consciousness as opposed to self-knowledge, to experience of knowing contrasted with explicit cognitional structure, to religious experience contrasted with religious creeds. See *A Third Collection*, 54–57, 112–15.

that this is enriching and not diminishing. The religious dimension to life is the apex of human development, the fullness of one's potential. In this sense to be fully human is to be more than human. The desire to know God is natural. Wonder and religious awe are natural. Every culture and civilization has had a religious aspect. Attacking religion as a delusion, as superstition, as irrational, simply does not fit the facts. Humans were religious, are religious, and will forever be religious.

Conclusion

We differentiate in order to integrate, we take apart in order to put together again, we analyze in order to synthesize. I hope all the pieces of this worldview fit together into a coherent, correct, helpful whole and will provide the assumptions and principles on which our knowledge of common sense, our work in all the sciences, and our work to improve the life of human persons, can be built upon further. It is possible to see common sense, the sciences, philosophy, and religion and all the disciplines involved in making the world a better place, as distinct, but also mutually interdependent and complementary. In principle there can and should be no conflict between them. We generalize on the basis of what the specialists tell us. Our policy has been to give a general picture of the universe within which specialists of all kinds can collaborate, knowing that their basic assumptions are true and clear and correct. Specialists work on the basis of general assumptions which they presume are correct, and which direct the questions they ask, the manner of studying, the presentation and interpretation of their results. Endless confusion arises from mistaken assumptions, from lack of common understanding of basic method, and from mistaken or truncated worldviews. I hope to have made a positive contribution to seeing through that confusion.

Bibliography

Alvira, Tomas, et al. *Metaphysics*. Manila: Sinag-Tala, 1991.

Aristotle. *Metaphysics*. Translated by Hippocrates Apostle. Iowa: Peripatetic, 1966.

———. *Nicomachean Ethics*. Translated by Hippocrates Apostle. Iowa: Peripatetic, 1984.

———. *On the Soul (De Anima)*. Translated by Hippocrates Apostle. Iowa: Peripatetic, 1981.

Augustine, Saint. *The Confessions of St. Augustine: Modern English Version*. Grand Rapids: Spire, 2005.

Barnes, Jonathan. *Aristotle*. Oxford: Oxford University Press, 1982.

Barrow, John. *Theories of Everything: The Quest for Ultimate Explanation*. Oxford: Clarendon, 1991.

Beards, Andrew. *Method in Metaphysics: Lonergan and the Future of Analytic Philosophy*. Toronto: University of Toronto Press, 2008.

Becker, Adam. *What Is Real? The Unfinished Quest for the Meaning of Quantum Physics*. New York: Basic, 2018.

Bedau, Mark, and Paul Humphreys. *Emergence: Contemporary Readings in Philosophy and Science*. Cambridge: MIT Press, 2008.

Behe, Michael J. *Darwin's Black Box: The Biochemical Challenge to Evolution*. New York: Free, 2006.

Bellah, Robert. *Habits of the Heart: Individualism and Commitment in American Life*. New York: Harper and Row, 1985.

Bhaskar, Roy. *A Realist Theory of Science*. Sussex: Harvester, 1978.

Blanchette, Oliva. *Philosophy of Being: A Reconstructive Essay in Metaphysics*. Washington, DC: Catholic University of America Press, 2003.

Bryson, Bill. *A Short History of Nearly Everything*. New York: Broadway, 2003.

Burtt, Edwin Arthur. *The Metaphysical Foundations of Modern Physical Science*. London: Routledge and Kegan Paul, 1980.

Butterfield, Herbert. *The Origins of Modern Science*. New York: Free, 1965.

Calder, Nigel. *Einstein's Universe: The Layman's Guide*. New York: Penguin, 1979.

Chalmers, Alan. *Science and Its Fabrication*. Minneapolis: University of Minnesota Press, 1990.

———. *What Is This Thing Called Science? An Assessment of the Nature and Status of Science and Its Methods*. Indianapolis: Hackett, 1994.

Clarke, W. Norris. *The One and the Many: A Contemporary Thomistic Metaphysics.* Notre Dame: University of Notre Dame Press, 2001.

Clayton, Philip, and Paul Davies. *The Re-emergence of Emergence: The Emergentist Hypothesis from Science to Religion.* Oxford: Oxford University Press, 2006.

Clegg, Brian. *A Brief History of Infinity: The Quest to Think the Unthinkable.* London: Robinson, 2003.

Conee, Earl, and Theodore Sider. *Riddles of Existence: A Guided Tour of Metaphysics.* Oxford: Clarendon, 2005.

Coreth, Emerich. *Metaphysics.* New York: Herder and Herder, 1968.

Cottingham, John. *In Search of the Soul: A Philosophical Essay.* Princeton: Princeton University Press, 2020.

Cronin, Brian. *Foundations of Philosophy: Lonergan's Cognitional Theory and Epistemology.* Nairobi: Consolata Institute of Philosophy, 1999.

———. *Phenomenology of Human Understanding.* Eugene, OR: Wipf and Stock, 2017.

———. *Value Ethics: A Lonergan Perspective.* Nairobi: Consolata Institute of Philosophy, 2006.

Davies, Paul. *God and the New Physics.* London: Dent, 1983.

Dawkins, Richard. *Climbing Mount Improbable.* London: Penguin, 1997.

———. *The Selfish Gene.* Oxford: Oxford University Press, 1976.

Deacon, Terrence. *Incomplete Nature: How Mind Emerged from Matter.* New York: Norton and Co., 2012.

Dear, Peter. *The Intelligibility of Nature: How Science Makes Sense of the World.* Chicago: University of Chicago Press, 2006.

Delio, Ilia. *Making All Things New: Catholicity, Cosmology, Consciousness.* Maryknoll, NY: Orbis, 2015.

Descartes, René. *Philosophical Works.* Vol. 2. Translated by Elizabeth S. Haldane and G. R. T. Ross. Cambridge: Cambridge University Press, 1931.

Desmond, William. *God and the Between.* Oxford: Blackwell, 2008.

Doran, Robert. *Subject and Psyche.* Milwaukee, WI: Marquette University Press, 1994.

Eagleton, Terry. *Materialism.* New Haven: Yale University Press, 2016.

Einstein, Albert. *Relativity: The Special and the General Theory: An Exposition for the Layman.* New York: Bonanza, 1961.

Eliade, Mircea. *The Sacred and the Profane: The Nature of Religion.* Translated by Willard Trask. New York: Harvest, 1957.

Emonet, Pierre-Marie. *The Dearest Freshness Deep Down Things: An Introduction to the Philosophy of Being.* New York: Herder and Herder, 1993.

Feyerabend, Paul. *Against Method.* London: Verso, 2010.

Francis, Pope. *Laudato si': Praised Be: Encyclical Letter on Care for Our Common Home.* Dublin: Veritas, 2015.

Frankl, Viktor. *Man's Search for Ultimate Meaning.* New York: Insight, 1997.

Gadamer, Hans-Georg. *Truth and Method.* London: Sheed and Ward, 1975.

Garrett, Brian. *What Is This Thing Called Metaphysics?* London: Routledge, 2006.

Gleich, James. *Isaac Newton.* New York: Vintage, 2003.

Green, Brian. *The Fabric of the Cosmos: Space, Time, and the Texture of Reality.* New York: Knopf, 2005.

Gribbin, John. *In Search of Schrodinger's Cat: Quantum Physics and Reality.* London: Corgi, 1983.

———. *Science: A History, 1543–2001.* London: Lane, 2002.

Grondin, Jean. *Introduction to Metaphysics: From Parmenides to Levinas*. New York: Columbia University Press, 2012.

Gschwandtner, Christina. *Postmodern Apologetics? Arguments for God in Contemporary Philosophy*. New York: Fordham University Press, 2013.

Guthrie, W. K. C. *A History of Greek Philosophy: The Presocratic Tradition from Parmenides to Democritus*. Vol 2. Cambridge: Cambridge University Press, 1965.

Hacking, Jan, ed. *Scientific Revolutions*. Oxford: Oxford University Press, 1981.

Harari, Yuval Noah. *Sapiens: A Brief History of Humankind*. New York: Harper, 2015.

Harris, Henry. *The Birth of the Cell*. New Haven: Yale University Press, 1999.

Hasker, William. *Metaphysics: Constructing a World View*. Downer's Grover, IL: InterVarsity, 1983.

Hawking, Stephen. *Brief Answers to the Big Questions*. New York: Bantam, 2018.

———. *A Brief History of Time: From the Big Bang to Black Holes*. Toronto: Bantam, 1988.

———. *The Theory of Everything: The Origin and Fate of the Universe*. Beverly Hills, CA: New Millenium, 2002.

Hawking, Stephen, and Leonard Mlodinow. *The Grand Design: New Answers to the Ultimate Questions of Life*. New York: Bantam, 2010.

Hector, Kevin. *Theology without Metaphysics: God, Language, and the Spirit of Recognition*. Cambridge: Cambridge University Press, 2011.

Heidegger, Martin. *Being and Time*. Translated by Joan Stambaugh. Albany: State University of New York Press, 2010.

———. *Introduction to Metaphysics*. New Haven: Yale University Press, 2000.

———. *What Is a Thing?* South Bend, IN: Gateways Editions, 1967.

Heisenberg, Werner. *Physics and Philosophy: The Revolution in Modern Science*. New York: HarperPerennial, 1958.

Henig, Robin Marantz. *The Monk in the Garden: The Lost and Found Genius of Gregor Mendel, the Father of Genetics*. Boston: Houghton Mifflin, 2000.

Holland, John H. *Emergence: From Chaos to Order*. New York: Basic, 1998.

Hull, David L., and Michael Ruse, eds. *The Cambridge Companion to the Philosophy of Biology*. Cambridge: Cambridge University Press, 2007.

Hume, David. *A Treatise of Human Nature: Book One*. London: Fontana/Collins, 1962.

Kant, Immanuel. *Critique of Pure Reason*. Translated by Norman Kemp Smith. New York: St. Martin's, 1965.

———. *Prolegomena to Any Future Metaphysics That Will Be Able to Come Forward as Science*. Translated by James Ellington. Indianapolis: Hackett, 1977.

Kauffman, Stuart A. *At Home in the Universe: The Search for the Laws of Self-Organization and Complexity*. Oxford: Oxford University Press, 1995.

———. *Reinventing the Sacred: A New View of Science, Reason, and Religion*. New York: Basic, 2008.

Korner, Stephan. *Metaphysics: Its Structure and Function*. Cambridge: Cambridge University Press, 1984.

Krauss, Lawrence. *A Universe from Nothing: Why Is There Something Rather Than Nothing*. New York: Atria, 2012.

Kuhn, Thomas S. *The Structure of Scientific Revolutions*. Chicago: University of Chicago Press, 1970.

Lawrence, Frederick. *The Fragility of Consciousness: Faith, Reason, and the Human Good*. Toronto: University of Toronto Press, 2017.

Lawson, Hilary. *Closure: A Story of Everything*. London: Routledge, 2001.

Levinas, Emmanuel. *Existence and Existents*. Translated by Alphonso Lingis. Pittsburgh: Duquesne University Press, 1978.

Liddy, Richard. *Startling Strangeness: Reading Lonergan's Insight*. Lanham, MD: University Press of America, 2007.

Locke, John. *An Essay concerning Human Understanding*. Lexington: WLC, 2009.

Lonergan, Bernard. *Collection*. Edited by Frederick F. Crowe and Robert Doran. Collected Works of Bernard Lonergan 4. Toronto: University of Toronto Press, 1988

———. *Insight: A Study of Human Understanding*. Edited by Frederick E. Crowe and Robert Doran. Collected Works of Bernard Lonergan 3. Toronto: University of Toronto Press, 1992.

———. *Method in Theology*. Edited by Frederick E. Crowe and John Dadosky. Collected Works of Bernard Lonergan 14. Toronto: Toronto University Press, 2017.

———. *A Second Collection*. Edited by Robert Doran and John Dadosky. Collected Works of Bernard Lonergan 13. Toronto: Toronto University Press, 2016.

———. *A Third Collection*. Edited by Robert Doran and John Dadosky. Collected Works of Bernard Lonergan 16. Toronto: Toronto University Press, 2017.

———. *Understanding and Being*. Edited by Elizebeth Morelli and Mark Morelli. Collected Works of Bernard Lonergan 5. Toronto: Toronto University Press, 1990.

———. *Verbum: Word and Idea in Aquinas*. Edited by Frederick E. Crowe and Robert Doran. Collected Works of Bernard Lonergan 2. Toronto: University of Toronto Press, 1997.

Lyotard, Jean-François. *The Postmodern Condition: A Report on Knowledge*. Minneapolis: University of Minnesota Press, 1984.

Macdonald, Cynthia. *Varieties of Things: Foundations of Contemporary Metaphysics*. Malden, MA: Blackwell, 2005.

Maor, Eli. *To Infinity and Beyond: A Cultural History of the Infinite*. Boston: Birkhäuser, 1987.

Marion, Jean-Luc. *God without Being*. Chicago: Chicago University Press, 1991.

Maritain, Jacques. *A Preface to Metaphysics*. London: Sheed and Ward, 1945.

Mathews, William. *Lonergan's Quest: A Study of Desire in the Authoring of Insight*. Toronto: University of Toronto Press, 2005.

Mayr, Ernst. *What Evolution Is*. New York: Basic, 2002.

McGrath, Alister. *The Twilight of Atheism: The Rise and Fall of Disbelief in the Modern World*. London: Rider, 2004.

Midgley, Mary. *Are You an Illusion?* Durham: Acumen, 2014.

Miller, Mark. *The Quest for God and the Good Life: Lonergan's Theological Anthropology*. Washington, DC: Catholic University of America Press, 2013.

Monod, Jacques. *Chance and Necessity: An Essay on the Natural Philosophy of Modern Biology*. Translated by Austryn Wainhouse. New York: Knopf, 1971.

Morowitz, Harold J. *The Emergence of Everything: How the World Became Complex*. Oxford: Oxford University Press, 2002.

Mounier, Emmanuel. *Personalism*. Notre Dame: University of Notre Dame Press, 1952.

Mouroux, Jean. *The Meaning of Man*. New York: Doubleday, 1961.

Nietzsche, Friedrich. *Beyond Good and Evil: Prelude to a Philosophy of the Future*. Translated by Walter Kaufmann. New York: Vintage, 1966.

Noble, Denis. *Dance to the Tune of Life: Biological Relativity*. Cambridge: Cambridge University Press, 2017.

Otto, Rudolf. *The Idea of the Holy: An Inquiry into the Non-rational Factor in the Idea of the Divine and Its Relation to the Rational*. Translated by J. W. Harvey. Oxford: Oxford University Press, 1923.

Pascal, Blaise. *Pensées*. Translated by A. J. Krailsheimer. London: Penguin, 1966.

Penrose, Roger. *The Emperor's New Mind: Concerning Computers, Minds, and the Laws of Physics*. Oxford: Oxford University Press, 1989.

Potter, Christopher. *How to Make a Human Being: A Body of Evidence*. London: Fourth Estate, 2014.

Reale, Giovanni. *The Concept of First Philosophy and the Unity of the "Metaphysics" of Aristotle*. Albany: State University of New York Press, 1980.

Ridley, Matt. *Genome: The Autobiography of a Species in 23 Chapters*. London: Fourth Estate, 1999.

Rorty, Richard. *Philosophy and the Mirror of Nature*. Princeton: Princeton University Press, 1979.

Rosenbarg, Alex, and Daniel W. McShea. *Philosophy of Biology: A Contemporary Introduction*. New York: Routledge, 2008.

Rovelli, Carlo. *Reality Is Not What It Seems: The Journey to Quantum Gravity*. London: Penguin, 2014.

Ruse, Michael. *The Gaia Hypothesis: Science on a Pagan Planet*. Chicago: University of Chicago Press, 2013.

Schilpp, P. A. *Albert Einstein: Philosopher-Scientist*. New York: Open Court, 1949.

Schrodinger, Erwin. *What Is Life? With Mind and Matter*. Cambridge: Cambridge University Press, 1967.

Singh, Simon. *Fermat's Last Theorem: The Story of a Riddle That Confounded the World's Greatest Minds for 358 years*. London: Harper Perennial, 2005.

Smith, Christian. *What Is a Person? Rethinking Humanity, Social Life, and the Moral Good from the Person Up*. Chicago: University of Chicago Press, 2010.

Sokol, Alan, and Jean Bricmont. *Fashionable Nonsense: Postmodern Intellectuals' Abuse of Science*. New York: Picador USA, 1998.

Stewart, Ian. *Does God Play Dice: The New Mathematics of Chaos*. London: Penguin, 1990.

Stoljar, Daniel. *Physicalism*. London: Routledge, 2010.

Swinburne, Richard. *Are We Bodies or Souls?* Oxford: Oxford University Press, 2019.

Taylor, Charles. *Sources of the Self: The Making of the Modern Identity*. Cambridge: Cambridge University Press, 1989.

Teilhard de Chardin, Pierre. *The Phenomenon of Man*. London: Fontana, 1955.

Vaske, O. Martin. *An Introduction to Metaphysics*. New York: McGraw-Hill, 1963.

Vélez, Francisco Vicente Galán. *Una metafísica para tiempos posmetafísicos: La propuesta de Bernard Lonergan de una metametodología*. Mexico City: Universidad Iberoamericana, 2014.

Vertin, Michael. "Acceptance and Actualization: The Two Phases of my Human Living." *Method: Journal of Lonergan Studies* 21 (2003) 67–86.

———. "Lonergan's Metaphysics of Value and Love." *Lonergan Workshop Journal* 13 (1997) 189–219.

———. "Lonergan's Three Basic Questions and a Philosophy of Philosophies." *Lonergan Workshop Journal* 8 (1990) 213–48.

Ward, Keith. *God, Chance, and Necessity*. Oxford: Oneworld, 1996.

Watson, James. *DNA: The Secret of Life*. New York: Knopf, 2003.

Watson, Peter. *Convergence: The Idea at the Heart of Science*. New York: Simon & Schuster, 2016.

Weinberg, Stephen. *The Discovery of Subatomic Particles*. New York: Freeman, 1990.

———. *Dreams of a Final Theory: The Search for the Fundamental Laws of Nature*. New York: Vintage, 1992.

Wilber, Ken. *A Brief History of Everything*. Dublin: Gill and Macmillan, 1996.

———. *Eye to Eye: The Quest for the New Paradigm*. Boston: Shambhala, 1990.

Wilczek, Frank. *The Lightness of Being: Mass, Ether, and the Unification of Forces*. New York: Basic, 2008.

Wilson, Edward O. *Consilience: The Unity of Knowledge*. London: Abacus, 1998.

Wojtyla, Karol. *The Acting Person*. London: Reidel, 1979.

———. *Person and Community: Selected Essays*. New York: Lang, 1993.

Zimmer, Carl. *Evolution: The Triumph of an Idea: From Darwin to DNA*. London: Arrow, 2002.

Index